Henri-Dominique Lacordaire

**Jesus Christ, God, God and Man**

Henri-Dominique Lacordaire

**Jesus Christ, God, God and Man**

ISBN/EAN: 9783743477988

Manufactured in Europe, USA, Canada, Australia, Japa

Cover: Foto ©Lupo / pixelio.de

Manufactured and distributed by brebook publishing software (www.brebook.com)

Henri-Dominique Lacordaire

**Jesus Christ, God, God and Man**

# JESUS CHRIST
# GOD
# GOD AND MAN

CONFERENCES DELIVERED AT NOTRE DAME IN PARIS

BY THE

REV. PÈRE LACORDAIRE,

OF THE ORDER OF FRIAR-PREACHERS.

*Translated from the French, with the Author's permission, by a Tertiary of the same Order.*

NEW EDITION, IN ONE VOLUME.

LONDON:
CHAPMAN AND HALL, Limited,
1884.

CHARLES DICKENS AND EVANS,
CRYSTAL PALACE PRESS.

# TRANSLATOR'S PREFACE.

THE subject of the following Conferences is daily attracting increased attention in England—so justly famed for her religious feeling and strong sense, yet so distracted by divisions which contradict the authority, the object, and the work of Jesus Christ. Many minds that know not the repose of divine faith, are—timidly perhaps, but anxiously—watching this great question; requiring, not only to believe, but also, and rightly, to know why they should believe.

Humbly desiring to discharge a part of the deep debt of gratitude which he owes to the author of these celebrated discourses, the translator respectfully offers them to his well-beloved country, as a guide in her present religious confusion and a support in her manifest and perplexing doubts, hoping and believing that they will be to others what they have been to him, namely, heralds of that "glorious liberty" which is the ever-blessed fruit of Catholic Christianity.

# DECLARATION.

ALTHOUGH I have constantly taught under the authority and in the presence of the Archbishops of Paris, and my doctrine has never been criticised or called in question by them; although that same doctrine, published by the press, has excited neither reproach nor discussion: yet, lest in treating so many theological questions some involuntary error may have escaped me, and this I must and do readily presume from my weakness, I declare that I submit my Conferences to the Catholic Church, whose son I am, and in particular to the Holy Roman Church, the mother and mistress of all Churches, wherein resides the plenitude of the authority founded upon earth by our Lord Jesus Christ.

I also declare again that I do not acknowledge the pretended reproductions of my Conferences which have been made by various periodicals, whatever be their form or name. I once more protest against that violation of literary rights, whose result is to place under the name of a preacher discourses imperfectly reported amidst an immense auditory, and not less imperfectly corrected by the authors of such speculation. Should the doctrine contained in these publications be attacked, I decline the responsibility thereof as of a work which is not mine, and for which I can be held responsible only by a violation of all right and equity.

FR. HENRI-DOMINIQUE LACORDAIRE,
*Prov. des Fr. Prêcheurs.*

NANCY, at the Convent of Notre-Dame-et-Chêne.

# CONTENTS.

JESUS CHRIST:

                                                                          PAGE

    The Inner Life of Jesus Christ . . . . . . 3

    The Public Power of Jesus Christ . . . . . 24

    The Foundation of the Reign of Jesus Christ . . . 40

    The Perpetuity and Progress of the Reign of Jesus Christ . 58

    The Pre-existence of Jesus Christ . . . . 76

    The Efforts of Rationalism to Destroy the Life of Jesus Christ . . . . . . . . . . 96

    The Efforts of Rationalism to Pervert the Life of Jesus Christ . . . . . . . . . . 116

    The Efforts of Rationalism to Explain the Life of Jesus Christ . . . . . . . . . . 134

GOD:

    The Existence of God. . . . . . . . 153

    The Inner Life of God . . . . . . 168

    The Creation of the World by God . . . . 185

    The General Plan of Creation . . . 204

    Man as an Intelligent Being . . . . . 221

    Man as a Moral Being . . . . . . 242

    Man as a Social Being . . . . 262

    The Double Work of Man . . . . . . 280

GOD AND MAN:

|  | PAGE |
|---|---|
| The Supernatural Intercourse between God and Man | 297 |
| Two Objections against the Supernatural Intercourse between God and Man | 316 |
| The Need of Supernatural Intercourse between God and Man | 337 |
| Prophecy | 353 |
| Mystery as the Object of Prophecy | 371 |
| The Human Act corresponding to Prophecy | 386 |
| Sacrament | 404 |

# JESUS CHRIST.

# JESUS CHRIST.

## THE INNER LIFE OF JESUS CHRIST.

My Lord*—Gentlemen,

In demonstrating the divinity of Christianity we have not taken our starting-point in the profound depths of metaphysics or in the distant regions of history, but in a living, palpable phenomenon, which has been for ages before the world; we have analyzed this phenomenon, we have shown you that under the intellectual, moral, and social points of view, the Catholic Church is a phenomenon unique here below, and therefore divine. For whatsoever is human is multiple, since whatsoever men have been able to accomplish in a given time and place, other men are able to accomplish in other times and places. We have then changed the ordinary tactics—instead of starting from the basis, we have started from the summit, instead of digging about the foundations of the pyramid, we have examined its apex and its crown, beginning by that which is most visible, to return afterwards to that which is most hidden, and which bears the whole mass. A writer of our times has said: Christianity is the greatest event which has passed in the world. We have said otherwise, and perhaps better: "Christianity is the greatest phenomenon which has been naturalized in the world, the greatest intellectual phenomenon, the greatest moral phenomenon, the greatest social phenomenon," something unique, in a word, and yet once more consequently divine.

* Monseigneur Affre, Archbishop of Paris.

But what is the primary cause of this phenomenon? Every phenomenon has a cause. After having examined its visible side, we should evidently examine that which has produced the spectacle, that which explains and supports it. Who, then, has made the Catholic Church? Who has founded that society which rules minds by certainty, regulates souls by the highest virtues, blesses the human race by the new elements it has given to civilization? Who has formed, under a hierarchy spiritual and unarmed, that body wherein conviction, holiness, unity, universality, stability, and life, form a tissue of superhuman and incontestable beauty? Who has designed and produced it? Is it time, or chance? Is it the work of many, or of one alone? It is but one, yes, one alone, a man, that is to say, nothing; the word of a man, which is but a passing breath. Behold the artist! God has so willed it, then, that the foundation of this great work should be something resembling ourselves, and that man, so weak, so vain, should, like Atlas, bear heaven and earth upon his shoulders. Who is this man? What name does he bear on the tongues and in the memorials of the human race? I have no need to tell you: his name speaks and resounds of itself. Every man knows it from love or hatred, and in naming Jesus Christ I am but the remote echo of all ages and all minds. Jesus Christ, then! Jesus Christ! He is the artist! It is He who founded that Church whose ineffable architecture we have contemplated together: I speak of the Church under her present form, for the Church has existed upon earth from the day when God first spake to man, and when man first responded from his heart to God.

The artist found, gentlemen, it is needful to study his history, that we may be able to judge whether the workman answers to the work, and whether, after having seen that the work is divine in itself, its divinity will receive confirmation from the life of him who produced it. In order to do this we must first learn where to seek for the elements of that life. This difficulty is not great. Like every man who appears at an epoch which is historical and rendered famous by his works, Jesus Christ has a history, a history which the Church and the world possess, and which, surrounded by countless memorials, has at least the same authenticity as any other history formed in the same countries, amidst the same peoples, and in the same times. As, then, if I would study the lives of Brutus and Cassius, I should calmly open Plutarch, I open the Gospel to study Jesus Christ, and I do so with the same composure. We will afterwards examine whether I have erred in admitting this preliminary authenticity; I assume it now, being in possession of it, subject to my returning to it by retracing our steps at a future period, in order to verify the documents and base them upon a degree of certainty worthy of the sacred object of our investigation. I take the Gospel, then, provisionally, for my historical title. You are free to make what reserve you please as to its authenticity and veracity; it is a right which I do not dispute, as I know you will also be just enough to respect in the Gospel, at least provisionally, the faith of twenty centuries, and the natural weight of that which forms so conspicuous a part of the world's history.

Lord Jesus, for ten years I have spoken of Thy Church to this auditory, yet it is indeed of Thee that I have always spoken; but now, and more directly, I come to Thyself, to those divine features, which are the daily object of my contemplation, to Thy sacred feet, which I have so often kissed, to Thy divine hands, which have so often blessed me, to Thy forehead, crowned with glory and with thorns, to that life whose sweetness I have respired from my birth, which my youth disregarded, which my manhood regained, which my riper age adores and proclaims to every creature. O Father! O Master! O Friend! O Jesus! second me now more than ever, since, being closer to Thee, it is meet that my hearers should perceive it, and that the words which fall from my lips should manifest the nearness of Thy adorable presence!

There are two lives—the outer life and the inner life. The outer life would be nothing without the inner life. The inner life is the support of the other, and therefore, desiring to study the life of Jesus Christ, I must begin by examining His inner life. But what is this inner life? It is the converse between ourselves and ourselves. Every man converses with himself, every man speaks to himself, and that converse with himself is his inner life, as that which, from all eternity, God makes with Himself in the mystery of His three divine persons is His inner life. Every man, every intelligent being, holds this inner converse with himself, which forms his real life. The rest is but a semblance, when it is not the produce of that inner life. The inner life is the whole man, and forms all the worth of man. One is clothed in purple, and yet he is worthless, because his converse with himself is that of a worthless being; and another passes along our streets barefoot and in rags, who is a great man, because his inner converse is that of a hero or a saint. On the day of judgment we shall see this changing being within and without, and the mysterious colloquy of each man being known, his history will then begin. Now, we proceed as best we can from the outer to the inner life; for, if this gift of judging the inner by the outer life had not been granted to us, if our outer life were any other thing than a permanent transpiration of our inner life, we should be but spectres to each other, we should pass by without knowing one another, as maskers who pass each other in the night. Happily, and thanks to God, there are orifices through which our inner life constantly escapes, and the soul, like the blood, hath its pores. The mouth is the chief and foremost of these channels which leads the soul out of its invisible sanctuary; it is by speech that man communicates the secret converse which is his real life. And although every man thus speaks from within to without, there are men in whom this manifestation of themselves is more especially called for, more needful, more authentic. They are those who come before the world with doctrines destined by them to become laws. For the first question put to them is: Who are you? What say you of yourselves? As the priests of Jerusalem sent men to ask John the Baptist in the desert: TU QUIS ES? QUID DICIS DE TEIPSO?* First of all, since you are not a man like other men, tell us what you are, what you affirm of yourself: QUID DICIS DE TEIPSO?

And it is not a slight thing, gentlemen, to force a man to say what he is, or what he believes himself to be; for that supreme word of man, that single expression which he utters of and upon himself is decisive. It lays down the basis upon which all judgment of him is to be formed. From that moment all the acts of his life must correspond to the answer given by him to the question: QUID DICIS DE TEIPSO? And therefore Jesus Christ, appearing amongst men to bring them new laws, a new order of things, had to submit to that necessity of declaring what He was, and therewith to undergo the unfailing test to which it subjected Him. It was to His friends

---

* St. John i. 22.

and disciples that He had first to declare Himself, by telling them what He thought of Himself. What said He to them?

One day, at Cæsarea Philippi, He asked His disciples: "Whom do men say that I, the Son of Man, am? And they said, Some say John the Baptist; others, Elias; others, Jeremias, or one of the prophets. Jesus saith to them: But whom say ye that I am? Simon Peter answered, and said: Thou art the Christ, the Son of the living God." Jesus Christ, so far from rejecting these words as blasphemous, accepted them as expressing a truth which filled Him with delight, and He said to Peter: "Blessed art thou, Simon Bar-jona: for flesh and blood hath not revealed it to thee, but My Father which is in Heaven." And He then added, as a reward for the faith of His disciple: "And I say unto thee that thou art Peter, and upon this rock I will build my Church, and the gates of hell shall not prevail against it." *

Jesus Christ then presented Himself to His disciples as the Son of God—not as the Son of God in the sense in which we are all sons of God, but as the Son of God in its true and proper sense: had it been otherwise, He would not in so marked a manner have manifested to His apostle the joy He felt at his confession. Moreover, on other occasions He spake, if possible, more clearly to them. Philip said to Him: "Lord, show us the Father, and it is enough for us." Jesus Christ grew indignant at his demand, and said to him: "So long a time have I been with you, and you have not known me? Philip, he that seeth me, seeth the Father also. How sayest thou, Show us the Father? Believe you not that I am in the Father, and the Father in Me?" † And, at another time, manifesting His divine filiation yet more clearly, He said to one of His disciples who still wavered: "God so loved the world as to give His only-begotten Son.... He that believeth in Him is not judged; but he that doth not believe is already judged, because he believeth not in the name of the only-begotten Son of God." ‡ Jesus Christ stood forth then as the Son of God without equal or rival, and in so strict a sense, that He was in His Father and His Father in Him, and that to see Him was to see His Father.

So much for friends and disciples. But, besides friends and disciples, there is another tribunal before which every new

\* St. Matt. xvi. 13-18. † St. John xiv. 8-10.
‡ St. John iii. 16, 18.

doctrine must appear, namely, the tribunal of the people. After having spoken in secret to the chosen ones, it becomes needful to quit the chamber, to appear in public, to speak to mankind of all ages and conditions, to those who have not leaned upon the bosom of the Master, who have not received the education of friendship, who know not what is required of them, who oppose to the word of doctrine a host of passions blended with as many prejudices. Jesus Christ did this ; He heard the murmurs of the crowd around Him, and was undaunted before the account which He had to give them of Himself. "How long," cried they to Him, "dost Thou hold us in suspense ? If Thou be the Christ, tell us plainly." Jesus Christ answered them : " I speak to you, and you believe not ; the works that I do in the name of My Father, they give testimony of Me.* I and the Father are one." † At that saying, which expressed all, the Jews took up stones to stone Him, and Jesus said to them : "Many good works I have showed you from My Father ; for which of these works do you stone Me ?" The Jews answered Him : " For a good work we stone Thee not, but for blasphemy ; and because that Thou, being a man, makest Thyself God." ‡ The language which Jesus Christ held towards the people in order to make known to them the origin and mission of their new spiritual Master, was, then, language free from all constraint and obscurity. He fearlessly uttered to them that terrible phrase : " I and my Father are one "—EGO ET PATER UNUM SUMUS.

But above the people—that confused mass whose voice is at the same time the voice of God and the voice of nothingness ; above the people—who form at the same time the highest and the lowest authority—rises, with calm vigilance and self-respect, the highest representation of right and truth. Every nation possesses a supreme magistracy which concentrates in itself the glory and enlightenment of the country, and before it every doctrine claiming to rule, either by doing apparent or real violence to received traditions, must at last appear. Jesus Christ could not escape from this general law of the human order. He is called before the council of the elders, the priests, and the princes of Judæa. After hearing evidence more or less inconsistent, the high priest at length resolves to place the question in its true light ; he stands up

* St. John x. 24, 25.    † *Ibid.* 30.    ‡ *Ibid.* 32, 33.

and addresses this solemn charge to the accused : " I adjure Thee by the living God that Thou tell us if Thou be the Christ, the Son of God."* Jesus Christ calmly replies in two words : EGO SUM—" I am ! " And He immediately adds, in order to confirm His avowal by the majesty of His language : " I am ; and you shall see the Son of Man sitting on the right hand of the power of God, and coming with the clouds of heaven." † Then the high priest rends his garments. " What need we any further witnesses ? " he exclaims. " You have heard the blasphemy ! What think you ? " ‡ And they all condemn him, as guilty, to death. He is then brought before the Roman governor, who, not finding good reasons for His condemnation, wishes to release Him ; but the princes of the people persist : " We have a law," say they, " and by that law He ought to die, because He made Himself the Son of God." § Pilate so fully comprehends this, that his Roman, and therefore religious, ear is all attention; he draws Jesus Christ aside, and timorously asks Him whence He is : UNDE ES TU ? || Jesus Christ is silent; He confirms by His silence all that He is accused of having said of Himself, and what, in fact, He has said. The people who witness His crucifixion understand His condemnation in the sense in which it was pronounced ; they insult Him even in death by these expressive derisions : " Vah, Thou that destroyest the temple, and in three days dost rebuild it, save Thy own self; if Thou be the Son of God, come down from the cross." ¶ And, when darkness covers the earth, when the rocks are broken in pieces, when the veil of the temple is rent in twain, and all Nature proclaims to mankind that a great event is in action, the lookers-on and the Roman centurion strike their breasts, saying: "Indeed, this was the Son of God ! " ** And the apostle St. John concludes his gospel in these words: "These things are written that you may believe that Jesus Christ was the Son of God." ††

Thus, before His friends, before the people, before the magistracy, in His life, in His death, Jesus Christ everywhere declares that He is the Son of God, the only Son, a Son equal with His Father, one with His Father, being in His Father, and His Father in Him. This is the testimony which He renders of Himself, His answer to that imperious question :

\* St. Matt. xxvi. 63.   † St. Mark iv. 62.   ‡ St. Mark xiv. 63, 64.
§ St. John xix. 7   || St. John xix. 9.   ¶ St. Matt. xxvii. 40.
\*\* St. Matt. xxvii. 54.   †† St. John xx. 31.

QUID DICIS DE TEIPSO? And what an answer, gentlemen! What! a man, a creature of flesh and blood, who has before him, not only the weaknesses of life, but those also of death; a man! and he dares to call Himself God! It is the first time in all history. No historical personage, before or since, has set himself up as God. Idolatry had numberless gods; but it had a supreme God, to whom none other was equal; and when the most shameful flattery decreed apotheosis to emperors convicted of every crime by their lives and of complete nothingness by their death, none saw in the incense offered to their ashes anything but a poetical figure, a last act of adulation rendered by bondage to tyranny. Mahomet, come to replace the reign of idols, did not call himself God, but a simple envoy of God; and if we would go back beyond idolatry in search of the arrogant impostures, we shall find even in the heart of India nothing but narrations without consistency, ages without date, a shapeless abyss in which our vision will be totally unable to discover any authentic mortal bold enough to declare that he was God, formally and distinctly, by those two ineffable words: EGO SUM. Man is not capable of uttering so bold a falsehood, the improbability is too striking.

It is also and too manifestly useless, for what would it profit? What end could it serve a man to call himself God? Would he establish laws, found an empire? It is a human ambition; and I can well understand why he would not call himself a philosopher, since any one versed in history knows that whoever sets himself up as a philosopher is sure to remain alone upon his pedestal. A man, then, having great ambition would never advance such pretensions. God is the cornerstone of every lasting edifice. His name, even when invoked by imposture, serves as a solid cement; and it was natural that before and after others Jesus Christ should call Himself the envoy of God. Men have often accepted that idea; they readily believe in the intervention of the Divinity in human affairs, and their faith, thus deceived in its application, is never deceived as to the reality of a Providence eternally watchful over their condition. Jesus Christ, in calling Himself the Man of God, would have proclaimed something probable and serviceable; but the very title of God, the apotheosis of Himself by Himself, added nothing but difficulties to His enterprise. Thenceforth it became necessary that in all His actions he should sustain the part of the Infinite, that even in His death

He should maintain proofs of His divine nature, and that His tomb, as well as eternity, should bear witness of Him. Was this humanly possible?

Add thereto a third consideration relative to the state of religious belief among the Jews. That people had in their law only one explicit dogma—all the others, although they possessed them in their traditions, were, so to say, veiled and obscure. The unity of God, graven at the head of the tables of Sinai, was their chief dogma; the one that recalled and included all the others, such as the creation, the fall of man, the immortality of the soul. To attack this, even remotely, was to attack Moses, Sinai, all the treasured memorials of the children of Israel, all their customs, every object of their veneration. Now the name of Jesus Christ as the Son of God, even without destroying the divine unity, did not enter naturally into the ears of this people, accustomed by their lawgiver and their prophets to know only the God who had brought them out of the land of Egypt, and who had so often said to them: "I am the Lord thy God; thou shalt have no other gods before me."*

If, then, Jesus Christ falsely called Himself God, He needlessly created for Himself unaccountable difficulties.

But let us pass on from these preliminary reflections, and see what account we have to render of the life we are contemplating. Whatever motives Jesus Christ might have had against calling Himself God, He did call Himself God; such is the fact. Before we examine whether what He said was true, an intervening question arises: we have to learn whether in calling Himself God He believed what He said. Between the affirmation and the reality, between saying, I am God and being God, stands the question of good faith and sincerity. Did Jesus Christ believe in His divinity? Was He convinced of the truth of that vital dogma which He laid down as the basis of His teaching and for which He died? Was He sincere, or—pardon the expression—was He an impostor? We cannot advance a step further in His life before we solve this doubt. All mankind, without distinction of time, place, nations, laws, or religions, is divided into two ranks, the rank of impostors and that of sincere men: in these each individual marks his own place. The impostors have too often led the

* Exodus xx. 2, 3.

sincere, but their reign sooner or later betrays itself; and sincerity in regard to man is a requirement which honours him; to error, an aroma which renders it less bitter; to truth, a crown which is the first object of our search. Let us then first of all learn whether Jesus Christ wears this crown; whether He is anointed with this aroma; whether He possesses this honour, without which there is no honour. What think you? Must we place Him with the impostors or with the sincere? Was He of those who have covered their ambition with the veil of hypocritical sanctity, or of those who have preferred the honour of irreproachable language even to success, and who have chosen for their device the motto of the Maccabees: MORIAMUR IN SIMPLICITATE NOSTRA?—Let us die in our simplicity.

This is the great question.

It is answered by the character of the man, and hence I may conclude that the cause is judged in favour of Jesus Christ; for no more venerable form has dawned upon the horizon of history. The simple course of time has placed Him above all, leaving nothing visible that can approach it. By the consent of all, even of those who do not believe in Him, Jesus Christ is a good man, a sage, an elect, an incomparable personage. He has done such great, such holy things, that even His enemies pay constant homage to His work and to His person.

It is true that in the last century there was a man who chose for his motto—designating Jesus Christ—the words: *Écrasez l'infâme!*—Crush the wretch! But this phrase, gentlemen, had not strength enough to pass the bounds of the century in which it was uttered; it halted trembling on the frontiers of our own; and since then no human voice, even among those which are not respected, has dared to repeat that signal of impious revolt. It has fallen back upon the tomb of him who first uttered it, and there, after having been judged by the posterity which has already followed, it awaits the still more stern judgment of posterity yet to come.

I may, then, stop here, since nothing is higher than a universal judgment, and since all demonstration appears weak before a conclusion which forms part of the common sense of mankind. But I wish to afford you the gratification of analysing the character of Christ, and of examining by what harmony of moral beauties that physiognomy infinitely surpasses the most illustrious forms which time has produced.

The human character is composed of three elements, namely, the intelligence—the seat of its thoughts; the heart—the seat of its feelings; the will—the seat of its resolutions. It is the fusion of these three elements which, by its measure, determines every moral type and fixes its value. We have no need to seek elsewhere the secret of that perfection which we find in the hero of the Gospel. Doubtless, for those who believe Him to be God, His divinity supports and shines through the whole visible tissue; but without changing anything of the nature of the soul any more than of the body. Jesus Christ has nothing in Himself to constitute His physiognomy but thoughts, feelings, and resolutions; but the harmony and blending of these form that peculiar charm which it is now our purpose to examine.

I shall not mislead you, gentlemen, in saying of His intelligence, that in character and sign it possesses that which we call the sublime. The sublime is elevation, profundity, and simplicity, blended together in a single trait. When the aged Horatius was told that his son had fled from the combat which decided the supremacy between Alba and Rome, and, seeing his indignation, they asked him what his son should have done against three, the old man replied: "He should have died!" This is a sublime exclamation; it is the cry of duty springing at once from a great soul, and bearing us in a moment above all the weaknesses which plead within us against self-sacrifice. Nothing is more simple, but nothing is higher or more profound. God has given to man the faculty of reaching the sublime in his actions and in his writings; but these occasions are rare and fugitive. The greatest men have been sublime four or five times in their lives; such was Cæsar saying to a boatman who brought him through a tempest: "What fearest thou? Thou carriest Cæsar!" Simplicity is too often wanting to the greatest actions, or, when they are simple, they do not raise us sufficiently out of ourselves, or they are not profound enough to give us sufficient food for thought. It is the same with our writings. It is not rare to find in them harmony, grace, beauty, and, as it were, a flowing stream which bears us along between sweet and flowery banks. We are thus carried on through whole pages. Suddenly, and as by chance, a powerful emotion seizes upon us, and seems to pierce even to our soul. The sublime has appeared. But it is only an apparition;

and this is why it draws us out of our natural state, by producing within us a sudden and passing shock.

It is not so in regard to Jesus Christ. His actions and His language are stamped with a continuous elevation, profundity, and simplicity, so that the sublime is, as it were, naturalized in them, and no longer excites our wonder; nevertheless, its empire over the soul is undiminished. For this reason, after so many famous masterpieces of literature, the Gospel has remained a unique book in the world, a book acknowledged to be above all imitation. " Blessed are the poor in spirit,"* said Jesus Christ. What can be more simple? And yet how suddenly it bears us away from earth! The angel who seized Habakkuk and carried him from his fields to Babylon was not more rapid. Three simple words suffice to change all our notions of beatitude, of the value of earthly things, of the object and end of life—to bear us above worldly cupidity, and cause us to hover joyfully, like the eagle, above the kingdoms of the world. " Blessed are the poor in spririt !" These words will resound throughout the world ; the soul, having once heard them, will constantly recall them, and never fail to find hidden in them a powerful hand, ready to its rescue. Meditation, in sounding their depths, will open treasures of profundity, a new social economy destined to change the relations of men with each other, ennoble labour and suffering, abolish slavery, and make a beneficial and holy profession even of poverty. Such is the Gospel—that is to say, Jesus Christ, from beginning to end ; and that sovereign intelligence cannot be better defined than by saying that it had received from God the gift of continuous sublimity.

Great minds generally exhaust their whole power in their thoughts, and are unable to impart more than a feeble and secondary action to their hearts. This is especially remarkable in founders of empires and doctrines—cold, haughty men, masters of themselves, looking down upon mankind and urging them to and fro in their hidden designs, as the wind waves a field of corn, ripe and ready for the sickle. The conception of their plans absorbs them ; success corrupts them by flattering their pride: reverse sours them, and all things combine to make them scornful of mankind, which is for them only a pedestal, erect or overthrown. Even if they do not fall

* St. Matt. v. 3.

so low in the degradation of the heart, they are not permitted to raise their faculty of loving as high as their faculty of thought. The piercing glance of the eagle is not naturally given to the eye of the dove. These distinctions are perceptible even in authors. Racine—pardon these comparisons—is tender; Corneille is much less so, because his genius draws nearer to the sublime. We feel in him something heroic and austere, like those Romans of whom he said:

> Et je rends grâce au ciel de n'être pas Romain
> Pour conserver encor quelque chose d'humain.

Now, Jesus Christ, under this head, is an ever-memorable exception, and far above successful imitation, even by those who adopt Him as the Master of their souls. He carried the power of loving even to tenderness, and to a kind of tenderness so new that it was needful to create a name for it, and that it should form a distinct species in the analysis of human feelings—I mean the evangelic unction. Jesus Christ was tender towards all men; it was He who said of them: "Whatsoever you shall do to the least of these my brethren, you will have done it unto me;"* an expression which introduced Christian fraternity into the world, and which still daily engenders love. He was tender towards sinners; He sat at meat with them, and, when doctrinal pride reproached Him for it, He replied: "I am not come for those that are in health, but for those that are sick." † Perceiving a publican who has climbed up into a tree to see Him pass by, He says to Him, "Zacchæus, make haste and come down; for this day I must abide in thy house."‡ A sinful woman approaches Him, and ventures even to anoint His feet with ointment, to the great scandal of a large assembly; He reassures her by that immortal allocution: "Her sins, which are many, are forgiven, because she has loved much."§ They bring before Him a woman taken in adultery, in order to force a judgment from Him, which by its very leniency may compromise Him; He answers: "He that is without sin among you, let him cast the first stone at her."‖ He was tender towards His ungrateful and parricidal country; and, beholding its walls from afar, He wept, saying: "Jerusalem! Jerusalem! thou that killest the prophets, and

---

\* St. Matt. xxv. 40.  † St. Matt. ix. 12.
‡ St. Luke xix. 5.  § St. Luke vii. 47.  ‖ St. John viii. 7.

stonest them that are sent unto thee, how often would I have gathered together thy children, as the hen doth gather her chickens under her wings, and thou wouldst not!"* He was so tender towards His friends as to wash their feet, and to permit a very young man to lean upon His breast on one of the most solemn occasions of His life. Even at His crucifixion he was tender towards His executioners, and, lifting up His soul to His Father for them, He said: "Father, forgive them; for they know not what they do."† No earthly life shows such a blending of light and love. Every word of Jesus Christ is an expression of tenderness and a sublime revelation; at the same moment when He opens the Infinite to us by His look, He folds us in His arms and presses us upon His bosom. We soar away in thought, and are retained by love.

And it must not be forgotten that the tenderness of Jesus Christ, although boundless, is of spotless virginity. It is difficult for those who have received a soul apt for love to hold that precious gift within chaste limits; it is the object of a supreme struggle, in which one may be sometimes tempted to regret the gift, or to desire more liberty in its use. Jesus Christ seems to know nothing of this; He bears His love in a vase so pure that the shadow even of doubt does not approach His heart, and posterity, which, for eighteen centuries, has sought for faults in Him, has never dared to utter a word of suspicion against His virtue. The character of His tenderness is that of ineffable chastity.

There remains yet one thing, gentlemen, to complete our estimation of the character of Jesus Christ, and to enable us to judge by His character, of His sincerity. A sublime intelligence, a tender heart, do not suffice to form a will capable of great resolutions. The will is a distinct world, where, notwithstanding our views and our feelings, the helm is too often guided by a feeble hand. The character of Jesus Christ on this head is that of absolute certainty of Himself. None ever ventured upon a more difficult design; He claimed to be acknowledged as God, loved as God, served as God, adored as God; it would seem that the will should sometimes have yielded under so heavy a load, and that at least Jesus Christ should have employed all the human means capable of insuring the success of such gigantic ambition. It is not so,

---

\* St. Matt. xxiii. 37.  † St. Luke xxiii. 34.

gentlemen ; Jesus Christ despised all human means, or rather He abstained from employing any.

Politics rank among the highest of these. It is the art of seizing the tendency of minds at a given moment, of bringing together opinions and interests which seek to be satisfied, of anticipating the will of a people before they have a clear consciousness of it themselves; of assuming, by the help of circumstances, the post of their natural representative, and of placing them upon a course in which we shall be borne along with them for half a century. Such is the art of politics—an illustrious art, which may be used for good or evil, and which is the source of prosperous and lamentable vicissitudes among nations. Jesus Christ was admirably placed for becoming the instrument of a revolution favourable to His religious designs. The people from whom He had sprung had lost, under the Roman yoke, the remains of their ancient nationality; hatred of Rome was then at its height among them, and, in the deserts and mountains of Judæa, bands of liberators were daily formed under the command of some patriot, distinguished for his boldness or some other characteristic. These movements were seconded by celebrated prophecies, which had long announced a chief and a saviour to the Jewish people. The relation of these ideas and interests to the new kingdom, the coming of which Jesus Christ proclaimed, was evident. Nevertheless, so far from conniving at and employing them, He trampled them under foot. In order to prove Him, He is asked whether it is needful to pay tribute to Cæsar; He calls for a piece of money, and, on being told whose image and superscription it bears, He calmly replies: "Render then to Cæsar that which is Cæsar's, and to God that which is God's." * He goes still further. He announces the temporal ruin of His nation, He speaks against the temple—the object of religious and patriotic veneration among the Jews—and He openly predicts that there shall not remain of it one stone upon another; therefore this charge was numbered amongst the accusations brought against him before the supreme magistracy.

His doctrine, so favourable to the people and to the poor, was of a nature to obtain great popularity for Him : this is a powerful mainspring for revolutions. In fact, He gained such an ascendency over the people that they wished to elect Him

* St. Matt. xxii. 21.

King of Israel; but He fled in order to avoid that honour, and broke with His own hands an instrument which great men would commonly have valued as a gift and a sign from Heaven.

Next to the art of politics comes power, one of its adjuncts, but which may be considered without reference to the causes that generally communicate it. Jesus Christ had nothing so much at heart as to prevent His disciples from trusting to power and from exercising it. He sends them forth, He says, like lambs; He announces to them all kinds of troubles, without giving them any other help than patience, meekness, and humility. If, unmindful of His lessons, they would call down fire from heaven, he reproaches them with not yet knowing "of what spirit they are."* At the moment of His arrest, when He might have defended Himself, and an apostle drew the sword, Jesus Christ says to him: "Put up thy sword again into its sheath; for they who draw the sword shall perish by the sword."† Whilst the authors of other doctrines seek a sanction from victory—rashly forgetting that victory is variable and conscience immutable—Jesus Christ chooses the Cross for His standard, and protests against all triumph of power by the triumph of His crucifixion.

He also despises science and philosophy—those nobler and truer means of imparting conviction. He surrounds Himself with fishermen instead of *savants*, and, avoiding even the appearance of a scientific and philosophical organization of His doctrine, He teaches it by parables and detached sentences. He leaves to His disciples and to His Church the future charge of blending reasoning with them, and of ranging the whole in order.

In fine, the most ordinary skill seems to be unknown to Him; He makes of His death—of the time when He should have received therefrom so terrible a check to His divinity, and when He would no longer be present to sustain His followers—He makes, I say, of His death a snare for the faith of His disciples, in promising them to rise from the dead, and in leaving the confirmation of His whole life to that test, which, if He were not God, could result only in a base fraud, or a flagrant contradiction.

I know no other human means, gentlemen, of founding anything here below, than those I have just cited, namely,

---

* St. Luke ix. 55. † St. John xviii. 11.

politics, power, science, philosophy, skill. Jesus Christ abstained from employing any of these, and yet, confidence in Himself, absolute certainty of Himself, never failed Him for a single hour or a single moment. This very forbearing to employ any human means proves to the highest evidence His inflexible resolution, and the omnipotent energy of His will. Nevertheless, nothing can be accomplished without means, without instruments. What means, then, what instruments did Jesus Christ employ? Ah! gentlemen, what means? Do you not see what means? It was Himself, His inner force, the converse which He held with Himself, the sure possession of His essence. Men tremble because they see themselves. Jesus Christ did not tremble because He saw Himself. He knew that His very word was "the Way, the Truth, and the Life;"* He gave it to all who came, as the husbandman sows corn; the husbandman has no more need of politics, power, science, philosophy, or skill; he has the corn, the earth, and the heavens; he opens his hand and casts forth life. And whilst human politics pursue their course, whilst power struggles with power, whilst science exhausts science, the philosophy of to-day buries the philosophy of yesterday, and the skilful are taken in their own nets; the wheat fallen from the hand of God into the hand of man, and from the hand of man into the bosom of the earth, vegetates, grows up, and ripens; it is gathered in, eaten, and mankind lives! So did Jesus Christ; so does everyone who believes that he holds the truth from God: he first lives by it, then he sows it, and the world—"which is the field"†—the world lives by it in its due time.

We have then before us, gentlemen, the character of Jesus Christ, as the Gospel shows it to us. With regard to His intelligence—continuous sublimity; with regard to His heart—chaste and ineffable tenderness; with regard to His will—absolute certainty of Himself. Now this character is incompatible with the ignoble vice which I no longer dare even to name, so far is it already removed from your thoughts. Jesus Christ was sincere because He was a sublime intelligence; He was sincere because His heart was open to men as a sanctuary of tenderness and chastity; He was sincere because He possessed absolute certainty of Himself, because He had faith in

* St. John xiv. 6.     † St. Matt. xiii. 38.

His doctrine, because He believed in Himself. Jesus Christ, like the Gospel—which is no other than Himself—Jesus Christ was sincerity itself, and the invincible charm which is felt in contemplating and in listening to Him comes from the inmost brightness of His physiognomy, by which He is seen from without wholly as He is.

Granted, say you, Jesus Christ was sincere. What then? So many others have also been sincere! Reflect a moment, gentlemen; remember that Jesus Christ, being sincere, believed what He said. Now, He said that He was God; He declared this to His disciples, to His friends, to the people, to the supreme magistracy of His country; He was condemned, and He died for that affirmation; therefore He believed that He was God. But He could not believe this if He were not God, because it is impossible to be deceived in such a matter as that of consciousness of one's own personality, without being mad. Now, Jesus Christ was not a madman, and He was sincere: then He was God. Here, by an exception which belongs to the very nature of the subject, the question of sincerity blends with the question of reality. And this is no new discovery, no vain idea of my mind. Through ages past, gentlemen, the Gospel, in proving to the minds of its attentive readers the sincerity of its hero, convinced them of His divinity without any other argument. Whilst the Catholic Church, the daughter and spouse of Jesus Christ, demonstrates the divinity of her founder by the divinity of her own characteristics, the Gospel, in another manner, proves to the children of the Church the divinity of Him who founded it. And this impression is common to different ages—to the three ages of man—so natural is it, and so based upon truth.

At the age of twelve, in the first bloom of life, we heard the Gospel read, we heard of Jesus Christ; His works appeared to us most simple, gentle, and loving; we believed in them in the simplicity, the gentleness, the love of our young souls. But that first impression too often fades and vanishes; reason grows strong with its real rights; outward prejudices penetrate within us; inward passions are drawn forth by the sun of our ripening years, and Jesus Christ falls gradually from the altar whereupon our first adorations had placed Him. This time has its day. Years pass over our bondage, up to the time when reason, become more personal and more powerful, makes us ashamed of our faith in lessons without authority, and when our very passions, enlightened by their domination, incite us by lassitude to instincts of governance, of duty, and of greater self-respect. This time is hallowed amongst all others; it is the time when we enter into order by liberty itself, by that divine liberty of youth which Providence has prepared for us, and which no law can snatch from us. If the Gospel then fall into our hands, and we read it a second time, Jesus Christ often touches us again, and with a mastery which we no longer contest, because we yield it to Him of ourselves at an age when nothing any longer pleads against Him but passions judged and ignorance overcome. It is the second reading of the Gospel, gentlemen, that we are now accomplishing together.

There is a third, less fortunate than the two former, because it is more tardy; but it brings to Jesus Christ the homage of man in his maturity, and has produced avowals worthy of eternal remembrance. Whilst the eighteenth century heaped insult upon the Son of God, in the very midst of that school which attacked him, there was a man who believed no more than the rest, a man as celebrated as the rest—the most celebrated amongst them, with one exception—and who above them all was privileged with sincere impulsions. God so willed it that His name might not be left without a witness even amongst those who laboured to destroy His reign. That man, then at the height of his glory, acquainted by his studies with past ages, and by his life with the age of which he was an ornament, had to speak of Jesus Christ in a profession of faith in which he desired to sum up all the doubts and convictions which his meditations on religious matters had left in his mind. After having treated of God in a worthy, although in a confused manner, he came to the Gospel and Jesus Christ. There, that soul, floating between error and truth, suddenly lost its hesitation, and with a hand firm as a martyr's, forgetting his age and his works, the philosopher wrote the page of a theologian—a page which was to become the counterpoise of the blasphemy: *Écrasez l'infâme!* It concluded by these words, which will resound throughout Christendom until the last coming of Christ: "If the life and death of Socrates be those of a sage, the life and death of Jesus Christ are those of a God."*

It might well have been thought that the force of that con-

---

* Rousseau, "Emile."

fession would never have been surpassed, whether in regard to the genius of the man who wrote it, the authority of his unbelief, the glory of his name, and the circumstances connected with the age which received it; but it would have been an error. Another man, another expression, another glory, another phase of unbelief, another age, another avowal met, were greater altogether, if not in each separate part, than those you have just heard. Our age commenced by a man who outstripped all his contemporaries, and whom we, who have followed, have not equalled. A conqueror, a soldier, a founder of empire, his name and his ideas are still everywhere present. After having unconsciously accomplished the work of God, he disappeared, that work being done, and waned like a setting sun in the deep waters of the ocean. There, upon a barren rock, he loved to recall the events of his own life; and, from himself, going back to others who had lived before him, and to whom he had a right to compare himself, he could not fail to perceive a form greater than his own upon that illustrious stage whereon he took his place. He often contemplated it; misfortune opens the soul to illuminations which in prosperity are unseen. That form constantly rose before him—he was compelled to judge it. One evening in the course of that long exile which expiated past faults and lighted up the road to the future, the fallen conqueror asked one of the few companions of his capitivity if he could tell him what Jesus Christ really was. The soldier begged to be excused; he had been too busy during his sojourn in the world to think about that question. "What!" sorrowfully replied the inquirer, "you have been baptized in the Catholic Church, and you cannot tell me, even here upon this rock which consumes us, what Jesus Christ was! Well, then, I will tell you;" and, opening the Gospel, not with his hands, but from a heart filled by it, he compared Jesus Christ with himself and all the great characters of history; he developed the different characteristics which distinguished Jesus Christ from all mankind; and after uttering a torrent of eloquence which no father of the Church would have disclaimed, he ended with these words: "In fine, I know men, and I say that Jesus Christ was not a man!"

These words, gentlemen, sum up all I would say to you on the inner life of Jesus Christ, and express the conclusion which, sooner or later, every man arrives at who reads the Gospel with just attention. You who are yet young have life before you; you will see learned men, sages, princes, and their ministers; you will witness elevations and ruins; sons of time, time will initiate you into the hidden things of man; and when you have learned them, when you know the measure of what is human, some day, perhaps, returning from those heights for which you hoped, you will say also, "I know men, and I say that Jesus Christ was not a man!"

The day too will come, when upon the tomb of her great captain, France will grave these words, and they will shine there with more immortal lustre than the sun of the Pyramids and Austerlitz!

THE
# PUBLIC POWER OF JESUS CHRIST

My Lord—Gentlemen,

Jesus Christ declared that He was God, and by His character He proved the sincerity of that declaration; therefore He was God. But is this all the proof of His divinity? Doubtless the first manifestation of beings endowed with intelligence is their word, the affirmation which they give of themselves; doubtless the expression of what they are by their moral physiognomy, or character, is the second and natural manifestation of the same beings: but is this all? Is there nothing beyond this? And even should this demonstration suffice as to the ordinary relations between men, will it be sufficient when it is a question of intercourse between God and men? Evidently not. For it requires a certain amount of penetration, and time also, in order to judge a character; a moral physiognomy is not fully disclosed in a single day, and when God appears, gentlemen, when He deigns to come to us, it is manifest that, at the first glance, there should be in His appearance something exclusive of doubt, or discussion, or time, or even science, something recognisable immediately by all; something, in a word, manifesting openly the public power of God, and infallibly revealing His presence and action. Even as there is a certain expression of the majesty of temporal sovereignty, there should be for God an eminent and adequate means, by which, as soon as He appears, every intelligent being, not in mad revolt against Him, should bend before Him and exclaim: It is God! What is this mode of manifestation, which I have called the public power of God? In what does it consist? Did Jesus Christ possess it? What objections does it raise, and how are they answered? Such, gentlemen, is the vast field we are about to traverse to-day.

No being can manifest itself save by the elements contained within itself, and which constitute its nature. Now all beings, of what kind soever, contain but three elements, namely, substance, force, and law; substance, which is their centre of being; force, which is their action; law, which is the measure of their action. If we cast a glance upon the lowest in the scale of beings, upon that which approaches nearest to nothingness, we shall find in it these three elements. Thus the atom has a substance, something which adheres, which holds its place, something which we cannot analyse, but which we have called by a mysterious name, signifying that which is under and sustains what is above. The atom possesses a resisting force: in order to displace it, a movement, however slight it may be, is required; and without that movement it remains stationary. It possesses a cohesive force by which its parts hold together, a force of affinity by which it attracts other atoms to itself; for it is its vocation, as it is yours, to increase. It possesses a force of passibility by which it receives light, heat, and all the fluids of which its obscure, yet mysterious and profound life, has need. In fine, its substance and its force are regulated by a law; it is not alone in the world, it is connected with other beings, it is subject to other influences, as its own influence is exercised; its action is measured, as the action of others upon itself is measured. Substance, force, law; all these are in an atom, and all these are in God, who is the Father of the atom. God is the fulness of substance, the fulness of force, the fulness of law; He is infinite substance, absolute force, eternal law. He is yet more: He is the centre of all substances, their creator and preserver; the centre of all forces, their beginning and their end; the centre of all laws, their principle, their sanction, and their majesty.

As beings are thus formed, from the atom even to God, every being is able to manifest itself in a threefold manner, namely, by its substance, by its force, or by its law. By its substance: thus bodies appear to us; by its force: thus the soul reveals itself to us; by its law: thus the heavenly bodies, even when invisible, are anticipated by the astronomer through the general movement that governs them, withholding or bearing them away from our view. And consequently God may manifest Himself as substance, as force, and as law; as the centre of all substances, of all forces, and of all laws. For if an atom possesses the magnificent power of disclosing itself, if from its very dust and nothingness it imposes itself upon our vision, enters our academies, provokes discussion, exhausts our learning for ages, how much more should God possess the right and power to disclose Himself! A being that does not do this, is not. For the vocation of every being, without exception, is to appear, to take a field of action and to act in it; and as there is no action without manifestation, to appear is to live. And as God is life, His sole work is evidently His appearing, radiating, conquering; in a word, being in all what He is, namely, the King of substances, the King of forces, the King of laws.

It is true He now hides His substance from us men, and we may exclaim with the prophet: "Verily, Thou art a hidden God!"\* But if He withholds from us that direct vision of Himself, it is not from weakness or from envy, it is from respect for our liberty and for the very intercourse which He would hold with us. Had we at once seen His substance, the overwhelming splendour of that manifestation would have taken from our soul all its freedom of action; we should have adored God in spite of ourselves, whilst the adoration which God claims from us, and which He has a right to claim, is an adoration of choice and love, springing from our soul and reaching to his own. It was needful, then, that God should manifest Himself without dazzling our vision and making us the slaves of His beauty; it was needful that we should see Him without seeing Him, that we should be sure of His presence without being oppressed by it; and this is why He has hidden His substance from us whilst He leaves to us His light, as the sun sometimes gathers clouds to lessen his splendour, remaining still visible in the midst of heaven.

If the manifestation of God by His substance would have been too powerful for our liberty, there was another reason against His manifesting Himself only by His law. The law of God is truth, that is to say, the sum of all necessary and possible relations, of all uncreated and creatable relations. In revealing truth, God indeed reveals Himself to us, but under a form which permits us easily to disregard Him, because we detach truth from the living source which bears it, and because

\* Isaiah xlv. 15.

we make of it, so to say, a creation, an idol of our own mind; or, being unable in certain cases to hail it as the offspring of our own intelligence, we rid ourselves of it as a stranger who offends and contradicts us. Doubtless, God is able to raise truth to the state of prophecy, by announcing beforehand relations that will result in the course of ages between events and empires whose names do not yet exist; but prophecy needs time for its fulfilment and confirmation; up to the latest moment it remains suspended in history as a dream unworthy of our attention, and, were it to apply to events too near at hand, it would lose force, wanting anteriority. Therefore, even in the prophetic state, truth would be insufficient as the instantaneous sign of the divine presence. So that, whilst the manifestation of God by His substance would be too powerful, that which He gives to us by His law, or truth, is too feeble to produce immediate conviction.

Force then remains to God, as a means of revealing himself with a degree of splendour which brings neither too much nor too little light.

But God possesses force itself, and can exercise it in three different orders: in the physical order, which includes all the kingdoms of nature; in the moral order, which includes whatever relates to the soul; in the social order, which comprises the soul and the body ranged under the laws of unity. Now God, by Jesus Christ, has visibly applied His force to the two last orders, that is to say, to the soul and to society, as we have shown in our preceding conferences in treating of the virtues reserved to the action of Catholic doctrine, and of the social effects produced by that same doctrine, the offspring of Jesus Christ. This sign, however, was insufficient to form at once a halo of divinity for Jesus Christ, when on His first appearing among men, He had to present His credentials to them in the name of the Father, of whom He called Himself the august and only Son. The conversion of the soul, its exaltation to the highest virtues, needs time, and the cooperation of man himself; the foundation of a visible society, endowed with privileges of unity, universality, stability, holiness, needs yet more time, and the co-operation of an innumerable multitude of men spread over the field of ages and space. God does not create a society in a day, He does not even so convert a soul; and when perchance He works this last prodigy, He who has been its object, and who has the most steadfast consciousness thereof, does not suddenly become a burning and a shining light, enlightening the world with the splendour of His virtue. Men hide the mystery of God, and keep it long from the eyes of the world; like St. Paul, they withdraw into the desert, and that desert—were it even the busy throng—remains long in presence of a transfigured soul before recognizing in it the divine sign.

What remains then to God, gentlemen, as His eminent mode of appearing, His own and inimitable sign, the public expression of His physiognomy in space and time? There remains to Him His physical force, or, in other words, His sovereignty over nature, a sovereignty which, in the matter and order forming its field of action, meets with no liberty to respect, no co-operation to solicit or wait for, but simply an immense energy, whose instantaneous submission announces the Master of heaven and earth to every man who is not afraid to encounter God. The proper character of this sovereign act is that it requires from the beholder neither study, nor science, nor any preparation requiring time or distinction, but sincerity only. It is so foreign to all human action that, at least, it confounds, even when it does not produce conviction, so that the rebel has no resource but silence against the upright man who exclaims: DIGITUS DEI EST HIC!* Therefore, human tongues, the mysterious organs of truth, have given a singular name to the act by which God exercises his sovereignty over nature, and instantaneously manifests His presence to men: they have called it a *miracle*, that is, the marvellous in the highest degree, the act which constitutes the public power of God.

But does Jesus Christ bear upon His brow this sign of absolute force? Did he work miracles? Did He exercise the public power of God?

One day John the Baptist sent his disciples to ask him: "Art Thou He that should come, or look we for another?" Jesus Christ answers them: "Go, and tell John what you have heard and seen; the blind see, the lame walk, the lepers are cleansed, the deaf hear, the dead rise again, to the poor the Gospel is preached."† That is to say, Jesus Christ, the man whom we have acknowledged as the most admirable character shown in history, was not afraid to give as proof of His mission and divinity, a whole series of miraculous acts wrought by Him-

---

\* Exodus viii. 19. † St. Luke vii. 20-22.

self. And indeed, the Gospel, from beginning to end, is a series of simple sayings, which pierce to the very centre of the soul, and of prodigious sayings, which agitate nature even to its foundations. Vainly have men endeavoured to separate these, and see two works in one single work; the Gospel resists that analysis which pretends to extract from it the moral substance and put aside the miraculous substance, to take from the worker of miracles the support of the sage, and from the sage the support of the worker of miracles. Both of these remain firmly united against the wily efforts of Unbelief; the doctrine supports the miracle, the miracle justifies the doctrine, and the Gospel circulates in the world with an invincible character of unity, which permits and obtains for Jesus Christ only absolute hatred or complete adoration.

This unity is of itself a demonstration for all who reflect seriously. Nevertheless, Unbelief, amazed at its powerlessness to divide Jesus Christ, falls back upon itself, and anxiously exclaims : Is it then really true that Jesus Christ gave sight to the blind, made the lame to walk, cleansed the lepers, gave hearing to the deaf, and life to the dead? Is it true that He acted as the Master of nature, and that daily, before the eyes of the people, in the light of heaven, His creating hand proved that a divine virtue dwelt in Him? Is there not a horrible falsehood engrafted upon the sincerity of that life?

Gentlemen, the Gospel is from a period in history : it is a history. The miracles of Jesus Christ were wrought in the public squares, before multitudes of all conditions, before numerous and bitter enemies. They formed the basis of a teaching which divided a whole country, and which soon divided the universe. If, notwithstanding the character of truth which distinguishes the Gospel from all other books, you suspect its testimony as the work of those who believed in Jesus Christ, you cannot, by a contrary reason, suspect the recitals and impressions of those who did not believe in the new Master, and who everywhere persecuted His disciples, His doctrines, and even His name. A public discussion was raised, a man called himself God; He died for having done so ; His nation, divided upon His tomb, appealed from that blood, and from His nation men appealed to that blood shed, which on all sides found adorers. Now publicity is a power which forces the enemies of a cause to pronounce openly, and in spite of themselves to concur in the authentic formation of a history which they detest and would fain utterly destroy. It is in vain; publicity forces them, they are compelled to speak, and even in calumniating they are compelled to speak enough of truth to save it for ever from perishing. This it is, gentlemen, that saves history. Nothing in the world is more hated and more feared; the oppressors of nations and the oppressors of God labour at nothing more vigorously than in endeavouring to prevent the existence of history; they silence the four winds of heaven against it; they shut up their victim within the narrow and deep walls of their dungeons; they surround it with cannon, lances, and all the instruments of menace and fear; but publicity is stronger than any empire; it bears along even those who hold it in execration; it constrains them to speak; the cannon turn, the lances fall, and history passes on!

So, gentlemen, has the history of the miracles of Jesus Christ advanced? It has advanced by His very enemies; by the Pharisees, who crucified Him, by the Pagan rationalists, who crucify His memory. The deicidal Jews, in the face of publicity filling the whole world, could not avoid expressing their sentiments and opinions upon the miraculous life of Christ; they were compelled to pronounce an affirmation or a denial, and a denial they dared not pronounce, because no one in the world can impose absolute falsehood in regard to public facts after the world has spoken. Absolute falsehood is no more possible in the order of history than is absolute error in the order of speculation. The Jews have perverted the miracles of Jesus Christ; they have not denied them; they have written that Jesus Christ assumed in the temple the incommunicable name of God, and that by that sovereign name He commanded nature. This explanation is deposited in the most grave monuments of their tradition, and this is all they have been able to do against the accusing memory of Jesus Christ, against the blood which the whole universe reproached, and still reproaches, them for shedding. But what more could they do? Publicity is master of men who have seen; it becomes changed into tradition upon their tomb, and pursues them from age to age, from justice to justice, even to their latest posterity.

The Pagan rationalists came in their turn to deal with the history of Jesus Christ. Doubtless they had taken no part in His crucifixion, and it was not His blood that alarmed them; but, with His blood, Jesus Christ had shed upon the world a truth which condemned to nothingness the wisdom of the wise;

could the wise of this world forgive Him? They also then had to give a critical text of His life, and, in order to depreciate it, they had to employ all the resources which the traditions and discussions of their times afforded them. What have they said of the miracles of Jesus Christ? What have Celsus, Porphyrius, Julian—names for ever illustrious, because from the earliest Christian ages they have been the heralds of the Son of God in the incomparable offices of enmity—what have they said of Him? Have they denied that Jesus Christ wrought miraculous works in support of His doctrine? No more than the Jews; they have simply made a skilful magician of Him. Why a magician, and not a sage? What need was there of so strange an expression? It is because history was there. It was possible to pervert the miraculous works of Jesus Christ; it was not possible to be silent in regard to them.

It is then clear, gentlemen, by the very testimony of the enemies of Jesus Christ, that His preaching was accompanied by superhuman prodigies. But we must not separate these exterior incentives to faith, strong as they are, from the intimate character of the Gospel and Jesus Christ. In an edifice all is bound together from the base to the summit. If Jesus Christ was sincere, as we have shown, if His nature was stamped with the character of divine superiority, His sincerity and His superiority call for confidence in His miracles, as well as in the affirmations which he made of Himself. If Jesus Christ did not speak falsely in declaring that He was God, by a stronger reason He did not lie in acting as God. For it is more shameful, more contrary to sincerity, to perform impostures, that is to say—pardon the expression, but by its force, that very expression shows the scorn in which mankind holds imposture—it is more shameful to be a juggler than a knave. The knave deceives only by his speech, the juggler adds thereto miserable manipulations in order to dazzle the eyes of ignorant spectators. It is a lie heaped upon a lie, an indignity upon an indignity. And this is why human tongues—so skilful in expressing scorn—have created that odious name of juggler, to mark all who dare to employ illusion in aid of imposture.

The superiority of Jesus Christ is no less favourable to the reality of His miracles than His sincerity. No grave and learned man will ever employ juggles to support a doctrinal teaching. For what is jugglery? It is the use of a power unknown to the science of the times in which it is practised.

But science will not be slow to arrive at it; absent for a moment, it is inevitable in the course of mankind; a day comes when it rises radiant, and, casting back its investigating lustre upon the past, it judges, weighs, verifies all, and, whilst it brings to the true works of genius or of the Divinity their final consecration, it reduces to dust the puerile practices which had imposed upon the faith of untaught generations. Therefore nothing great in the world has ever been founded upon impostures of this kind; every work possessing any force or dignity, even if not altogether free from falsehood, has gathered its meed of stability from something ancient and true. Mahomet is a memorable example of this. Author of a religious revolution in a country unenlightened by science, he employed every human means to insure success, but he did not employ jugglery, because it is not a human means. I have recently read through the Koran. Every twenty pages Mahomet touches the question of miracles; he objects, or he is reproached with not performing them; never does he once venture to say that he had performed or ever would perform them; he constantly eludes the question. He invokes Abraham, Moses, all the patriarchs; an event in his life when God protected him; a victory which had crowned his arms and justified his doctrine; he loudly affirms that God is God, and that Mahomet is His prophet; this is all. And this scorn of miserable imposture, this respect for general ideas in regard to Providence and traditional memorials, is not an insignificant mark of his skill, and even of his genius.

And we are to believe that Jesus Christ, the author of the Gospel, stooped to the most unworthy imitations of the omnipotence of God, that He passed the time of His public mission in deceiving the eyes of His contemporaries by phantoms as despicable as they are powerless! We are to believe that such miserable trickery could have obtained the greatest success of faith which the human race has ever wrought! It is not possible. Common sense, as well as history, condemns such a supposition. The public life of Jesus Christ answers to His inner life, and His inner life confirms His public life. He declared Himself to be God, He was believed to be God, He acted as God, and precisely because that position is one of marvellous strength, men have been forced to try their greatest efforts against it; history and common sense speaking too loudly in favour of Jesus Christ, it was needful to have recourse to metaphysics and physics in order to snatch from His hands at least the sceptre of miracles. Let us see whether they have succeeded.

Two things are advanced against Him. First, Jesus Christ wrought no miracles, because it is impossible. Secondly, His working miracles is of no importance, since everybody can work them, everybody has wrought them, everybody works them.

First, Jesus Christ wrought no miracles because it is impossible. And why? Because nature is subject to general laws, which make of its body a perfect and harmonious unity where each part answers to all, so that if one single point were violated the whole would at once perish. Order, even when it comes from God, is not an arbitrary thing able to destroy or change itself at will; order necessarily excludes disorder, and no greater disorder can be conceived in nature than that sovereign action which would possess the faculty of destroying its laws and its constitution. Miracles are impossible under these two heads; impossible as disorder, impossible because a partial violation of nature would be its total destruction.

That is to say, gentlemen, that it is impossible for God to manifest Himself by the single act which publicly and instantaneously announces His presence, by the act of sovereignty. Whilst the lowest in the scale of being has the right to appear in the bosom of nature by the exercise of its proper force; whilst the grain of sand, called into the crucible of the chemist, answers to His interrogations by characteristic signs which range it in the registers of science, to God alone it should be denied to manifest His force in the personal measure that distinguishes Him and makes Him a separate being! Not only should God not have manifested Himself, but it must be for ever impossible for Him to manifest Himself, in virtue even of the order of which He is the Creator. To act, is to live; to appear, is to live; to communicate, is to live; but God can no longer act, appear, communicate Himself; that is denied to Him. Banished to the profound depths of His silent and obscure eternity, if we interrogate Him, if we supplicate Him, if we cry to Him, He can only say to us—supposing, however, that He is able to answer us: "What would you have? I have made laws! Ask of the sun and the stars, ask of the sea and the sand upon its shores; as for Me, My condition is fixed; I am nothing but repose, and the contemplative Servant of the works of My hands!"

Ah! gentlemen, it is not thus that the whole human race has hitherto understood God. Men have understood Him as a free and sovereign being; and, even if they have not always had a correct knowledge of His nature, they have at least never refused to Him power and goodness. In all times and places, sure of these two attributes of their heavenly Father, they have offered up their ever fervent prayer to Him; they have asked all from Him, and daily, upon their bended knees, they ask Him to enlighten their minds, to give them uprightness of heart, health of body, to preserve them from scourges, to give them victory in war, prosperity in peace, the satisfaction of every want in every state and condition.

There is perhaps some poor woman here who hardly understands what I say. This morning she knelt by the bedside of her sick child; and, forsaken by all, without bread for the day, she clasped her hands and called to Him who ripens the corn and creates charity. "O Lord," said she, "come to my help; O Lord, make haste to help me!" And even whilst I speak, numberless voices are lifted up towards God from all parts of the earth to ask from Him things in which nature alone can do nothing, and in which those souls are persuaded that God can do all. Who then is deceived here? Is it the metaphysician, or the human race? And how has nature taught us to despise nature in order to trust in God? For it is not science that teaches us to pray, we pray in spite of science; and as there is nothing here below but science, nature, and God; if we pray in spite of science, it must be nature or God that teaches us to pray, and to believe with all our heart in the miracles of divine power and goodness. After this, whether nature become disorganised or not, or even if it must perish whenever the finger of God touches it, it is assuredly the very least concern to us. Nevertheless, out of respect for certain minds, I will show that miracles do no violence to the natural order.

Nature, as I have already said, possesses three elements; namely, substances, forces, and laws. Substances are essentially variable; they change their form, their weight, combining and separating at each moment. Forces bear the same character; they increase and diminish, cohere, accumulate, or separate. They have nothing immutable but the mathematical laws, which at the same time govern forces and substances, and whence the order of the universe proceeds. The mobility of forces and substances spreads movement and life in nature; the immutability of mathematical laws maintains there an order which never fails. Without the first of these all would be lifeless; without the second all would be chaos. This established, what does God do when He works a miracle? Does He touch the principle of universal order, which is the mathematical law? By no means. The mathematical law appertains to the region of ideas—that is to say, to the region of the eternal and the absolute; God can do nothing here, for it is Himself. But He acts upon substances and upon forces —upon substances which are created, upon forces which have their root in His supreme will. Like ourselves, who, being subject to the general combinations of nature, nevertheless draw from our interior vitality movements which are in appearance contrary to the laws of weight, God acts upon the universe as we act upon our bodies. He applies somewhere the force needful to produce there an unusual movement: it is a miracle, because God alone, in the infinite fount of His will—which is the centre of all created and possible forces—is able to draw forth sufficient elements to act suddenly to this degree. If it please Him to stop the sun—to use a common expression— He opposes to its projective force, a force which counterbalances it, and which, by virtue even of the mathematical law, produces repose. It is not more difficult for Him to stop the whole movement of the universe.

It is the same with all other miracles; it is a question of force, the use of which, so far from doing violence to the physical order—which indeed would be of little moment— returns to it of its own accord, and, moreover, maintains upon earth the moral and religious order, without which the physical order would not exist.

This objection answered, gentlemen, let us proceed to examine the second. We are told that miracles prove nothing, because all doctrines have miracles in their favour, and because, by the help of a certain occult science, it is easy to perform them.

I boldly deny that any historical doctrine, that is, any doctrine founded in the full light of history by men authentically known, possesses miraculous works for its basis. At the present time, we have no example of it; no one, before our eyes, among so many instructors of the human race whom we see around us, has as yet dared to promise us the exercise of a power superior to the ordinary power which we dispose of. No one of our contemporaries has appeared in public giving sight to the blind and raising the dead to life. Extravagance has reached ideas and style only; it has not gone beyond. Returning from the present age back to Jesus Christ, we find no one, amongst the innumerable multitude of celebrated heresiarchs, who has been able to boast that he could command nature, and place the inspirations of his rebellious pride under the protection of miracles. Mahomet, at the same time heretic and unbeliever, did not attempt it any more than the others: this I have already said, and the Koran will more fully prove it to any one who will take the pains to read that plagiarism of the Bible made by a student of rhetoric at Mecca. Beyond Jesus Christ, in the ages claimed by history, what remains, if we put aside Moses and the prophets—that is, the very ancestors of Jesus Christ? Shall we notice certain strange facts connected with Greece and Rome? Shall we speak of that augur, who, says Livy, cut a stone with a razor; or of that vestal who drew along a vessel by her girdle, or even of the blind man cured by Vespasian? These facts, whatever they may be, are isolated and belong to no doctrine; they have provoked no discussion in the world, and have established nothing; they are not doctrinal facts. Now we are treating of miracles which have founded religious doctrines—the only miracles worthy of consideration; for it is evident that if God manifests himself by acts of sovereignty, it must be for some great cause, worthy of himself and worthy of us, that is to say, for a cause which affects the eternal destinies of the whole human race. This places out of the question altogether all isolated facts, such as those related in the life of Apollonius of Thyana.

This personage is of the first century of the Christian era, and his life was written at a much later period by an Alexandrian philosopher called Philostratus, who designed to make of it a rival to the Gospel, and of Apollonius himself the counterpart of Jesus Christ. A most singular physiognomy is here presented to us, but that is all. What has Apollonius of Thyana accomplished in regard to doctrine? Where are his writings, his social works, the traces of his passage upon earth? He died on the morrow of his life. Instead of certain equivocal facts, had he removed mountains during his life, it would but have been a literary curiosity, an accident, a man, nothing.

Where then shall we look for doctrines founded in the light of history upon miraculous events? Where in the historical world is there another omnipotence than that of Jesus Christ? Where do we find other miracles than His and those of the saints who have chosen Him for their Master, and who have derived from Him the power to continue what He had begun? Nothing appears upon the horizon; Jesus Christ alone remains, and His enemies, eternally attacking Him, are able to bring against Him nothing but doubts, and not a single fact equal or even analogous to Him.

But do there not at least exist in nature certain occult forces which have since been made known to us, and which Jesus Christ might have employed? I will name, gentlemen, the occult forces alluded to, and I will do so without any hesitation; they are called magnetic forces. And I might easily disembarrass myself of them, since science does not yet recognise them, and even proscribes them. Nevertheless I choose rather to obey my conscience than science. You invoke then the magnetic forces; I believe in them sincerely, firmly; I believe that their effects have been proved, although in a manner which is as yet incomplete, and probably will ever remain so, by instructed, sincere, and even by Christian men; I believe that these effects, in the great generality of cases, are purely natural; I believe that their secret has never been lost to the world, that it has been transmitted from age to age, that it has occasioned a multitude of mysterious actions whose trace is easily distinguished, and that it has now only left the shade of hidden transmissions because this age has borne upon its brow the sign of publicity. I believe all this. Yes, gentlemen, by a divine preparation against the pride of materialism, by an insult to science, which dates from a more remote epoch than we can reach, God has willed that there should be irregular forces in nature not reducible to precise formulæ, almost beyond the reach of scientific verification. He has so willed it, in order to prove to men who slumber in the darkness of the senses, that even independently of religion, there remained within us rays of a higher order, fearful gleams cast upon the invisible world, a kind of crater by which our soul, freed for a moment from the terrible bonds of the body, flies away into spaces which it cannot fathom, from whence it brings back no remembrance, but which give it a sufficient warning that the present order hides a future order before which ours is but nothingness.

All this I believe is true; but it is also true that these obscure forces are confined within limits which show no sovereignty over the natural order. Plunged into a factitious sleep man sees through opaque bodies at certain distances; he names remedies for soothing and even for healing the diseases of the body; he seems to know things that he knew not, and that he forgets on the instant of his waking; by his will he exercises great empire over those with whom he is in magnetic communication; all this is difficult, painful, mixed up with uncertainty and prostration. It is a phenomenon of vision much more than of operation, a phenomenon which belongs to the prophetic and not to the miraculous order. A sudden cure, an evident act of sovereignty, has nowhere been witnessed. Even in the prophetic order, nothing is more pitiful.

It would seem that this extraordinary vision should at least reveal to us something of that future which may be called the present future. It does nothing of this. What has magnetism foretold during the last fifty years? Let it tell us, not what will happen in a thousand years, not what will happen the day after to-morrow even, but what will happen to-morrow morning. All those who dispose of our destinies are living; they speak, they write, they alarm our susceptibility; but let them show us the certain result of their action in a single public manner. Alas! magnetism, which was to change the world, has not even been able to become an agent of police; it strikes the imagination as much by its sterility as by its singularity. It is not a principle; it is a ruin. Thus, on the desolate banks of the Euphrates, in the place where Babylon once stood, and where that famous tower was begun which, to speak like Bossuet, was to bear even to heaven the testimony of the antique power of man, the traveller finds ruins blasted by the thunderbolt, and almost superhuman in their magnitude. He stoops, and eagerly gathers up a fragment of brick; he discovers characters upon it which belong, doubtless, to the primitive writing of the human race; but vain are his efforts to decipher them; the sacred fragment falls back again from his hands upon the colossus calcined by fire: it is nothing now but a broken tile, which even curiosity despises.

I look around, gentlemen. I see nothing more: Jesus Christ is alone.

Perhaps, however, you may yet say to me: If Jesus Christ wrought miracles during His life, and even in the early days of the Church, why does He do so no longer? Why? Alas! gentlemen, He works miracles every day, but you do not see them. He works them with less profusion, because the moral and social miracle, the miracle which needed time, is wrought, and before your eyes. When Jesus Christ laid the foundations of His Church, it was needful for Him to obtain faith in a work then commencing; now it is formed, although not yet finished: you behold it, you touch it, you compare it, you measure it, you judge whether it is a human work. Why should God be prodigal of miracles to those who do not see *the* miracle? Why, for instance, should I lead you to the mountains of the Tyrol, to see prodigies which a hundred thousand of your contemporaries have witnessed there during the last fifteen years? Why should I pick up a stone in the quarry when the Church is built? The monument of God is standing; every power has touched it, every science has scrutinized it, every blasphemy has cursed it; examine it well, it is there before you. Between earth and heaven, as says the Comte de Maistre, it has been suspended these eighteen centuries; if you do not see it, what would you see? In a celebrated parable Jesus Christ speaks of a certain rich man who said to Abraham: "Send someone from the dead to my brethren." And Abraham answers: "If they hear not Moses and the prophets, neither will they believe, though one rose from the dead."* The Church is Moses, the Church is all the prophets, the Church is the living miracle: he who sees not the living, how should he see the dead?

* St. Luke xvi. 31.

# THE FOUNDATION OF THE REIGN OF JESUS CHRIST.

My Lord—Gentlemen,

We have seen that in His public as well as in His inner life, Jesus Christ lived as God. But to live is only the first act of life, the second act of life is that of outliving ourselves. For all life has an object, and it is the accomplishment of that object which judges the life. Consequently, it is not enough for me to have proved to you even with the highest evidence that the inner life of Jesus Christ, and His public life possessed a divine character; for if that life has not attained its object, if it has left no traces, whatever else we may think of it, it has been vain. It is needful then that Jesus Christ, after having lived as God, should have perpetuated himself as God; if He has not done this, all the conclusion we should be able to draw from that disproportion between His life and the effects of His life, would be that He was the most magnificent and the most inexplicable nothing that the world has ever seen. But what had Jesus Christ to do in order to perpetuate Himself as God? He had to fulfil the object of His life, such as He had publicly announced and represented it, which was to found here below the kingdom of God. "After John was put in prison," says the evangelist St. Mark, "Jesus came into Galilee, preaching the gospel of the kingdom of God, and saying, The time is fulfilled, and the kingdom of God is at hand: repent ye, and believe the gospel."* And sending forth His disciples to take their part in the apostolate, He thus set forth their mission: "Into whatsoever city ye enter, and they

* St. Mark i. 14, 15.

receive you, eat such things as are set before you: and heal the sick that are therein, and say unto them : The kingdom of God is come nigh unto you. But into whatsoever city ye shall enter, and they receive you not, go your ways out into the streets of the same, and say, Even the very dust of your city, which cleaveth to us, do we wipe off against you : yet know this, that the kingdom of God is come nigh unto you."\*
And what was this kingdom of God preached by Jesus Christ, as being the object of His coming upon earth? It was Himself, inasmuch as that He was to be recognised as God, loved as God, adored as God, the founder and chief of a universal society, of which His divinity was to be the cornerstone through faith, love, and adoration. I ask you, gentlemen, is this work accomplished? Has Jesus Christ, living and dead, founded here below a kingdom of which He is the God? Has He founded the kingdom of souls? Is He amongst us the one and only King of souls? I no longer need to demonstrate this; during ten years I have shown its marvels to you; and had I not done so, this spiritual kingdom is before your eyes, many among you are its members and its subjects; it is a thing that speaks of itself and is above all demonstration. Yes, there exists in the world—in this world of mire and change—a kingdom of souls wherein God is worshipped in spirit and in truth, where men wrestle with flesh and blood, and pride ; where nothing resembles what is elsewhere to be found, and of which Jesus Christ is the author, the chief, the king, the God. And as the angel of the Apocalypse, on beholding the last triumph of that dominion, proclaimed its glory beforehand by that unparalleled expression uttered before astonished worlds: FACTUM EST—"It is done!"† so, henceforth, as a disciple of Jesus Christ, a son of this kingdom, an adorer of the King of souls, I say also to you: FACTUM EST—" It is done!"

The fact is then no longer in question between us; it is proved, it is palpable, it is here before us, and I may thus conclude : "After having lived as God, Jesus Christ has perpetuated Himself as God." But it may not be unprofitable to show you how greatly this work surpasses all created power ; and I will endeavour to do this by exposing to you the double difficulty which Jesus Christ had to overcome. I will call one

---

\* St. Luke x. 8-11. † Apocalypse xi. 15,

of these the inner difficulty, and the other the public difficulty; their explanation will occupy the hour which God now permits me to devote to you.

The first condition of the kingdom of souls and of its establishment was that of obtaining faith in its founder, that is to say, that Jesus Christ should become for an innumerable multitude of men the rule of all their thoughts, and that, renouncing themselves in regard to their most necessary and most profound attribute—which is their own judgment—they should accept that of Jesus Christ as their own, even to the point of being able to say with St. Paul: "I live; yet not I, but Christ liveth in me."\* Not, gentlemen, that Jesus Christ required from us the sacrifice of our reason in order to establish His reign by faith; for He is Himself reason, and it is He who gives us ours by a reflection of His own, as it is expressly written in the Gospel of St. John. But He had to require from us the sacrifice of our own judgment, which is a very different thing from the sacrifice of our reason. In fact, reason does not exist in us in its pure state; were it so, enlightened as we should be by a single and an undivided light, we should advance in the most perfect unanimity. Instead of this, although participating in reason, one and universal, without which we should not be intelligent beings, we mix up with it weaknesses, obscurities, habits, resolutions, numberless mysterious circumvallations which bar up its great outlets, lessen its light, and make of our reason that limited and personal thing which we call private judgment. It is this judgment, the result of our servitude and liberty, which divides men in the house of their common mother, and hinders them from founding here below, by themselves, the holy republic of truth. We cleave, in fact, to our own judgment in a twofold manner, because it is based upon reason, and nothing is more just than to hold to reason; and we cleave to it still more, perhaps, by that individuality which distinguishes us, and which is made up of the innumerable impressions which the ebb and flow of the intelligence have deposited in us from the day when we first exercised that admirable faculty of seeing, hearing, judging, reasoning, and feeling. Now, by the faith in Jesus Christ, necessary to the constitution of the kingdom of souls, we must abdicate that personal judgment which is so

---

\* Gal. ii. 20.

natural and so dear to us; we must found our reason in the superior reason of Christ, we must break in pieces the personal mould—more or less false and narrow—which makes us what we are, and enter into the wide and deep mould whence the Gospel has come, and which is the very mind of Jesus Christ.

This sacrifice, gentlemen, is infinitely painful to us, because, in order to tear us from ourselves, it touches the root of our spiritual being. It is still more painful under another head. Not only do we cleave to ourselves as nature and liberty have made us, but we strive also to impose ourselves upon others, to become their models, their masters, and to create a kingdom of minds in order to govern them. In whatever degree man may have received from Heaven an elevated mind, this is his propensity; in the mental order, as in all the orders of action, the will of man is to reign. If he be favoured by what is called birth, or fortune, or power, his will is to be supreme in them; in fine, if he be gifted in the intellectual order, he thirsts to govern minds. This last royalty is the most courted of all, and its most absolute sovereigns are not satisfied if they do not bring all minds into subjection to their own. When, therefore, Jesus Christ requires from us the sacrifice of our judgment to His supreme reason, He requires from us the abdication of the royalty which we have most at heart; He enters into a conspiracy, the object of which is to humble us before the most rightful throne to which we could aspire: for what sovereignty is more lawful than the sovereignty of the mind—that gift which does not come to us from chance or election, or the efforts of others, but from our own selves, from what is sown in us by nature and cultivated by us? And in proportion as we possess this, whether by science or philosophy, so are we the more incensed against that usurper called Christ, who pretends to nothing less than to set up His mind in the place of our own, than to cause us to think His thoughts and speak His words. This, gentlemen, is the secret of that aversion which so many learned men and philosophers feel towards Jesus Christ; they are men who will not submit to be dethroned, and, naturally, they are in the right.

Nevertheless, it has been necessary that, for eighteen centuries, all of us, whoever we may be, who are the children of Christ, should consent to be dethroned, to become little, to be taught, not only during our childhood, but throughout our lives; and, laden with years and honours, having governed men otherwise than by the mind, in our last moments, when about to appear before God, we have again been required to abdicate that reign of the judgment, so dear to pride, in order to repose in Jesus Christ as little children, and charge Him to bear us in His blessed hands to the throne of that pure and eternal reason, who is God His Father.

None other upon earth, gentlemen, none other, has obtained that supreme dictatorship of the understanding. Tyrants have oppressed human thought by hindering its manifestation, they have never governed it; it eludes all the devices of the most subtle rule. Sages have formed schools, but ephemeral schools, whose laws have been disowned even by their disciples. Should we wonder thereat? The disciple of the sage is a man like himself; he idolises the idea of the master until the day comes when his own idea, ripe for an act of legitimate ingratitude, enables him to attain to the honours of teaching, and mark his place in the history of the unstable dynasties of human knowledge. The religious sects, although standing upon more solid ground, have, however, met with no better success. Heresy leaves us our own judgment, Protestantism leaves us our own judgment; all these doctrines, so far from enchaining faith, have had for object its emancipation. Even Mahometanism, like idolatry beforehand, was unable to constitute a doctrinal authority, and consequently it leaves its followers to the chance of their personal direction. All, save Christ, either leave to us or restore to us our judgment, and here lies the eternal charm of error. What do we now hear around us? What does the present age, uncertain of its course, and almost alike incapable of boldness in evil and in good, demand of Christ with supplication? Is it not to slacken the bonds of His rule, to retrench certain articles of the ancient Christian constitution, to revise the primitive pact of the Gospel, to sign, in fine, a compromise between time and eternity? But Christ smiles at those frail desires which do not spring from entire obedience to His adorable reason; between Him and ourselves, nothing can exist but Himself or ourselves, the abdication of our own judgment, or the reign of our own judgment: between these we have to choose.

It is not even enough for Jesus Christ to set up His judgment in place of our own; as King of our minds, He is as yet only at the beginning of His ambition; He requires more than our minds; He requires our hearts; He requires affection. And what affection, great God? A love which is the fulness of human love, and before which all history of love is as nothing. And that you may judge of what a prodigy this is, let us examine closely the difficulty which we ourselves find in exciting love during our lives.

Hardly has the flower of sentiment germinated within us before we seek in the companions of our youth sympathies which seize upon our hearts, and draw them forth from their dear and lonely solitude. Thence, in the history of all generous lives, come those youthful times, those early remembrances, which none other will ever efface, and which, even in extreme old age, leave in our souls a perfume of the past. Yet, notwithstanding the strength of these young ties, the simple course of time suspends their progress: our eyes, in growing stronger, become less sensible to the beauties of our age, something no longer of childhood delivers us from that first charm, which perhaps none will ever equal, but which no longer suffices for us. Affection cools into grave and virile confidence, and our soul, having mounted a step upon the cycle of life, needs a new attraction, which, in filling it, brings it into subjection. Shall I pronounce its name? And why not? There are two things before which, by the help of God, I will never shrink, namely, duty and necessity. It is needful in my discourse that I should pronounce the name, too much profaned, of the second sentiment of man; I name it then, and I say, that man rising from youth to manhood, needs an attraction capable at the same time of satisfying his youth and his strength, his need of renovation and of future. God has prepared for him love; which, if it be true, that is to say pure, should complete the education of his life and render him worthy of having a posterity. But, O weakness of our nature! the cares of manhood soon furrow our brow, and its wrinkles stamp upon it a worthy testimony to thought; what more do we need? Henceforth, incapable of obtaining the interchange of an infatuation already appeased for us, and which no longer possesses illusions enough for its own nourishment, we rest in an attachment more calm, more serene, still possessing its charm, but which no longer merits to be compared to the ardour of that passion which I have just called by its proper name.

All the resources of the soul are not, however, yet exhausted: as the offspring of eternal love, the genius of its source inspires it even unto the end. With the first shadows of age the sentiment of paternity descends into our heart, and takes possession of the void left there by its former affections. It is not a state of decadence—beware of thinking so; after the regard of God upon the world, nothing is more beautiful than the regard of the aged upon the young, so pure is it, so tender, so disinterested, and it marks in our life the very point of perfection and of the highest likeness to God. The body declines with age, the mind perhaps also, but not the soul whereby we love. Paternity is as superior to love as love itself is superior to affection. Paternity is the crown of life. It would be full and stainless love, if from the child to the father there were the same equal return as from friend to friend, from the wife to the husband. But it is not so. When we were children we were loved more than we loved, and, having grown old, we also love more than we are loved. We must not complain of it. Your children take the very road upon which you have passed before them, the road of affection, the road of love—eager courses which do not permit them to reward that grey-haired passion which we call paternity. It is the honour of man to find again in his children the ingratitude which he showed to his fathers, and thus to end, like God, by a disinterested sentiment.

But it is nevertheless true that, although pursuing love all our lives, we never obtain it save in an imperfect manner, and which wounds our hearts. And even had we obtained it during life, what would remain of it to us after death? I know that fond prayers may follow us beyond this world, that our names may still be pronounced in pious remembrance; but soon heaven and earth will have advanced another step; then comes oblivion, silence dwells upon us, the ethereal breeze of love passes over our tomb no more. It is gone, it is gone for ever; and such is the history of man in regard to love.

I am wrong, gentlemen; there is a Man whose tomb is guarded by love, there is a Man whose sepulchre is not only glorious, as a prophet declared, but whose sepulchre is loved. There is a Man whose ashes, after eighteen centuries, have not grown cold; who daily lives again in the thoughts of an innumerable multitude of men; who is visited in His cradle by shepherds and by kings, who vie with each other in bringing to Him gold and frankincense and myrrh. There is a Man whose steps are unweariedly retrodden by a large portion of mankind, and who, although no longer present, is followed by that throng in all the scenes of His bygone pilgrimage, upon the knees of His mother, by the borders of the lakes, to the tops of the mountains, in the byways of the valleys, under the shade of the olive-trees, in the still solitude of the deserts. There is a Man, dead and buried, whose sleep and whose awaking have ever eager watchers, whose every word still vibrates and produces more than love, produces virtues fructifying in love. There is a Man, who eighteen centuries ago was nailed to a gibbet, and whom millions of adorers daily detach from this throne of His suffering, and, kneeling before Him, prostrating themselves as low as they can without shame, there, upon the earth, they kiss His bleeding feet with unspeakable ardour. There is a Man, who was scourged, killed, crucified, whom an ineffable passion raises from death and infamy, and exalts to the glory of love unfailing which finds in Him peace, honour, joy, and even ecstasy. There is a Man, pursued in His sufferings and in His tomb by undying hatred, and who, demanding apostles and martyrs from all posterity, finds apostles and martyrs in all generations. There is a Man, in fine, and one only, who has founded His love upon earth, and that Man is thyself, O Jesus! who hast been pleased to baptize me, to anoint me, to consecrate me in Thy love, and whose name alone now opens my very heart, and draws from it those accents which overpower me and raise me above myself.

But among great men who are loved? Among warriors? Is it Alexander? Cæsar? Charlemagne? Among sages? Aristotle? Plato? Who is loved among great men? Who? Name me even one; name me a single man who has died and left love upon his tomb. Mahomet is venerated by Mussulmans; he is not loved. No feeling of love has ever touched the heart of a Mussulman repeating his maxim: "God is God, and Mahomet is His prophet." One Man alone has gathered from all ages a love which never fails; Jesus Christ is the sovereign Lord of hearts as He is of minds, and by a grace confirmatory of that which belongs only to Him, He has given to His saints also the privilege of producing in men a pious and faithful remembrance.

Yet even this is not all; the kingdom of souls is not yet established. Jesus Christ, being God, should not be satisfied with steadfast faith and immortal love; He must exact adoration. Adoration is the annihilation of one's self before a superior being; and this sentiment, gentlemen, is not a stranger to us.

It lies, like all the others, in the very depth of our nature, and plays a more important part there than you are perhaps aware of. Let us not disguise this truth from ourselves; all of us, more or less, desire to be adored. It is this innate thirst for adoration which has produced every tyranny. You sometimes wonder that a prince should weave together numberless intrigues in order to emancipate himself from human and divine laws; that he should add violence to cunning, shed streams of blood and march onward to the execration of mankind; you ask yourselves why he does this. Ah! gentlemen, for the very natural object of being adored, of seeing every thought subject to his own, every will in conformity to his will, every right, every duty emanating from him, and even the bodies of men bent like slaves before his mortal body. Such is the depth of our heart, as was Satan's. But by a counterpoise due to that frightful malady of pride, we can only desire adoration for ourselves by abhorring the adoration of others. Thence springs the execration that follows despotism. Mankind, abased by a power despising all law, concentrates its secret indignation within itself, awaits the inevitable day of the despot's weakness, and, when that day comes, it turns upon and tramples under foot the vile creature who had disdained it even to demanding incense from it. A great orator once said to a celebrated tribune: "There is but one step from the Capitol to the Tarpeian rock." I shall say with as much truth, although in less grand expressions: There is but one step from the altar to the common sewer. Whosoever has been adored will sooner or later be hurled by the hand of the people from the lofty summit of divine majesty usurped, to the execration of eternal opprobrium. Such do we find history—that power charged with the promulgation of the judgments of God upon the pride of man.

In spite of history, however, Jesus Christ is adored. A man, mortal and dead, He has obtained adoration which still endures, and of which the world offers no other example. What emperor has held His temples and His statues? What has become of all that population of gods created by adulation? Their dust even no longer exists, and the surviving remembrance of them serves but to excite our wonder at the extravagance of men and the justice of God. Jesus Christ alone remains standing upon His altars, not in a corner of the world, but over the whole earth, and among nations celebrated by the cultivation of the mind. The greatest monuments of art shelter

His sacred images; the most magnificent ceremonies assemble the people under the influence of His name; poetry, music, painting, sculpture, exhaust their resources to proclaim His glory and to offer Him incense worthy of the adoration which ages have consecrated to Him. And yet, upon what throne do they adore Him? Upon a cross! Upon a cross? They adore Him under the mean appearances of bread and wine! Here, thought becomes altogether confounded. It would seem that this man has taken delight in abusing His strange power, and in insulting mankind by prostrating them in wonder before the most vain shadows. Having by His crucifixion descended lower than death He made even of ignominy the throne of His divinity; and, not satisfied with this triumph, He willed that we should acknowledge His supreme essence and His eternal life by an adoration which is a startling contradiction to our senses! Can such success in such daring be in any way understood?

It is true many have endeavoured to overthrow His altars; but their powerlessness has but served to confirm His glory. At each outrage He has seemed to grow greater; genius has protected Him against genius, science against science, empire against empire; whatever arms have been uplifted against Him He has made His own; and when apparently vanquished, the world has still beheld Him calm, serene, Master, adored!

Thus has He founded the kingdom of souls by a faith which costs us the sacrifice of our own judgment, by a love which exceeds all love, by an adoration which we have given to Him alone; a triple mystery of a force which reveals His divinity to us, and which will yet more clearly reveal it when we shall have taken account of the public difficulty that stood in the way of the establishment of this supernatural kingdom.

The place was filled, gentlemen, when Jesus Christ came into the world; the place was filled because it is never void. Even had He pretended to establish between Himself and us secret relations only, a kind of obscure worship, this design would sooner or later have encountered fears and jealousies, manifested by public opposition. But Jesus Christ was far from desiring to hide His reign; He had said: "That which you hear in the ear, preach ye upon the housetops;"* and He

---

* St. Matt. x. 27.

Himself, the enemy of all mysterious initiation, had constantly spoken and acted before the eyes of the multitude and the authorities. He willed a visible reign, a social constitution of His doctrine, a recognised priesthood, temples, laws, rights; and consequently it was inevitable that He should find in His way the religious and political establishment which preceded Him. That establishment had two names; it was called idolatry, and the Roman Empire. Idolatry was the worship that assembled the universe under one and the same religious form; the Roman Empire was the power that governed all known mankind, or nearly so. The one and the other were incompatible with the establishment of the reign of Jesus Christ, and that reign could only begin by abolishing idolatry as a false religion, and by modifying the Roman Empire so as to fit it for the laws promulgated by the Gospel.

You have, perhaps, hitherto considered idolatry as a religious organization easy to overthrow; you have greatly deceived yourselves. Of all the forms of worship that have taken possession of man, none, save Christianity, has possessed more extent and solidity than idolatry. This is because it fully satisfied the three great passions of man. What are these three passions? The first, and perhaps it will surprise you, the first is the religious passion, the want of intercourse with God. Yes, gentlemen, the religious passion precedes all others, even the passion of sensuality. For sensuality touches only the senses which are fragile, which soon become exhausted, which tire of themselves; while the religious want, a sort of divine hunger, has its source in the most profound depths of our being, and gathers nourishment there from all those miseries which excite in us a continuous distaste for the present life. Even pride comes but after it; however active it may be, it is subject here below to too many humiliations not to second and bear before itself in our soul a better and a gentler sentiment, that which draws us near to God, and causes us to seek our own dignity in his greatness. Religion is the first and oldest friend of man; even when he wounds it, he still respects and cultivates secret intimacies with it. Let not the state of our country, gentlemen, deceive us on this point; do not think because there are some millions of men around us who are besotted in practical atheism, that this is the natural condition of the human race. It is the result of extraordinary circumstances, and notwithstanding the irreligion of some of her children, this same France has never for a single day ceased to bear in her glorious womb a multitude of souls who serve God ardently, and honour their faith by works known throughout the world.

Now, idolatry, in spite of its slight doctrinal character, gave satisfaction to the religious want; it had temples, altars, a priesthood, sacrifices, prayers, public and pompous ceremonies, a very great station in the world, and the shreds of its mythology still contained sufficient remembrance of God to keep the soul from fasting and without food.

But it must not be forgotten that idolatry, in giving satisfaction to the elevated inclinations of our nature, did not disdain the most abject, and abundantly dispensed sacred nourishment to them. A most profound and subtle art had blended together God and matter, religion and sensuality, causing grave thoughts and shameful solicitations to descend from the same altars. The idolater had all in his gods; whatever he willed, heaven obeyed his desires. What a masterpiece, had heaven in its turn been obeyed! In addition, the third passion of man, the pride of domination, found also in this worship, which was erudite by its very degradation, an ample satisfaction. Idolatry was not distinct from the empire; the prince, the senate, or the people, conferred the sacerdotal magistracy, named the pontiffs, regulated the ceremonies, took pleasure in covering the robe of their consuls with the mantle of their gods. Religion was country also. The fasces and the altars were seen advancing together before the republic: the fasces, the symbol of its justice and power; the altars, the symbol of that mysterious alliance which united the destinies of the State to the very destinies of the gods.

No, you will never adequately represent to yourselves the force of that institution. Ah! if a pagan ceremony were to rise up again before you; if you could see all Rome mounting to the temple of Jupiter Capitolinus, that concourse of people, those legions, that senate, all those patriotic memorials mounting with them, and all together bearing to the gods the new victory of Rome! If you could hear the silence and the sound of unanimity, that hum of all the passions convinced of their rights and satisfied with their triumph, pride as well as sensuality, sensuality as well as religion, the elevated and the abject, heaven and earth, all at once, all in a single day and in a single action: if you had seen and heard this, you, perhaps, yielding to that total intoxication of the human faculties, would for a moment have bowed the head, and adored in the hands of Rome the antique gods of the world!

However, they were not to be adored, they were to be destroyed; such was the order of Jesus Christ. They were to be destroyed throughout the world, since the whole world was subject to idolatry. And what was to replace it? A Man, humbled even to the punishment of slaves; a Man, come from a country upon which the Romans showered floods of ridicule with oppression; a Jew, and a Jew crucified! This is what the fishermen of Judæa brought to Rome, to the Capitol, to replace the statue of Jupiter Capitolinus! Judge, then! Here was ignominy instead of greatness, penance and mortification instead of sensuality. Penance and mortification; what words! After eighteen centuries of naturalization, I hardly dare to pronounce them before you, without disguising them to your ears, which have nevertheless been nourished by the language of the Gospel; and it was necessary to reveal these to the Romans! It was necessary to say to them: We bring you a religion all pure and holy, founded upon the immolation of the body by chastity, and not only by chastity, which is only a simple retrenchment, but by the direct hatred of the senses. We come, with the scourge in our hands, to teach you to treat your body as a slave, because it is the slave of the most vile inclinations, and because you can only deliver your souls from it by keeping it in the respect and chastisement of obedience. It was necessary to say these things to a people puffed up by seven centuries of arrogance and domination, plunged in sensuality as well as in pride, and accustomed to find in their gods, which were to be destroyed, the justification of their pompous ignominy. But Jesus Christ had so ordered it; all that was said, believed, adopted, and the reign of idols fell before the reign of the cross, in spite of the Roman Empire.

The Roman Empire and idolatry were as one; but it was not less inimical to the Christian establishment on another hand. That empire had been founded slowly by the prudence and stability of its councils, the courage of its armies, the abnegation of its chiefs, until, having become master of the world, it bent under the very weight of its greatness, and lost in corruption all the public liberties which had formed its glory and its welfare. Nothing of this remained when Jesus

Christ came into the world, save a few already dishonoured
symbols; and when He died, the empire had passed from
Augustus to Tiberius by a decadence which foreshadowed
Nero. The orators' tribune was mute, the people consoled
themselves for the loss of the Forum with a crust of bread
thrown to them; the senate, mangled and decimated in its last
illustrious men, opposed to despotism only the promptitude of
an obedience which sometimes even wearied the insolent
caprice of the master. A single man was all, and that man
could hurl with impunity any defiance to servitude. One day,
it pleased him to assemble the senate, that is to say, the relics
of all the great Roman families, the descendants of those
conscript fathers who had borne war and liberty so proudly
within the folds of their togæ; it pleased him to call them
together to deliberate about the composition of a fish sauce!
I thank you, gentlemen, for refraining from laughter; this is
the greatest insult which has ever been offered to human
nature in the person of the greatest political body it has ever
produced. God permitted it, gentlemen, in order to teach us
how low man falls by the corruption of riches and apostasy
from liberty, that guardian of all rights and of all duties. Such,
then, was Rome when Jesus Christ sent His disciples to convert her to Himself, and such was with Rome the whole universe.
Mistress of the world, after having enchained nations to her
greatness, she held them enchained to her humiliations; and
for the first time in the history of the human race liberty had
no longer an asylum upon earth.

I say, for the first time. Until then, by a providence worthy
of all our thanksgivings, God had so provided that there was
always some free land where virtue and truth could defend
themselves against the designs of the stronger. Whilst the East
was fertile in tyrannies, Egypt possessed institutions worthy of
esteem, and judged her kings after their death; Greece defended
her tribune against the ambition of the kings of Persia; Rome
protected her citizens by laws which surrounded their lives
with many sacred ramparts. If from ancient we pass to modern
times, we shall find there the same care of Providence in not
permitting despotism to reign everywhere at the same time.
The present world is divided into three zones, the zone of unlimited tyranny which has nothing to envy from the most cruel
histories of the past, an intermediate zone where some action
is still permitted to thought and to faith; and, in fine, that

generous western zone of which we form a part, those great kingdoms of France, England, the United States of America, Spain, where rights and duties have guarantees; where men speak, write, discuss; where, whilst power oppresses the majesty of God and man in distant regions, we defend it before the world, and we defend it without glory, because nothing in that office menaces either our heads or our honour!

A unique moment arrived when, with a map of the world open before you, you would have sought in vain for a mountain or a desert to shelter the heart of Cato of Utica, and when Cato of Utica thought it necessary to ask from Death that liberty which no spot upon earth could any longer give to him. At that unique and terrible moment, Jesus Christ sent His apostles to announce the Gospel to every creature, and to found in their faith, love, and adoration, the kingdom of souls and of truth.

Let us see what this kingdom was to the Roman Empire.

First, it was the liberty of the soul. Jesus Christ claimed the soul; He claimed that it should be free to know Him, to love Him, to adore Him, to pray to Him, to unite with Him. He did not admit that any other than Himself had right over the soul, and above all the right of hindering the soul from communicating with them. Yet much more: Jesus Christ claimed the public union of souls in His service; He knew nothing of secrecy; He demanded a patent and social worship. The liberty of the soul implied the right to found material and spiritual churches, to assemble, to pray together, to hear in common the Word of God, that substantial food of the soul which is its daily bread, and of which it can be deprived only by an act of sacrilegious homicide. The liberty of the soul implied the right of practising together all the ceremonies of public worship, of receiving the sacrament of eternal life, of living together by the Gospel and Jesus Christ. None upon earth possessed any longer the government of sacred things but the anointed of the Lord—the elect souls—initiated into a larger faith and love, tested by the successors of the apostles, sanctified by ordination. All the rest, princes and peoples, were excluded from the administration of the body and blood of Jesus Christ, that divine centre of the kingdom of souls, and which it was not meet to deliver to dogs, according to the forcible expression of the most gentle Gospel.

But as the soul is the basis of man, by creating the liberty of the soul, Jesus Christ, at the same time, created the liberty of man. The Gospel, as the regulator of the rights and duties of all, rose to the power of a universal charter, which became the measure of all legitimate authority, and which, in hallowing it, preserved it from the excesses into which human power had everywhere fallen. On this account, the kingdom of souls was absolutely the very opposite of the Roman Empire, and it was impossible to imagine a more complete antagonism. The Roman Empire was universal servitude; the kingdom of souls, universal liberty. Between them it was a question of being or not being. The struggle was inevitable; it was to be a deadly struggle.

Now, what force did the kingdom of souls dispose of against that empire covered with legions? None. The Forum? It was no more. The senate? It was no more. The people? They were no more. Eloquence? It was no more. Thought? It was no more. Was it at least permitted to the first Christians whom the Gospel had raised up in the world to gather one against a hundred thousand for the combat? No, that was not permitted to them. What then was their strength? The same that Jesus Christ had before them. They had to confess His name and then to die, to die to-day, to-morrow, the day after, to die one after another, that is to say, to vanquish servitude by the peaceful exercise of the liberty of the soul; to vanquish force, not by force, but by virtue. It had been said to them: If for three centuries you can boldly say: "I believe in God the Father Almighty, Maker of heaven and earth, and in Jesus Christ, His only Son our Lord, who was born of the Virgin Mary, was dead, and is risen again;" if for three centuries you can say this openly, and die daily after having declared it, in three centuries you shall be masters, that is to say, free.

And this was done.

And this was done in spite of the fury of the Roman Empire converting the universe into a headsman, and losing its terrified reason in the emptiness of its cruelties. I will say no more of the martyrs; they conquered, as the whole world knows. And this kingdom of souls, founded by their blood; this kingdom of souls, which was to destroy idolatry, and which has destroyed it, which was to overthrow the Roman Empire, and which has overthrown it in all that was false and unjust in it; where did this kingdom of souls set up its capital? In Rome! The seat of virtue was placed in the seat of power; the seat of liberty in the seat of bondage; in the seat of shameful idols the seat of the cross of Jesus Christ; in the seat whence the orders of Nero issued to the world, the seat of the disarmed and aged pastor, who, in the name of Jesus Christ, whose vicar he is, spreads throughout the world purity, peace, and blessing. O triumph of faith and love! O spectacle which enraptures man above himself by showing him what he can do for good with the help of God! My own eyes have seen that land, the liberator of souls, that soil formed of the ashes and blood of martyrs; and why should I not recur to remembrances which will confirm my words in reinvigorating my life?

One day, then, my heart all trembling with emotion, I entered by the Flāminian Gate that famous city which had conquered the world by her arms, and governed it by her laws. I hurried to the Capitol; but the temple of Jupiter Capitolinus no longer crowned its heroic summit. I descended to the Forum; the orator's tribune was broken down, and the voice of herdsmen had succeeded to the voices of Cicero and Hortensius. I mounted the steep paths of the Palatine; the Cæsars were gone, and they had not even left a prætorian at the entry to ask the name of the inquisitive stranger. Whilst I was pondering those mighty ruins, through the azure of the Italian sky, I perceived in the distance a temple whose dome appeared to cover all the present grandeurs of that city upon whose dust I trod. I advanced towards it, and there, upon a vast and magnificent space, I found Europe assembled in the persons of her ambassadors, her poets, her artists, her pilgrims —a throng diverse in origin, but united, it seemed, in common and earnest expectation. I also waited, when in the distance before me an old man advanced, borne in a chair above the crowd, bareheaded and holding in his two hands, under the form of mysterious bread, that Man of Judæa aforetime crucified. Every head bent before Him, tears flowed in silent adoration, and upon no visage did I see the protestation of doubt, or the shadow of a feeling which was not, at least, respectful. Whilst I also adored my Master and my King, the immortal King of souls, sharing in the triumph, without seeking to express it even to myself, the obelisk of granite standing in our midst sang for us all, silent and enraptured, the hymn of God victorious: CHRISTUS VINCIT, CHRISTUS REGNAT, CHRISTUS IMPERAT, CHRISTUS AB OMNI MALO PLEBEM SUAM LIBERAT! And, lest an enemy should have been found in that multitude, it answered itself by another celebrated hymn, which warned us to fly from the lion of Judah if we would not adore him in his victory. After many years, which have already whitened my brow, I repeat to you those threats and those songs of joy; happy are you if you do not fly, but if, drawing nearer, you repeat with us all, children of Christ and members of His kingdom: CHRISTUS VINCIT, CHRISTUS REGNAT, CHRISTUS IMPERAT, CHRISTUS AB OMNI MALO PLEBEM SUAM LIBERAT!

# THE PERPETUITY AND PROGRESS OF THE REIGN OF JESUS CHRIST.

My Lord—Gentlemen,

According to His design and according to His declaration, Jesus Christ established upon earth the kingdom of God, the kingdom of souls; He established it, notwithstanding the difficulty of reigning over men by faith, love and adoration, and notwithstanding the public difficulty which the state of political and religious society then presented to him. But, gentlemen, to enable us to affirm that Jesus Christ has outlived Himself as God, is it enough that His work is stamped with a character which can be only divine? No; for although His success was prodigious, regarding it at the point where we left it, namely, at the accession of Constantine, yet it is the lot of every power that makes its appearance here below to have its struggle and its triumph—a struggle and a triumph, I grant, not all of the same measure, but which have, at least, this in common, that they appear, contend, and reach a favourable moment, which will be called success. What is more difficult and more necessary for the confirmation of victory is to resist victory itself. A celebrated diplomatist has said: "Time is the great enemy." Has Jesus Christ then overcome the great enemy? After idolatry, after the Roman Empire, has He overcome that other power, which is but eternity disguised, the power of time? At the end of a more or less prosperous career, has He not, like all the rest, felt that icy hand which, sooner or later, dishonours the greatest events, and hurls the most stable dynasties from their throne? Is He not visibly struck by that slowly advancing thunderbolt which spares nothing? Such is the question which now claims our attention. In a word, I am about to lay before you the balance-sheet of Jesus Christ, and I invite you to examine it.

Why is time the great enemy? Because, gentlemen, it is endowed with a double power, the power of destroying and of building up. What was it that overthrew those primitive empires of Assyria and Chaldæa? It was time. What overthrew that empire of Cyrus, vainly raised up again by Alexander? It was time. What overthrew that empire, increased by the ruins of all the others, and which we should rather call the world than an empire, the Roman world? It was time. What overthrew all those republics of the Middle Ages whose vestiges, surviving in marbles and paintings, we so much admire? It was time. And, on another hand, what has built up those new kingdoms whose sons we are, the kingdoms of the Franks, the Germans, the Anglo-Saxons, and the rest? It is the same hand, skilful in creating after having destroyed, and which, from the very dust where it has revelled with so much pride, draws forth substance, order, and solidity. Time destroys with one hand and rebuilds with the other, enemy alike to both, since the edifice it raises up does but sink deeper the edifice it overthrows, for, with time, to found is also to destroy.

Nevertheless, gentlemen, let us not halt at those splendid images, which only reveal to us the inimical power of time by outward appearances. Let us endeavour to unveil its secret by analysis, in order that, having learned whence time derives its double power of destruction and edification, we may consider whether Jesus Christ has not been subject to the exercise of that formidable action, and why He alone has been able to escape from it, should we at length prove that He has escaped from it.

The action of time results from five causes, the first of which is novelty. Time is always young, and yet it ages all things. Each of its steps is the advance of dawn, but it leaves darkness and night behind. Restless child of eternity, it borrows unfading youth there, but has no power to communicate it, save but for a moment, to the things measured by its course. It passes, it sheds life; but that life of to-day soon becomes that of yesterday, of the day before, of bygone times, a remembrance, a relic of the past, and yet time is not impoverished; it is ever fertile and young, causing the new to follow the old. Now, the new possesses a charm which seduces the mind as well as the senses, and which enables doctrines bearing its impress easily to prevail against doctrines become superannuated by the simple fact of their duration. Remark what happens around us. As soon as a man is able to give a new form to ideas, and appropriate them to the course of time, he inevitably has disciples. Why? Because he has said something which had not been said before, or had been forgotten. We have the passion for novelty in ideas as in all the rest, and it is not difficult to understand why it is so. Predestinated as we are to enjoy the infinite, the infinite is our want, and we pursue it everywhere. Now, novelty is the only thing here below which gives us some sensation of the infinite. As soon as we have considered an object, we say: It is enough. Who will turn the page? Novelty turns it, and in turning it, disguises its feebleness to our intelligence by a false gleam of progress, which enchants us.

Above all others, gentlemen, Jesus Christ had to fear this inclination of our souls, which arms time with a power so dangerous to doctrinal sterility. However merciful the Gospel may be, it was not to bend to the inconstancy of our mind; "heaven and earth shall pass away," said Jesus Christ, "but my words shall not pass away."* It was to traverse all ages, losing daily the force of its novelty without losing any of its precept, or rather, like God, "who," said Saint Augustin, "is beauty ever ancient and ever new," the evangelic word was to infuse into its progressive antiquity a youthfulness which should charm the heart of all new generations.

This first advantage obtained over time, a second remained to be gained. The second power of time is in experience, that is to say, in the revelation that results from the application of doctrines to the positive life of mankind. Every doctrine is a body of laws, which is of value only in so much as it is considered to contain true relations of beings; it is like the creation of a world. As long as that creation remains in the mind in the state of pure conception, we may be deceived as to its real merits, because it is difficult to judge a great assemblage of ideas; but it is no longer so when, entering into the domain of reality, they are required to found or to maintain a positive order; experience infallibly manifests their

* St. Matt. xxiv. 35.

weakness or their falsity; for a false or powerless law is incapable of establishing durable relations, and as a house based upon false mathematical principles falls to the ground, so no order whatever could subsist based upon ideas wanting the equilibrium of truth.

Now, who had ever more reason to fear this terrible test of experience than Jesus Christ? For, with the Gospel, he had not placed in the world a society confined within the narrow limits of a race and a country, but a universal society, wherein every soul wheresoever born, could claim the rights of citizenship; and consequently, if the Gospel were false, its ruin should have been as great as the universe, and as rapid as time, acting at once upon numberless places and minds.

The third power of time is in corruption. Everything, having reached a certain point of prosperity, decays, because as soon as man is master he wills to enjoy, and because the inevitable result of enjoyment is that decomposition of the soul and body which we call corruption. The history of all successes is the history of Hannibal at Capua. Men grow listless and forgetful, they think themselves secure, they become intoxicated with success; the slow poison of ease relaxes all the springs of their activity; and the being who is nothing save by activity, falls little by little into the shame of slumbering effeminacy. Nimrod begins, Sardanapalus ends. It is the high road of great fortunes; labour and virtue form them, enjoyments annihilate even their last traces. Religion, even more than any other empire, is subject to this great law, and above all the Church, or the religion of Jesus Christ, was firmly chained to it. For the blood of the cross had given her life; having sprung from the crucifixion of a God, she could not fail, in the days of her prosperity, to remember the cruel humiliations of her cradle. And, on another hand, the temptations which her triumph prepared for her were far to surpass any temptations until then known. She was to see the kings of the earth at her feet, to issue orders from one end of the world to the other, to behold ages bending before her teaching and her action, to cover the earth with sumptuous monuments, and see it become a tributary to all the wants of unlimited power and glory; and under the weight of such success, reaching even to heaven, to preserve upon her brow, as in her heart, the sign of penance and humility. Or, if in one of the long days of her life she was about to yield, and to feel the attack of corruption, from that very corruption she was to resuscitate her life, not another life—as we see in nature—but her own life; and, like the eagle of Scripture, recovering the charm of her youth, soar aloft with outstretched wings, invigorated and renewed by her very poverty and by the shedding of her own blood.

The fourth power of time is chance, that is to say, certain conjunctures which do not blend with anything that genius is able to combine and foresee, and which suddenly overthrow the most ably concerted designs. History is full of these. Human prudence makes shipwreck upon shoals imperceptible to the keenest eye. It is the grain of sand of which Pascal speaks, which one morning threw Cromwell into disorder, and destroyed plans destined to change the face of Europe.

You sometimes wonder, perhaps, at a certain equilibrium visible in the world, and which keeps the strong from destroying the weak at will. Why have those great empires not yet crushed the small neighbouring States? It is because those great empires have Cromwell's grain of sand against them. At the very moment when their combinations are ready to succeed and bring about the destruction of all rights upon earth, the obscure son of some peasant, in the corner of a hut, sharpens his knife on a broken millstone; at the noise of war he dons his cap, slips his knife into his girdle, and goes out to see something of what is passing between Providence and the kings of the earth. The smoke of powder opens his eyes; the sight of blood elates him; God makes him the instrument of a brilliant action; behold him a great captain; empires recede a step before him : that knife, that peasant, is chance.

Judge now how much of this Jesus Christ has had to encounter in the course of a reign of eighteen hundred years. Consult simply the history of the papacy, and see what a slender thread has held the destinies of that throne, always surrounded by enemies, yet always enduring. It has constantly had to contend against the most skilful combinations; but what is still more terrible is that conspiracy of chance, that enemy which might at any time have destroyed it, and which, strange to say, has always respected it.

The fifth power of time is war. No earthly power can avoid combat; it necessarily has enemies, not only on account of its faults and abuses, but by the simple fact of its existence. To exist is to combat, because to exist is to take from the common seat of life a part of the substance destined for all; and if this be true of the most feeble being, how much more so must it be of an assemblage of beings raised to the state of power! Therefore Jesus Christ declared "that He came not to send peace, but war,"* a terrible war, and upon a scale so vast as to astound our imagination. For it is the war of the spirit against the flesh and of the flesh against the spirit, that is to say, of the two elements which constitute man, neither of which can ever completely vanquish the other. When the body is victorious, the soul struggles against it, and when the soul is the stronger, the body watches for the moment when its yoke may be broken. But this internal struggle does not cease here, it necessarily produces a war as general as it is deeply seated. Souls unite with souls and bodies with bodies; it is the union of bodies against the union of souls which forms the great war of mankind. Jesus Christ at the head of one army, and Satan at the head of the other; the army of the passions, pride, sensuality, hatred, on one side; the army of the spirit, humility, chastity, obedience, mortification, charity, on the other. All these are in action in the formidable regions of the finite and the infinite, in the depths of God, of the soul, and of the senses, amidst a thousand secondary causes which add to the gloom and the chances of the struggle; and if Jesus Christ be God, He must in the end be victorious, His form remaining unchangeable, although continually insulted, upon the venerable summit of time and things.

Has it been so, gentlemen? Can we testify of Jesus Christ that He has been more powerful than novelty, than experience, than corruption, than chance, than war, than all these causes banded together against Him during a course of eighteen centuries? Can we do this?

Yes, gentlemen, I can do this; I can even show you three degrees in this triumph of Jesus Christ over time. For, in the first place, He lives, His work is before you; although it has undergone more or less of attack in that long pilgrimage under the rebel hand of time, it is nevertheless still before you. It remains surrounded by sufficient glory to attract all eyes, and to be still the object of veneration to which there is no rival, as nothing is comparable to the hatred of the enemies who have not accepted in its temporal duration the proof of its origin in

* St. Matt. x., 34.

the very bosom of eternity. But this is not all. Not only is Jesus Christ living in His Church and His Church in Him, but, since the Christian era, no religious establishment has been founded in the world of which Jesus Christ has not been the basis and the bond of union.

The first in the order of time is Islamism. Now, the basis of Islamism, as Grotius long ago remarked, is entirely biblical. It is Abraham, Isaac, Jacob; it is Moses, Mount Sinai, the Jewish people in the most memorable events of its history; it is Jesus Christ Himself, come after the prophets, and greater than they. At each page of the Koran, Mahomet inscribes a recital drawn from Christian antiquities or makes some allusion to them. Why is this? Why is it that, aspiring to the honour of founding a religion, Mahomet did not base it entirely upon himself! Why, gentlemen? Because he could not. Man can no more build in the air in the order of spirits than in the order of bodies; he must however find a basis. Now, according to the expression of Fontenelle, "the Christian religion is the only religion which possesses proofs," and wherever it has appeared with the authority of its history, error must take its support and be grafted into that mighty trunk which alone throws out its roots in antiquity. Mahomet lived in an age and in a land already impregnated with the sap of Christianity; he touched Abyssinia, a great seat of Christendom, Egypt, a metropolitan church, Judæa, where all the great Christian mysteries were accomplished; the blood of his people remounted with omnipotent celebrity to the blood of Abraham; he could only, in such conditions, found a heresy, or, if you prefer it, establish himself upon Jesus Christ by an infidelity which still rendered immense homage to Him. This is why Mussulmans have always permitted Christians to live in their territory, and adore Jesus Christ, not from toleration resulting from fear, but from respect for the common traditions of the two religions and the formal recommendations of the Koran. There has been a struggle for supremacy between Mussulmans and Christians; but there has been no persecution, properly so called, of Christians by Mussulmans. Ishmael reclaimed only his right of primogeniture over Isaac. And this, gentlemen, explains to you the strange spectacle which Constantinople now presents to us, where, although the penalty of death is decreed against any Christian who should convert a Mussulman, Christians of every communion have nevertheless full liberty to exercise their worship, even publicly.

After Islamism came the Greek schism. Now the Greek schism is the whole Catholic Church save two points—the supremacy of the sovereign Pontiff, and the procession of the Holy Ghost. All the rest, dogmas, morals, sacraments, hierarchy, customs, have been preserved by the descendants of Photius. They have rejected the vicar of Jesus Christ, but they have not rejected Jesus Christ. Jesus Christ is the object of their faith, their love, and their adoration, the corner-stone of their religious edifice.

It is the same, although in a minor degree, with Protestantism. Protestantism has denied the Church, but not Jesus Christ. Jesus Christ remains the Doctor and King of souls, and even for a great number of Protestants He is still the only Son of God, worthy as such of supreme adoration.

No other religious establishment has been raised up in the world since the Christian era. Brahminism and Buddhism were anterior to Jesus Christ; and if some movement was visible in the last of these at a nearer epoch, it was owing to the intercourse between Christians and the distant regions of India and Tartary. Thus, in the mountains of Thibet, since our celebrated embassies of the Middle Ages, a puerile imitation of the papacy has been witnessed. Jesus Christ no sooner dawned upon the world than His light caused the clouds of false religions to recede; many have entirely disappeared, and none has been formed but upon His name and history. He has become the trunk of error as well as of truth, and whoever totally denies Him, opens an abyss for himself where nothing but death will ever fructify. His tomb is now the centre of the religious world; Mussulmans, Greeks, Protestants, Catholics, guard it. All, gathered together from the four winds of heaven, agree to venerate the inanimate stone upon which the mangled body of Christ for three days and nights reposed. A hundred battles have been fought around it; the destinies of the world have a score of times changed their aspect there; but defeat or victory has ever borne to it the homage of nations, and so many struggles have but served to glorify that fragile tomb where all come to prostrate themselves. If Catholics alone had guarded it, it would have been an ordinary protection, like all the rest that is measured by the sword; it was more fitting to the designs of God that Jerusalem "should be trodden under foot of nations," * as the Gospel had foretold, and that the Holy Sepulchre, held up by a thousand hands, should appear amidst all the events as the indicative sign that no religious establishment is thenceforth possible save on condition of participating in Christ by something at least of His blood, His doctrine, and His memory.

Time, gentlemen, will bring you new proofs of this. You will see the fading away of the miserable vestiges of religions without foundation, as the civilization advances of which Jesus Christ is the Creator and the Head. Fable cannot keep ground against history, antiquity empty against antiquity filled, the vague against the certain, death against life. Jesus Christ pursues his course even by the very unfaithfulness which pride brings to Him; He makes use of schisms and heresies as of tainted water which still contains Him for a multitude of souls armed against poison by the simplicity of ignorance and good faith. But at the same time—and this is His third triumph over time—He maintains incorruptible and above all His true Church, the Catholic, Apostolic, Roman Church. He insures to her even a numerical superiority; for Islamism counts but a hundred millions of followers, the Greek schism, sixty millions, Protestantism a like number, whilst the Catholic Church holds a hundred and sixty millions of souls subject to her government. Hierarchical superiority; for neither Islamism, nor the Greek schism, nor Protestantism has been able to create a papacy. Superiority of independence; for no spiritual community has been able to preserve inviolable the sanctuary of the soul, save the Catholic Church, which, by constantly giving her inexhaustible blood for that cause, has kept her teaching and her action free from the yoke, and has merited the honour of being here below the bulwark of right and the virgin soil of holy liberty.

I shall not enlarge further, gentlemen, upon the marks of the true Church of Jesus Christ. I have already done this, and I hastily refer to it now only to demonstrate the sovereign providence by which Jesus Christ has maintained them on the brow of His Church against all the efforts of time.

Thus then a threefold perpetuity is acquired for Jesus Christ

* Isaiah v. 5.

from the scrutiny to which we have subjected Him : perpetuity of life ; perpetuity of exclusive irradiation of life; perpetuity of superiority in life.

But you may reply : This is not questioned. Jesus Christ has lived ; He has infused His life into all religious establishments which have come after Him, and He has even maintained His Church above all the rest. Yet do you not now perceive signs of decadency in His work? Have not a multitude of souls emancipated themselves from His rule? And when signs of decrepitude begin to appear, may we not foresee a near and an inevitable dissolution?

This may be your idea, gentlemen ; mine is that Jesus Christ is at the apogee of His glory and power; and this, with the help of God, I shall now proceed to show you.

Three things constitute power, and the progress of these three things constitutes the progress of power, namely, the territorial state, the numerical state, and the moral state. Now, I affirm that, under this threefold relation, Jesus Christ has never attained a higher point than that at which we at present contemplate him.

In the first place, what was the territorial state of Jesus Christ under Constantine? It was nearly included even in the boundaries of the empire, between the Rhine, the Euphrates, and the Atlas. If it passed beyond, that addition was compensated for by the many parts of the empire of which the Gospel held but an imperfect and uncertain possession. But what do you now see? It is true Jesus Christ has lost some of his former territories, now occupied by Mussulmans; although it must be remarked that Christians exist upon the whole surface of the Islamic soil, and that Islamism itself recognises Jesus Christ and His ancestors.

But turn your eyes to the west, to the east, to the north, to the south, and in every direction of the globe you will find the conquering steps of the Saviour. He has crossed the Rhine ; He has subjected Germany, Poland, All the Russias, the three kingdoms of Great Britain, and has borne even to the pole, across the mountains and ices of Sweden, the sun of His dominion. The Atlantic Ocean opened before Him ; He has passed the Cape of Good Hope, has joined to the sceptre of his children that famous peninsula of India, which from antiquity was looked upon as the reservoir of all the treasures of nature. He has founded establishments along the coast of Africa, and rejoined by the Red Sea His old possessions of Abyssinia. He has made the tour of the two Americas, and from one pole to the other, ranging them under His laws, He has raised up together republics, missions, and bishoprics. He has retaken Spain from Mahomet, and everywhere shaken the territory of Islam. But yesterday, again, when the chief of the house of Bourbon was descending from the throne and about to carry His noble old age into exile, we saw Jesus Christ, by the arm of the old Frank king who thus wrote his testament among us, conquer two kingdoms from infidelity, the kingdoms of Greece and Algeria. Still more recently, China has opened to Him her ports, which had so long been shut; New Holland becomes peopled under the shadow of His cross; the islands of Oceania transform their savage inhabitants into humble and meek adorers of His Gospel. There are no longer any seas, or solitudes, or mountains, or inaccessible places where Jesus Christ does not hoist the bold standards of His children blended with His own.

Return now back to Constantine; weigh the Christian world of that epoch with the Christian world of the present time, and judge of the territorial progress which Jesus Christ has made.

It is the same with the numerical state. I said just now that the Catholic Church counts a hundred and sixty millions of children, the Greek schism sixty millions, Protestantism sixty millions more. This is a total of two hundred and eighty millions of men who acknowledge Jesus Christ for their Saviour and their spiritual head. Doubtless, there are some among these who do not bear His yoke from clear and positive conviction; but the Christian's life must be judged as a whole, and especially at the hour of death. Among the many who think themselves unbelievers there are few who resist Christ to the last, and who do not ask Him to forgive their errors much more than their apostasy. Their soul, moreover, was formed by the Gospel, and it is still their nourishment even when they think they despise it. The numerical state of Jesus Christ was never more flourishing, and it daily tends to increase by the development of Christian populations. Whilst the Mahometan races become impoverished and the remains of the idolatrous nations vegetate in their immobility, the Christian blood, blessed by God, prospers beyond measure, and continual emigrations carry its superabundance into distant lands, and with it the precious seeds of faith.

If you perceive a disproportion between the territory and the population of Jesus Christ, it is easy to be explained. The power of Christians grows yet faster than their blood; they conquer and govern space with a handful of men, and their genius fills it long before their posterity. I do not think this observation is prejudicial to Jesus Christ. But there is another which you certainly expect from me, and which I also expect from you. Whatever may be the state, say you, of the territorial and numerical progress of Jesus Christ—a phenomenon which may be explained by the ascendency of the Christian races—you cannot deny the invasion and progress of unbelief in the very midst of Christianity. If Jesus Christ has overthrown the religions which were before His own, unbelief, more powerful than He, overthrows in its turn the work which He had built up, and overthrows it with still more terrible effects, since it is doubt and negation which take the place of faith. Like those lands exhausted by a substance that has devoured all their sap, and which can no longer produce anything, the land over which Christ has passed is a land cursed; it no longer produces anything but doubt and negation. Thus we advance to a state worse than any of which mankind has been the witness and the victim. Like that conqueror who caused Jerusalem to be razed and salt to be cast upon its ruins, Christ has exhausted the convictions of the human race, and cast upon its intelligence the salt of absolute unbelief. Woe to us, doubtless, woe to us who can no longer believe! But to whom do we owe that incapacity, if not to the tyranny of Christ, who has not been powerful enough to bend for ever our minds to His dogmas, and who is powerful enough to keep us from ever holding any other faith than His own?

I grant, gentlemen, that after seventeen centuries during which Jesus Christ was not denied, He was at length denied in the last century; He is denied even now. But so far from that accident menacing the work of Christ, it derives a glory therefrom, which it will be easy for you to recognise and appreciate. Three countries formed the seat of the total revolt against Jesus Christ—England, France, and Germany. As to England, unbelief has long ago ceased to possess any power or renown there. If your ears are attentive to the echoes of the British Parliament, that highest of all expression of national opinions, you will not have heard, since the birth of the present century, a single word of insult or menace to Christ. England has emancipated Catholics; she has recalled to the tribune of her Parliament the proscribed voices of the defenders of the papacy; she has opened her fields to the labour of monks, and her schools to the learning of the Roman clergy. The old walls of Oxford have heard the most celebrated doctors of Anglicanism speaking of Jesus Christ like the Ancient Church, they have witnessed the retreat of many who have passed from the rostrum to the humble cell, there to recite the office after the manner of the religious orders, and to pray at the foot of a crucifix for the return of their soul and of their country to the old faith of the Anglo-Saxons. Catholic churches, and even cathedrals, have risen up full of splendour from the land of proscription, and Jesus Christ has marched triumphantly with His bishops and priests in the very places where stones and the sword had pursued Him. In fine, England is won back from unbelief, she who was the first to shelter it under the protection of her nobles and her men of genius.

If we turn next to France, doubtless we shall not find there in the same fulness the signs of a return to faith. Yet none of you, knowing the history of the past and the present, would compare the two positions. In the last century, unbelief was absolute mistress of minds, alone it guided the pen and spoke with eloquence; its books were public events; its great men ranked with the old families of the monarchy, and held familiar intercourse with all the kings of Europe; a flagrant and an overwhelming conspiracy hurled to heaven every insult against Jesus Christ. Is it so now, gentlemen? Has not Jesus Christ His writers, His orators, His party, His youth, His glory, among us? And if unbelief still exists, do we not well know how to make it bend before us, and how to march on in the strength of our souls, against its now decrepit successes and its ill-judged expectations? We do, gentlemen; the watchword of the faith in all its most militant action comes from France; our missionaries, our sisters of charity, our brothers of the Christian schools, bear it to the ends of the world, and whoever loves Jesus Christ upon earth keeps his hand upon our heart to feel there the pulsations of faith, and to thank the God who strikes and who heals.

I shall say nothing of Germany; she remains, doubtless, although with certain modifications, the seat of the war against

Jesus Christ. Our unbelievers go there to seek the arms which the genius of France refuses to them yet more and more; but the fall is great, and the thunder that comes from the clouds of the Rhine is not destined to produce such effects as that double voice of England and France, whose future alliance in favour of the Church and Jesus Christ the great Comte de Maistre has long ago foretold.

However, gentlemen, let us not be content with proving by facts the progressive decrease of the forces of unbelief; let us endeavour to trace its causes in order to draw conclusions which may embrace the future as well as the past.

God, then, seeing the darkness of men's minds, has caused three suns to rise slowly upon the horizon of the Church: the sun of history, the sun of science, and the sun of liberty. History was ill-understood; great research, aided by great social revolutions, has enlightened its sombre mysteries, and Jesus Christ, calumniated in the works of His Church, has retaken in the realities of the world a place which men willed to dishonour. Whilst history returned to him by the labours of Protestants and unbelievers, as much as by those of Catholics, science did not serve Him with a lesser return of justice and fidelity. Did it dig in the bowels of the earth, it found again there the first page of Moses; did it descend to the foundations of the temples and monuments of Egypt, it found there the points of junction between Egyptian history and the history of the people of God; did it succeed in deciphering the language of hieroglyphics, those signs, recalled to the vigour of their expression, bore testimony to the newness of the world, compromised by the calculations of astronomy; did it discover and bring to light ruins and inscriptions, those ruins and those inscriptions spoke for us; nature interrogated in every sense, gave back a Christian note from all its pores, as if it had been created or charmed by Jesus Christ.

Liberty also has rendered us signal services. It has loosened the bonds with which unbelief had bound the Church by the hand of kings, and permitted Jesus Christ to resume the sceptre of speech, too long enfeebled from respect which was no longer merited.

Unbelief has, however, received a heavier blow than all these. For the causes I have just enumerated act only in the higher ranks of the world; they do not strike at the heart of the human race, and that central shock is necessary to all extended action. The centre of the world, the heart of the human race, is the people. The people then should have had a sign against unbelief, and that sign was given to them in order that nothing might be wanting to the causes of salvation which God prepares for us. What sign then was given to the people? What sign, gentlemen? It is this: the soul and the body of the people have gained nothing from unbelief, and they know it. The people had a God in heaven; when the earth, so sparing towards them, overtasked their strength, they clasped their hands, and in looking upwards and in appealing to God from their very wretchedness, they felt dignity and consolation reaching to them. The people had a God, not only in heaven, but nearer to them, a God who had become man and was poor, who was born in a stable, whose body had been laid upon straw, and who had suffered in this life more than they. The people had a God, not in heaven only, not only in the flesh and in poverty, but they had a God upon the same cross which they themselves bear, and when they beheld themselves with their two arms extended in their suffering, they found on their right hand their God who was crucified for them, and who bore them company. The people had a God, not only in heaven, not only in their flesh, in their poverty, and in their own cross, but they had a God living in the Church to teach, to protect, and to console them; they had a God living in their priest to receive the oppressive secrets of their hearts; they had a God living in the sister of charity to bind up their wounded limbs when they could no longer serve them, and to honour their souls in the miseries of their bodies. The people had a God in heaven and upon earth; you have taken away from them the God of heaven, and you have not preserved for them the God of earth. What then did you give them in His stead? What other God have you made for them? Ah! I am wrong, for God you have given them doubt, and for goddess negation! You said to them: "Perhaps!" And finding that too much, you spoke again with authority, and said: "No!" Why should they complain? There is no longer any God, or Christ, or Gospel, or Church; but you remain to them, and with you the worms which brought them into the world, and the worms which will prey upon their dead bodies. Is not this enough to satisfy a soul?

Perhaps, unable to bear the sight of that merciless spoliation wrought by your hands, you will turn to the bodies of the people and boast of what they owe to you, for the temporal well-being which you have procured for them in exchange for what they have lost. Ah! I expected as much from you! The bodies of the people! But listen to the sounds which rise from Manchester, Birmingham, Flanders, the cry, not of poverty and want—they are the words and things of bygone times—but the cry of pauperism : that is to say, the cry of distress having reached the state of system and power, and rising by an unexpected malediction, from the very development of wealth itself. The political economy of unbelief has been destroyed by facts upon every seat of human enterprise and activity ; it still struggles against these results, as terrible as they were unlooked for ; but it is the hydra of Lerne against the arm of Hercules: the blow which it has received is a mortal blow because it has been dealt by the hand of the people !

In a word, the bodies and the souls of the people have gained nothing from unbelief; and the people know it.

But if you have done nothing as yet for the souls and bodies of the people, perhaps it is to come, perhaps you will some day set up a doctrine in the place of the doctrine of Christ? I must deprive you of that last hope ; and without even trusting to the nothingness of your past efforts, I must show you that it is impossible for you to found a doctrine. In fact, unbelief rests upon two general principles, of which this is the first: man should not believe in man, because one man is as good as another, and his most precious treasure is the independence of his mind. Your second principle is : Man should not believe in God, because God does not speak to man. But if man ought neither to believe in God nor in man, in whom then should he believe ? Your answer is : In himself, and in himself alone. Now wherever men believe only in themselves, there are no disciples ; where there are no disciples, there is no master ; where there is no master, there is no unity ; where there is no unity, there is no doctrine. You would not then found a doctrine, even had you a thousand years multiplied by another thousand before you. If you quit the principles of unbelief, at that very moment you fall back upon Jesus Christ, the only possible Master for whosoever acknowledges an authority, because without Him there is nothing which holds together upon any foundation.

But after all let us admit that you may found a doctrine. Even should you succeed it would not be sufficient to dethrone Jesus Christ; your doctrine must be more perfect than that of Jesus Christ. Now listen to what I have just experienced. Three months ago I read for your sake the author who in this age seems to have had the distinction of writing against Jesus Christ with the greatest boldness, if not with the greatest ability: I mean Dr. Strauss. After having, with heated forehead, waded through four large volumes of transcendental weariness, as the Germans say, I reached, at length, the last chapter, entitled *Conclusion*. There Dr. Strauss, starting from the idea that Jesus Christ is completely vanquished, asks himself whether some man, capable of equalling and even of surpassing Jesus Christ, will not appear upon the empty stage of mankind. That question asked, a kind of tardy and eloquent justice seizes upon the author, and, in a page which I read again more than once, the only one in which the soul makes itself felt, he declares that it is not probable that any man will ever be able to equal Jesus Christ, but he is absolutely certain that no man will ever surpass Him.

Such is the conclusion.

To sum up, gentlemen, I find in Jesus Christ a threefold perpetuity: perpetuity in His life, perpetuity in the exclusive irradiation of His life, perpetuity in the superiority of His life. I also find in Him a threefold progress: progress in the territorial state, progress in the numerical state, progress in the moral state. Jesus Christ has, then, overcome time; he has overcome the great enemy, and, beholding Him upon the summit of ages in all the serenity of His imperturbable youth, I remember what Saint Paul said of Him in another sense: "Christ, risen from the dead, dieth no more."* Once He descended into the tomb; but the human race, for whom He died, bent towards Him, and, raising Him up with a love which has never grown cold, bears Him in its hands, risen again to life. Behold Him, gentlemen, examine Him well, He lives! Look again, He dieth no more, He is young, He is King, He is God! He lived as God, He has outlived Himself as God; to-morrow I will show you that He pre-existed as God. Nothing will then be wanting to that threefold act of life, living, surviving, pre-existing; nothing will be found in Him

---

* Rom. vi. 9.

which is not stamped with the seal of divinity, and which hinders me from proclaiming with the sovereignty of certainty that other expression of Saint Paul: "Jesus Christ was yesterday, He is to-day, and the same for ever!"*

* Heb. xiii. 8.

THE
# PRE-EXISTENCE OF JESUS CHRIST.

My Lord—Gentlemen,

All life is not yet comprised in living and in outliving that life; the third act of life, which is the first in the order of time, is that of pre-existence. Every being, save God, pre-exists in its germ, and man in particular pre-exists in his ancestors. No one appears here below whose reign has not been prepared long beforehand; and the more important the destiny designed for him by Providence, the more important also is the preparatory action of his ancestors. Jesus Christ, as man, should therefore have pre-existed after the manner of men; and, inasmuch as He was greater than all men by His destiny, He should also have pre-existed in a manner peculiar to Himself alone. I remark then, in the first place, that alone amongst all the great names, He possesses an authentic genealogy which remounts from Him even to the father of the human race, and that He is thus, undoubtedly, the first gentleman in the world. It is but little, I grant, and therefore His pre-existence should not be limited to this alone.

Ancestry, we have said, is proportionate to posterity. Whosoever has no ancestry, will have no posterity; and this explains to you the weakness of doctrines which unceasingly appear and disappear before you. They begin in the man who advances them, and, beginning with him, they die with him. As soon as a man without antecedents in his teaching, a man, the last who has sprung up in this world, dares to bring to mankind doctrines which he calls new, that single word is the foreboding of his powerlessness and the expression of his condemnation. For if the doctrines claimed by him as his own possessed any importance, they would inevitably have pre-existed him, he would at most be but their renovator; to say that an important thing begins in one's self, is to take nothingness for starting-point, for horizon, and for end.

But if ancestry be proportionate to posterity, it follows that Jesus Christ must have pre-existed in His ancestors with incomparable greatness. And, to speak more precisely, since Jesus Christ has had for His posterity the most important social and religious work of the times which have followed Him, He should also have had for His ancestry the most important social and religious work of the times which preceded Him. The Catholic Church being the fruit of His coming, we must find before His coming something that worthily prepares the Catholic Church, and that comprises Jesus Christ between a past and a future—doubtless not of equal proportions, but so balanced that that which preceded Him was beyond all comparison with the rest, as well as that which followed Him. The Jewish people, gentlemen, fulfil these conditions. The Jewish people was the most important social and religious work of the times preceding Jesus Christ, as the Catholic Church is the most important social and religious work of later times; and, as Jesus Christ is the soul of the Catholic Church, in which His life is perpetuated, so He was the soul of the Jewish people in whom He pre-existed. I must explain this double proposition to you, and so succeed in surrounding the sacred head of Christ with all the promulgatory rays of His divinity.

That the Jewish people was the greatest social and religious work of antiquity, I shall not, I think, have much difficulty in proving. Let us begin by its superiority in the social point of view. Legislation is the highest element of the life of a people, and, in legislation, the first point to consider is the constitution of the law itself. Now the Hebrew law possesses two characters which belong to it alone, and which place it beyond all comparison; they are universality and immutability. It has for its basis something universal, namely, the general relations of man with God and with mankind. The tables of Sinai, which form its prologue and its fundamental page, exist even now as the most memorable expression of all the great duties; and the Catholic Church, even after the promulgation of the Gospel, has not been able to substitute in place of the Decalogue anything which she has judged worthy to set it aside. Those ten decrees form the basis of Christian morals, as they formed the basis of Hebrew morals. In the second place, the Jewish law, although including the whole political, civil, criminal, commercial, judicial, and even ceremonial order—things essentially variable in their nature—was endowed with an immutability of which there is no other example in any legislation whatsoever. In Moses the legislative power of the Hebrews began and ended. Whilst every human society has in its centre a permanent legislative power which retrenches, adds, corrects, according to times and necessities, and an exceptional legislative power, which goes so far as to reform even the constitution itself, affected by the change of habits and customs, the Jewish people, from Moses, remained contented in regard to law, with a simple regulating faculty. The hand that had graven the tables of Sinai and penned that vast legislation comprised in the Pentateuch was strong enough permanently to consolidate a whole nation, how long soever it might endure; and three thousand years passed over his work have never once borne to it the slightest contradiction. Above all others, gentlemen, after the last fifty years of our history, we can appreciate the superhuman genius of such a foundation.

The constitution of authority in legislature follows in importance the constitution of law; for authority is the living guardian of the dead text of law. Now, what was the constitution of authority among the Hebrews? It has been often said, if I mistake not, that it was theocratic; this is an error. From the earliest times, Moses and Aaron divided the power; one was the military and civil chief, the other the religious chief, and that distinction between the temporal and spiritual order —deeply traced by the double memorial of the legislator and the pontiff—continues throughout the whole history of the Jewish people, notwithstanding the accidental gathering of the whole authority in one and the same hand. If the pontificate and the supreme judicature blend together in Samuel, they become separated in the times of David and the kings; if they are found united after the captivity, they separated again before Jesus Christ. The Hebraic community, like the Catholic community, was based upon the distinction between the spiritual and the temporal powers, a distinction without which a nation would neither be able to preserve truth nor liberty. Truth, because being of a higher order, it could not keep its place under a sceptre transmitted by purely human means; liberty, because all the social and regular forces, being concentred under the sceptre of one single mind and one single action, it becomes impossible for any one to defend his feeble personality against the omnipotent personality of the State. The people, crushed under the weight of such a formidable unity, would doubtless writhe like the giant under the weight of Etna; but their force, not being united under a stable and recognized organization, their efforts would result only in futile shocks, by which, if they succeeded in overthrowing the order that weighed upon them, their very victory would still cost them their liberty; for to destroy order is also to destroy liberty. By the division of power into two branches, not opposed to each other—not even rivals, so much do their attributes differ—opinion obtains a pacific support against force, right against oppression, and society, notwithstanding its vicissitudes, being united without violence, duly performs its office for time and for eternity.

However, this admirable order has nowhere been able to establish itself, save among the Jewish people and in nations entirely Christian, that is to say, Catholic. Everywhere else, the State has not failed to absorb the whole of human nature in its rapacious unity. And this, gentlemen, should not excite our wonder: the spiritual power, being by its very essence a disarmed power, God alone is able to communicate to it the inner force which it needs peacefully to resist the temporal power. Where God is not, intrigue, baseness, fear, soon bend mind to matter; and the spiritual order, should it still exist, remains but a miserable phantom, to which the State leaves a reed for sceptre, contempt for protection, and a little gold for pay. Inasmuch, then, as the Jewish people, as well as the Catholic nations, possessed the prerogative of a true spiritual power, it is stamped with a character of pre-eminence, which no other people can dispute with it in the times anterior to Christ.

The constitution of family was not less remarkable in the Jewish people than the constitution of law and authority. The individuals whose union forms families, and whom we may call domestic individuals, namely, the father, the mother, the child, and the servant, stood there in relations full of order and equity. Moses, it is true, did not formally substitute the unity of the conjugal tie in place of Eastern polygamy; but he instilled the practice of it by establishing the faculty of repudiation for certain cases, by forbidding the future kings of

Israel to have a great number of wives, like the princes of the East, and in supposing but once only in his whole legislation that a man may have two wives. Thus, save a few examples noticed in the course of Scripture, the Hebraic family appears to us, under this head, in a state analogous to that of the Christian family. The unity of marriage was a custom among them. The authority of the father over the child was great, without extending to that right over life and death which too often made an executioner's office of paternity among the ancients. The servant belonged to the family by virtue of a voluntary agreement; no Hebrew could be the slave of another Hebrew; and even engagements for perpetual service were permitted by law only after the trial of seven years. The stranger alone, by right of conquest, was liable to slavery, properly so called; and even this bondage, kept within certain limits, was far from producing that contempt and that abuse of man which we remark among the peoples anterior to Jesus Christ. All the Jewish families were ranged in twelve tribes, corresponding to the twelve patriarchs, sons of Jacob, and forming of the nation twelve great families, united in the bond of the same blood, and so much the more strongly, as it flowed from the same father by twelve perfectly recognizable sources. Nothing in antiquity is comparable to this constitution of the Hebraic family.

It is the same in regard to the bases upon which the system of proprietorship rested among them. Houses and lands could only be alienated for a lapse of forty-nine years. After that they returned to their former possessor, or to his heirs. The object of this singular arrangement was to prevent the ruin of families and the too great inequality of fortunes, without hindering, however, the necessary movement of commerce and industry. The rich man bought of the unfortunate or erring man the whole or a part of his patrimony, and enjoyed possession of it for half a century; but the son or grandson of the despoiled proprietor cherished in his heart the hope of returning again to the roof of his ancestors. By a second and no less remarkable regulation, the fields could not be cultivated more than six years in seven; they rested the seventh year, and all the fruit which they bore naturally in a land covered with vines and olive trees belonged to the poor, as their share in the common patrimony of Israel.

Such was, in the most fundamental matters, that celebrated

legislation of Moses, the invulnerable stability of which time has respected, and which has placed that great man at the head of all those who have had the rare distinction of giving laws to nations.

But legislation is only the first element of the life of a people; art is the second. Legislation classes a people in the order of acts, art determines its rank in the order of ideas and of their expression. The greater the idea the greater is the visible monument it raises up, and which causes it to subsist even after it has perished in the mind that conceived it. Now the monument of Hebraic ideas is a book which forms part of the Book of books, a book which forms the preface to the Gospel, and which in that illustrious vicinity obtains respect as the finished pedestal of a faultless statue. As history, the Hebrew Bible precedes all histories by its antiquity, continuity, and authenticity; alone it mounts to the cradle of the human race, and lays down the first stone of the whole edifice of the past. As a juridical compilation, it is without equal in any of the collections containing the laws of great communities. As moral philosophy, it opposes its books of wisdom to all the maxims of the most renowned sages, and a presence of God is felt in them which elevates the soul above the natural reach of reason. As poesy, it contains the hymns of David and the Prophets, repeated after two or three thousand years by all the echoes of the Christian world, and become creators of a language which has passed into all human tongues for lauding and blessing God. Other peoples have had historians, jurisconsults, sages, poets, but which are their own, and form, as it were, a separate glory; the Jewish people has been the historian, the jurisconsult, the sage, the poet of mankind.

Its territory also answered to that great place which we behold it occupying. For the support and nourishment of its body, it had received a land equally illustrious with its legislation and its art. Cast a glance upon a map of the world, and you will quickly perceive there a point which forms the centre of Asia, Africa, and Europe; which, washed by the waves of the Mediterranean, touches by them those healthy and genial climates where in the plenitude of human activity the hardy race of Japhet exercises its energy; whilst on another hand, the river Euphrates and the Gulf of the Red Sea open to its inhabitants the routes of the Indian Ocean, permitting them to seek under the equatorial zones those fabulous riches which

Solomon explored, which Alexander desired to see, which the Romans coveted, which the Middle Ages discovered anew, which the British power now guards with such supreme jealousy. In close vicinity also to that favoured point of the globe, you will perceive Memphis, the Nile, the Pyramids, and those sublime deserts which to the present time have rebelled against the most courageous curiosity; so that its boundaries, having gates open to all, had them also closed against all. There, as at an inevitable rendezvous indicated by nature and God, all the conquerors have appeared. The primitive monarchies of Assur and Chaldæa unceasingly sent there their generals. Alexander was halted there before Tyre, and went to read in Jerusalem the history of his triumphs written beforehand like those of Cyrus; his successors contested desperately for this remnant of his crown; the Romans took possession of it; all the chivalry of the Middle Ages pressed there during two hundred years; Napoleon caused a gleam of his sword to shine upon its sands; in fine, but yesterday the last thunder of European cannon awakened the old echoes of that proud land; and the discerning finger of those who observe the future points to it as the future battle-ground for the combats reserved to our descendants. You have named Syria, gentlemen, and with it the territory given to the Jewish people as the temporal complement of those magnificent graces which they had received in the mental order.

Nevertheless, gentlemen, a people is not yet fully known when we know its territory, its art, and its legislation; it is necessary also to know its history. The history of a people is the course of its acts for the preservation of its laws, ideas, customs, territory—all, in fine, that constitutes its proper life and civilization. The more magnificent its endowments, the more is it accountable towards God and man for the devotedness shown by it in defence of the gifts which are not only its personal patrimony, but which form part of the general dotation of mankind, and enter into the plans by which Providence conducts all things to their end. And, according as a people acquits itself well or ill of this great task, it marks in history its degree of shame or renown. What, gentlemen, has formed the dignity of our history? It is that having received from God a territory which is the heart of Europe, we have held it under faithful guardianship for fourteen hundred years, permitting none but ourselves to settle between the Alps and the Pyrenees;

it is that having among all the barbarous nations received the firstfruits of the Catholic faith, we have preserved it to the end, neither permitting this, the elder kingdom of Christendom, to be entirely corrupted by heresy nor overcome by doubt; it is that having received, in fine, the most ancient, and the most free monarchy of Europe, we have preserved in a happy balance, although it has been often troubled, the double spirit of authority and liberty, being equally incapable of supporting anarchy or absolute power. We have, in a word, preserved in the body of Europe a land of faith, order, and liberty.

The Jewish people had yet greater duties, and a more perilous position imposed upon it. Feeble in number, and cast upon a part of the world which by its position tempted all the neighbouring empires, it had to protect against them, with its independence, laws and traditions upon which the destinies of the world depended. No people entrusted with a more precious charge, in more favourable conditions, has shown such remarkable and persevering magnanimity in defending it. Not to see this would be an act of blindness, not to acknowledge it an act of ingratitude. Nineveh, Babylon, Memphis, by turns, and sometimes together, conspired for the destruction of that handful of Israelites; innumerable armies, led by powerful kings, invaded their territory, and laid siege to their capital; often victorious, they often purchased their glory at the cost of cruel reverses. Ten of their tribes, carried into captivity, have disappeared from history; the two others afterwards followed the same road of exile from whence nations never return. But seventy years of adversity far from their country did not weary the hearts of the captives; by science and beauty they penetrated into the palace of kings, and governed their conquerors. Cyrus delivers them, Alexander visits them, and when, in the heart of Asia, a new and a more terrible persecution brings into their temple the desolation of impiety, they raise up in their midst to save their country and religion, that race of the Maccabees whose name has become for peoples oppressed by stronger than themselves the very name of courage and right. And this heroic spectacle, gentlemen, lasted fifteen hundred years! For fifteen hundred consecutive years Israel held her place against the great empires of the world; and when at length Rome had surmounted all and subjected all, when the whole earth had kept silence before her for more than a century, Israel still struggled in the mountains and valleys of Judæa for the remnants of her liberty. Rome was forced to send her legions and her captains against such memorable perseverance, and Jerusalem, yet once more besieged, sent up to heaven, in an implacable defence, the last generous cry which the Romans were destined to hear.

Was it ended, gentlemen? Did not this people, without territory and without princes, wander to die in obscurity upon the vast surface over which the still timid will of their conquerors had scattered it? For any other, indeed, the hour of death would have come. But the Israelites remembered the days of their captivity, when they hung their harps upon the willows of Babylon, because they could not sing the songs of Sion in a strange land; as they had then carried their laws and traditions with them to be their eternal principle of life, they again bore them over the whole earth. They demanded their subsistence from labour, their dignity from the memorials of their ancestors, their consolation from the God who had brought them out of Egypt by Moses, out of Chaldæa by Cyrus, and who was able, when He willed, to bring them back again to that Jerusalem already raised from its ruins, and become the object of the combats of all Christendom. This people, whom their founder called a hard people, and who in fact opposed to adversity a soul of granite, this people still lives—lives everywhere. Disinherited from their country, the children of Israel have sought in commerce that movable wealth which may be hidden more quickly than persecution advances; and we now see kings tributaries to their activity, unblushingly recurring to the venerated purse of some Hebrew for the accomplishment of their designs and the aggrandisement of their glory. Yet once more, Israel lives; she has lived for seventeen centuries without chief, without temple, without territory, often persecuted, but preserving, as in Jerusalem, her antique and immovable ideas, and having in addition that unique glory of subsisting from an inner force sustained by nothing from without, and which nourishes itself at the mysterious altar of a superhuman past. Do you not see that she defies you? That alone among nations she counts four thousand years of duration? That nothing prognosticates the end of such a scandal against the nature of things? Dig out her tomb if you can; set your surest seal upon it; place your guards around it: she will but laugh at you and rise again, proving to you yet once more that she lives of a spirit which you have not, and that matter can do naught against spirit.

I have the right to conclude, gentlemen, that the Jewish people, under the social point of view, is the most important monument of the times anterior to Christ. It is not less so under the religious point of view; and here I shall need but very short observations.

For, remark that whilst all nations were plunged in the darkness of idolatry, Greeks, Romans, Assyrians, Egyptians, that little people adored one only God; and antiquity spake with wonder of the empty temple of Jerusalem, because it did not see God represented there by any image capable of impressing the senses—not that such representation is an evil in itself, as long as it does not touch the true character of the Divinity; but the Hebrews had such a horror of idols that they preferred, according to the order of their legislator, to leave God in their temple in His total invisibility rather than expose their faith to the impressive charm of some striking representation. For idolatry not only attacked them from without, it seized upon their heart, and they often fell before it. But, notwithstanding this double temptation, they never failed to return to that God of their fathers of whom they were the sole adorers.

By the dogma of creation they had an idea of Him which always completely separated them from idolaters. These rendered no account to themselves of the existence of the universe, or if they sought to penetrate its secret, they willingly believed it to be contemporary with their gods, giving to them at most some secondary action upon universal substance. The Jews had quite another doctrine, expressed from the first sign of their sacred Scriptures by that astounding phrase: "In the beginning God created the heavens and the earth."\* Had they possessed but that single doctrinal expression, they would have been richer in knowledge of God than all the schools and all the religions of antiquity. In a word, the Jewish people was the only people before Jesus Christ which had a clear notion of the Divinity, and which rendered to Him a worship free from the puerile dreams of the imagination and the taint of shameless sensuality. I may then conclude that in the religious, as in the social point of view, the Hebrew nation was

---

\* Gen. i. 1.

the most important monument of the times anterior to Jesus Christ.

I add that Jesus Christ was the soul of that nation, and pre-existed in it by a life which we are about to verify.

I ought to have grown weary, gentlemen, of pointing out to you the peculiarities of the Jews. There is one, however, which surpasses all the rest, and of which I have as yet said nothing. I mean the Messianic idea which circulated in their veins as their purest blood, and without which it is impossible to explain either their faith or their destinies. The Messianic idea is composed of four elements. Under its influence, the Jews believed, in the first place, that the one God and Creator adored by them would some day become the God of the whole earth. In addition, they believed that that revolution would be brought about by a single man, called the Messiah, the Holy One, the Just, the Saviour, the Desired of nations. They believed that this Man would be a Jew of the tribe of Judah, and of the house of David. They believed, in fine, that this predestinated Man would suffer and die in order to accomplish the work of transformation with which Providence had charged Him.

That such was their faith it is easy for us to learn even of themselves, since they still live, and since, notwithstanding four thousand years of expectation which, in their eyes, has not been realised, they have never ceased to render unshaken testimony to the hopes of their ancestors. But, gentlemen, let us not be content with their present testimony; let us open the monuments of their history, and follow the progress of the Messianic idea through the principal phases that mark the development of the nation itself, such as its birth, its formation into a people, the point of its maturity, its decadence, its captivity, and its restoration at the foot of the second temple, raised up by Zorababel.

Behold us in the fields of Chaldæa with Abraham! We are about to hear the first words, which formed, as it were, the seed of the Hebrew race. Observe, gentlemen, that we are not now examining whether these words are true, whether they were from God; we have now simply to show the idea which the Jewish people had of themselves, and of their mission here below. Whether they deceived themselves in this idea is another question, to be judged afterwards.

God, then, according to the Hebrew monuments, says to

Abraham : " Go forth out of thy country, and from thy kindred, and out of thy father's house, and come into the land which I will show thee ; and I will make of thee a great nation, and I will bless thee, and magnify thy name, and thou shalt be blessed. I will bless them that bless thee, and curse them that curse thee, and in thee shall all the kindred of the earth be blessed." * Thus at the same moment, and in an inseparable manner, two thousand years before Jesus Christ, the Jewish people appeared in the world, and therewith the Messianic idea—the idea that Israel was the depositary of a blessing which was to spread over the whole universe.

Abraham goes forth from Chaldæa, and settles in the land promised to his posterity. He waits there even to an advanced old age for the son to whom he is to transmit the Messianic heritage ; that son is given to him ; and when the child has attained all the graces of youth, God calls upon the patriarch to offer him in sacrifice upon a mysterious mountain. With unshaken faith in the wisdom and goodness of God, the old man raises his hand upon his only and well-beloved son, and he hears that second declaration, stronger and more distinct than the first : " By my own self have I sworn, saith the Lord, because thou hast done this thing, and hast not spared thy only-begotten son for my sake : I will bless thee, and I will multiply thy seed as the stars of heaven, and as the sand that is by the sea-shore ; thy seed shall possess the gates of their enemies, and in thy seed shall all the nations of the earth be blessed." † An oath is added to the force of the promise ; and it is more clearly indicated that the Messianic benediction should spread over the whole human race, not by Abraham himself, but by his posterity.

Isaac, the son of Abraham, hears the same promise and the same prophecy ; they are repeated to Jacob, the son of Isaac. The three first Hebrew generations, thus confirmed in the hope of the Messiah, spread out in twelve patriarchs, father of twelve tribes ; and Jacob, about to die, assembles them around his bed to close the first Messianic age by a solemn prophecy, which sums up the preceding ones, giving, at the same time, additional precision to them. Surrounded, then, by his twelve children, he announces to each of them, by some characteristic traits, what will be his lot in the future. Having arrived at

---

\* Gen. xii. 1–3. † Gen. xxii. 16–18.

Judah, he says these memorable words to him : "Judah, thee shall thy brethren praise : thy hands shall be on the necks of thy enemies; the sons of thy father shall bow down to thee. Judah is a lion's whelp : to the prey, my son, thou art gone up: resting thou hast couched as a lion, and as a lioness : who shall rouse him? The sceptre shall not be taken away from Judah, nor a ruler from his thigh, till he come that is to be sent, and he shall be the expectation of nations."* Thus, at the moment when the patriarchal inheritance becomes subdivided into twelve branches, the branch from which the Messiah is to be born is designated ; it is to be that of Judah ; and the day predestined for the appearance of the Messiah is marked by a sign which posterity will easily recognise.

The blood of Abraham, Isaac, and Jacob is henceforth fertile ; it multiplies in a land which has given it hospitality ; and having soon become an object of fear and jealousy, it passes from exile to bondage, in order to serve in tribulation an apprenticeship necessary to its high destinies. Its enemies think to destroy, they do but strengthen it. The Israelites are a people. Moses brings them out of Egypt, and leads them across the desert to the foot of Sinai, from whence come the laws which are to govern them. Follow, gentlemen, follow that marvellous march of so great a people ; the eyes of your childhood formerly gazed upon its wonders, look at them again with the thought of riper years. From encampment to encampment the children of Israel arrived before Jordan, to the frontiers of that territory inhabited by their first ancestors, and the possession of which is promised to their posterity. There they meet a whole people in arms awaiting those adventurers who despoiled Egypt, and whose march has resounded from the desert even to the hills of Judæa. Moab has ranged her battalions, she has raised her altars, convoked her chiefs ; the children of Israel are afoot, with their wives, their children, their soldiers, their Levites, bearing, hidden under the skins of animals, the tabernacle of the God who has just spoken to them from Sinai. A man of the East advances between the two peoples. "Balak," says he, "Balak, king of the Moabites, hath brought me from Aram, from the mountains of the east : Come, said he, and curse Jacob ; make haste and detest Israel. How shall I curse him whom God hath not

* Gen. xlix. 8-10.

cursed? By what means shall I detest him whom the Lord detesteth not? I shall see him from the top of the rocks, and shall consider him from the hills. This people shall dwell alone, and shall not be reckoned among the nations. Who can count the dust of Jacob, and know the number of the stock of Israel?"* These unexpected blessings alarmed Moab; the prophet is implored to change his language; if he will not curse, they pray him at least not to bless. Thrice Balaam opens his mouth; thrice he blesses the conquering people before him; and at last the Messianic prophecy escapes from him as in spite of himself: "I shall see him, but not now: I shall behold him, but not near. A star shall rise out of Jacob, and a sceptre shall spring up from Israel, and shall strike the chiefs of Moab, and shall waste the children of Seth. . . . Alas! who shall live when God shall do these things? They shall come in galleys from Italy, they shall overcome the Assyrians, and shall waste the Hebrews, and at last they themselves also shall perish." †

Observe again, gentlemen, that we are not now examining whether Balaam was or was not a prophet, but simply showing the course of the Messianic idea in the historical life of the Jewish people. You see this idea taking here a new development; it is no longer a patriarch of Israel who announces the coming of the Messiah, and the establishment of His reign over all the children of Seth, that is to say, of Adam, but a stranger. And he marks the circumstances of His coming with most strange perspicacity, since he even designates the domination of the Romans over the East and over the Jewish people as the precursory sign of the Messiah's appearance.

David and Solomon mark the highest point of the Hebrew monarchy, and with them commence the national and religious hymns known by the name of psalms. Sung in the temple of Jerusalem on the great feast days, they publicly expressed the inner feeling, the hopes and desires of the whole nation. Now it is easy to recognise here the Messianic idea disclosing itself on all occasions in the soul of poet and people. On reading them you will remark passages such as this: "All the ends of the earth shall remember and shall be converted to the Lord: and all the kindreds of the Gentiles shall adore in His sight, for the kingdom is the Lord's; and he shall have

* Numb. xxiii. 7-10.   † *Ibid.* xxiv. 17, 23, 24.

dominion over the nations. All the fat ones of the earth have eaten, and have adored: all they that go down to the earth shall fall before him."\*

Later also, at the approach of the decadence and captivity —seven hundred years, however, before Jesus Christ—the Messianic idea assumed in Isaiah a clearness and an abundance of expression which it is impossible to render to you, since I should weary you by the number and length of the passages I should have to cite. It is he who sees the Messiah springing from the race of Jesse, the father of David, and who at the same time describes, as if from Calvary or the Vatican, the glory of the sufferings and triumphs of Jesus Christ. "Arise, arise, put on thy strength, O Sion; put on the garments of thy glory, O Jerusalem, the city of the Holy One: for henceforth the uncircumcised and unclean shall no more pass through thee."† "How beautiful upon the mountains are the feet of him that bringeth good tidings, and that preacheth peace: of him that showeth forth good, that preacheth salvation, that saith to Sion: Thy God shall reign!"‡ "The Lord hath prepared His holy arm in the sight of all the Gentiles, and all the ends of the earth shall see the salvation of our God."§ "Behold my servant shall understand, he shall be exalted and extolled, and he shall be exceeding high. As many have been astonished at thee so shall his visage be inglorious among men, and his form among the sons of men. He shall sprinkle many nations. Kings shall shut their mouth at him: for they to whom it was not told of him have seen, and they that heard not have beheld."|| And immediately after, Isaiah begins the description of the sufferings and ignominies of Calvary, which he completes in twelve consecutive verses. Then he continues, resuming his hymns of triumph: "He that hath made thee shall rule over thee, the Lord of hosts is his name; and thy Redeemer, the Holy One of Israel, shall be called the God of all the earth."¶

But it is at Babylon, during the captivity, six hundred years before Jesus Christ, that the Messianic idea becomes invested with a form which attains to mathematical clearness and precision. Must I recall to you the prophecy of Daniel? Listen then to it: "Seventy weeks are shortened upon thy people, and upon the holy city, that transgression may be

---

\* Ps. xxi. 28–30.  † Is. lii. 1.  ‡ *Ibid.* 7.  § *Ibid.* 10.
|| Is. lii. 13–15.  ¶ *Ibid.* liv. 5.

finished, and sin may have an end, and everlasting justice may be brought, and vision and prophecy may be fulfilled, and the Saint of saints be anointed. Know thou therefore and take notice that from the going forth of the word to build up Jerusalem again unto Christ the Prince, there shall be seven weeks and sixty-two weeks : and the street shall be built again, and the walls in the straitness of times. And after sixty-two weeks Christ shall be slain : and the people that shall deny him shall not be his. And a people with their leader that shall come shall destroy the city and the sanctuary : and the end thereof shall be waste, and after the end of the war the appointed desolation. And he shall confirm the covenant with many, in one week : and in the half of the week the victim and the sacrifice shall fail : and there shall be in the temple the abomination of desolation : and the desolation shall continue even to the consummation, and to the end." *

I do not stop, gentlemen, to examine the striking features of this discourse, which resembles less a vision of the future than a narration of the past. The course of my subject bears me on and brings me to the foot of the second temple, to hear, five hundred years before Jesus Christ, those last words of the prophet Aggeus: " Yet one little. while, and I will move the heaven, and the earth, and the sea, and the dry land, and I will move all nations ; and the Desired of all nations shall come ; and I will fill this house with glory, saith the Lord of Hosts. . . . Great shall be the glory of this last house more than of the first, and in this place will I give peace."†

What continuity, gentlemen, through so many eventful centuries ! What fidelity to one and the same idea from so many men separated by ages ! But the Messianic idea was not even confined to the special tradition of the Jewish people; it passed over Jordan, the Euphrates, the Indus, the Mediterranean, all the oceans, and, borne upon the invisible wings of Providence, it penetrated all the most diverse and most distant nations, to create among them a uniform hope and a universal remembrance. Confucius, at the eastern extremity of Asia, spoke of a saint who, he said, was the true saint, and who would appear in the West. Virgil, translating into verse the oracles of the Cumæan Sibyl, announced to the Augustan Age the coming of a mysterious child, a son of

* Dan. ix. 24-27.   † Aggeus ii. 7-10.

Jupiter, destined to banish from the world the vestiges of iniquity, and to commence an order of things as great as new. Tacitus, on the reign of Vespasian, thus expresses himself: "It was a widely-spread belief that, according to ancient sacerdotal writings, at that very epoch, the East should prevail, and that men come from Judæa should seize the government of things." The rationalists of the eighteenth century, constrained by evidence, have often avowed that unanimity of the Messianic expectation. Voltaire said: "From time immemorial it was a maxim among the Indians and the Chinese that the sage would come from the West; Europe, on the contrary, declared that the sage would come from the East."\* Volney said: "The sacred and mythological traditions of former times had spread throughout Asia the belief in a great mediator who was to come, a final judge, a future saviour, king, God, conqueror, and legislator, who would bring back again the golden age upon earth, and deliver men from the empire of evil."† Boulanger, under a still more general form, confessed that all nations held "an expectation of that nature;" and he adds this astounding phrase: that the East may be said to be "the pole of the hope of all nations."‡ It is the very saying of Jacob on his death-bed.

It is then certain, gentlemen, that the Messianic idea was the life of the Jewish people during the course of the two thousand years which preceded Jesus Christ; and that idea was held among all the nations of the earth with such unanimity, that it is not even possible to account for it by the communications of the Hebrews with the Gentiles, but it is necessary to suppose a diffusion of that idea even anterior to Abraham. And that Messianic idea, so extraordinary in its universality, its progress, its perseverance, and its precision, is it at length fulfilled? Yes, it is fulfilled; the one God, creator of the Hebraic Bible, has become the God of nearly all the earth; and the very nations that have not yet accepted Him render homage to Him by a certain number of adorers whom Providence elects from their midst. And who has accomplished this incredible revolution? One single Man, Christ. And whence came this Man, Christ? He was a Jew, of the tribe of Judah, of the house of David. And how has He accomplished

---

\* "Additions à l'Histoire Générale," page 15.
† "Les Ruines," page 228.
‡ "Recherches sur l'Origine du Despotisme Oriental," section x.

this prodigious social and religious revolution? By suffering and dying, as David, Isaiah, Daniel, had foretold.

And now, gentlemen, what think you of it? Here are two parallel and corresponding facts, both certain, both of colossal proportion, one which lasted two thousand years before Jesus Christ, the other which has lasted eighteen hundred years since Jesus Christ; one which announces a great revolution, and a revolution impossible to foresee, the other which is its accomplishment, both having Jesus Christ for principle, for end, and for bond of union. Yet once more, what think you of it? Are you bold enough to deny it? But what would you deny? The existence of the Messianic idea? It is in the Jewish people, still living, in all the continuous monuments of its history, in the universal traditions of the human race, in the most positive avowals of the most profound unbelief. Would you deny the anteriority of the prophetic details? The Jews, who crucified Jesus Christ, and who have a national and traditional interest in depriving Him of the proofs of His divinity, declare to you that their Scriptures were formerly what they are now, and for additional certainty, two hundred and fifty years before Jesus Christ, under Ptolemy Philadelphus, king of Egypt, all the Old Testament, translated into Greek, fell into the possession of the Greek world, the Roman world, and the whole civilised world. Would you turn to the other pole of the question, and deny the accomplishment of the Messianic idea? The Catholic Church, the offspring of that idea, is before your eyes—she has baptized you. Would you stand upon the point of junction of those two formidable events? Would you deny that Jesus Christ has verified the Messianic idea in His person, that He was a Jew, of the tribe of Judah, of the house of David, and the founder of the Catholic Church upon the double ruin of the synagogue and idolatry? The two interested parties—and they are irreconcilable enemies—confess all this. The Jew affirms it, and the Christian affirms it. Would you say that this juncture of colossal events at the precise point of Jesus Christ is the result of chance? Were it even so, chance is but a brief and fortuitous accident—its definition excludes the idea of continuity; there is no chance of two thousand years' duration and of eighteen centuries added thereto. In fine, would you say that it is the result of a long conspiracy, by which the ambitious and theological Jewish people sought to create for itself a great existence? What! a conspiracy lasting two thousand years founded upon a chief whom sixty generations had to wait for, and whom it was necessary to create after having so patiently waited for him! Alas! it is no easy matter to conspire in favour of a living man; what must it be to conspire in favour of a man who does not exist, and who, it is supposed, will be born at an indefinite epoch? And remark that when that Man came, the Jews crucified Him —doubtless because His crucifixion formed part of the conspiracy. Observe also that they denied Him after as well as before the crucifixion—doubtless in order to secure the final success of the conspiracy and all the success of ambition and theology which they expected therefrom!

Gentlemen, when God works there is nothing to be done against Him. The proportions of the work of Christ in the times which preceded Him are yet more striking than all the divine proportions of His life and His after-life. For, in fine, when a man lives, He is a power, He has an action; it is possible to conceive that certain circumstances may have favoured a man of rare genius, and have given him great ascendency over his contemporaries. Even after death there remain friends, disciples, the remembrance of an existence which was real, and consequently a surviving means of action. But what are we able to do upon that which precedes us, upon the past? Who among us, however eminent he may be, is able to make an ancestor for himself? Who among us, desiring to found a doctrine, is able to create for himself an *avant-garde* of generations already faithful to a teaching which had not yet been heard? Who among us will present his doctrinal ancestry to the world, if he be not truly the son of a doctrine anterior to himself? Ah! the past is a land closed against us; the past is not even a place wherein God can act, unless He act there beforehand, and by way of preparation. Had Jesus Christ been like one of us, fallen without a providential pre-existence between the past and the future, He would in vain have demanded from history accomplished and closed a pedestal which would bear Him back twenty centuries beyond His cradle. Instead of this, Abraham, Isaac, Jacob, David, Isaiah, Jeremiah, Ezekiel, Daniel, a whole people, the human race itself, came to meet and salute Him in the arms of the aged Simeon, exclaiming in the name of all the past, of which he is the last representative: " Now lettest thou thy servant depart, O Lord, according to thy word, in peace. Because mine eyes have seen thy salvation, which thou hast prepared before the face of all people : a light to lighten the Gentiles, and the glory of thy people Israel."*

We have reached the summit, gentlemen; Jesus Christ appears before us as the moving principle of the past as well as of the future, the soul of the times which preceded Him as well as of the times which follow Him. He appears before us in His ancestry, upheld by the Jewish people, the most important social and religious monument of ancient times ; and in His posterity, upheld by the Catholic Church, the greatest social and religious work of modern times. He appears before us, holding in His left hand the Old Testament, the greatest book of the times which preceded him, and in His right hand the Gospel, the greatest book of the times which come after Him. And yet, so preceded and so followed, He is still greater in Himself than His ancestors and His posterity, than the patriarchs and the prophets, than the apostles and the martyrs. Supported by all that is most illustrious before and after Him, His personal physiognomy still stands out from this sublime scene, and, by outshining that which seemed above all, reveals to us the God who has neither model nor equal. Therefore, in presence of this triple sign of divinity—before, during, and after—in ancestry, in posterity, and even during life, let us stand up, gentlemen, let us all stand up together, whoever we may be, believers and unbelievers. Let us stand up, believers, with feelings of respect, admiration, faith, love, for a God who has revealed himself to us with so much evidence, and who has chosen us among men to be the depositaries of that splendid manifestation of his truth ! And you who do not believe, stand up also, but with fear and trembling, as men who are but as nothing with their power and their reasoning, before facts which fill all ages, and which are in themselves so full of the power and majesty of God !

* St. Luke ii. 29-32.

# THE EFFORTS OF RATIONALISM

TO DESTROY THE

# LIFE OF JESUS CHRIST.

My Lord—Gentlemen,

Jesus Christ lived as God, He has outlived Himself as God, He pre-existed as God; He pre-existed in the Jewish people, He has expressed His life in the Gospel, He has out-lived that life in the Church; and it is this triple circle of His manifestation that has rendered His divinity triumphant here below. As soon as the human race possessed full consciousness of this, it became, so to say, overwhelmed by such a demonstration, and from Theodosius to Louis XIV.—for the space of thirteen hundred years—discussion seemed impossible against Christ—in this sense at least, that all yielded to Him, or accepted Him as their foundation. But, this time having passed, rationalism, which had been dethroned by Jesus Christ, attempted to claim again the empire it had lost; it thought that, as ages had covered all that formidable edifice with their billows, some chances were possible in favour of doubt and negation, and that the eighteenth century of the Christian era could be called upon to render willing reprisals and new judgments against a doctrine grown old by time. Rationalism thus found itself again in presence of Jesus Christ, standing Himself between the Catholic Church and the Jewish people, as between the right and left wings of truth; and a triple war was planned, in order to overthrow the work whose building up was in past times accomplished in spite of the powerless efforts which were now to be renewed. The Jewish people was described as a vile, an ignoble, an odious race, unworthy of any credit or respect;

the Catholic Church as an instrument of misery for the people, of bondage for the intelligence, of subjection for nations and kings. I have defended the Church before you, gentlemen, for many long years; yesterday, I restored the true physiognomy of the Jewish people; I shall not return to either of these during these discussions. Jesus Christ calls me to-day into the very heart of the combat of which He is the object and the chief. The Jewish people was composed of men, and so is also the Catholic Church; and, however great men may be, they are not altogether exempt, even when bearing in their hearts the Spirit of God, from some failing and some infirmity; it is not so with Christ. Miraculous in His perfection, He does not suffer, as the Gospel shows Him, any human doubt; and if He really stands upon that faultless pedestal, it is vain for rationalism to fulminate, on the right hand and on the left, its powerless thunder against Him. Christ, impassible in the centre of Catholic truth, shelters all under His impregnable divinity. It was, then, necessary to destroy Jesus Christ, either by annihilating His life, by perverting it, or at least by explaining it away. This has been attempted, gentlemen; and the exposition of this triple effort will terminate our conferences for this year. Let us commence with the most decisive of the three—that which had for its object the annihilation of the life of Christ.

Is Christ a chimera or a reality? Does He belong to fable or to history? This is the question. It may astonish you, gentlemen, and yet it is serious; for clever men have boldly denied the existence of Jesus Christ; and others, without venturing to this extreme audacity, have sought at least to weaken the certainty of His life, and artfully to lessen its historical splendour. It becomes necessary, then, to place, or rather to maintain, Jesus Christ in history; and to this end we must first of all learn the nature and the laws of history; for as long as we are unacquainted with them, it will be impossible for us to decide whether Jesus Christ is or is not an historical personage. I proceed, then, to treat of history; we shall afterwards see whether Christ is present in it or absent from it.

Man lives in time, that is to say, in a singular element, which causes him at the same time to live and to die; he advances between a past which is no more and a future yet to come; and if he did not possess the faculty of concentrating in himself these three states of his existence, he would be but incessantly coming into the world without ever attaining to the possession of life. For hardly would he have made a step in advance before forgetfulness would have obliterated its traces, and thus he would be constantly before himself like a vapour rising from the earth and vanishing away. Against this terrible power of time, God has given him memory, by which man lives in the past as well as in the present; so that resuscitating his ancient days at pleasure, he beholds himself in the plenitude of his personality, like an edifice whose stones have been placed successively, but which the eye surveys and perceives entire. Now the memory that suffices for the life of a single man is not sufficient for mankind; whilst man is one, with a memory subsisting as long as himself, mankind is multiple, and its memory expires with each generation, or at most but little of it is transmitted to the future generation. The father tells the son what he has seen, the son relates it to the grandson, but at each stage remembrance grows more obscure, and little by little the light of that tradition brightens only the distant heights of the most important events. It ends, however, by becoming defaced; its lines grow confused to the eyes of a posterity continually retreating before them; and if God did not intervene to bring help to the human race losing all traces of itself, we should be living in an eternal state of infancy, between a past about which we are untaught and a future entirely unknown to us. Experience, the source of all progress, would constantly be wanting. Neither truth nor error, neither good nor evil would be known, save by a puerile combat recommencing always at the same point—a spectacle unworthy of man, unworthy of God—where truth and good, having no adequate field of action, would never be able to display their characters of stability and immortality. God, who, by memory, had provided for the progressive identity of man, should evidently have provided also for the continuous perpetuity of the human race by a memory conformable to the destinies of this vast body, that is to say, by a united, a universal, a certain memory, capable of giving to mankind complete consciousness of its works from the beginning to the end. In so speaking, gentlemen, I have defined history.

History is the life of mankind present to itself, as our life is present to us; history is the memory of the world. But what difficulties lie in the way of its formation! God lights a torch in our intelligence which enlightens our past, because He is our intelligence itself, one and indivisible; but how is the human race, multiple and divided, to be endowed with a similar light? How is an immortal memory to be given to the human race which dies daily? An immutable memory to that which is but change? A certain memory to that which doubts so easily about all that it does not see? God provided for this in giving us writing. By means of writing, a thing once said may be always heard, a spectacle once witnessed may be always visible; writing seizes the passing wave and renders it eternal. This is already immortality and immutability; but it is not yet certainty. For the false can be written as well as the true. A thing may indeed be written, but who will guarantee its truth to us? A man two thousand years ago writes a book, wherein he relates things which he says he witnessed: who will prove to us that he speaks the truth, and that a fable has not reached us under the seeming garb of history? Evidently, writing alone does not answer to this question; history begins with it, but it is not history in all its elements. History, if there be any, should command our minds with the same authority as the other powers which have received a mission to govern them. As there is a moral force in the world which does not permit us to say it is lawful for the child to kill his father, a mathematical force which does not permit us to build a house upon a plan without equilibrium, so also there should exist in the world a historical force which would not permit us to say to history: Thou hast spoken falsely. If this force exist not, there is no history.

What are, then, the conditions of history; or rather, what are the conditions of an historical writing? For writing is the fundamental, persisting, substantial element of history. Without writing, there remains to us nothing but tradition more or less confused; but as writing may deceive, it is needful that we should know the conditions which elevate writing to the state of historical writing, that is to say, to the state of authentic, certain, infallible, true writing. These conditions are three in number.

In the first place, writing must be public. All that is secret is without authority; every mysterious document is valueless because it has not been verified. Nothing of this is powerful but by public verification. The people form the only notary capable of certifying their own history, because they form the assemblage of all ages, of all ideas, of all interests, and because a popular conspiracy formed to lie to posterity is even impossible to conceive. A man fabricates error; a people has too many diverse ideas and passions to be able to combine together to deceive future generations. Moreover, a people never stands alone; it exists among contemporary peoples whose history is blended with its own: and even were it capable of unanimous falsification, it would inevitably call forth the protestation of the very age under whose eyes it would have inaugurated its conspiracy.

The second condition of writing, in order for it to attain to the state of history, is that it must bear upon public events. Every fact that is not public does not belong to the domain of history, for the reason I have just given; for who has witnessed a fact that is not public? A single man, three men if you will, but history cannot be based upon the testimony either of a single man, or of three men; this is not history, it is only memory. Memory bears upon private facts, whilst history bears upon public events. For example, that Louis XIV. conquered Flanders, Alsace, Lorraine, that he joined these provinces to the kingdom of France, first by force of arms, then by treaties, is history; these are events which interested France and all the nations of Europe, and which had a hundred millions of men for spectators. But that Louis XIV. in his chamber at Versailles said something in presence of M. le Duc de Saint Simon, which is related in the works of that talented person, is nothing more than memory. Doubtless this secondary element enters largely into the formation of the annals of the human race, because we should not be satisfied with recitals wherein only the main features of historical architecture would be visible; we are attracted more even by the private details than by the general movements of the world; they approach nearer to our personal existence, and cause the most eminent personages of past times to descend even to us. Moreover, although destitute of the solemn certainty of history, they are not always without a grave sanction, although of an inferior order; private acts become interwoven with public acts; numerous concurring witnesses establish each other's statements; and the whole advances in a manner not too unequal. Nevertheless, as soon as absolute historical certainty is aspired to, it is necessary to separate the two elements, and to give to the former, by that separation, all its force, and all its lustre.

The third condition necessary to raise writing to the state

of history, is that the events should blend together and form a public and general web. Nothing is isolated in the events of this world; they are connected with each other by a chain of succession similar to that which unites ideas in the logical tissue of a discourse. History should reproduce that continuous generation in such a manner that all the facts it relates should enter naturally into the course of things of which the progressive whole constitutes the life of the human race. A solitary fact is not an historical fact; it has no real place, it floats in air. Still much less should we give this name to a fact which cannot take its place in the general web of history without deranging its whole economy; this is the infallible sign of imposture. The force of history, like the force of every other real order, is in its completeness and unity. When a man stands alone, he is nothing; when a fact stands alone, it is nothing. But let a man enter into association with others, they form a family, a people, the whole human race. And, in like manner, when a fact enters into historical association with others, and not with others only, but with all the rest, let it become necessary to the general web of history, so that history cannot be constructed without that fact, then it possesses not only the force of an historical fact, but the force of all history; we must accept it or deny the entire life of the human race.

The three elements of history are, then, public writing, public events, public web of events; and when these three elements are united, I affirm that history exists, and that it cannot be resisted without resisting the very force of common sense. In effect, gentlemen, for history to be false in this case see what must be possible: that a man, no matter who, relating in public events of a public nature, those events supposed to be false must be received as true, and, notwithstanding their falsity, be interwoven in the general web of history. Now this is altogether impossible, and nothing is more easy than to prove it to you. Allow me only one supposition. I suppose that to-morrow morning it may please me to publish a work the substance of which I thus sum up. On the 1st of January, 1847, France declared war against the three great Continental Powers of Europe. The object of this war was to re-establish the rights of nations and faith in treaties compromised by acts of violence. The hostile armies met on the plains of Mayence. France had six hundred thousand men under arms, the enemy had a million. The battle lasted ten consecutive days; on the morning of the tenth day the French were victorious. The plenipotentiaries of Europe assembled at Mayence, and signed a treaty which put an end to the war by a new partition of the European continent.

I ask you, gentlemen, do you believe that this political romance would have any chance of imposing upon posterity? Is it not manifest that France would treat it with the deepest scorn? If France accepted it, is it not manifest that the whole of Europe would hold it up to public derision? And if, by an act of universal folly, France and Europe consented to invest it with an absurd authority, is it not manifest that it would be found impossible to introduce it into the web of history, since the state of all contemporary affairs, and, consequently, of all future affairs, would be in contradiction with that pretended war and that fictitious treaty? To sustain falsehood, perpetual falsehood is necessary; and the conspiracy of a single moment against truth would require a conspiracy continued to the end of the world. The impossibility of such a concurrence and of such perseverance in a universal imposture is not only a moral impossibility, but a metaphysical and an absolute impossibility.

Now, gentlemen, to whatever epoch in the history of mankind we may turn, that impossibility would be the same. In all times and places, public writing describing public events which naturally arrange themselves in the general course of history would be authentic and true, because in all times and places it would have been impossible under such circumstances to deceive the human race in regard to its own life, or to persuade it to deceive itself without object and against all reason. And—mark it well, gentlemen—history once existing, time has not the privilege of lessening its force; so far from lessening, it confirms it. I say, first, that it does not lessen its force; and as proof I propose this to you: Think of Cæsar, then think of Louis XIV., and ask yourselves whether the historical certainty of Louis XIV. and the historical certainty of Cæsar differ in the slightest degree in your mind. Evidently, they do not differ; and yet seventeen centuries separate Louis XIV. from Cæsar. But those seventeen centuries vanish from your thought by the electrical glance which suddenly carries it from the one to the other, and causes it to perceive not only that the historical basis of Cæsar is the same as the historical basis of Louis XIV., but also that in doubting in regard to the first it would be needful to doubt the second, since without Cæsar history would lose all its connection, and therewith the principal cause of its reality. I say still more, I say that time confirms, instead of lessening, the certainty of history. And why so? Because time at every step unfolds the historical canvas, and because each point of history entering into participation with the united force of the whole, the more that force increases by the repercussion of events upon each other, the more each particular point becomes settled, sustained, and extended. Thus, Moses has been consolidated by Jesus Christ; for although Moses wrote publicly on public events, the web of history was short in his time, and wanted breadth; and when Jesus Christ took His place there, His presence lighted up the Mosaic past, as the Christian future had in its turn to reflect back again even to Jesus Christ. Whence it follows that we do not advance a step in the present time without again bearing to Moses the glory of a new confirmation, because in all that we do he supports us, and we in our turn explain all that he has done. The thread of history unceasingly goes and returns from the past to the future, from the future to the past; and that which we see with our eyes will be more clear to our posterity than it is to us, because upon the canvas which represents us they will complete designs which have not yet left the hands of the workmen. Like a building that covers its foundations, so is history; as land that grows firm by being trodden upon, so also is history under the footsteps of generations. In a word, Time, which seemed the greatest enemy of history, as soon as history is founded, protects and consolidates it.

But does history exist? Is all that we have just said anything but a magnificent speculation? Does the human race know its own life? Is there in the world a history of the world? This, gentlemen, is to ask if there exist public writings containing a long web of public events; now these writings and this web of events are before your eyes. Mankind learns its primitive life by certain fundamental traditions collected in due time, and confirmed by their universality; it learns its subsequent life from Moses by an unbroken history which advanced in constant development. From Moses to Herodotus is the dawn of history; from Herodotus to Tacitus its morning; Tacitus is its noon, and that noonday still lasts. It is even become more striking for the last three centuries, through a celebrated invention which has greatly increased the publicity and immortality of writing. As God had given writing to our fathers when tradition was in danger of growing obscure, he gave printing to them when writing itself was also menaced with becoming forgotten and confused from the superabundance of documents. Printing saved history fifteen hundred years after Jesus Christ, as writing saved tradition fifteen hundred years before Him.

Such being the case, gentlemen, and history having existed for thirty centuries, it remains to be seen whether Jesus Christ does or does not form a part of history. I affirm that He is in history, and that none other in the world holds in it a place more important or more certain than His own.

What have I to do, gentlemen, in order to prove this? Evidently three things: I have to show that the life of Jesus Christ is contained in a public writing; that it is a tissue of public events; and that it enters naturally into the public web of history.

Now the life of Jesus Christ is contained in the Gospels, and the Gospels form a public writing; this is my first proposition. But you at once ask me where I find the proof that the Gospels form a public writing. Is it not, say you, in the Gospels themselves? And do you not thus prove the question by another question? Gentlemen, if the Gospels commenced or formed the whole of history it would, perhaps, be difficult to reply to you; but you have not, I think, so soon forgotten that history existed before Jesus Christ; and God, who willed to give us the certainty of the existence and works of His Son, had apparently prepared the ground upon which we were one day to meet Him. That ground is history; and at the time in which the life of Jesus Christ is placed, that is to say, about the time of Augustus, history held a position in the world which did not depend upon us. It is not Catholics who make history; it is made without us and against us. It was in the hands of our enemies, and if we then began the history of the Church, that of the world continued its course upon a plan which was not ours, and in which no power was reserved to us. Now this is the history that I invoke to establish the publicity of the Gospels; and first of all I rest upon an observation which I consider fundamental; the Gospels, I say, were public writings, because they belonged to a public doctrinal society.

That the first Christians formed a doctrinal society is clear of itself; that that society was public is also beyond doubt; nevertheless, it is necessary to establish this in the most positive manner, for it is the groundwork of the whole matter. It can indeed be conceived that a few men, secretly united, and preaching a secret doctrine, may have been able secretly to prepare a mysterious book, which had not been subject to any investigation, and which was spread from hand to hand, gaining authority with time. But if the Christian community was from the very first public; if, from the morrow of the death of Christ, His Apostles appeared in the public places of Judæa, and soon after in the public places of the Roman empire, provoking, not an occult war, but a visible and notorious struggle; if they said boldly to the Jews: "Jesus of Nazareth, a man approved of God among you, by miracles and wonders and signs, which God did by Him in the midst of you, as you also know; this same being delivered up, by the determinate counsel and foreknowledge of God, you, by the hands of wicked men, have crucified and slain. Whom God hath raised up;" * if, being dragged before all the tribunals of the empire, when asked who they were, they answered: We are Christians, that is to say, the children of Christ, who has been put to death, but whom the arm of God—more powerful than all the conspiracies of men—has raised from His tomb, and elevated to be for ever the head and chief of all nations. If they said this, if it be certain that they said this—certain, not only from our writings, but from writings derived from strangers, from our enemies, by a multitude of documents—I shall have the right to conclude that the Christian society, at its beginning, was a public society, and that, differing from so many things formed in secret—because they have no faith in their strength and legitimacy—the Catholic Church began in publicity, as she has continued in publicity.

Let us come to the proof, and hear Tacitus, the most celebrated of historians—Tacitus, charged by God to grave in history the certificate of the birth and death of His only Son Jesus Christ. Twenty-seven years after that great drama of

---

* Acts ii. 22-24.

Calvary, Nero was pleased to burn Rome; and to hide the horror of that abominable action, he caused to be seized, says Tacitus, an *immense multitude of men*—INGENS MULTITUDO. Who were those men? Tacitus defines them: they were men *whom the common people called Christians*—QUOS VULGUS CHRISTIANOS APPELLABAT. Remark this word VULGUS; twenty-seven years after the death of Christ the name of His disciples was common in Rome, the capital of the world. But what were Christians? Tacitus tells us: *the author of this name was Christ*—AUCTOR NOMINIS HUJUS CHRISTUS. You hear, gentlemen, you hear; and the date of this text, which has never been contested by anyone, is authentic; it is marked by the burning of Rome, in the year 64 of the Christian era, that is to say, twenty-seven years after the death of Jesus Christ. But is this all? No; you will hear more, you will hear the Apostles' Creed, written by the pen and with the ink of Tacitus. The historian had to say who Christ was; he continues, then: *They derived their name and origin from Christ, who, in the reign of Tiberius, had suffered death by the sentence of the procurator Pontius Pilate*—AUCTOR NOMINIS HUJUS CHRISTUS, QUI, TIBERIO IMPERITANTE, PER PROCURATOREM PONTIUM PILATUM SUPPLICIO AFFECTUS ERAT. Once more, is it Tacitus who speaks, or is it the Apostles' Creed? The Apostles' Creed says: QUI PASSUS EST SUB PONTIO PILATO; Tacitus says: QUI PER PROCURATOREM PONTIUM PILATUM SUPPLICIO AFFECTUS ERAT. It is indeed Tacitus—a stranger, a Pagan, a man who, in writing these things in indestructible memorials, did not even know what he said. And what said he of the Christians, of that immense multitude whom the common people called Christians? He said this of them, in the same text: *For a while this dire superstition was checked; but it again burst forth, and not only spread itself over Judæa, the first seat of this evil, but even in Rome*—REPRESSAQUE IN PRÆSENS EXITIALIS SUPERSTITIO RURSUS ERUMPEBAT, NON MODO PER JUDÆAM ORIGINEM HUJUS MALI, SED PER URBEM ETIAM. What a text, gentlemen! what precision! what matter in two lines! Twenty-seven years, then, after the death of Christ, the Christians formed an immense multitude in Rome, they were commonly known by their true name; even before this epoch they had already been repressed by public authority, but that repression did not hinder them from spreading such power, that Tacitus calls it an irruption; they appeared before the tribunals, and there bore testimony to their faith; for Tacitus adds that they were seized *by their own avowal*—PRIMO CORREPTI QUI FATEBANTUR. They were *odious to all*—INVISOS: and their morals differed so much from general morals that, according to the remark of the historian, *they were less convicted of the crime of revolt than of hatred of the human kind* —HAUD PERINDE IN CRIMINE INCENDII, QUAM ODIO HUMANI GENERIS CONVICTI SUNT.* And Tacitus knew all this; he knew the life of Jesus Christ; he knew Pontius Pilate; the drama of Calvary was present to him.

Would you have another proof of the public life of Christians from the very origin of Christianity? God and history will not refuse it to you. In the year 98 of the Christian era—sixty-one years after the death of Jesus Christ—Trajan mounts the throne; and history brings us a letter of one of his proconsuls on the subject of the Christians, the proconsul of Bithynia and Pontus, Pliny the Younger, a celebrated man. For observe, gentlemen, when God wills to write history, he is not unskilful in choosing his historians. We have just heard Tacitus; let us now hear Pliny the Younger, in an official letter to Trajan. He writes to the emperor to consult him about the measures to be taken against Christians; for, says he, " I have never had to deal with cases of this kind, and I know not what it is the custom to pursue and punish in them, or in what degree. I have no little difficulty in ascertaining whether it is needful to take account of difference of age or to be indifferent to it; whether pardon is to be granted on repentance, or whether it is useless to cease to be a Christian after having once professed Christianity; whether it is the name which is to be pursued, even when exempt from crime, or the crime attached to the name." What questions, gentlemen, for an able and good man! A name criminal! Crimes attached to a name! But what could he do? Pliny found in his way customs already inveterate against a society of men in open struggle with the Roman empire; and we perceive, even in the absurd things which he says, a desire to be as lenient as possible without offending the emperor. His letter ends with the remark, "that a great number of persons of every age, rank, and sex, were compromised, and that others would be; that not only

* *Annals*, Book 15.

the cities, but the towns and villages, were overrun with that contagious superstition; that, in fine, the deserted temples, and the sacred ceremonies which had for a long time been interrupted, began to revive, in consequence of the measures taken against the Christians."

This picture, gentlemen, joined to that of Tacitus, leaves no doubt upon the capital point before us, namely, that from the origin of Christianity, the Christians lived in a publicly-constituted society. And, moreover, the very result obtained by them in the short space of three centuries is a superabundant proof of it. At the end of three centuries, the Christians were masters of the Roman empire; they bore to the throne the first Cæsar who embraced their faith, and, not content with this prodigy of their power, they said to Constantine: "Withdraw to the Bosphorus, for here, in Rome, the chair of St. Peter, the fisherman of Galilee, must be placed." And Constantine, from instinctive obedience to that unexpressed command of Providence, withdrew, and so bore, even to the borders of the Euxine, a proof, still subsisting, of the social mission of Jesus Christ. Now, gentlemen, no secret society has ever been capable of such success. All that begins in secret is accomplished in secret. When men speak to you of a secret society, it is as if they told you that nothing had formed an association. Doubtless these secret conspiracies may work secretly, shake the foundations of states, prepare the day of ruins; but they never attain to a regulated and public life. All that begins in darkness is struck with incapacity to live in open air and in open day. Therefore the attainment of empire by the Christian society, under Constantine, is of itself a sufficient proof that the Christian work was a constantly public work.

But if the first Christians formed a public society, and at the same time a doctrinal society, it necessarily follows that their writings were public. Endeavour to conceive a public doctrinal society which hides its writings; you will never succeed. For how would it be public, if it did not boldly proclaim what it believed, and how would it proclaim what it believed, if it secreted its writings, and those even which formed the foundation of its faith? Although the Gospels may not have been written on the very instant after the death and resurrection of Jesus Christ, they were published over the whole world by the preaching of the Apostles, and when they appeared successively, the young and living tradition became blended with them in one and the same authenticity. A contest of nearly three hundred years began upon the very text of the Gospels between Catholics on one hand and heretics and philosophers on the other. This contest has left very numerous monuments. We see, then, Celsus and Porphyry following step by step upon the Gospels, the life of the Saviour. They do not dispute their publicity or their authenticity. Heretics do something more. Not only do they discuss upon the text consecrated by the adhesion of the Church, but they fabricate for themselves apocryphal Gospels to oppose them to the approved Gospels, so true is it that the whole discussion bore upon those fundamental texts. They were simple enough to make for themselves an arm against us of apocryphal Gospels, that is to say, to invoke against Jesus Christ books wherein the principal mysteries of His life and death were recognised, and where the very alteration of certain passages served but to prove so much the more the truth of the whole. It is very natural that great publicity should call forth counterfeits; this is even the greatest sign of success. Every idea, every style, every fashion that succeeds, raises up a cloud of imitators or speculators. But what is that to the man or to the thing which is the object of such effort? At least, it is not publicity which suffers from it; now, the publicity of the life of Jesus Christ by the Gospels and the primitive Christian books is precisely the point that I desire to establish, and I do not think you will require more from me.

The life of Jesus Christ was, from the first, surrounded by immense publicity. His disciples, from the first, formed a public society; their profession of faith, their writings filled all the tribunals and all the schools of the earth; and finally, in three centuries, the emperor was publicly Christian, and the vicar of Jesus Christ was publicly seated in Rome. All this is as certain in profane history as in Christian history. This first point is gained.

As to the events which compose the very life of Jesus Christ, their nature is also that of manifest and striking publicity. What was in question? Was it a philosopher teaching certain disciples under a porch or in a garden? Was it but a Socrates, however celebrated he may be? No; it was a question of a Man, the founder of a new religion, a thing that touched all—traditions, laws, customs, sentiments, even the most sacred interests; it was of a Man the founder of an exclusive religion, and who designed nothing less than the overthrow of all existing religious and sacerdotal bodies; it was of a Man working, it was said, in public unheard-of miracles, and accompanied everywhere by an innumerable multitude, attracted by His works and His doctrine; it was of a Man called before the supreme tribunal of His country, condemned, put to death, and afterwards, it was said, raised again from the dead, and who sent His disciples to the moral conquest of the world; it was of a Man having succeeded in raising up an unshaken faith in the hearts of a multitude of men of all nations, and become, by His name alone, the rallying-point of a new society. If ever there were public events, assuredly they were these.

And these events, which contradicted all the past life of the human race—which must, consequently, if they were false, have been rejected from the general web of history by an invincible impossibility of ever forming a part therein—have they or have they not taken their place in that rigorous chain of the human life during three thousand years? They have done more than this, gentlemen; without them history is an incomprehensible enigma. What, indeed, is the principal question of history, from Moses to Pius IX., those two extreme terms of the world's annals? Is it the rise and fall of the empires of Assyria, the Trojan war, the conquests of Alexander, the fortunes of the Romans, the rise of modern nations, the discovery of America, the progress of science and history in modern times? No; none of these questions, however vast they may be, is the principal question of history, the one that embraces the totality of the three thousand years that live in the memory of mankind. The principal question, because it contains all the past, the present, and the future, is this: the world having lived in idolatry in the times before Augustus, how has it become Christian since His time? These are the two sides that divide all history, the side of antiquity, and the side of later ages; the one idolater, plunged into the most licentious materialism; the other Christian, purified at the sources of a complete spirituality. In the ancient world the flesh publicly prevailed over the spirit; in the present, the spirit publicly prevails over the flesh. What has caused this? Who has produced a change so great and so general in extent between the two periods of mankind? Who has so greatly modified the human form and the course of history? Your fathers adored idols; you, their posterity, descended from them by a corrupted blood, you adore Jesus Christ. Your fathers were materialists even in their worship; you are spiritualists even in your passions. Your fathers denied all that you believe; you deny all that they believed. Again I ask what is the reason of this? There are no events without causes in history, any more than there is movement without a motive power in mathematics. What is this historical cause which converted the idolatrous world into the Christian world, which gave Charlemagne as a successor to Nero? You are compelled to know or at least to seek it. We Catholics say that this prodigious change corresponds to the appearance upon earth of a Man who called Himself the Son of God, sent to take away the sins of the world—who preached humility, purity, penance, gentleness, peace; who lived piously among the poor and the lowly; who died on a cross, with His arms extended over us to bless us; who left us His teaching and His example in the Gospel; and who, having thus touched the souls of many, subdued their pride and corrected their senses, has left in them a tranquil joy so marvellous that its perfume has spread to the ends of the world, and has won even sensuality. We say this. Yes, a man, a single man, has founded the empire of Christians upon the ruins of the idolatrous empire; and we do not marvel thereat, because we have remarked in history that all good as well as evil invariably springs from a single principle, from a man, the depositary of the hidden force of the demon, or of the invisible force of God. We say this, and we base our declaration upon uninterrupted monuments which begin with Moses and reach to us; we appeal also to a publicity of thirty-two consecutive centuries; we join together the Jewish people, Jesus Christ, the Catholic Church, or rather we do not join these, they appear before us closely linked together in a course of things sustained the one by the other; we appeal, in fine, to the whole web of history, and in the name of that immense monument which it is absolutely necessary to admit and to explain, we say to you: Jesus Christ is the supreme expression of history, He is its key and its revelation. Not only does He form a part of history, He has taken His place in it in the midst of all its events, without difficulty and without effort, but history is not possible without Him. Endeavour, in following the line of these monuments, to pass from the ancient to the new world, and to explain to yourselves how, without Jesus Christ, the Pope has replaced the Cæsars at the Vatican. Is it possible to do this? And if a gleam of good faith remain in the depths of your soul, will you not be compelled to say with us: Yes, it is in Christ on Calvary, in that blood which was shed, that the renovation of the human race began?

Therefore, gentlemen, before our epoch, none dared to deny the historical reality of Jesus Christ, not one. Before you, long before you, Jesus Christ had enemies; for before you pride existed, and pride is the chief enemy of Jesus Christ. Before you Jesus Christ had enemies; for before you sensuality existed, and sensuality is the second enemy of Jesus Christ. Before you Jesus Christ had enemies; for before you egotism existed, and egotism is the third enemy of Jesus Christ. And yet, when He appeared for the first time, when He came with His cross to sap your pride, to insult your senses, to drag down your egotism to the very dust, what was said to Him? Pride, sensuality, egotism, had then as now able men in their service —Celsus, Porphyry, all the Alexandrian school, and the lovers of this life, and the throng of courtiers, ever ready to find in truth a secret enemy to power. What said they of Christ? They pursued Him by putting His followers to death; by deriding His life; by disputing His dogmas; by oppression called to the help of a cause which betrayed liberty; but their books, subsisting in a thousand remains by the aid of printing —which I just now called the salvation of history—their books confirm Him; not one of them has denied the reality of the life of Jesus Christ. You alone, coming eighteen centuries after, and thinking that time, which confirms history, is its destroyer, you have dared to battle against the very light of the sun, hoping that every negation is at least a shadow, and that human folly, seeking a refuge against the severity of Jesus Christ, would accept of any arm as a defence, and of any shield as a protection. You have deceived yourselves. History subsists in spite of negation, as the heart of man subsists in spite of the debauchery of the senses; and Jesus Christ remains under the shelter of unexampled publicity, and of a necessity to which there is no counterpoise, upon the summit of history.

Nevertheless, as a last hope you say to me: If it were a question of human events only, such as those of which the ordinary annals of nations are composed, it is manifest that the life of Jesus Christ contained in the Gospels would be beyond all discussion. But in that life it is a question of events which bear no comparison with those we habitually witness. It is a question of a God who made Himself Man, who died and rose again; how is it possible for us to admit such strange things upon a mass of human evidence? For in fine, public writings, public events, the public and general web of history, all this assemblage of proofs is purely human; and it is upon this mortal foundation that you base a history where all is superhuman. The base must evidently sink under such a weight.

Gentlemen, I do not undervalue the force of that objection. Yes; I understand that when it is a question of the history of a God it needs another pen than that which traces the history of the greatest man in the world; this is true. But I also believe that God has solved this objection by creating for His only Son, Jesus Christ, a history which is not human, that is to say, which, in its proportions, is so much above the nothingness of man, that the ordinary power of history would evidently not have sufficed for it. Where indeed will you find such connection as that of the Jewish people, Jesus Christ, and the Catholic Church? Where is there anything to be compared to it? And, moreover—without returning to what has already been said—where, amongst all the histories known to you, do you find any which for three centuries had witnesses who gave to it the testimony of their blood? Where are the witnesses who have given their lives in favour of the authenticity of the greatest men or the greatest events? Who died to certify the history of Alexander? Who died to certify the history of Cæsar? Who? No one. No one in the world has ever shed his blood to add another degree of evidence to the historical certainty of anything whatever. Men leave history to take its course. But to form it with their blood, to cement historical testimony with human blood for three centuries, is what has never been witnessed, save on the part of Christians for Jesus Christ. We were interrogated during three centuries, and asked to declare who we were; we answered: Christians. They then said to us: Blaspheme the name of Christ; and we replied: We are Christians. They put us to death for this in frightful tortures; and in the hands of our executioners our last sigh exhaled, as a balm for the dying and a testimony for the living to all eternity, the name of Jesus Christ. We did not die for opinions, but for realities

—the very name of martyrs proves it; and Pascal has well said: "I believe in witnesses who give the testimony of their blood." And although there may be presumption in attempting to speak better than Pascal, I shall however say something better: I believe in the human race dying for its faith.

Shall I give you another sign which shows the elevation of Jesus Christ, in history, above all history? Tell me which amongst the ancient peoples of the world, the most celebrated in your eyes, has left guardians upon its tomb to protect its history? Where are the survivors of the Assyrians, the Medes, the Greeks, the Romans? Where are they? What defunct people renders testimony to its life? One alone, the Jewish people, at the same time dead and living, a relic of the ancient world in the new, and a self-accusing witness in favour of Christ—by the Jews crucified. God has preserved them for us as an irreproachable witness; I produce them, they are there. Behold them! The blood is in their hands. And we also, Catholics, we the Church, we are by their side, we speak with them and as loudly as they. As a living and a universal society we bear, in the wounds of our martyrs, the blood shed by us to render testimony to the history of Jesus Christ; and on their side, as a society, living also, universal also, the Jewish people bear blood which is not their own, but which is not less eloquent than ours. There are two witnesses here, and two streams of blood. Behold them! Look on the right hand and on the left of Christ, behold the people who crucified him! Behold the people who sprang from his cross! They both speak the same thing to you, both, during eighteen centuries, suffer a martyrdom which is not the same, but which has the same source, both are enemies—they meet but in one single thing, Jesus Christ! Ah! you would defy God! Learn that when man defies God, his Providence inevitably prepares an answer for him; and you have just heard, on the subject of Jesus Christ, the answer He has given to you.

I conclude, gentlemen. To deny the historical reality of the life of Jesus Christ is an act of folly, an act of desperation. And you wonder perhaps why this has been done, directly or indirectly, with or without precaution. It is, because the historical reality of Jesus Christ once admitted, or taken for granted, the sentiment of His divinity begins to shine in the mind, and it is difficult not to yield more or less. It was necessary to gather clouds around an existence so remarkable, connected, moreover with so many things which are remarkable also. Were the result of negation only to call forth proof of the fact, it would already have provoked discussion, and discussion is of value on unattackable ground; its prestige seems to be thereby lessened. It is better, in fine, to attempt something than to remain inactive. Then, hatred blinds, it renders the vision insensible to the clearest evidence; and, in this sense, it was fitting that the historical reality of Jesus Christ should be attacked, as a proof of the intellectual diminution of those who become His enemies. Truth gains by the attacks of the mind as by those of the body; and, tranquil in the inaccessible eyrie where God has placed her, sure of herself, however she may be attacked, she can say to man, imitating a celebrated line:

*Contest*, if thou canst; and if thou dar'st, *consent!*

# THE EFFORTS OF RATIONALISM
## TO PERVERT
# THE LIFE OF JESUS CHRIST.

My Lord—Gentlemen,

In our last conference I proved to you the historical reality of Jesus Christ. But what is it to have proved to you the historical reality of Jesus Christ? Does it mean that a Man called Jesus Christ undoubtedly lived at a certain epoch? If we have proved but this we shall have proved nothing, for a name is nothing. To prove the historical reality of a personage is to prove the reality of the living type which constitutes that personage. Thus, when I name Cæsar, I do not name an indifferent person, I name the Roman who, before Augustus, conquered and governed the Gauls, who, recalled by the Senate, passed the Rubicon, assumed the dictatorship, and at last fell under the daggers of a band of conspirators. So also, when I name Jesus Christ, I name Him who, in the time of Tiberius, preached a religious doctrine in Judæa, supported His preaching by acts, about which you reserve your judgment, but which were at least extraordinary, who was surrounded by disciples, and, after a condemnation followed by His death, was presented to the whole world as living, and who, in fine, founded that hierarchy, that dogma, that worship, that Catholic Church, which we see still living before our eyes. And to have proved the historical reality of Jesus Christ is to have proved the reality of this type whose leading features I have just traced. I have done more, gentlemen; I have at the same time proved the authenticity of the Gospels. For a book is authentic when it is historical; and I have shown that the Gospels possess all the characters of history, that is to say, that they were public writings, containing public events adapted to the general and public web of the annals of the human race. This is its great authenticity. There is another, secondary and of little importance, which consists in knowing the precise date of a book and the exact name of its author. I place it below the former, because a book may have a certain date and a certain author, without possessing any historical value, whilst an historical book bears with itself the date and the course of things authentically promulgated by invincible publicity. The Gospels are authentic in both ways; but as the first and great authenticity is of itself sufficient, I have confined myself chiefly to establishing it.

Perhaps in listening to me, gentlemen, you have asked yourselves whom I was addressing, why I took so much pains about a thing which did not seem to be contested. In this you would have deceived yourselves. Not only in a celebrated work on the "Origin of all Religions" has Dupuis denied the historical reality of Jesus Christ, but so also in some degree does every unbeliever, endeavouring to raise up clouds between his mind and that formidable figure of the Son of God manifest in the flesh. Hence it is that you hear it so blandly and so falsely repeated that no contemporary testimony, out of the Christian school, attests the presence of Jesus Christ upon the stage of history. Hence it is that the famous text of Flavius Josephus on the life and death of Christ has been made the object of so much suspicion. There are no unbelievers whom the historical certainty of the early times of Christianity does not disturb and importune, and who do not set a high value upon the slightest doubt in regard to it. It was necessary then to take away this consolation from them—the more so, gentlemen, as in demonstrating to you the divinity of Jesus Christ I had previously supposed the authenticity of His person and history, and because if I had not retraced my steps in order definitely to establish this, the whole edifice of my demonstration would have rested upon a gratuitous hypothesis. Let us to-day complete the substitution of the reality for the hypothesis by treating of another effort of rationalism, no longer to destroy the life of Jesus Christ, but to pervert it. For, after having said or suggested that the life of Christ was a fable, rationalism itself perceived that it was too much to ask of human credulity: it feared the all-powerful light of common sense; and at the beginning of this century, not in England, not in France, but in Germany, a new system has been developed. The life of Christ, they say, is not a fable, but a myth. What is a myth? Is the life of Christ a myth? Such is, gentlemen, the object of this conference and of your attention.

Let us first clearly understand the causes which have kept rationalism from sanctioning, by its adhesion, the historical reality of Jesus Christ. Assuredly there remain many questions to solve, even when it is admitted that Jesus Christ lived, that His history is authentic, that publicity sheds the clearest light upon the origins of Christianity and Christendom. Yet, gentlemen, when we have advanced thus far, we immediately find ourselves before a very simple dilemma: either Jesus Christ and His apostles were sincere, or they were impostors. To say they were sincere is in the main to admit the divinity of their work; for, the reality of the life of Christ being established on the one hand, and the sincerity of their work being admitted on the other, we cannot, before the nature and the course of events which form its tissue, avoid this conclusion: Jesus Christ is God. If, on the contrary, it is affirmed that Jesus Christ and His apostles were impostors, the position is one which the mind will hardly accept. And why? Because all that belongs to Jesus Christ, all the apostles, all the martyrs, manifest the sincerity of man in its highest degree; because God has placed in the person of Jesus Christ, in the life of His apostles, in the death of His martyrs, a character of truthfulness, which leaves no room for the supposition that all that beautiful history, for three whole centuries, is nothing but a mass of imposture steeped in blood. Moreover, Christianity is now sincere; it is impossible to accuse of falsehood the multitude of civilised men who believe in Jesus Christ, who profess to have the daily demonstration of His divinity, who say that, even independently of the Gospel history, the action alone of Christ upon them manifests its all-powerful reality; and it is the thesis of a celebrated German, who, having made the historical void around him, and inwardly verifying to his mind the influence of the Saviour of men, said to Germany: But I who live, who feel, who think, I live with Jesus Christ, I feel with Jesus Christ, I think with Jesus Christ; He raises me above myself, He purifies me, He gives me that which nothing in this world has ever given me; He is then more than myself, more than the world, more than the soul, He is God. Yes, we are sincere; and if all Christians do not prove their sincerity by their virtues, many of them at least render to Jesus Christ this testimony of their faith. Will you dare to charge them with hypocrisy? Will you dare to insult the hearts and actions of so great a number of men bound to you by so many ties? Hypocrites! And why? With what object? What pleasure is there in being chaste from hypocrisy? What a strange design, and what a strange salary for such a sacrifice! We are then sincere, and we are able to say of Jesus Christ, the spouse of our souls, that which Pauline said of Polyeuctes, and with the same feeling:

> My spouse in dying has left me his light,
> I see, I know, I believe!

But if Christianity is now sincere, how is it possible that, from the highest of all imposture, namely, that of assuming the name of God, this torrent, this sea of sincerity, should have spread its bays and horizons even to us, to the very centre of existing mankind? An impure cause cannot produce a pure effect; and if Christianity is now sincere, it was so yesterday, the day before, in the days of its youth; it was so in Jesus Christ, in the first heart whence it issued to fire our own and render it true. Or, if you deny the consequence under that form, recognise at least in Jesus Christ, in His apostles and martyrs, signs of sincerity still greater even than those of Christianity in the present time, and learn why unbelief needs to reject from history the primitive times of Christianity—fearing lest, having once given admission to them, they would too readily attain the crown of incontestable divinity. Yes, our ancestors, the unbelievers of France, showed the necessary boldness; they placed the question in its true light, and whosoever does not follow them, at all risk and peril, is a coward or an infant in the order of negation. Our fathers, here as elsewhere, advanced straight to the heart of things; with the native intrepidity of their minds, they comprehended that it was needful to deny all or to admit all. I laud them for it; for, after all, when men love error it is better to steer in it like Columbus than like those timid barks which fear to brave the ocean, and break up on the very edge of the shore. By advancing boldly, the end is sooner reached, and the very mind which pursued error has thus greater chances of entering in full sail into the harbour of truth.

German genius is not, it seems, endowed with this advantage of brightness and rapidity. It is this genius which has created the theory of the myth around which it has hovered for fifty years. But what is a myth? Sweep away the vaulted roof of this cathedral, and gaze upon that other vault of which Pascal said: "The eternal silence of that unknown space terrifies me." Beyond the luminaries which your eye easily discovers there as it were on the extreme frontier of space, you will still perceive an array of unknown stars. Are they the result of vision deceived by distance? Have they a total subsistence? Or rather is the cause of their apparition at the same time an optical illusion and a certain reality? So will it be if, instead of exploring the profound regions of the firmament, you cast a prying glance upon the frontiers of antiquity. You will find there recitals which will trouble your mind, uncertain whether to reject or to admit them. I take Prometheus, for example. You all know the story of Prometheus—that daring man who stole fire from heaven, and whom Jupiter, in punishment for so great a sacrilege, caused to be chained to a rock, where his liver is devoured by a vulture. Antiquity was full of this story, upon which Æschylus formed one of the most remarkable tragedies of the Greek stage. What in fact was Prometheus? Was it a pure fable? It is very difficult to think so, gentlemen; man always founds the objects of his belief upon some reality, and when these objects have a universal character it is not logical to treat them with absolute disdain. But, on another hand, would you range the story of Prometheus in history? This is equally impossible. How can we admit that a man stole fire from heaven, that God chained him to a rock, and that his liver, never diminishing, was ever preyed upon there by an insatiable vulture? We are here evidently between fable and history. An event relative to the religious destinies of the human race occurred in the depths of primordial ages; the people carried its remembrances in their emigrations; but as the shadow of the past deepened upon the world, the true physiognomy of that antique tragedy lost its clearness; imagination came to the help of memory, and Prometheus chained to his rock became the popular expression of a great crime followed by a great expiation. This is a myth. A myth is a fact transfigured by an idea; and the frontiers of antiquity—I repeat the expression—appear to us as it were guarded by a legion of myths, which are all adulterated expressions of certain truths.

Such being the case, says Dr. Strauss—one of the most celebrated masters of the mythic school—why should not Jesus Christ be a myth? Why should not the Gospels be a collection of myths, that is to say, of real facts transfigured by ideas? Let us see if this be not possible; and, in the second place, if it be not real.

That it is possible, in the first place, analogy leaves us hardly room for doubt. Is there a religion, whether idolatry, or Brahminism, or Buddhism, which subsists otherwise than by a vast assemblage of facts and ideas adulterated the one by the other? If you deny this, Christians, you will inflict a heavy blow upon yourselves. For you would thereby affirm that mankind is so wanting in common sense as to be capable of adoring for centuries fables devoid of every kind of foundation, traditional or ideal. Evidently you cannot deny it; you must admit, under pain of wounding your own selves, that wherever men have bent the knee with some universality and perpetuity they have had before them facts incrusted in conceptions. But if this be the general phenomenon, why may not Christianity have been produced under the empire of the same law? Doubtless Christians adore realities; Jesus Christ is a reality; but with the course of time and the fascination of a preconceived idea, as in all occasions of like nature, the primordial fact, although certain, has undergone modifications in the idea of its adorers which take it from pure history and range it in the category of myths. That Jesus Christ has not undergone so complete a transformation as the more distant events of remote antiquity, may be readily granted; but the degree of more or less is a secondary question only; and it nevertheless remains that the person of Christ and the Christian event are comprised in the general law which links to the myth all known religions.

So much the less is this to be doubted, as the publication of the Gospels is not contemporary with Jesus Christ. From the very avowal of Christians, many years of tradition and preaching preceded the era of the evangelical writings; and, if we come to exact criticism, we shall not be able to place the assured reign of the New Testament before the middle of the second century. What a space left to the imagination and to faith for transforming Jesus Christ!

It is especially worthy of remark that this transformation was so much the more easy, as the Messianic idea pre-existed Jesus Christ. Long before He appeared that idea flowed in the veins of the Jewish people; a vast number of men, attentive to the voice of the prophets, looked for the Messiah who was to come; and after Christ had attributed this mission to Himself it was natural that all its features should be applied to Him. The Messianic idea was the mould in which, for three centuries, the myth of Jesus Christ was formed. Jesus Christ had, so to say, but to leave things to their own course, and when He died His life entered of itself, like matter in fusion, into the mould of the Messianic idea, whence at length it came forth such as it now is before the astonished eyes of generations.

Analogy, the time, the preconceived idea of the Messiah, all these circumstances lead to the conclusion that Christianity may have been found, like all the religions of antiquity, by the principle of mythical transfiguration. But a closer examination will lead us far beyond that conclusion, and cause us to perceive in the New Testament all the characters of an accomplished myth.

In the first place, the life of Jesus Christ, as related in the Gospels, is stamped with a character of continuous marvel. From the angel who announced His conception in the womb of the Virgin Mary, up to His resurrection and ascension, not a single event in the whole of that existence is conformable with the course of nature. Every word develops a prodigy, every step is a miracle, and the miracle seems constantly struggling to surpass itself and to confound the last hopes of reason. Now, the marvellous is precisely the inseparable companion of the myth, and its seat is the same. Where, in fact, do we find the marvellous? Is it before our eyes—near to us, in the modern world? Never. All that we see is simple and natural; general laws, whence proceeds a constant order, governing the world which is before us; God does not act in it by any sudden and capricious intervention, but he leaves to secondary causes their indissoluble succession. Where then do we find the marvellous? There—even where we find the myth—in antiquity. Antiquity is the seat of the one and the other; and the myth itself is revealed to us only by the presence of the marvellous. For if nothing were marvellous in antiquity, all would be history. But what then is it that distinguishes the marvellous in regard to Jesus Christ from the marvellous elsewhere? In Himself, nothing; as to place, nothing still, since that place is antiquity. Why, then, may we ask, do you divide antiquity in twain, and call one false and the other true? Why reject in the myth that which was marvellous before Jesus Christ, and raise to the rank of history the marvellous which is contemporary with Him? Reason seizes no motive for this distinction, if it be not that you call the time of Jesus Christ an historical period, in opposition to other epochs which you call fabulous. But the marvellous is the very character that distinguishes fabulous from historical ages; for, without this, where would be the principle of their distinction?

In the second place, it is manifest, on the first reading of the Gospels, that they present no chronological suite, nothing which announces history, but that they are simple materials collected in minds at hazard, without the slightest attempt having been made to give them any appearance of harmony. All is in confusion and contradiction there. Dr. Strauss has had but to read and let his pen run freely, to form four volumes of the inconceivable blunders of which they are full. And we must not blame the evangelists for this; it is the very proof of their sincerity. They took the myth as they found it, vague, indefinite, contradictory—like all that comes from the gloomy confluence of facts and ideas. More than a century had passed over the life of Jesus Christ; shreds of that life had been carried from the East to the West, under the impression of sentiments and ideas of diverse origins; and, although the type possessed some unity because of the Messianic form which was the primitive starting-point, it was nevertheless impossible for the final elaboration of so many elements not to bear visible marks of disagreement and variety.

Such, gentlemen, is the reasoning of the mythic school. I believe I have not hidden any of its force from you; I do not like to depreciate the enemies of truth. Why should I? Were I to succeed for a moment in abusing your penetration and memory, on returning to your homes a glance at the work of Dr. Strauss would reveal to you my want of sincerity, and the cause I defend, for the half-hour it may have gained, would have lost a century in your minds. No, gentlemen, it is less than a duty, it is a pleasure to be sincere when we have truth on our side; and if the arguments of the mythic school have wanted force in passing by my mouth, it is because, after three months devoted to the study of them, it is not possible for me to impart to them more attractiveness and more authority. Do not, however, deceive yourselves; the work is as skilful as it could be. You perceive that the historical reality of Jesus Christ is no longer denied; they no longer rush to their destruction against the very constitution of history; and yet Jesus Christ, although remaining as a reality, is disarmed of the power of that position. On another hand, it is no longer necessary to combat the impression of sincerity which results from His life and that of His disciples. That sincerity is admitted. Jesus Christ believed in Himself, and men believed in Him. They believed in Him before Cæsar, they believe in Him before incredulity. Your fathers gave their blood for realities and ideas; you do the same. Only you do not properly understand them; and it is permitted, it is honourable, it is glorious, to live and die for things which we do not properly understand.

Gentlemen, I believe this exposition is sufficient. I will now meet this great engine of Germanic warfare.

Shall I deny the existence of myths? No, gentlemen; the myth appears to me historically as of all things in the world the most veritable. I admit that man, left to tradition during a long course of ages, ends by no longer clearly perceiving the limit and the primitive text of events. Like a picture before which the spectator constantly retreats, the human race retreats before the past; and however attentively it may be watched, at length it becomes obscure. The imagination, however, dwelling upon this now distant scene, adds new features to it, the idea governs the fact, and something is produced which is neither history nor fable, but that which we call a myth. Mythology is the assemblage of all the creations of the human mind between the gloom and the light of antiquity. For, remark where is the theatre of myths. It is antiquity, or rather it is tradition abandoned alone to the course of mankind, which bears it along in advancing and pressing onward. The seat of the myth is in pure tradition. But wherever writing appears, wherever there is a fixed recital, wherever the indelible record is placed before the eyes of generations, at that moment the mythic power of man vanishes. For then the reality remains before him in its true proportions, it remains in command of his imagination, and a thousand years can do no more against it than a single day. Never, since the time of Herodotus and Tacitus, has anyone shown you myths in history. Has Charlemagne become a myth after a thousand years? Clovis after thirteen hundred years? Augustus, Cæsar, in retreating into the past, have they assumed any mythical appearance? No; the most distant point where the modern historian seeks to discover the myth is, for example, the beginning of Rome, Romulus and Remus. And why? Because although they approached writing, although it existed before them in other countries, it had not yet received the guardianship of Roman history. But, as soon as writing exists, as soon as it seizes the general web of history, the mythical mould is from that moment broken.

Now, Jesus Christ does not belong to the reign of tradition, but to the reign of writing. He was born at a period when writing was fully established, in a land where it was impossible for the myth to take root and grow. Providence had foreseen all and prepared all beforehand; and if you have sometimes wondered why Jesus Christ came so late, you now see a reason for it. He came so late not to be in antiquity, to have his place in the centre of writing; for He does not stand first there; He was careful to provide against being so placed; fifteen hundred years preceded Him, and if you count only from Herodotus, five hundred years preceded Him. Therefore He is modern, and even should the world last for numberless ages, as by means of writing all is present, since at a glance and with the rapidity of lightning we survey the whole chain of history, Jesus Christ is ever new, standing in the full reality of the events which compose the known and certain life of the human race.

I might stop here, gentlemen; for you see clearly that the mythic engine is overthrown, since the fundamental condition of the myth, which is the absence of writing, is wanting in regard to Jesus Christ. Dr. Strauss himself expressly admits that the myth is not possible with writing, therefore he endeavours to strip Jesus Christ of the scriptural character by placing at as remote a period as possible the publication of the Gospels. We shall soon see the weakness of that resource, if you will permit me to follow step by step the trace of his reasoning.

Analogy, says he, is against Jesus Christ, since the myth is the basis of all known religions. This I deny. The myth is the basis of all the religions of antiquity, save the Mosaic, because all those religions plunged their roots in a tradition of which writing had not fixed the shadows, and so rendered deflections impossible. But writing having appeared, even the false religions, such as that of Mahomet, have taken an historical consistency which manifestly separates them from the priesthoods and corrupted dogmas of antiquity. The difference is clear. This is why we Christians, and you who fight against Christianity, never think of combating Mahomet by making a myth of his person, and of the Koran a mythical compilation. The force of writing, under the empire of which he lived, interdicts to us even the thought of such chimerical temerity. We are constrained to avow that he is a real personage, that he wrote or dictated the Koran, organised Islamism; and our sole resource against his pretensions in regard to us is to treat him as an impostor, to say boldly to him: Thou hast lied! But here the difficulty is greater, the success much more costly; and this is why rationalism disputes with so much art the powerful reality of Christ. However this may be, the analogy which is invoked to spread over Him the clouds of the myth is an analogy without foundation. A great line of demarcation separates into two hemispheres all known religions—the mythic hemisphere and the real hemisphere; the former contains all the religions formed in primitive times under the empire of floating traditions, the latter contains the true or false religions which writing has enchained in a settled history and dogma. To reject the former, it suffices to oppose to them their mythical nature; to reject the latter, it is necessary to enter into the discussion of their historical, intellectual, moral, and social value.

It is true that the scriptural character of Jesus Christ is contested, but how? Because, say they, it is impossible to prove that the promulgation of the Gospels took place before the year 150 of the Christian era, whence it follows that the type of Christ floated, during more than a century, at the mercy of tradition. Suppose, gentlemen, that I admit this; suppose that I admit that our Gospels did not appear before the year 150. Bear in mind that before 150 writing existed elsewhere than in the Christian school; it existed among the Jews, the Greeks, the Romans; over the whole space upon which the question of Christianity was disputed; history was founded by the publicity and immutability of the monuments. Before 150, Jesus Christ, dead and risen again, was announced in all the synagogues that covered the surface of the Roman world, and even beyond it; He was publicly announced in the palace of the Cæsars, and in the prætorium of all the proconsuls. Before 150, I have cited Tacitus and Pliny the Younger, who attest that it was so. That preaching, those testimonies, those discussions, that struggle, that blood, all was public, was written; it was not a dead tradition left to the chances of time and imagination during a thousand years of indifference and peace. At the same moment men gave their teaching and their life; and three communities together, supremely interested in what was passing—the Christian community, the Jewish, and the Roman—met upon the battlefield, the traditional limit of which you circumscribe within the period of little more than a century. What! those Jews to whom it was said: You have killed Jesus Christ; those princes and those presidents whose orders were trampled under foot in the name of Jesus Christ; not one of them perceived that it was all only a myth in the state of formation? No; all was steeped in blood, and consequently in reality; all was in discussion, and consequently in the strength and glory of publicity, which is the foundation of all history. It matters little then what date the Gospels bear, for history supports the Gospels. If they did not appear before a hundred and twenty years after Jesus Christ, they existed before they appeared, they lived in the mouth of the apostles, in the blood of the martyrs, in the hatred of the world, in the breasts of millions of men who confessed Jesus Christ dead and risen again! What a pitiable resource, gentlemen, what weakness! To compare a religion whose origin is so public and militant, and whose tradition could have preceded writing only a hundred and twenty years, to those religions without history, plunged for two thousand years in the still waters of a tradition which was confided to no one, and for which no one ever gave a drop of his blood!

I hardly need to tell you, gentlemen, that we do not accept the date which they attempt to assign to the promulgation of the Gospels. The Gospels are public writings, containing public facts which enter into the public web of history; they bear the names of three apostles, and of a celebrated disciple, who were public men in a public society; now, it is impossible that such an attribution, under such circumstances, should be contrary to truth. The mathematical laws of publicity do not permit it. The Gospels are apostles; they possess the value of their testimony, and the date of their life, that is to say, the date of a contemporary life, and the value of a contemporary testimony. This detail of authenticity blends itself with the general authenticity of the Christian origin, and it is not separable therefrom. Judge yet once more of the relation existing between such monuments and the obscure myths emerging from the silent and dark abyss of remote antiquity.

In vain, in order to place Jesus Christ in a more remote period than His time, have they had recourse to the Messianic idea which prepared His coming. In the first place, the Messianic idea was not a myth; it appertained to a scriptural people, a people who wrote and who were written about; and the Messianic idea itself was a part of their writing. The idea and the fact were fixed. But even had Messianism primitively been a myth, it could no longer preserve that character in its application to Jesus Christ. For that application to Jesus Christ was modern; it took place at a scriptural and public epoch, and, consequently, whatever it may have been in the past, the myth disappeared in the broad day of Jesus Christ and of His age. The real question extinguished the chimerical question.

There remain, gentlemen, the mythic characters which they pretend to discover in the very history of Jesus Christ. The first of these characters is the marvellous. The marvellous, say they, is the mythic character, properly so called; wherever it shows itself history disappears; for a miracle being impossible in itself, every narration containing it would evidently not be historical. Therefore, says Dr. Strauss, I overthrow your dogmatism by this single expression: The Gospel is a tissue of miracles; now miracles are impossible, their history is then impossible also, and consequently that history does not exist. It can be but a myth.

Whether a miracle be impossible or not, is a metaphysical question of which I have already treated, and to which I shall not return. But, at least, it is a question. You rationalists do not admit the possibility of the sovereign action of God in this world; we Christians admit that possibility. Now, we are men like yourselves, intelligent beings like yourselves; if you are numerous, we are more so than you; if you are learned, we are as learned as you. And whilst you deny the possibility of a miracle, we daily ask God to perform miracles, being fully persuaded that He thus manifests His power and goodness towards us, even in the present day. We go further, we do not comprehend the idea of God without the idea of a sovereignty able to manifest itself by the omnipotence of its action; so that, for us, the negation of the possibility of the miracle is the negation of the very idea of God. God, according to us, is miraculous in His nature; and if history ceases by miracles, we think that God ceases without them. You see that an abyss separates these two sentiments. What follows? It follows that the possibility of miracles is a question; and consequently to determine the reality of history by the presence or absence of miracles, is but to decide one question by another question—a mode of proceeding which is contrary to the rules of logic and common sense. What! documents are authentic, they are linked together and form a visible and continuous order, they blend with the whole course of the public life of mankind, they are irrefragable, certain, sacred, it is an act of folly to assail them; but the finger of God is seen in them, that power which created the world—and that is enough, history has disappeared! You will not ask me, gentlemen, even supposing that miracles may be problematical in themselves, to deny the certain because of the uncertain. We Christians admit the uncertain on the faith of the certain: each has his own logic.

Nevertheless, say they, the marvellous is the only character that distinguishes fable from history. It is not so, gentlemen, the line of demarcation between history and fable lies elsewhere; it lies in the difference between things without continuity and without any public monuments, and things which possess continuity, and are firmly based on all sides upon publicity. I have already said this; I shall not repeat it.

Is Dr. Strauss more fortunate in that which forms the basis of his work—the exposure of innumerable mistakes and contradictions of our evangelists? I think not. I have read his work with attention and labour, and I did so in this manner. After having studied a paragraph—always a very long one—and there are a hundred and forty-nine of them, filling four volumes, I closed the book in order to recover a little from fatigue and from a kind of involuntary terror caused by the abundance of erudition. Then opening the Gospel—which I kissed respectfully—I read the texts under discussion, to see if by the simple aid of ordinary literature, and without the help of any commentators, I could not succeed in unravelling the difficulty. With the exception of three or four passages, I have never required more than ten minutes to dissipate the charm of vain knowledge, and to smile within myself at the powerlessness to which God has condemned error. I cannot, gentlemen, pass in review before you all that legion of texts distorted by rationalism; I will limit myself to two examples taken at hazard.

Saint Luke, having to narrate the birth of Jesus Christ at Bethlehem, away from the country of His parents, writes in these terms: "And it came to pass that in those days there went out a decree from Cæsar Augustus that the whole world should be enrolled; this enrolling was first made by Cyrinus the governor of Syria." Upon this Dr. Strauss, after having first shown very learnedly that the enrolling was not possible, opens the "Judaical Antiquities" of Flavius Josephus, and shows by a formal text that Cyrinus did not govern Syria until ten years after the birth of Jesus Christ. Judge what a triumph this was! Now, how was this difficulty to be solved? You think, perhaps, that we shall have to change a word or a letter? No; it is less than that. You all know the value of an accent in the Greek language; change then an accent, and see what will be the meaning of the evangelist: "And it came to pass that in those days there went out a decree from Cæsar Augustus that the whole world should be enrolled; this is the same first enrolling which was made by Cyrinus the governor of Syria." That is to say, that the order having been given to number the Roman Empire, and the execution of that order having been commenced, it was not, however, accomplished until ten years after, under Cyrinus the governor of Syria. And if the sacred historian makes mention of the name of Cyrinus, it is precisely to give an authentic character to his declaration; for had he been content with saying: "There went out a decree from Cæsar Augustus that the whole world should be enrolled," it might have been said that the enrolling did not take place at the time of the birth of Christ. He anticipated the objection then by saying: "This is the same first enrolling which was made by Cyrinus the governor of Syria."

Here is another example: It is said, in regard to the resurrection of our Lord, that the holy women went to the tomb, according to St. Mark, the sun being then risen, and according to St. John, when it was yet dark. Dr. Strauss notices this contradiction amongst a great number which he pretends to discover in the event of the resurrection—and he does not fail to turn them to account. But how shall we solve this terrible difficulty? It suffices to comprehend that when a distance is to be reached early in the morning it is possible to start before sunrise, and to arrive at daybreak.

I assure you, gentlemen, that, save a very few passages, nothing has caused me any greater trouble. So that after the work had often left my hands from weariness, my hands fell from me again when I thought that this was learning, German learning—that learning in whose name they pompously defy Catholic preachers and writers, saying to us: You speak of Christ and the Gospel—you cite them; but you are behind your age, Germany has now destroyed Christ and the Gospel; she has examined them by the light of criticism, and all that is nothing but a shadow, a dream, a myth!

Let us leave this triumph to pride; and with our sounder sense let us seek why the history of Jesus Christ lends itself to the attacks which I have just pointed out to you. Had Providence so willed it, Jesus Christ would have had but one single historian, conducting from one end to the other the thread of His life with a chronological clearness which would have given to each part its true place, and have raised the whole above any possible discussion. But Providence did not so will it. Providence desired that the Gospel should be the work of several men differing in age, in genius, in style, and in judgment, and not one of whom should collect under his pen all the materials of the life of Christ, but only simple fragments, the very choice of which was arbitrary. The idea of God in this was to make of the biography of His Son a miracle of intimate truth which the most vulgar eye might discern, and which was to be found in no other life of any man whatever. Indeed, from the first glance, the multiplicity of the Gospels is striking, not only from the title-page, which bears different names, but from the reflection of their personal nature in each of the Gospels. We see and feel that St. Matthew, St. Mark, St. Luke, St. John, are different souls, and that each traces in his own manner the likeness of his beloved Master, without taking the least account of what his neighbour is doing, or even of what the continuity of chronology requires. Thence an arbitrary choice of fragments, a default of connection, apparent contradictions, details omitted by one and related by another, a multitude of varieties of which men render no account to themselves. This is true. And yet in these four evangelists there is the same portraiture of Christ, the same sublimity, the same tenderness, the same force, the same language, the same accent, the same supreme singularity of physiognomy. Open St. Matthew the publican, or St. John the young man, chaste and contemplative; choose whatever passage you will in the one or in the other, different alike in matter and expression, and speak it before a thousand men assembled together, all will raise their heads; they recognise Jesus Christ. And the more the exterior disagreement of the Gospel is shown, the more that intimate agreement whence the moral unity of Christ springs will become a proof of their fidelity. If they unanimously represent so well the inimitable features of Christ, it is because He was before their eyes; they saw Him such as He was and such as they were not able to forget Him. They saw Him with their senses, with their hearts, with the exactitude of a love which was to give its blood; they are at the same time witnesses, painters, and martyrs. That sitting of God before man has been witnessed only once, and this is why there is but one Gospel, although there were four evangelists.

And what soul is insensible to this? What soul will not one day forget science at the feet of Jesus Christ, represented by His apostles? To close this subject, listen to the words of a Frenchman, which will console you for the frenzies of that learning which the Gospel has not disarmed. They are those of a man whose judgment upon Jesus Christ I have already cited to you, and they express in clear and forcible language the impression which the reading of the Gospel leaves in the mind of the profane as well as in that of the Christian: "Shall we say that the Gospel history is a pure invention? My friend, men do not invent in this way, and the acts of Socrates, which no one doubts, are less fully proved than those of Jesus Christ. In truth, it is to push aside the difficulty without destroying it; it would be much more inconceivable that several men together should have fabricated that book than that only one should have furnished the subjects of it. The Jewish authors would never have acquired that tone or that morality; and the Gospel possesses characters of truth so great, so striking, so perfectly inimitable, that the inventor of it would be more marvellous than the hero!"

This is French language and French genius; and therefore you should not be surprised at returning to Christ after having quitted Him. The lucidity of our national intelligence sustains within you the light of grace, and causes you like giants to cross those thorny abysses of science, but of a science which braves the soul. Be faithful to this double gift which bears you towards God; judge of the power of Jesus Christ by the efforts, so contradictory and so vain, of his adversaries; and permit me to recall to you in terminating this discourse a celebrated trait which paints that power, and the eloquent prophecy which fifteen centuries have confirmed.

When the Emperor Julian attacked Christianity by that stratagem of war and violence which bears his name, and, absent from the empire, had gone to seek in battles the consecration of a power and popularity which he thought would achieve the ruin of Jesus Christ, one of his familiars, the rhetor Libanius, on meeting a Christian, asked him derisively and with all the insolence of assured success, what the Galilean was doing; the Christian answered: He is making a coffin. Some time afterwards Libanius pronounced the funeral oration of Julian over his mutilated body and his vanished power. What the Galilean was then doing, gentlemen, he does always, whatever may be the arm and the pride men may oppose to His cross. It would require much time to deduce all the famous examples of this; but we possess some which touch us closely, and by which Jesus Christ, at the extremity of ages, has confirmed to us the nothingness of His enemies. Thus, when Voltaire rubbed his hands with joy, towards the close of his life, saying to his followers: " In twenty years, God will see fine sport;" the Galilean prepared a coffin: it was that of the French monarchy. Thus, when a power of another order, but sprung, in some degree, from the same, held the Sovereign Pontiff in a captivity which threatened the fall at least of the temporal power of the vicar of Jesus Christ, the Galilean prepared a coffin: it was that of Saint Helena. And now, on seeing Germany agitated by the convulsions of unregulated science, of which you have just witnessed so lamentable a production, we may say with as much certainty as hope : The Galilean prepares a coffin, and it is that of rationalism. And you all, sons of this age, ill-instructed by the miseries of past errors, and who seek out of Jesus Christ the way, the truth, and the life, the Galilean prepares a coffin for you; and it is that of all your most cherished conceptions. And so it will ever be, the Galilean ever working but two things, living of Himself, or either by blood, oblivion, or shame, entombing all that is not of Him.

# THE EFFORTS OF RATIONALISM
### TO EXPLAIN
# THE LIFE OF JESUS CHRIST.

My Lord—Gentlemen,

Rationalism has then made but vain efforts to destroy and to pervert the life of Jesus Christ. Jesus Christ is not dethroned; the power of history protects and upholds Him against all these attacks. Therefore rationalism has been forced to attempt a last and supreme effort to explain at least that life which it was unable either to destroy or to dishonour. We Catholics explain the life of Christ, we explain the success He has obtained—the greatest of all success, that of producing in minds the rational certainty of faith; in the soul, holiness by humility, chastity, and charity; in the world, a spiritual community, one, universal, and perpetual—we explain it by that single expression: Jesus Christ is the Son of God. But if it be not so explained; if it be supposed that Christ is but a man, it is nevertheless necessary to give a reason for that greatest success ever obtained, which is His own. Now, as after the power of God there remains only the power of man, if Jesus Christ did not act by the power of God, He acted by the power of man. But the power of man in its results being manifestly inferior to that which Jesus Christ has accomplished, it follows that we must seek in man a certain root of power which, in rare cases, may suddenly appear and explain what Christ was, and what he has accomplished. That is to say, that Jesus Christ, not being the Son of God, nor, as He Himself said, the Son of man, He is the Son of mankind, the illustrious production of that silent and progressive action which is the life of mankind, and which, on certain solemn occasions, buds forth, so to say, blossoms, produces an extraordinary being, and surrounds him with a halo which all who come after Him will confirm, up to the time when mankind, ever pregnant with the future, feels that it is imperfectly represented by the heroic and sovereign being it has produced, and at length salutes Him with a last mark of respect, brings Him down to the level of earthly things, and says to Him: Adieu.

I shall devote our last conference of this year to the refutation of this system. This done, all that belongs to the constitution and character, alike of the Church and of Christ, having been manifested to you in our teaching, it will only remain for us to enter upon the doctrine itself of the Church and of Christ, in order to present it to you in all the fulness of its harmony; after which we shall have but to repose, you, gentlemen, from your attention, and I from the happiness of having taught you so long.

Three things have to be explained in the life and success of Jesus Christ: His doctrine, which appears to surpass all others; the faith which the world has given to that doctrine; and, thirdly, the union of that doctrine and faith in a body hierarchically constituted, which is the Church. This triple phenomenon, it is said, is easily explained by the general state of doctrines, minds, and nations, at the time when Jesus Christ appeared. First, by the general state of doctrines. That of Jesus Christ is ordinarily considered to be a new doctrine, unknown, creative, as something which had neither root nor model in the past; this, as rationalism says, is a very palpable error. The human race has never been without doctrine; it is a necessary part of its life. That some simpleton, satisfied in the debauch of pride and of the senses, may pass through the world without troubling himself about doctrine, as a grain of dust carried along by the unstable wind passes and disappears, no one will deny. But mankind has other desires and other destinies. Mankind requires to know, to seek, to render account to itself of itself and of the universe, to possess a faith; and never, in reality, has it lived without that spiritual element. As men dig the earth that bears them, as they scan the sky that covers them, so they unceasingly labour upon the fertile soil of doctrines in order to draw from them an aliment which they deem divine. This working is not less active in itself than that which is external and scientific, and they form together a tissue of unwearied action. Now there were three principal theatres of this action before Jesus Christ, the East, the West, and Judæa, which was the connecting link between the two others.

The East preserved doctrine under this form: that man had fallen, that he needed an expiation to return to a better condition—an expiation which, from cycle to cycle, favoured mysterious incarnations of God. The Eastern incarnation, its expiation, its metempsychosis or trial—nothing is more famous than these in the history of doctrines; and it will suffice to place these terms before your minds for you to perceive in a single moment, on penetrating to the heart of Judæa, this order of ideas still existing. In the West, a work of another nature had been accomplished. Under the reign of free discussion, it more effectually stripped itself of past myths; it sought wisdom, founded less upon tradition than upon the decisions of pure reason; and Plato was the most memorable instrument of these explorations of the human mind. He comprehended that God was in communication with man, not only by corrupted or lost traditions, but by the perpetual effusion of his Verb or Word within us, the Divine Word, the eternal *Logos*, absolute reason—of which our reason and our word are the transparent image, so that in contemplating his own ideas, man beheld, as in a mirror, the very ideas that are in God, and form there the first Word. And this theory of the manifestation of God by His Word, of which the word of man is but the diminutive and the reflection, had become the most elevated point of the doctrines of Greece and of the West. The Jewish people, on their part, had maintained, with extraordinary fidelity, the dogma of the unity of God, that of the creation, and in addition a certain hope of the fundamental unity of man, which should eventually be restored as it existed in the original family.

This was evidently the general state of doctrines at the time of Christ, and these doctrines, long isolated, each in its place, had at length met together after the conquests of Alexander and the invasions of Rome reaching to Asia. The East, the West, Judæa, and with them the Brahmins, the prophets, the sibyls, the sages, all the documents, and all the efforts of the past, had, as it were, met together by common accord before the throne of Augustus, on the day when he closed upon the world the prophetic gates of the temple of war. At that moment Jesus Christ was born. Endowed with a genius answering to the marvellous circumstances of His age, He saw with a sure glance the confluence of doctrines; in that confluence He unravelled more than one fortuitous junction, He discovered there the germs of deeply-seated unity, and imagined that by giving satisfaction to all, by engrafting the East upon the West, the West and the East upon the Hebraic trunk, He should attain to a doctrine which would at least captivate a great multitude of minds in the divers parts of the world. He laid down as a foundation the Eastern dogma of the fall, and declared that He Himself, the last incarnation, superior to all that had preceded Him, had come definitively to expiate the fault of the human race, and to restore to men with their native purity all their birthrights. Next, as the Eastern incarnation was dishonoured by too many fabulous elements, He based the idea of His own incarnation upon that Word of Plato, who had detached the communication between God and man from the traditional myth, in order to reduce it to a permanent communication of ideas in the very seat of the understanding. He declared that He was the Word of God, the reason of God, the one who, by His nature, enlightened every man coming into the world; and who, by the effective presence of His personality, by the exterior lights of His teaching, brought to the mind a more complete vision of truth. The Divine Word was thenceforth in presence of the human word; the image had but to look upon the model, the consequence had but to consult the principle, and from that confronting of within to without, of light to light, the supreme enlightenment of the human race would come. Plato thus became allied to the Brahmins of India, the West to the East; and, in fine, to give satisfaction to the Hebraic ideas, Jesus Christ not only proclaimed Himself the Messiah, He also accepted the dogmas of the unity of God and of the creation, which were inscribed in the first pages of the Bible, and which were the special patrimony of the Hebrew people.

Such was, gentlemen, according to rationalism, the theme of Jesus Christ, the mode of the formation of His doctrine, and of the efficient cause of His doctrinal success. He was not creator, but electric; His success was not a success of creation, but of fusion. Before seeking to discover how far this is confirmed by comparing the Christian doctrines with the doctrines of antiquity, let us first see how Jesus Christ declared Himself. Did He declare Himself as a creator? Did He say: I am the inventor of truth? No, gentlemen; He said: "I am the truth."* He said: "I am not come to destroy the law, but to fulfil it;"† which means: I am the truth of all times and places; I am that truth which was in the bosom of the Father; which appeared to the first man in the innocence of the terrestrial paradise; which the patriarchs, his successors, knew; which Noah, on quitting the ark, received and promulgated afresh; which Abraham, in the fields of Chaldæa and Syria, saw and heard; which Moses, at the foot of Sinai, received, graven by the hand of God. I am that truth which is the first and the last, and which no man has ever been able totally to set aside. Behold, gentlemen, what Jesus Christ said of Himself, and what the Church still says of Him daily. He did not seek, nor do we seek for Him, a success of creation; we have never pretended that Christianity commenced with the appearance of Christ under Augustus. To have given it a character of novelty would have been to ruin Christianity. From the first day of the world, from the first word of God, from the first divine ray which shone in our soul, it was Christ who acted, who spake, and who revealed Himself; and that revelation spread over the whole earth with the dispersion of the primordial branches of the human race.

However, by the side of this phenomenon of the primitive and universal propagation of Christianity, we must remark that there grew up another of a very different character: I mean the progressive adulteration and corruption of Christianity by forgetfulness, reasoning, and unbelief. So that Jesus Christ, although not new, brought into the world something which the world no longer knew save by ill-defined hopes and disfigured recollections. And, to begin by the East: it is true, the East had preserved the idea of the fall, of expiation, of the divine intervention for the restoration of man—no one will contest it; but the East had stifled that idea between two absurdities, namely, pantheism and metempsychosis; the one and the other affirming that the purification of man had for object and for effect the return of man to the very substance of the Divinity, from whence He had sprung, and that after cycles of trials, more or less prolonged, the final state of mankind

---

\* St. John xvi. 6.   † St. Matt. v. 17.

would be that of the external and absolute repose of complete deification. Now, did Jesus Christ admit this doctrine? Did He compromise with the East in regard to pantheism or metempsychosis? No, He taught the very opposite; He said to us: You are but nothingness which has responded to the creating power of God; and your destiny, although great, is not to attain to God by confounding your substance with Him, but by simple vision. You will one day see Him, if you have believed in Him; you will possess Him present, if you have loved Him absent; but your nature and your personality will subsist before Him. Pantheism bears you alike too high and too low—too high in promising you that you are one in substance with God; too low in taking from you your proper nature and your principle of distinction. Your place and truth are not there. God and man are for ever two; two in their essence; two in their personality; two in their love, for God made man from love; and if man correspond to that love which sought him the first, that same love will eternally reward him. If, on the contrary, man be unfaithful and ungrateful, that love will reject him eternally.

I ask you, gentlemen, was this the Eastern dogma, or was it not rather its destruction?

And as to the West, they speak of Plato. But, in the first place, was Plato the whole West? Did he resume the West in himself? Did not Aristotle, Epicurus Zeno, Pyrrho, exist by the same title, and did not their doctrines share with those of the Academy the empire of minds? You say that Plato was the highest expression of Western wisdom; let us not contest it, and in seeing what he thought, let us see what Jesus Christ owed to him. In the metaphysical order, Plato believed in the eternity of matter and of chaos, placing the world in presence of God as a substance inferior, but parallel and uncreated; in the moral order, he denied the existence of freewill, and affirmed in proper terms that no one was voluntarily bad, because the principle of all evil is an indeliberate error of the mind. Dualism and fatalism, such is that Plato so much admired—whom I have lauded myself, whom I shall still praise, a man admirable indeed, who, being plunged like all the others in the faint and almost extinguished light of antiquity, caught here and there glimpses of the shadow of truth, and made plaintive cries to it, as if he had beheld it; but being unable to seize it, had thrown again over his desires and his regrets that royal vestment which has become the charm of his thoughts, the beauty of his discourse, and the majesty of his renown. No sage ever equalled him in the invocation of truth, none foresaw its future more clearly, none ever tinged the twilight of error with a halo more gorgeous or better formed to solace the soul for wedding but a dream. But to make him an ancestor of Jesus Christ, and the tie by which the Gospel attached the West to itself, is to expect too much from his glory. Jesus Christ denied the Platonic dualism and fatalism, as He also denied the pantheism and metempsychosis of India; and if He called Himself the Word, the Son of God, that expression sprang from a mystery which, to Plato, was unknown—the mystery of a triple personality in the substance, one and indivisible, of God.

The Jews, in their turn, although possessors of primitive Christianity and the expectation of the Messiah, had corrupted this deposit in their ideas, by making of Christian truth—which is the patrimony of all—their own special heritage, by substituting the idea of the law for the idea of faith—Moses for Christ, the personal for the universal. This is what St. Paul reproaches them with in the Epistle to the Romans, where he takes so much pains to explain to them the inferiority of the law to faith; how Christ was the principle of salvation from the time of Abraham, and how the works of the law, understood and performed without Jesus Christ, were a cause of death. The Jews rebelled against that forcible teaching; already steeped in the liberating blood, and even in communion with it, they persisted in venerating the idol which raised their national pride to the rank of a duty and a virtue, and persuaded themselves that Judaism was to subjugate the universe. In the Christian sense, this was true; in the sense in which they held it, it was false. Jesus Christ had then to combat Judæa as well as the East and the West. And if you would see yet more clearly that Christian doctrine was not a success of fusion, but a success of contradiction—of contradiction to the East, to the West, to the Hebrew people—you have but to study pantheism as the East has preserved it, Judaism as the remnant of Israel still understands it, and Platonism as it has been resuscitated before our eyes.

Pantheism lives in India. India is now, as in past times, its land of predilection, it lives there under the same forms and in the same doctrines as in the time of Jesus Christ. Now, no country, no system, has offered more resistance to the Christian apostolate. For three centuries the great Indian peninsula has been open to us; many European nations have together and successively governed it. England is now its mistress; we hold it by our missionaries as by our arms under the grasp of our domination, and nowhere, not even in that China which is closed to us, has the action of Jesus Christ been less rewarded with success. Brahminism has resisted example as well as discussion; it has been like granite against truth, like a thing incompatible with another thing, and which rejects it so much the more as it approaches nearer. Many reasons have been given for this, such as the rule of caste, and the aversion resulting therefrom for our principles of equality. It may be also that on account of the many traditions it has preserved on the fall and reparation, Brahminism has been less sensible to the mystery of redemption by the blood of Jesus Christ, as we see men in whom the possession of a certain measure of truth serves as an obstacle to the acquisition of the rest. The honest man is often in this state, gentlemen, when he has the misfortune not to be a Christian; his probity keeps him from God, whilst the unworthy sinner, looking upon himself, sees nothing within that raises an illusion for him. This is why Jesus Christ said: "Those women whom you call lost will go into the kingdom of heaven before you."\* They are, in fact, nearer to good by being far from it; they touch the feet of Jesus Christ by humiliation; and when we are at the feet of Jesus Christ we are very near to His heart. So perhaps is it with nations that have lost all truth; they feel the need of regaining it, whilst those who still preserve vestiges of truth, grow proud with the little they have, scorning to desire and seek that which they have not. Be that as it may, Indian pantheism has not changed; it is now what it was in the Augustan Age; and whatever may have been the cause of its insensibility towards Jesus Christ, it no less proves to us how chimerical is the idea of that fusion of doctrines by which it is desired to explain the formation of the Christian dogma.

The spectacle of Judaism as it lives before us leads us to the same conclusion. And as to Platonism, God has permitted it to resuscitate in our time, so that on witnessing it in action we may be able to judge of its doctrinal sympathy for Jesus

---

\* St. Matt. xxi. 31.

Christ. You all know to what school I allude; you know how that school has restored Platonic dualism to honour, by rejecting from its philosophy the fundamental dogma of the creation of the world by God, and you know also how it treats the rest of Christianity. In contemporary literature we have no more avowed enemies than the friends of Plato. Whether then we regard pantheism, Judaism, or Platonism—all three subsisting before us as in the time of Jesus Christ—it is easy for us to judge that Christianity was not the result of a fusion between the doctrines of the ancient world, but a work of renovation and of contradiction. The Gospel has renewed all, because all had been forgotten; it has contradicted all, because all had been denied or disfigured; it has had all doctrines for adversaries, because it has disavowed and rejected all. And as it was aforetime, so it is now. The dogmatic intolerance of which it is accused defines its nature and proves its originality.

But the success of Jesus Christ was not only realised in the powerful and aboriginal formation of His doctrine; it was also a success of faith. A doctrine is as nothing as long as it has not taken possession of minds by faith, which gives it life and action. How did the ancient world believe in Jesus Christ? How did the men of the East and the West, the learned or the unlearned, and, in fine, the great nations, abdicate the teaching they had received from the past, in order to become the disciples of a Jew crucified in Jerusalem? Rationalism explains it thus: At the epoch of Augustus the human mind was weary. On the one hand, it no longer accepted idolatry, which was the popular form of ancient doctrines; and on the other, philosophy having founded nothing, a double lassitude of the intelligence ensued—lassitude as to public religion, and lassitude as to the powerless efforts of philosophy. Men wandered in the void and at hazard, invoking a new faith. Jesus Christ came; He inaugurated before the world, fatigued and ready to receive it, an affirmation which did but slight violence to general opinion; He was listened to, men wanted to believe, and they believed in Him.

For my part, gentlemen, I have no belief in this genesis of the Christian faith. When an epoch has lost faith it is not so easy to give it back again; and we have some proof of this before our eyes. Rationalism, in such times, invades all hearts; and rationalism is never convinced of its impotency, or weary of itself. If four or five centuries of useless efforts before

Jesus Christ had discouraged it, it should now, when it counts eighteen centuries more of vain endeavours, be on the eve of abdicating its pretensions. Does it, I ask you, even dream of so doing? Do we not see it more affirmative, more arrogant, more sure of itself than ever? So will it be a thousand years hence. A thousand years hence our posterity will see masters who will ascend the rostrum and say to them with imperturbable self-possession: Gentlemen, we are about to create philosophy, or at least, if we have not that honour, we touch the fortunate epoch which will place the crowning stone upon its edifice. Such is rationalism. No experience has wearied or will ever weary it of itself; it rises anew from its ashes, or rather, it neither lives nor dies, but is a credulous infant who aspires to maturity without ever once leaving its cradle. Let us not wonder thereat: it takes its starting-point in a principle which excludes life, because it excludes faith; and yet faith will destroy it. It has but the choice of death; and it naturally prefers that which leaves to it the appearance of being something, were it but a doubt and a negation. Rationalism is incorrigible, because to correct itself it must cease to exist.

To admit, then, that the general state of minds, in the Augustan Age, was a state of void and lassitude, is by no means to explain the propagation of the Christian faith then accomplished with so much power and rapidity. But I do not admit that such was, under Augustus, the general state of minds. Doubtless idolatry had become an object of contempt to a great number of enlightened men, but the people did not despise it. The popular mind sympathised with idolatry, which more than ever included all the recollections which the multitude adored, and all the spectacles they needed. The political spirit favoured that tendency; it supported idolatry as a State necessity. And when Jesus Christ came to ask from Rome that right of citizenship which she had refused to none of the gods she had vanquished, it was easy to see what was the state of the popular and political spirit upon this head. Do we not know what answer she gave to Him? Do we not know who replied to the martyrs of Christ, in the amphitheatres, by insults and cries of death? Whilst the emperors and the proconsuls gave sentence against them in the name of the political spirit, the people issued theirs also in the form and power peculiar to them. The empire shed the blood, the people called for it; and, after having obtained it, they threw it at the face of Christ. And, behind the empire and the people, rationalism, forming the rearguard of idolatry, eagerly fed its pen from the sources of error. Those Platonists, so puffed up with their spiritualism, were seen tearing up the Gospel page by page, perverting its meaning, and launching forth their maledictions against it; they were seen parading their affection for Jupiter and all the old gods, writing genealogies for them, consecrating a new philosophy, bearing offerings to them; nothing was left untried—neither science, nor sarcasm, nor energy—nothing that could be turned into an outrage or an argument against Christianity. Is this what they call the lassitude of minds? Is this the tacit conjuration of the times in favour of Christ? Ah! when at length He had won the faith of the world, and when the successors of His apostles appeared at Nicæa, their mutilated visages showed whether they came from peace or war, whether they had been favoured or persecuted, whether the popular spirit, the political spirit, the rationalist spirit, had or had not been their servitors, and what was the real value of those systems invented after the fact, by which the life of the patient is explained by the tyrant who caused His death. Julian, at least, said what was true: "Galilean, thou hast conquered!"

Here we find again in regard to the formation of the Christian dogma, not the principle of fusion, but the principle of contradiction. Jesus Christ contradicted all minds as He contradicted all doctrines, He conquered all minds as He conquered all doctrines: such is the truth.

It was not, however, enough for Him to found a doctrine and obtain faith; it was not enough to found a doctrine in contradicting all other doctrines, to found a spirit of faith in contradicting every other spirit. He had in addition to found a Church, that is to say, a society of men living by that doctrine and faith. Rationalism, in order to explain His success, invokes here the general state of nations. It says that in the time of Augustus a double want was felt, namely, a want of liberty and unity. The nations one after another had borne the yoke of the Romans; and, stripped of their independence, victims of the increasing rapacity of the proconsuls, they marked the progress of Roman corruption, watching, like all who are in bondage, for that hour of weakness which inevitably follows prosperity when it is without limit or counterpoise. That hour advanced rapidly; Jesus Christ came also, at the same time, at the precise moment. And what brought He? The elevation of the lowly, in the idea of a common origin and a holy brotherhood; strength to the weak, to women, to children, in the idea of a new domestic right; help to oppressed peoples, in the idea of a universal republic founded by God Himself and governed by Him. What could be more attractive, more sure of success? When then Jesus Christ appeared, and when from the heart of Judæa the very air had borne even to the ends of the world His emancipating word, with what a thrill of sacred hope must the world have stood up and watched! What wonder if women, children, those who toiled, the slaves, the poor, the despised of every kind and of every country, went forth to meet Him, cast their garments under His feet, cut down branches from the trees and strewed them in His way, not once only, when He entered into Jerusalem on the eve of His death, but even after His death, unwilling to believe He was dead, and crying to His disciples as to Him: "Hosanna to the Son of David! Blessed is He that cometh in the name of the Lord."* That hosanna was the cry of deliverance, the response to Him who had heard the groanings of men; and from wheresoever He came, whatsoever name He took, whatsoever His race or His design, Man or God, it was impossible for Him not to be accepted as He presented Himself. What matters it to the prisoner, set free, whence liberty comes to him? To the miserable, to the oppressed, whence the deliverer comes?

Who saves his country is inspired from Heaven!

I grant, gentlemen, that these ideas are full of charm; it touches us to think that when nations are slaves and corrupted, they aspire to their emancipation. But, alas! history pronounces another judgment than the heart of man. We learn from history that nations fallen into servitude do not desire liberty. As the apostate from truth inveighs against truth, so the apostate from liberty, the nation which has lost it by its fault—and it is always lost by its own fault, by taking the heart of a slave—that nation no longer aspires to regain it. It suffers, it is degraded; but to feel its misfortune and to reconquer the treasure it has lost requires the heart of a free man; that heart it has no longer. It loves the wages of servitude, and dreads

* St. Matt. xxi. 9.

the duties of liberty, especially of that which it has lost, and which is to be purchased at such a price. It would have to despise even its very life, to be ready to throw it to the winds, so that some slight lesson might be learned from its death, and that its last sigh, even remotely, might serve to bring about deliverance and honour. The enslaved nation knows not this heroism, and perhaps despises it. You have proofs of this, gentlemen, elsewhere even than in history; and passing over the continent of Europe, I will take you at once to the shores of Africa. Observe the negro there. You send your squadrons to protect his liberty against the conspiracy of the slave-dealer; doubtless you do well; it is perhaps a duty, it is certainly an honour. But are you simple enough to believe that you will prevent this traffic? Wherever man wills to sell himself, he finds buyers; wherever hearts of slaves meet together, they form masters, even when they do not find them already prepared. As long as the negro will sell the flesh and blood of his countryman, all the squadrons of the civilized world will not lift him from the consequences of that horrible baseness of heart; and it is the same, more or less, with all nations bent under the yoke of servitude and corruption. They seek no deliverance, but the price only of their soul and body; and they are sufficiently recompensed for the abjection of slavery by the abjection of vice. This was the state of the Roman world. Jesus Christ, it is true, brought them liberty, but with virtue and by virtue. The cost was too great for them; they did not accept it. Even after the Church was founded, the empire continued in decadence; it fell from Diocletian to the eunuchs of Constantinople; and when the West, renewed by the barbarians, willed to go to its help, even to the very centre of the East, when it armed all its chivalry to save it, that wretched people extended to the Latin hand only a hand incapable of sincerity. They treasonably rejected the blood given to it, fearing the too near approach of men who knew how to wield the sword and to devote themselves. ·

Jesus Christ may well found a Church, but not regenerate an empire. He formed free souls in forming pious souls, whom He drew to Himself from the midst of the general corruption; but the nations did not answer to His call, as nations, in order to manifest that His work was not the result of political circumstances in which the course of things had led mankind.

He had against Him the passion of servitude, instead of having in His favour the want of emancipation. And such is still the state of His Church here below. Although favourable to all the legitimate rights which together form the honour and liberty of nations, she unceasingly raises up against herself the instincts of servitude under the very name of liberty. They ask license from her, and propose to her oppression: it is the cry of nature in all times. In refusing both of these, now as heretofore, she doubtless responds to the real wants of mankind; but she responds to them after the manner of God, by a force which imposes itself and by a blessing whose glory none but the benefactor can claim.

It is the same in regard to unity. I do not deny that the Roman empire, by subjecting many diverse peoples under a common administration, had spread in minds the idea of a vast social organization. But that idea, in the degree in which it existed, did not pass over the very limited circle of a purely political domination. They did not perceive, even in the depths of that unity, the idea that the human race was a single being or a single body. By unity, they understood that one single nation became master of the others; one Cæsar, the Cæsar of the world; but of the spiritual unity of souls by faith, hope, and charity, under a single visible chief, the representative and vicar of God, they had not even the most confused notion. As soon as the universal Church had advanced a step in the world, and had thus revealed this secret of her destiny, it gave rise only to an immense fear, the enduring repercussion of which she still feels. The passion of nationality is as strong now against the Church as it was eighteen centuries ago; and those even who aspire to the social unity of the human race cannot endure the idea of the Christian republic, other than as a figure or a pattern which they use to represent their own conception. What philosopher or what statesman dreams of unity in the Christian sense, save to fear and detest it? You see, gentlemen, that in examining facts, not only ancient but present, we arrive at the same conclusion, namely, that the principle of the success of Jesus Christ, whether in regard to the formation of His doctrine, or to the propagation of His faith or the establishment of His Church, was not a principle of fusion, but a principle of contradiction. As He had contradicted all doctrines by His own, all minds by His own,

He has contradicted all nations by His Church, that is to say, He has braved and still braves, in the perpetuity of His work, all the combined forces of mankind.

Let us go further, gentlemen, and seek the supreme cause of that contradiction. Let us seek why Jesus Christ contradicts all and is contradicted by all—too often even by those who possess His faith, who belong to His Church, who eat His flesh and drink His blood. The cause of this is not in the region of the mind; rationalism deceives itself in seeking there the explanation of the Christian mystery. Jesus Christ advances beyond the intelligence, He reaches even the soul, which is the centre of all, and demands from it the sacrifice of its most cherished inclinations, in order to convert it from evil to good, from pride to humility, from sensuality to charity, from enjoyment to mortification, from egotism to charity, from corruption to holiness. And man opposes thereto an obstinate resistance; he arms against Jesus Christ his reason, his heart, the world, the human race, heaven and earth; and even when vanquished by the sense of his misery and by the tested gentleness of the yoke of the Gospel, he does not cease to feel within himself, even to his last moment, a possibility and a secret desire to revolt. Here the whole secret lies. And if you would understand how difficult is the triumph of Jesus Christ, I propose to you, not the conversion of the world, but of one single man. I ask you, princes of nations—you who command by intelligence, wealth, or power—I ask you to make a man humble and chaste, a penitent, a soul who judges his pride and his senses, who despises himself, who hates himself, who struggles against himself, and either as proof or as the means of his conversion, humbly avows the errors of his life. I ask but this from you. Can you accomplish it? Have you ever done so? Ah! if a king, radiant in the majesty of the throne, were to call you into his cabinet, and press you to confess your faults at his feet, you would say to him: Sire, I would rather confess them to the man who makes shoes for my feet! If the most famous philosopher of his age were to use all his eloquence to persuade you to kneel and confess your sins to him, you would not deign even to turn away from laughing in his face. Pardon these expressions, gentlemen, they would be ill-placed on other occasions; here, they are but just and grave. And yet, what kings, philosophers, and nations are unable to obtain, a poor priest, a man unknown, the most obscure among men, daily accomplishes in the name of Jesus Christ. He sees souls touched by their misery, coming to seek Him who knows them not, and avow to Him in all sincerity the degradation of their passions. It is the door by which men enter into Jesus Christ, by which they repose in Him, by which the Church herself enters; for the Church is but the world penitent; and that single word reveals to you the whole miracle of her foundation and perpetuity, as it will also explain to you the force of active and passive contradiction which is in Jesus Christ. Jesus Christ contradicts all doctrines, because His doctrine is holy and the world is corrupt; He contradicts every spirit, because His spirit is holy and the world is corrupt; He contradicts all nations, because His Church is holy and the world is corrupt; and for the same reason the world contradicts the doctrines, the spirit, and the Church of Jesus Christ.

It was then with justice, in a certain sense, that in the first proceedings directed against Christians, by the orders of Nero, they were convicted, according to Tacitus, of "hatred against the human race." They hated, in fact, all that the world esteemed; they pursued all its ideas and all its affections, in order to destroy them utterly; and although they did this from love for the world, the world was not bound to understand and thank them for it. Even charity, so new was it, clothed herself in hostile colours, and the death of Jesus Christ upon the cross —that masterpiece of love—appeared rather like an insult than devotedness. All was contradiction, because all was God; and in order to prove that nothing of this was of man, Jesus Christ was for ever to be recognised by this sign, according as it was said of Him at the moment of His first appearing among men: "This Child is set up for a sign which shall be contradicted." * And He Himself, recalling the prophecies, said to His enemies: "The stone which the builders rejected has become the corner-stone; the Lord hath done this, and it is wonderful in our eyes." † The prophecy is still accomplished daily; princes, nations, savants, sages, the skilful, the builders, in fine, reject the stone; they declare it to be unfit or worn out by time; they will accept it no longer; and yet it is still "the corner-stone, and it is wonderful in our eyes." It supports all, although it is rejected by all; it possesses the double character of necessity and impossibility. Recognise here,

* St. Luke ii. 34. † St. Matt. xxi. 42.

gentlemen, a struggle between two unequal wills—the will of man which revolts, and the will of God which causes itself to be obeyed by man, in man, and in spite of man. And you Christians, sons of this work wherein God gives you so favoured a place, learn the need of constant suffering, of not triumphing by triumph, that Jesus Christ may not be accused of owing something to man, but of triumphing upon the cross, so that your victory may be of God, and that you may be able, now and henceforth, to repeat those words which, after so many other signs witnessed by you, express the highest sign of the Divinity of Jesus Christ: "The stone which the builders rejected has become the corner-stone; the Lord hath done this, and it is wonderful in our eyes!"

# GOD.

# GOD.

## THE EXISTENCE OF GOD.

My Lord,[*]—Gentlemen,

We have proved the divinity of Christian doctrine in a twofold manner; by its results, in showing that it produces that marvel the Church, to which nothing is comparable, and which evidently surpasses all human power; and also by showing that her founder is Jesus Christ, the envoy of God and the Son of God. The effects and source of this doctrine being divine, it is manifestly stamped with the seal of divinity, or, in other words, it is divine. It would seem then that our task is ended, and that having crowned the doctrine whose minister we are with the most sacred and certain of all characters, we have but two things to demand from you, or rather to impose upon you, namely, silence and adoration.

But the human mind is so formed, it has been so steeped in light, that even if it saw the very hand of God bearing doctrine to it, it would not be willing to receive that doctrine without receiving therewith the right and power to sound its depths. The road of authority is doubtless a just, a natural road, and necessary for our present state; but it does not suffice for us. For our present state includes the foretaste of the future promised to us, and in regard to that future, nothing will fully satisfy us but light seen by us in the very essence of God himself. We do not desire henceforth to behold that light in its infinite fulness; we understand that limits have

[*] Monseigneur Affre, Archbishop of Paris.

been placed to our mental vision and to our horizon: but how feeble soever that vision may be, it is that of an intelligent being; how limited soever its horizon, it is an horizon traced by the hand of God. Our mind seeks light, and our horizon receives its rays. As soon then as a doctrine is proposed to us, from whatever hand it may come, we thirst to fathom it, to scrutinise it from within, to assure ourselves, in fine, that it possesses other marks of its truth than merely outward signs, however great they may be. I cannot escape from this law of our being, nor do I desire so to do. I respect it in you as in myself; I recognise therein our origin and our predestination. After having led you then for so many years through the externals of Christianity, I must now, under the eye of God, pass the threshold of the temple, and, without fear as without presumption, contemplate doctrine itself, the daughter of God and the mother of your soul.

I do not promise to show you its absolute superiority; this can be done only by leaving the present world and reaching the bright shores of the infinite. But I promise you that in comparing it with all the doctrines that have endeavoured to explain the mysteries of the world, you shall easily discover in it an unquestionable and a divine superiority. I promise you that a light shall shine from it, which, without always attaining to evidence itself, will form at least a glorious dawn of evidence, and perhaps even at times a blending, as it were, of the reason of man with the reason of God. Your soul elevated by veiled truths, will see them gradually growing clearer in the dawn of contemplation; in that holy exercise it will become accustomed to flights before unknown to it, and at length wonder at the sublime simplicity of the greatest mysteries.

But where shall we find a basis in order to found doctrine and appropriate it to ourselves? Where shall we find terms of comparison and means of verification? We shall not need to seek far. God has placed near to us the instruments destined by His Providence to lead us toward Himself. He has given them to us in nature and in intelligence, in conscience and in society. This is the quadruple and unique palace which he has built for us; quadruple in the diversity of its construction, unique in the relations which they hold to one another, and in our indivisible abode therein. As God is whole and ever present to every part of the universe, man is whole and always present to nature, to his intelligence, to his conscience, to society; he draws from them a life which constantly receives light from their reverberation, and which never leaves him in the solitary gloom of himself. Nature speaks to his intelligence, his intelligence responds to nature, both meet in his conscience, and society places the seal of experience to the revelations of all the three. Such is our life, and there all doctrine finds its verification. A doctrine contrary either to nature, intelligence, conscience, or society, is a false doctrine, because it destroys our life; a doctrine in harmony with these is a true doctrine, because it strengthens and enlarges our life, and because our life, taken in its totality, is heaven and earth, matter and spirit, time and space, man and mankind, whatever comes from God and bears with it a demonstration of Him and of ourselves.

It behoves me then to show you the conformity of Catholic doctrine with nature, intelligence, conscience, and society; and to draw from that comparison, unceasingly rising before you, rays of light which will lead us to the depths of the invisible and the immensity of the supernatural. This will form the last part of our conferences, and although it must necessarily employ several years, I cannot divest myself of a feeling of sadness in thinking that the day draws nearer when I must separate from you, and when I shall see no longer, save from a distance in the feebleness of remembrance, those great assemblies in which God was with us. Nevertheless some consolation is blended with the feeling of our coming separation; the consolation of the man who reaches his end, who has finished a career, and who foresees the hour when he will be able to say with Paul: "I have fought the good fight, I have finished my course."* Share with me this sadness and this joy; for our conferences belong to you as much as to me; they form a monument which has risen up from your hearts and from mine as from a single principle; and some day, if it please God to grant us the repose of old age, we shall each alike be able to say, on recalling the times which we loved: I formed part of those conferences of Notre Dame which held our youth captive under the word of God.

* 2 Tim. iv. 7.

MY LORD:

The Church and the country thank you together for the example you have given to us in these days of great and memorable emotion.* You have called us into this cathedral on the morrow of a revolution in which all seemed to have been lost; we have responded to your call; we are here peaceably assembled under these antique vaults; we learn from them to fear nothing either for religion or for country; both will continue their career under the hand of God who protects them; both render thanks to you for having believed in this indissoluble alliance, and for having discerned in passing things those which remain firm and become strengthened even by the changeableness of events.

Doctrine is the science of destinies. We live, but why do we live? We live, but how do we live? We, and all that is passing around us, move by a motion which never ceases. The heavens move onwards, the earth is borne along, the waves follow each other on the old shores of the sea; the plant springs up, the tree waxes great, the dust drifts along, and the mind of man, yet more restless than all else in nature, knows no repose. Whence and why is this? All motion supposes a starting-point, a term to which it tends, and a road by which it passes. What is then our starting-point? What our end? What our road? Doctrine must answer us; doctrine must show us our beginning, our end, our means; and, with them, the secret of our destinies. All science does not reach so far. The lower sciences teach us the law of particular movements; they tell us how bodies attract and repel each other; what orbit they describe in the undefined spaces of the universe; how they become decomposed and reconstituted, and numberless secrets of that restless and unremitting life which they lead in the fertile bosom of nature: but they do not make known to us the general law of motion, the first principle of things, their final end, their common means. This is the privilege of doctrine, a privilege as far above all the sciences as the universal is above the individual.

Now of these three terms which comprise the system of destinies, the one which doctrine should first reveal to us is doubtless the principle of things; for it is easy to conceive that upon the principle depends the end, that from the end

---

* The Revolution of 1848.

and the principle proceeds the means. The principle of beings evidently includes the reason of the end assigned to them, as their principle and their end determine the means by which they are to attain and fulfil their vocation.

I ask then this supreme question, I ask it with you and with all time: What is the principle of things? Catholic doctrine answers us in these three first words of its Creed: CREDO IN DEUM, PATREM OMNIPOTENTEM—*I believe in God, the Father Almighty.*

Hear its own explanation of this answer.

There is a primordial being: by that alone that it is primordial, it has no beginning, it is eternal, that is to say, infinite in duration; being infinite in duration, it is so also in its perfection; for if anything were wanting to its perfection, it would not be total being, it would be limited in its existence; it would not exist of itself, it would not be primordial. There is then a being, infinite in duration and perfection. Now the state of perfection involves the personal state, that is to say, the state of a being possessing consciousness and intelligence of itself, rendering an account to itself of what it is, distinguishing from itself that which is not itself, removing from itself that which is against itself; in a word, of a being who thinks, who wills, who acts, who is free, who is sovereign. The primordial being is then "an infinite spirit in a state of personality." Such is Catholic doctrine on the principle of things, the doctrine contained in that short phrase: CREDO IN DEUM —*I believe in God.*

Let us now hear the contrary doctrine, for there is a contrary doctrine; and you will never find Christianity announcing a dogma without at once meeting with a negation, a negation intended to combat it, but which must serve to prove it. For error is the counterproof of truth, as shadows are the counterproofs of light. Do not wonder then at so prompt an opposition to so manifest a dogma; invite it rather, and listen to the first expression of rationalism against the first expression of Christianity: CREDO IN NATURAM, MATREM OMNIPOTENTEM—*I believe in nature, the mother almighty.*

You hear then that rationalism, like Christianity, admits the existence of a principle of things; but for rationalism, nature is the primordial, necessary, eternal, sovereign being. Now, nature is not unknown to us, and it is evident to us that nature is in the state of impersonality; that is to say, nature has no consciousness of what it is, it does not possess that intellectual unity by which each of its members should live of the universal life, and the universe of the life of the least blade of grass comprised in its immensity. We are, so to say, immersed in nature, we draw from nature the aliment of our existence: but so far from forming there one single life by common knowledge, we know nothing even of the beings nearest to us. We pass each other by as strangers, and the universe answers to our laborious investigations only by the mute spectacle of its inanimate splendour. Nature is derived of personality, and this is why Rationalism, which declares that nature is self-existent, defines the principle of things as "an infinite force in a state of impersonality."

Such are the two doctrines.

And observe that the human mind could not conceive a third doctrine upon the principle of things. For either nature exists of itself and suffices to itself, or we must seek its cause and support above itself, not in an analogous nature subject to the same infirmity, but in a superior being answering in its essence to the idea and function of a principle. It is the one or the other. If we choose nature, as nature wants personality, we must say that the principle of things is "an infinite force in the state of impersonality. If we reject nature, we must say that the principle of things is a supernatural being, the logical conception of which necessarily leads to the conclusion that the principle of things is "an infinite spirit in the state of personality." Therefore human reason, in regard to the first question concerning the mystery of destinies, the question of principle, is inevitably condemned to one or the other of these professions of faith: "I believe in God ;—I believe in nature."

This is the reason why there are but two fundamental doctrines in the world: theism and pantheism. The first of these builds upon the idea of God, the second upon the fact of nature; one starts from the invisible and the infinite, the other from the visible and the indefinite. Whoever is not a theist is logically a pantheist, and whoever is not a pantheist is necessarily a theist. Every man chooses between these two doctrines, and the life of mankind cleaves to one or the other, as to the tree of life and the tree of death. Pantheism has perhaps been brought before you as a rare discovery of modern times, as a treasure slowly drawn forth from the fields of contemplation by the labour of sages: the fact is, it is as old as corrupted mankind, and the mind of a child is able to conceive that there is a God, or if there is not, that nature is itself its principle and its god.

It is a gift of truth, that upon a question so capital as that of the principle of things, you should have but to choose between two doctrines, and that on the rejection of one of these, the other becomes invested with the infallible character of logical necessity.

What do you now expect from me? You think perhaps that I am about to demonstrate to you the existence of God? I assure you I have no such intention, not because the thing is impossible, but because this is not the question before us. The existence of God is not a dogma overthrown, which it is needful to raise up again from the dust; it is a dogma standing erect, which holds its place between the Church, whose divine authority I have shown you, and Jesus Christ, whose personal divinity I have proved to you. God has been the basis of all that we have yet seen. He has revealed Himself to us as all beings reveal themselves, namely, by His action. If God had not acted upon earth, and if He did not still act here day by day, no one would believe in Him, whatever demonstration metaphysics and eloquence might make of Him. Mankind believes in God because it sees Him act. We have not, then, to demonstrate God, but to examine the idea of God, and to place it before our minds in all the splendour that we can draw from it.

Let us even put aside those positive proofs of God; let us forget His works in the world, and suppose that we have before us the bare question of His existence. The necessity of a direct demonstration of Him would not even then follow. For our mind carries in itself the certainty that a principle of things exists, and, in addition, that this principle is either God or nature. Nothing remains, then, but to choose between them, and a matter of choice is quite another thing than a position in which reasoning has all to create. I have to oppose theism to pantheism, this is my task; I have to seek which of these is in harmony with nature, intelligence, conscience, and society; such is the strength of my position.

Before entering upon this comparison, or rather on entering upon it, I will make one observation. It is that God is here below the most popular of all beings, whilst pantheism is a purely scientific system. In the open fields, resting upon his implement of toil, the labourer lifts up his eyes towards heaven, and he names God to his children by an impulse as simple as his own soul. The poor call upon Him, the dying invoke His name, the wicked fear Him, the good bless Him, kings give Him their crown to wear, armies place Him at the head of their battalions, victory renders thanksgivings to Him, defeat seeks help from Him, nations arm themselves with Him against their tyrants; there is neither place, nor time, nor circumstance, nor sentiment, in which God does not appear and is not named. Even love itself, so sure of its own charm, so confident in its own immortality, dares not to ignore Him, and comes before His altars to beg from Him the confirmation of the promises to which it has so often sworn. Anger feels that it has not reached its last expression until it has cursed that adorable name; and even blasphemy is the homage of faith that reveals itself in its own forgetfulness. What shall I say of perjury? A man possesses a secret upon which his fortune or his honour depends: he alone upon earth knows it, he alone is his own judge. But truth has an eternal accomplice in God; it calls God to its help, it places the heart of man to struggle against an oath, and even he who may be capable of violating its majesty would not do so without an inward shudder, as before the most cowardly and the basest of actions. And yet what is there contained in those words of an oath? Only a name, indeed, but it is the name of God. It is the name which all nations have adored, to which they have built temples, consecrated priests, offered prayers; it is the highest name, the most holy, the most efficient, the most popular name which the lips of men have received the grace to utter.

Is it so with pantheism? Where shall we look for it? Come with me, let us knock at yonder door; it is illustrious, and more than one celebrity has already been there. We are in the presence of a sage. Let us beg of Him to explain to us the mystery of our destinies, for He has sounded it. What says He to us? That there is in the world only one single substance. Why? Because substance is that which is in itself, and that which is in itself is necessarily unique, infinite, eternal, God. Behold then the whole explanation of our life based upon a metaphysical definition. I do not now examine whether it be true or false, whether the conclusions drawn from it are legitimate, whether it is easy otherwise to define substance, and so to overthrow the whole structure of this doctrine. I simply defy mankind to understand it; even you, who from your childhood have been initiated to speculations of words and ideas, you would not seize its tissue without great difficulty were I to expose it to you. Many of you, perhaps, would not succeed so far; for nothing is more rare than metaphysical sagacity, than that vision which dispels before it all realities and penetrates with a fixed regard the world of abstractions. You would soon feel the swelling veins of your brow, a kind of dimness would seize even upon the most hidden recesses of your thoughts, and all would disappear before you, the real and the ideal, in painful obscurity. And we are to believe that truth lies hidden in such subtle and inaccessible depths! That there it awaits the human race to declare to it its destiny! Can you believe it? For my part, I do not believe it. I believe in the God of the poor and the simple-minded; I believe in the God who is known in the lowly cottage, whom infancy hears, whose name is dear to misfortune, who has found ways to reach to all, how humble soever they may be, and who has no enemies but the pride of knowledge and the corruption of the heart. I believe in this God. I believe in Him because I am a man, and, in repeating with all nations and all ages the first article of the Church's Creed, I do but proclaim myself a man and take my rank in the natural community of souls.

Need I avow it?—Since I have been charged with the work of preaching the Divine Word, this is the first time that I have approached this question of the existence of God—if indeed it can be called a question! Hitherto I have disdained it as unnecessary. I have thought it needless to prove to a son the existence of his father, and that he who did not know him was unworthy of such knowledge. But the course of ideas constrains me to touch upon this subject. Nevertheless, in making this concession to logical order, I could not allow you to think that I purposed to satisfy a want of your hearts, or of the people and the age in which we live. God be thanked, we believe in Him, and were I to doubt of your faith in Him, you would rise and cast me out from amongst you; the doors of this cathedral would open before me of themselves, and the people would need but a look in order to confound me. That same people who in the intoxication of victory, after having overthrown many generations of kings, bore off in their submissive hands, and as the associate of their triumph, the image of the Son of God made man. (Applause.)

Gentlemen, let us not applaud the word of God; let us love it, believe in it, practise it; this is the only applause that mounts to heaven and is worthy of it.

I might here close this discourse, since you happily show me that it is needless. Allow me, however, before doing so, to seek why the idea of God is popular, and whether that popularity is but a vain illusion of mankind.

We have said that we possess four means of verifying doctrines; namely: nature, intelligence, conscience, and society. If the idea of God be legitimate, it should derive strength from these four sources of light, whilst pantheism should necessarily find its condemnation in them.

Nature is a grand spectacle which easily exhausts our vision and our imagination; but does it bear the stamp of a being without cause, of a being existing of itself? Can nature say like God, through Moses: EGO SUM QUI SUM—*I am who am?* Infinity is the first mark of the being without cause; does nature bear this sign? Let us examine it. All that we see there is limited, all is form and movement, form determined, movement calculated; all falls under the straitened empire of measure, even the distances which remain unknown to our instruments, but are by no means unknown to our conceptions. We feel the limit even where our eye does not perceive it; it is enough for us to seize it at one point, to determine it everywhere. The infinite is indivisible, and were but one single atom of the universe submitted to our feeble hands, we should know that nature is finite, and that its immensity is but the splendid veil of its poverty.

If nature existed of itself, it would moreover possess the character of absolute liberty, or sovereignty: for, what can a being be said to depend upon which has no cause? But do we find this in the operations that manifest the life of nature to us? The universe is a serf; it revolves in a circle wherein nothing spontaneous appears; the stone remains where our hand places it, and the planet describes an orbit where we always find it. Those worlds, so prodigious by their mass and their motion, have never revealed to the observer anything but a silent and blind mechanism, a slavish force, a helpless powerlessness to deviate from their law. And man himself—man in whom alone upon earth appears that liberty whose traces we vainly seek for in all the rest—is he a sovereign? Is he born at his own time? Does he die when it pleases him? Can he free himself from that which limits and embitters his existence? Like nature, of which he forms a part, he has his greatness, but it is a greatness which so much the more betrays his infirmity. He is like those kings who followed their victor to the Capitol, and whose abasement was but increased by the remnants of their majesty. The spectacle of the universe then awakens two sentiments, namely, wonder and pity. And these, strengthened by one another, together lead us to see the emptiness of nature, and to seek its author. Such is the language of worlds, their eternal eloquence, the cry of their conscience, if we may give such a name to the force that constrains them to speak for a greater than they, and to repeat to all the echoes of time and space the hymn of the creature to the Creator: NON NOBIS, DOMINE, NON NOBIS, SED NOMINI TUO GLORIAM—*Not unto us, Lord, not unto us, but to thy name be the glory!* Yes, sacred worlds that roll above us, brilliant and joyous stars that pursue your course under the hand of the Most High, happy islands whose shores are traced out in the ocean of heaven, yes, you have never lied to man!

It matters little whether pantheism does or does not endeavour to pervert the meaning of the spectacle of nature. It is of importance for us to know, however, that man, taken in general, the man of mankind, sees at a glance that the universe does not exist of itself. Metaphysics will never destroy that deep impression made upon mankind by the spectacle of things which forms the scene upon which we live. A child perceives the incapacity of the heavens and the earth; he sees, he feels, he touches it; he will always return to it as to an invincible sentiment forming a part of his being. In vain will you tell him that he is God, it is enough for him to have had but a fever to know that you are laughing at him.

In contemplating nature, man sees realities; in contemplating his intelligence, he sees truths. Realities are finite like the nature that contains them; truths are infinite, eternal, absolute, that is to say, greater than the intelligence in which we find them. Nature shows us geometrical figures; the intelligence reveals to us the mathematical law itself, the general and abstract law of all bodies. It does more, it reveals to us the metaphysical law, that is to say, the law of all beings of what kind soever, the law which is as applicable to spirits as to bodies. At this height, and in this horizon, the universe disappears from our mental vision, or, at least, we no longer perceive it save as the reflection of a higher world, as the shadow of a boundless light; the real becomes absorbed in the true, which is its root, really becomes measured by truth.

But where is truth? Where its dwelling-place, its seat, its living essence? Is it a pure abstraction of our mind? Is it nothing but the universe magnified by a dream? If it were so, our intelligence itself would be but a dream; truth, which appears to us as the principle of all things, would be only the exaggeration, and, as it were, the extravagance of sensible reality.

Shall we say that truth has its seat in our own mind? But our mind is limited, truth has no limits; our mind had a beginning, truth is eternal; our mind is susceptible of more or less, truth is absolute. To say that our mind is the seat of truth, is to say in obscure terms that our mind is truth itself, living truth: who is so mad as to believe this? Besides the contradiction existing between the nature of our mind and the nature of truth, do we not see the minds which form mankind engaged in a perpetual war of affirmations and negations? Truth would then be battling with itself? It would affirm and deny at the same time, although remaining absolute. It is the very height of folly!

If truth be not a vain name, it is in the universe only in the state of expression, and in our mind only in the state of apparition; it is in the universe as the artist is in his work, it is in our mind as the sun is in our eyes. But beyond the universe and our mind, it subsists of itself, it is a real, an infinite, an eternal, an absolute essence, existing of itself, possessing consciousness and intelligence of itself; for how could it be that truth should not understand itself, since it is the source of all understanding? Now, so to speak of truth is to define God; God is the proper name of truth, as truth is the abstract name of God.

There is then a God, if truth exists. Would you say that there is no truth? It is for you to choose. I do not deny your liberty.

Perhaps you will still better understand the force of this conclusion by applying it to the order of conscience. Even as truth is the object and life of the mind, justice is the object and life of conscience. Conscience sees and approves a rule of the rights and duties between beings endowed with liberty. That rule is justice. But where is justice? Is it a simple result of human will? In that case justice would be but a convention, a fragile law called into life to-day and which may fall to-morrow. Is it an order founded on the very nature of man? But that nature is variable, corruptible, subject to passions that lead it astray. What is order for one would be disorder for another. If then justice be a reality, it must be an eternal and absolute law, regulating the relations of free volitions, as mathematics are an eternal and absolute law regulating the relations of material beings, and metaphysics an eternal and absolute law regulating the relations of intelligent beings with all beings, either existing or possible. Beyond this notion, justice is but a name which arms the strong against the weak, the prosperous against the needy. Now, this notion necessarily calls forth the notion of God, since an eternal and absolute law could only be a reality in the person of a being subsisting of himself, possessing a will active and just, able to promulgate an order, to maintain it, to reward obedience and punish rebellion.

Truth is the first name of God; justice is the second.

Now it is easy to conceive that there may be men for whom truth and justice are nothing but philosophical speculations, men who shut themselves up in the proud solitude of their own thoughts, and build up in them their own glory upon systems that bear their names. But it is not so with poor and suffering mankind: it needs truth for its nourishment, justice for its defence, and it knows that the real name of both is the name of God, and that the real strength of both is the power of God. The poor and the afflicted have never been deceived herein. When they are oppressed, they lift up their hands towards God, they write his name upon their banners, they pronounce to the oppressor that last and solemn expression of the soul that believes and hopes: I cite you before the tribunal of God!

The time of that tribunal comes sooner or later, its temporal and visible, as well as its eternal time. Kings even here below are cited before it, and nations also. It is the permanent tribunal set up in the midst of error and wickedness, and which saves the world. In vain would pride destroy it; the people saved by it save it in their turn. If there were none but sages among us, the idea of God might perish here, for a man alone is always powerful against God; but happily nations are feeble against him, because they cannot do without justice and truth.

They protect him against the learned chimeras of false wisdom; they preserve his memory with a faithfulness which does not always preserve the perfect idea of him, but which at least has never yet permitted the sun and history to see a nation of atheists. Notwithstanding all that men have done, God remains as the corner-stone of human society; no legislator has dared to banish Him, no age has ignored Him, no language has effaced His name. Upon earth as in heaven, He is because He is.

But if God has on his side nature, intelligence, conscience, and society, what remains there to pantheism? Where is it to find its basis? It seeks its basis in the obscurities of abstruse metaphysics; withdrawing from all realities, from every feeling and every want, in order to form a labyrinth from whence thought can find no exit. It loses itself the clue, and, shut up in the subtle prison which it has made, takes refuge in the sneer of self-deceived pride, and calling to its help, from the corrupted depths of ages, the prying spirits of subtle doctrines, it hurls against God and mankind the anathema of scorn. God passes by without hearing and mankind without answering. Let us do likewise, let us pass by also.

We have a threefold intuition of God: a negative intuition in nature; a direct intuition in the ideas of truth and justice; a practical intuition in human society. Nature, in manifesting characteristics to us incompatible with a being existing of itself, causes us to mount to its source; the ideas of truth and justice name God to us, without whom they would be nothing; human society, which cannot do without Him, proves to us His existence by its need of Him. But besides these continuous and inadmissible revelations, there are others which Divine Providence scatters from time to time on the road of nations. He strikes with His thunders and rends the veils, He gives so full and deep a consciousness of His presence that none can be deceived, and causes a whole nation to utter from its inmost heart that unanimous and involuntary cry: It is the hand of God! We are witnessing one of those times when God unveils Himself; but yesterday He passed through our gates and the whole world beheld Him. Shall I then remain silent before Him? Shall I hold upon my trembling lips the prayer of a man who, once in his life, has seen his God before him?

O God, who has just dealt these terrible blows; O God, the judge of kings and arbiter of the world, look down in mercy upon this old Frank nation, the elder Son of Thy right hand and of Thy Church. Remember its past services, Thy first blessings ; renew with it that ancient alliance which made it Thy people ; touch its heart which was so full of Thee, and which now again, in the flush of a victory wherein it spared nothing royal, yielded to Thee the empire which it yields to none other. O God, just and holy, by the cross of Thy Son which their hands bore from the profaned palace of kings to the spotless palace of Thy spouse, watch over us, protect us, enlighten us, prove once more to the world that a people that respects Thee is a people saved !

# THE INNER LIFE OF GOD.

My Lord,—Gentlemen,

God exists, but what does He? What is His action? What is His life? This question at once rises in our thoughts. As soon as the mind has recognised the existence of a being, it asks how that being lives; and still more so in regard to God, who, as the principle of beings, excites within us a thirst for knowledge of Him, so much the more ardent and just as His action is the model of all action, and His life the pattern of all life. What then is the life of God? How does He employ His eternity? This is doubtless a bold question. Nevertheless it is a question which men ask and which they desire to solve. But how is it to be solved? How are we to penetrate the Divine Essence in order to catch a glimpse of the incomprehensible movement of an eternal, infinite, absolute, and immutable spirit?

Three doctrines come before us. One of these affirms that God is condemned by the sovereign majesty of His nature to isolation dreadful to imagine; that, alone in Himself, He contemplates Himself seeing only Himself, and loves Himself with a love which has no other object than Himself; that in this contemplation and this love, eternally solitary, the nature and perfection of His life consist.

According to the second doctrine, the universe shows us the life of God, or rather it is itself the life of God. We behold in it His permanent action, the scene upon which His power is exercised, and in which all His attributes are reflected. God is not out of the universe any more than the universe is out of God. God is the principle, the universe is the consequence, but a necessary consequence, without which the principle would be inert, unfruitful, impossible to conceive.

Catholic doctrine condemns these two systems. It does not admit that God is a solitary being eternally employed in a sterile contemplation of Himself; nor does it admit that the universe, although it is the work of God, is His proper and personal life. It soars above those feeble ideas, and, bearing us with the word of God beyond all the conceptions of the human mind, it teaches us that the divine life consists in the co-eternal union of three equal persons, in whom plurality destroys solitude, and unity division; whose thought corresponds, whose love is mutual, and who, in that marvellous communion, identical in substance, distinct in personality, form together an ineffable association of light and love. Such is the essence of God, and such is His life, both powerfully expressed in those words of the Apostle St. John: TRES SUNT QUI TESTIMONIUM DANT IN CŒLO: PATER, VERBUM, ET SPIRITUS SANCTUS—*There are three who give testimony in heaven: the Father, the Word, the Holy Ghost. And these three are one.*\*

Here, and very soon after having promised you light, it would seem that I am leading you into a maze of darkness; for, can anything be conceived more formidable to the mind than the terms by which I have just expressed, according to the Scriptures and the Church, the relations that constitute the inner life of God? Do not, however, yield to this first impression; trust rather to my promises, since they are those of the Gospel, wherein it is written: EGO SUM LUX MUNDI—*I am the Light of the World.* And again: QUI SEQUITUR ME NON AMBULAT IN TENEBRIS, SED HABEBIT LUMEN VITÆ—*He that followeth me walketh not in darkness, but shall have the light of life.*† Yes, be confident, count upon God, who has proposed nothing to you unnecessary to be believed, and who has hidden marvellous treasures in the most obscure mysteries, as He has hidden the fires of the diamond in the depths of the earth. Follow me, let us pass the pillars of Hercules, and, leaving truth to fill our sails, let us fearlessly advance even to the transatlantic regions of light.

We would understand something of the divine life: the first question, therefore, we have to ask is: What is life? For, as long as we do not know what life is in itself, it is clear that we shall not be able to form any idea of the life of God. What, then, is life? In order to comprehend this, we must learn

---

\* 1 John v. 7. † St. John viii. 12.

what being is; for life is evidently a certain state of being. We thus arrive at that first and supreme question: What is being? And we shall solve it by seeking for what is permanent and common in the infinitely varied beings which surround us. Now, in all of these, whatsoever their name, their form, their degree of perfection or inferiority, we find a mysterious force which is the principle of their substance and organization, and which we call activity. Every being, even the most inert in appearance, is active; it condenses, it resists foreign efforts, it attracts and incorporates to itself elements which obey it. A grain of sand is in contest and in harmony with the whole universe, and maintains itself by that force which is the very seat of its being, and without which it would become lost in the absolute incapacity of nothingness. Activity, being the permanent and common characteristic of all that is, it follows that being and activity are one and the same thing, and that we are warranted in making this definition: Being is activity. St. Thomas of Aquinas gave us an example when, having to define God, who is being in its total reality, he said: "God is a pure act."

But activity supposes action, and action is life. Life is to being what action is to activity. To live, is to act. It is true that spontaneous, and, above all, free action, being perfect action, the birth or apparition of life is generally marked at the point where that kind of action is manifested. Thus we say that the stone is, that the plant grows, that the animal lives; but these different expressions mark only the gradations of activity, whose presence, how feeble soever it may be, everywhere constitutes the living being.

We know what life is. Let us advance another step, let us learn what are its general laws, and then apply them to God.

The first general law of life is: *The action of a being is equal to its activity.* In fact the action of a being can be limited only by a foreign force, or by its own will. Now a foreign force checks it only at the point where its own energy ceases, and as to its own will, should it possess any, that necessarily bears it as far as it can reach by its own nature. An action superior to its activity is impossible to it; an action inferior is insufficient; an action equal to its activity is the only action that places it in harmony with itself and with the rest of the universe. Therefore whether you consider the general movement of worlds or the tendency of each being in particular, you will find them all acting according to the measure of their forces, and placing limits to their ambition only because they exist to their faculties. All, and man among the rest, advance as far as they can; all, having reached the point which exhausts and stops them, write like the poet, proudly accusing their own powerlessness:

SISTIMUS HIC TANDEM NOBIS UBI DEFUIT ORBIS.

This first general law being recognised, I at once draw some conclusions from it touching the life of God; for as the action of a being is equal to its activity, and as God is infinite activity, it follows that in God there is infinite action, or, to speak still more clearly, that infinite action constitutes in God the very life of God. But what is an action? Nature and mankind are composed only of a tissue of actions; we do nothing else from the moment of our birth to our death. Nevertheless, do you know clearly what an action is? Have you ever weighed the sense of that word which comprises all that passes in heaven and upon earth? An action is a movement; it is impossible for us to conceive its nature under a more clear and general form. The body moves when it acts, thought moves when it works, the heart moves when it conceives affections; from wheresoever the action comes, the tongue has but one term for expressing it, and the understanding but one idea for conceiving it. All is in movement in the universe because all therein is action, and all therein is action, because, from the atom to the planet, from the dust even to intelligence, all is activity. But movement supposes an object, an end to which the being aspires. I move, I run, I risk my life: Why? What do I seek? Apparently I seek something wanting to me and which I desire; for if nothing were wanting to me, my movement would have no cause, repose would be my natural state, immobility my happiness. Since I move, it is to act: to act is at the same time the motive and the end of movement, and consequently action is a productive movement.

Do not grow weary of following me; it is true I am leading you by ways whose outlets perhaps you do not yet see; you are passengers in the ship of Columbus, you seek in vain the star that announces the port to you; but take courage, you will soon hail the shore, it is already near.

Action is a productive movement, as I have just shown,

and, as action is the consequence of activity, it follows that production is the final end of activity; that is to say of being, since being and activity are one and the same thing. But in what proportion does being produce? Evidently in proportion to its activity; since, according to the first general law of life, the action of a being is equal to its activity. Therefore, to live is to act; to act is to produce; to produce is to draw forth from self something equal to itself. Doubtless we can conceive a production inferior to the being from whence it emanates; but that production, were it to take place, would not be the principal act of such life, it would but be accessory and accidental thereto. Every being tends to produce in the plenitude of its faculties, because it tends to live in the plenitude of its life, and it attains that natural term of its ambition only by drawing from itself something equal to itself. It is easy to prove this by observation, after having established it by reasoning. In what, for instance, consists the painful labour of the artist? The artist has had in his soul a vision of the Beautiful and the True; the horizon has opened before him, and in the luminous distance of the infinite he has seized an idea which has become his own, and which torments him day and night. What would he do, and what is it that troubles him? He would produce what he has seen or heard; he thirsts to make a piece of canvas, a stone, or words, express his thought as it is in himself, with the same clearness, the same force, the same poesy, the same tone. As long as he does not obtain that desired equality between his conception and his style, he is troubled and desponding, for he remains beneath himself, and sheds burning tears over the inefficacy of his genius, which is as a reproach and as death to him. "From him to whom much is given," says the Gospel, "will much be required." Such is the law of production, in the order of nature and art, as in the order of virtue.

But in order for life to produce something equal to itself, it must produce life; in order for the living being to produce something equal to itself, it must produce a being like itself, or, in other words, it must be fruitful. Fecundity is the extreme and complete term of production, which is itself the necessary term of activity. Thus we learn and lay down that second general law of life: "The activity of a being is resumed in its fecundity."

Here the spectacle of the world around us is so striking

that it is almost needless to invoke it. Where in nature can we find any being so abject and disinherited as not to have received from God the grace to produce a being like itself, to see itself in another emanating from itself? The plant ceases not to sow in the earth the germ that multiplies it; the tree sheds around it and confides to the winds of heaven the mysterious seeds that assure to it a numerous offspring; the animal gathers its little ones to its unfailing breasts; and last of all, man, spirit and matter, combines in his fragile life the double fecundity of the senses and thought. He bequeaths himself as a whole to a posterity which perpetuates him by the soul as much as by the body, a father twice blessed and doubly immortal. Shall I dare to advance further, and, passing from man to the opposite frontiers of life, show you the prodigy of fecundity even in those beings to whom science refuses organization, and which, notwithstanding their apparent insignificance, still find in themselves the power to seduce nature and be perpetuated in its bosom by alliances that manifest their vital energy? In vain, from one pole to the other, from man to the worm of the earth, I seek sterility. I find it only in one place and in one thing, in death. So that we may say with rigorous exactness, that life is fecundity, and that the fecundity is equal to the life.

Let us now lift up our eyes, for we can do so; let us turn them towards God. If what we have said be true, God, being infinite activity, is also, and even thereby, infinite fecundity. For, if He were active without being fruitful, if He were infinitely active without being infinitely fruitful, one of two things would follow, either His action would be unproductive, or He would produce only outside of Himself in the region of the temporary and the finite. To say that the action of God is unproductive is to say that He acts without cause, and that His life is consumed in the powerlessness of eternal sterility; to say that His action is only productive outside of Himself, is to say that His life is not His own, which is absurd, or that the universe is His life, which brings us to pantheism. We must then conclude that the life of God is exercised within Himself by an infinite and a sovereign fecundity. Do not seek beforehand how this adorable mystery is accomplished; do not hurry your curiosity beyond the light and the abyss. Be masters of yourselves, examine the point you are investigating, hear the sounds that you hear, and no more. The infinite, in heaven, is seen at a glance; here upon earth it is difficult for us to lift even a little of the veil that hides it from us.

I ask you now but one thing, I ask you if you can form any idea of being without the idea of activity; any idea of activity without the idea of production; any idea of production without the idea of fecundity? I ask you if your mind consents to pronounce this judgment: God is infinite activity which ends in infinite sterility. You may say: He sees and loves Himself, is this nothing? Yes, but His regard and His love are sterile; does that satisfy you? What! Your regard and your love are fruitful; they produce a living being like yourself, equal to you, in whom you see and love yourself; and God, the principle and pattern of all things, does not possess, under an infinite and a supernatural form, the mystery which you possess under a finite and natural form! His outer activity is great enough to give life to the universe, whilst his inner and personal activity is to produce nothing but the silence of unmeasured solitude! Is fecundity then a calamity, and sterility a state of perfection? If it be a state of perfection, do you not see that God contains them all in a supereminent degree? We must then conclude with St. Thomas of Aquinas, in his marvellous treatise on the divine persons: "The consequence of all action being something which proceeds from that action, even as there is an outer procession that follows the outer action, there is also an inner procession that follows the inner action . . . and thus the Catholic faith establishes a procession in God."\*

Let us still advance and ask why fecundity is the sum or term of the activity of beings? Why beings tend to produce other beings like themselves, and, in fact, do produce them? The reason of this is contained in the very idea of activity and action. For an action is a movement; a movement supposes a starting-point, which is the acting being; a point to be attained, which is the desired being; and a relation between the principle and the end of movement, between the acting being and the desired being. Without that relation there would be no cause of movement, and consequently no more action, no more activity, no life, no being, nothing. Relation is the very essence of life, and we have but to examine our

---

\* Question 27, art. 1.

own life to find abundant proof of it. What do we from the first of our days even to the last? We hold relations with God, with nature, with men, with books, with the dead, and with the living. The very time that measures our age is a relation, and our mind would lose itself in vainly endeavouring to imagine life otherwise than as an indivisible tissue of numberless relations.

What, then, is a relation? It is more than needful for us to know, since this is the last link of our whole being. A relation consists in the bringing together of two distinct terms. The perfect conjunction of these terms is unity, their perfect distinction is plurality, and consequently their perfect relation is unity in plurality. Survey the whole web of your relations, you will find nothing else there. The life of your intelligence is unity of mind in plurality of thoughts; the life of your body is unity of action in plurality of members; your life as a family is unity of affection and interests in plurality of persons; your life as citizens is unity of origin, duties, and rights, in plurality of families; your Catholic life is unity of faith and love in plurality of souls tending towards God; and so is it with all the rest. What am I now doing? Why are my words addressed to you? What is there between them and this auditory? Nothing, if it be not that my soul seeks yours to lead it to the seat of a light which, without destroying the distinction between your personality and mine, would, nevertheless, bring us together in the present unity of the same hope and in the future unity of the same beatitude.

Now this marvel of unity in plurality could be produced only by the likeness of beings, and the likeness of beings supposes their equality of nature by their community of origin. Fecundity, which produces beings like their authors and like each other, is then the natural principle of unity in plurality; that is to say, of the relations which form the life of beings by the continuous totality of their acts. It is true that we hold relations with beings to whom we are neither drawn by a similar origin nor by an exact likeness; but these relations are also feeble and distant, and the degree of likeness is always marked by the degree of kindred which measures the strength and intimacy of the relations. Thus members of the same family are nearer to each other than fellow-citizens; nations of the same race are more closely united than nations of different races; and all created beings derive from God, their common

Father, the reason of likenesses and relations, more or less direct, which bind them together in the vast unity of nature.

We are then entitled to lay down this third general law of life: "The end of fecundity is to produce relations between beings, that is to say, to give an object to and a reason for their activity."

Already you cease to wonder at those prodigious words by which the Apostle St. John defined the divine life for us: "There are three who give testimony in heaven, the Father, the Word, and the Holy Ghost, and these three are one." * You see that the mystery of life is a mystery of relations, that is to say, a mystery that involves these two terms—unity in plurality, plurality in unity. Before we arrive at a still more formal conclusion, let us halt for a moment to consider the effect of relations in beings.

Life is not the only phenomenon they offer to us. Above the movement that mingles and bears them onward, we find a charm which we call beauty. Beauty is the result of order; wheresoever order ceases, beauty vanishes. But what is order, if not the unity which shines in a multitude of beings, and which, notwithstanding their distinctions and their variety, brings them together again in the splendour of a single act?

Goodness is the sister of beauty. It is the gift which beings reciprocally make of their advantages, and consequently it is also the effect of relations. In order to give and to receive, it is necessary at least to be two.

Thus life, beauty, and goodness, have one and the same principle, which is unity in plurality; and to refuse this double character to God is at once to refuse life, beauty, and goodness to Him. Would you do this? Even should you not understand how one and the same being could realize in Himself one and many, unity and plurality, would that feebleness of your intelligence destroy the chain of the reasonings and observations which have initiated us into the most profound secrets of the nature of things? But let us meet the difficulty face to face.

God is one: His substance is indivisible because it is infinite; this is beyond doubt for faith as for reason. God cannot then be many by the division of His substance. But if he is not many by the division of His substance, how can He

---

* 1 John v. 7.

be many? How can a being who is one and indivisible at the same time be many? Gentlemen, I require but one word, and I ask you in return: Why should God need to be many? Is it not in order to possess relations in Himself, those relations without which we can neither conceive activity, nor life, nor being? Let the substance of God, then, remain what it is and what it should be—the seat of unity; and let it produce in itself, without being divided, terms of relation, that is to say, terms which are the seat of plurality in relation to unity. For these two things, one and many, are alike necessary in order to form relations; and if the substance of God were divisible, unity being wanting thereto, relations would be wanting also.

I divine your thoughts. You would tell me that you do not even understand the expressions which I employ, and that there is manifest contradiction between the idea of a unique substance and the idea of several terms of relation to be contained therein without dividing it. I will show you that it is not so, and had you but the intelligence of a child, it would suffice to enable you to follow me and to render justice to truth.

I stretch forth my hand. Where is it? In space! What is space? Philosophers have disputed about its nature: some have thought that it is an exceedingly delicate and subtle substance; others that it is something void, a simple possibility of receiving bodies. Whatever it may be, whether substance or not, space is manifestly a capacity constituted by three terms of relation, length, breadth, and height; three terms perfectly distinct, equal, inseparable save by an abstraction of the mind, and yet in their evident distinction forming together but one single and indivisible extent, which is space. I say that length, breadth, and height are terms of relation, that is to say, terms which relate to each other, since the sense of length is determined by the sense of breadth, and so on. I say that these terms of relation are distinct from each other; for it is manifest that length is not breadth, and that breadth is not height. I say, in fine, that these three terms, notwithstanding their real distinction, form but one single and indivisible extent. This, moreover, is perfectly clear to the senses and to the mind. There is then neither obscurity nor contradiction in this proposition: God is a unique substance, containing in His indivisible essence terms of relation really distinct in themselves.

Shall I give a more positive example than that of space? For, notwithstanding the reality of space, you may perhaps accuse it of being a kind of abstraction. Take then the first body you meet with. Every body, whatever it may be, a stone or a diamond, is comprised under the three forms of length, breadth, and height. Prisoner of extent, it bears it in its simple and triple form, and becomes wholly incorporated in it by a reciprocal penetration which makes of both one single thing. Body is space, and space is body. Length, breadth, and height are body, inasmuch as it is high. Divide the body as you will, change its inmost matter at pleasure, the same phenomenon of unity in plurality will always subsist; so that there is nothing in nature, space and body, that which contains and that which is contained, which does not fall under this definition as simple as it is marvellous—a unique substance in three terms of relation really distinct from each other.

The universe speaks then like St. John. Not only does it contain nothing contradictory to the logical rectitude of the expressions which represent the mystery of the divine life; not only do these expressions take in it the character of a general and algebraic formula of beings; but the force of analogy leads us also to apply this formula to the very principle of beings, to that being who should have placed in his works a copy only or a reflection of his own nature.

As soon, however, as we apply expressions or laws of the visible order to God, their proportions at once become changed, because they pass from the region of the finite to that of the infinite. You must not wonder then, if Catholic doctrine teaches you that terms of relation take, in God, the form of personality. Let us clearly understand this word. Every being, by that alone that it is itself and not another, possesses what we call individuality. As long as it subsists, it belongs to itself; it may increase or decrease, lose or gain; it may communicate to others something of itself, but not itself. It is itself as long as it is; none other is or will ever be so, save itself. Such is the nature and force of individuality. Suppose now that the individual being possesses consciousness and knowledge of its individuality, and it sees itself living and distinct from all that is not itself, it would be a person. Personality is no other thing than individuality having consciousness and knowledge of itself. Individuality is the characteristic of bodies: personality is the characteristic of spirits. Now God is an infinite spirit; all that which constitutes Him, substance and terms of relation, is spirit. Consequently each term of the divine relations possesses consciousness and knowledge of itself, sees itself distinct from the others as term of relation, one with them as substance: its distinction marks its relative individuality; consciousness and knowledge of its individuality make it a person. Imagine space become a spiritual being, you will have before you an analogous phenomenon. Length, breadth, and height would possess consciousness and knowledge of their relative individuality, consciousness and knowledge of their absolute unity in space; they would be one by substance, many by distinction raised to the state of personality.

It remains for us to consider how many persons there are in God, how and in what order they are manifested in Him.

Up to this point we have only employed analogies drawn from external nature, but now, having to consider the number and genesis of the divine persons, we must seek in more distant regions a light approaching nearer to the light of God.

Our horizon and light are not limited to external nature. We come in contact therewith by our body; but it is out of us, even of our body, and in addition, it is but dust and ashes; and if we possess something of God, it is but a vestige and not an image of Him. Let us leave the dust and limit, and enter into ourselves: Are we not spirits? Yes, I am a spirit! In this material sepulchre which I inhabit as a traveller, a light has been kindled, an immaterial and a pure light enlightening my life, which is my true life, which descends from eternity, and leads me thitherward as to my origin and nature. Why do I speak of time and space? Who shall stay me in these abject comparisons? Ah! I feel that you are ready to upbraid me. You wonder that I imprison my soul and your own in these inanities of the universe, where I see shadows only, and touch but the dead; from whence I have drawn only faint and defaced images of truth. You impatiently expect me to open to you the arena of a higher vision; I feel that it is there before us. I see that which is unseen, I hear that which is not heard, I read that which has neither form nor colour. Truth has still a veil, but it is its personality; it still has secrets, but they are the last. Nature, withdraw; and let us behold God in the spirit!

The mind lives, like God, of an immaterial life, and consequently it knows that life in which the senses have no part, and which is that of God. What, then, does the mind when, shut up within itself, imposing silence on all the rest, it lives of its own life? What does it, gentlemen? Two things only—two inexhaustible acts, which are constantly renewed, which never tire, and whose progress forms its whole labour and delight—it thinks and it loves. First it thinks, that is to say, it sees and combines objects divested of matter, form, extent, and horizon; a kind of universe before which the one that we inhabit by the senses is but a close and dreary dungeon. It dilates in that boundless sea of ideas. It calls into life, to form its own life, nameless and endless worlds which obey it with the quickness of lightning. It may be ignorant of their value and disdain them; pure contemplation will be so much the more burdensome to it as it exercises it the less and enchains its faculties to the abasements of the body. But I speak not of these treasons of the mind against itself; I speak of the mind as it is of its own nature, as it lives when it wills to live at the height where God has placed it. It thinks, then; this is its first act.

But thought; is it the mind itself, or something distinct from it? It is not the mind itself, for thought comes and goes, whilst the mind always remains. I forget on the morrow the ideas of the eve; I call them up and dismiss them; sometimes they beset me in spite of myself; my thought and my mind are two. I speak to myself in the solitude of my understanding; I interrogate myself. I answer to myself, my inner life is but a continual and mysterious colloquy. And yet I am one. My thought, although distinct from my mind, is not separate therefrom; when it is present, my mind sees it in itself; when it is absent, it seeks it in itself. I am at the same time one and two. My intellectual life is a life of relation; I find again therein what I have seen in external nature, namely, unity and plurality—unity resulting from the very substance of the mind, plurality resulting from its action. What, indeed, would the action of the mind be if it were unfruitful? What would be its reason, its end, its object? The mind, like the whole of nature, but in a much higher manner, is then prolific. Whilst bodies divide in order to multiply, the mind, created in the likeness of God, remains inaccessible to all division. It engenders its thought without emitting any of its incorruptible substance; multiplies it without losing anything of the perfection of unity.

You see that in rising from the outer to the inner life—from the life of the body to that of the mind—we find again the same law; but we find it, as was inevitable, with an increase of light and precision. Bodies, notwithstanding their marvellous revelations, kept us too far from God; the mind has borne us even to the sanctuary of His essence and His life. Let us enter, or at least, if we are forbidden to pass certain limits, let us approach as near as divine goodness will permit us.

God is a spirit; His first act, then, is to think. But His thought could not be like ours, multiple, unceasingly appearing but to vanish, and vanishing but to appear again. Ours is multiple, because, since we are finite, we can but represent to ourselves one by one the objects susceptible of being known to us; it is liable to perish, since in the crowding on of our ideas one upon the another, the second dethrones the first, and the third overthrows the second. On the contrary, in God, whose activity is infinite, the mind at once engenders a thought equal to itself, which fully represents it, and which needs no second expression, because the first has exhausted the abyss of things to know, that is to say, the abyss of the infinite. That unique and absolute thought, the first-born and the last of the mind of God, remains eternally in His presence as an exact representation of Himself, or, to speak the language of the sacred books, as "His image, the brightness of his glory, and the figure of his substance."* It is His word, His utterance, His inner word, as our thought is also our utterance and our word; but differing from ours inasmuch as it is a perfect word which speaks all to God in a single expression, which speaks it always without repetition, and which St. John heard in heaven when he thus opened his sublime Gospel: "In the beginning was the Word, and the Word was with God, and the Word was God."†

And even as in man the thought is distinct from the mind without being separated therefrom, so, in God, the thought is distinct without being separated from the divine mind which produces it. "The Word is consubstantial with the Father," according to the expression of the council of Nice, which is but the forcible expression of truth. But here, as in the rest,

* Cor. iv. 4.   Heb. i. 3.           † John i. 1.

there exists a great difference between God and man. In man the thought is distinct from the mind by an imperfect distinction, because it is finite; in God, the thought is distinct from the mind by a perfect distinction, because it is infinite: that is to say, that in man the thought does not attain to becoming a person, whilst in God it does attain thereto. The mystery of unity in plurality is not totally accomplished in our intelligence, and this is why we cannot live of ourselves alone. We seek from without the aliment of our life: we need a foreign support, a thought other than ours, and yet nearly allied to it. In God plurality is absolute as well as unity, and therefore His life passes entirely within Himself, in the ineffable colloquy between a divine person and a divine person, between a father without generation and a son eternally engendered. God thinks, and He sees Himself in His thought as in another so akin to Him as to be but one with Him in substance; He is Father, since He has produced in His own likeness a term of relation really and personally distinct from Him; He is one and two in all the force which the infinite gives to unity and duality; in contemplating His thought, in beholding His image, in hearing His word, He is able to utter in the ecstasy of the highest, the most real paternity: "Thou art my Son, to-day have I begotten thee."\*
To-day! In this day which has neither past, nor present, nor future; in this day which is eternity, that is to say, the indivisible duration of unchanging being. To-day! For God thinks to-day; He engenders His Son to-day, He sees Him to-day, He hears Him to-day, He lives to-day in that ineffable act which has neither beginning nor end.

But is this all the life of God? Is the generation of His Son His sole act, and does it consummate with its fecundity all its beatitude? No, gentlemen; for, in ourselves, the generation of thought is not the term where our life ends. When we have thought, a second act appears: we love. Thought is a movement which brings its objects into ourselves; love is a movement which draws us out of ourselves towards that object in order to unite it to us and ourselves to it, and thus to accomplish in its fulness the mystery of relations, that is to say, the mystery of unity in plurality. Love is at the

---

\* Psalm ii. 7.

same time distinct from the mind, and distinct from the thought; distinct from the mind in which it is engendered and in which it dies; distinct from the thought by its very definition, since it is a movement of drawing together, whilst the thought is a simple perception. And yet it proceeds from the one and from the other, and forms but one with both. It proceeds from the mind, whose act it is, and from the thought, without which the mind would not see the object which it should love; and it remains one with the thought and the mind in the same fount of life where we again find all the three, always inseparable, and always distinct.

In God, it is the same. From the coeternal regard interchanged between the Father and the Son, springs a third term of relation, proceeding from the one and the other, really distinct from them, raised by the force of the infinite to personality, and which is the Holy Ghost, that is to say, the holy, the unfathomable and stainless movement of divine love. As the Son exhausts knowledge, the Holy Ghost exhausts love in God, and by Him the cycle of divine fecundity and life closes. What more could be possible to God? As a perfect spirit He thinks and He loves; He produces a thought equal to Himself, and with His thought a love equal to both. What more could He desire or produce? And what more could you desire if, like Him, you possessed unbounded thought and unbounded love in the unity of your substance? But, poor as we are, thought and love are in our souls only a perception and a possession of a foreign object; we are obliged to leave ourselves in order to seek our life, to appease our thirst for knowledge, our hunger for love. And instead of turning to the only source of truth and charity, which is God, we wed ourselves to nature, which is but a shadow; to the life of time, which is but death. Or, returning to ourselves in a hopeless effort, we ask from our own powerlessness the accomplishment of the one and triple mystery which is divine felicity; we endeavour to satisfy ourselves in the pride of a solitary thought, in the delight of personal love, and, like dust which consumes itself, we waste away in a withering grasp of egotism which would be infinite if nothingness could be infinite.

Oh! lift up your eyes to heaven! There is life because there is true fecundity. It is there that the spectacle of the laws of nature, and the study of the laws of your own minds, lead you. All teaches you that being and activity are one and the same thing, that activity is expressed by action, and that action is necessarily productive or fruitful; that the end of fecundity is to establish relations between similar beings; that relation is unity in plurality, from whence results life, beauty, and goodness. And that thus, God, the infinite being, the pre-eminently good, beautiful, and living being, is infallibly the most magnificent totality of relations, perfect unity and perfect plurality, the unity of substance in the plurality of persons; a primordial mind, a thought equal to the mind that engenders it, a love equal to the mind and the thought whence it proceeds; all the three, Father, Son, Holy Ghost, ancient as eternity, great as infinity, one in beatitude as in the substance from whence they derive their identical divinity. Behold God! Behold God, the cause and pattern of all beings! Nothing exists here below which is not a vestige or an image of Him, according to the degree of its perfection. Space reveals Him in its single and triple plenitude; bodies proclaim Him in the three dimensions which constitute their solidity; the mind shows us a nearer vision of Him in the production of the two highest things of this world, if indeed they are of this world, namely, thought and love; in fine, the very tissue of the universe which is everywhere but relations, is before us, as it were, a picture which the divine light passes over, penetrates, and so gives to us above the visible heaven a glimpse of the invisible heaven of the Trinity.

All laws take their source in this seat of primordial relations. If human society would aspire to perfection, it has no other model to study and to imitate. It will find there the first social constitution in the first community; equality of nature between the persons who compose it; order in their equality, since the Father is the principle of the Son, and the Holy Ghost proceeds from the Father and the Son; unity, the cause of plurality; thought, receiving from above its being and its light; love, terminating and crowning all the relations. These laws are full of beauty, and if legislators could realise them upon earth, they would produce a work whose privilege and secret have until now belonged to the Catholic Church alone.

Let us halt here. I have not demonstrated the mystery of the Holy Trinity to you, but I have placed it in perspective, where pride will not mistake it without insulting itself. Let us forgive that satisfaction to pride if it be jealous of claiming it. For yourselves, inspired by humbler and higher wisdom, give thanks to God, who, in revealing to us the mystery of His life, has not overwhelmed our intelligence by a sterile light, but has given to us the key of nature and of our own mind.

# THE CREATION OF THE WORLD BY GOD.

My Lord,—Gentlemen,

We have penetrated even to the inner life of God; we know what He is, and what is His life. The course of ideas would lead us now to seek what is His character; but two words will suffice for us on this head. The character of God is perfection; whatever is included in the idea of perfection—immutability, wisdom, justice, goodness—must be attributed to God in an infinite degree, and forms His metaphysical and moral character. The difficulties which may spring from these divers attributes will naturally be solved when we come to treat of the relations between God and created beings. We pass over them then at a bound, and find ourselves logically in presence of this question: God being the admitted principle of things, how have they emanated from Him? By what process, and above all, from what motives?

Here we begin to touch more directly the secret of our destinies; for they unquestionably take their source in the process by which we have sprung from the bosom of our cause, and yet much more in the motives that led the self-existing being to produce something which was not himself. What then is this process? What are these motives?

Before I answer, I beg your particular attention to the state of the question. We are not now inquiring whether the world is or is not a work: that question is judged. Whosoever is not a pantheist is compelled to admit that the world has a cause, that it is the work of a superior intelligence and power; now we have discarded pantheism, we have recognised

God in the very infirmity of nature, and therefore we say of Him with the people and the poet:

"The Eternal is His name, the world is His work."

It is worthy of attention that the philosophers of antiquity who believed in the eternity of matter, such as Plato, could not however help recognising in the totality of visible things the character of a studied work, and they called God the great Architect of the universe. In fact the universe bears the visible sign of its personal powerlessness, if I may so speak; and those even who do not reach the idea of its creation, see in it the hand of the artist who formed and constructed it. They see it made, although they do not see it created, otherwise the idea of God would have no reason in their minds. The production of the world is a dogma which logically precedes the dogma of the existence of God. We say: The world is produced, therefore God is; and not: God is, therefore the world is produced. It is the reasoning of the ancient theist philosophers as well as of the Christian philosophers, only it was less complete in the former than in the latter. Aristotle, for instance, after having admitted the eternity of matter, could no longer mount to a supreme cause, save by discovering something in nature whose presence could not be explained without a higher principle. Such to him was the movement of bodies. The analysis of this phenomenon led him to see the necessity of a first motor, and he wrote this proposition, which is almost divine in its depth and originality: "There is something immovable which is the principle of movement."

Once more, then, we are not inquiring whether the world is produced, but how and why it has been produced.

Two systems have divided minds outside the pale of Catholic doctrine. The first affirms that the world has been produced by the co-operation of God and a certain inferior substance coeternal with God. Picture to yourselves, on the one hand, the absolute and perfect being: on the other, a vile, shapeless, lifeless substance, unable of itself to rise from that abject state, and yet uncreated like God, eternal like God, self-existing like God—matter, in a word, and yet matter stripped of the glory in which we see it clothed; that had God left it there, it would be there still, a sort of empty

and eternal tomb, receiving neither life nor death. But God
beheld it, He was moved with pity at the infinite greatness of
its poverty. He spake a word, and the world, bursting the
inflexible bonds of its conception, appeared as our eyes now
admire it, ancient in itself, new in form, father and son at the
same time, son of one more perfect than itself, father of itself
by co-operation.

This ingenious poesy has not satisfied all minds. Many
have refused to accept it. Before logic as well as in itself they
have seen the poverty of that singular substance, half God,
half nothingness—God in the eternity of its being, nothingness
in its powerlessness to give itself the mode of its existence—
and in order to explain the birth of the world they have
imagined the system of emanation. In this second order of
ideas God has drawn the substance of the universe from His
own substance, but without communicating to it His personality
or His divinity.

Catholic doctrine rejects this system as well as the other.
For either the divine substance is entire and indivisible in the
world, in which case the world is God; or the divine substance
is but in part in the world by virtue of emanation, and then it
loses the absolute character without which the mind cannot
conceive it.

It is not necessary to make a great effort of thought in
order to seize the vice or rather the absurdity of these theories
on the origin of the world. We find here a striking example
of the strength and the weakness of the human mind. It has
seen clearly that visible nature is inexplicable without the intervention of a higher nature; but—I know not why—it has not
been able to determine the mode and measure of that intervention. Struck by the poverty of the universe, it denied to
it self-existence in order to make it an emanation of the divinity;
then, not conceiving either that God could come forth from
Himself, or that His substance became impoverished by that
emission, it attributed to the world a fund of original vitality,
but poor and held within the most extreme limits of incapacity.
It is always the same contradiction. It would seem that only
a little logical vigour was needed in order to draw positive conclusions in the fulness of truth; man was unequal to this. His
eye, wandering between two abysses, dared neither to accept
the one nor the other, and sought between them an imaginary
resting-place.

Open now the Bible and read its first phrase: "In the beginning God created heaven and earth." What simplicity, and what certainty! Moses does not affirm even the existence of God; he names and defines by an action which at the same time explains the universe. The universe is not eternal, nor is it an emanation of the divine substance; it was made in the full meaning of the word, it was made by a pure act of will. "God spake, and all was made," said David; and this is the idea which the human mind was unable to discover, even in order to dispute it. The human mind ignored it, although it was the key of all, and, since it has been revealed, the human mind has rejected it as an incomprehensible fiction. What, says the mind, is it to make being by an act of the will? How can that magical operation be conceived? And what is an idea that offers no seizable image to the understanding? Man acts, but always upon a substance pre-existing his action; he produces, but only simple modifications in the subject where he exercises his power. Creation is an abyss in which he sees nothing but a name and despair; a name instead of an idea, despair instead of a solution.

What think you? Is it necessary for us to represent an act to ourselves in order to have an idea of it? Is it not enough that the force of logic constrains us to affirm its existence? I grant for the moment that reason in no way seizes the creating act; but it sees that the world is neither eternal, nor has it emanated from the substance of God, and, driven to the last extremity, concludes that it was made by means of creation; for what other issue remains to it? Assuredly if the mind sees anything here it sees but an impossibility, and therefore it takes the only road open to it, an obscure one however, but enlightened at least by the light contained in every logical necessity. Is it true moreover that the word creation represents nothing to our understanding? Is it true that we cannot conceive how the divine will is able to pronounce that sovereign word: FIAT! I should wonder if it were so; for, if we have unravelled in our intelligence images which have led us even to the sacred vestibule of the uncreated essence, why should not the mystery of our personal will teach us something touching the mystery of the divine will? The will is the seat of power; by it man commands and is obeyed. Command! What a word! Have you ever reflected upon it? One man utters a word: it is heard, and all is in motion. Another speaks:

nothing is done. Both pretended to command, only one has succeeded. It is because one only uttered the word that contains power, the word that expresses will. Many think they express it, because they speak the word; but few do so in reality. It is the most rare expression in the world, although it is the most often usurped; and when a man possesses its terrible secret, were he the poorest and the last of all, be sure that some day you will see him above you. Of such was Cæsar.

Have you ever remarked the part which the will plays in the occult sciences, and how no one becomes master of another there save by the energy of a kind of imperative fluid? Virile natures offer greater resistance to the perturbations of these secret arts, and this is why the ancient oracles chose the feeble mouth of the pythoness for their organ. Pardon this allusion to questionable mysteries; truth penetrates all, even those things whose nature is veiled and uncertain. Thus the clouds bear the sun in concealing it.

Be that as it may, none will dispute that the seat of power is in the will. It is by the will that man wields empire over his fellow-men, and by it also he moves his own body. Therefore, when Catholic doctrine teaches us that the world has sprung from an act of the divine will, it teaches us something which is verified by our own experience of the seat where lies the principle of our own force. In ourselves, as in God, the will produces force; but what is force? I stand still; suddenly my arm is raised, my hand is outstretched, my head is erect, my eye brightens: what has happened? Has any foreign power seized upon me and deprived me of my repose? No; within myself, in a calm and immaterial chamber, an act has been produced. I have said: Let my body move, and it has moved. At the same time I have conveyed to my members, and in an exact proportion, the quantity of force necessary to their movement; I have willed, and acted. Observe! the movement did not exist. It did not exist in my body, which was still: it did not exist in my soul, which is of a spiritual nature: I have produced it by a simple act of my will. I have created it. The proposition of Aristotle is verified in myself: "Immobility is the principle of movement." What is this but a creation? Say you that the motive power pre-existed in my will? Be it so; but what is the motive power but the principle that produces movement? Catholic doctrine does not teach that God creates without a creative power of which this will is the seat and the organ. The divine FIAT, like the human FIAT, has an efficient cause, without which it would be but an empty word, a fruitless desire.

Observe that the bodily movement is exterior to the soul which produces it by an act of the inner will. Herein lies the difference between generation and creation. When the mind conceives a thought, it engenders, because the thought is of the same nature as itself and dwells in itself; when the will suscitates the movement of the body, it creates, because the movement is not of the same nature as itself, and springs from without. These two acts have nothing in common. The first is the principle of the inner life; the second of the outer life. The first is the life of God and of our soul; the second is the life of the world and of our body. All activity is reduced to these two terms, to engender and to create, that is to say, to produce within and without. No being exists without this double faculty. Were the first wanting it would have no inner and personal life; were the second wanting it would have no outer life. Generation concentrates, creation dilates; they form together the mystery of all life.

Judge now whether reason forms no idea of the creating act. It is true that in God that act assumes a strength which surpasses our feeble powers. Whilst the movement created by us decreases and soon dies, the things created by God strengthen into a durable substance. This is the same difference which we have already remarked between the production of the divine thought and the production of human thought; the characteristic of the work of God is subsistency, whilst whatsoever man does passes from being to nothingness with lamentable speed. But this passing away of our works does not destroy their reality, or their analogy with the works of the infinite. We really engender like God, we really create like Him; we in an incomplete and a relative manner, God in a perfect and an absolute manner. And we understand the two mysteries of generation and creation, which form life, because we are really, though imperfectly, generators and creators.

This established, your place and your condition are henceforth known to you; you are not sovereigns, you are servants. Sovereignty is existence by itself; you do not possess it in any degree. You have been made, you have been "made out of nothing," according to the energetic expression of the mother of the Maccabees, and at the very most you can but pretend to the title of children of God. This is the extreme term of your ambition. If the divine goodness has shed in your soul and upon your brow some traces of likeness to Himself, you are His children, and He permits you, from your very dust, to address to His throne the name of Father. This is your highest glory. Pretend not then to sovereignty; what is sovereignty in a being who lives by another? And yet there are men who would invest you with it. For this, rationalism strains all its efforts to prove the eternity of the world, and to seek for signs of indefectibility in ruin and death. For do you think that the human mind would rush so eagerly upon these questions if they did not involve consequences for the direction of the soul and life? Be sure that all is there. To say that the world is uncreated is to say that man is sovereign; to say that it is created is to say that man is a servant, or at most a son. The first doctrine gives us the right to define ourselves like God: "I am who am."* The second places in our hearts the prayer of the Gospel: "Our Father who art in heaven."

Between these we have to decide; we must live here below as God or as creature, in the modesty of obedience or in the pride of sovereignty. Which will you choose? Some sages will tell you that you are great; they take the sublime part of your being, and would persuade you that there is nothing above you. Others will place a low and dishonoured image of yourselves before you; in the lowest regions of your nature they will discover secrets that will fill you with shame, and yet it is still but to flatter your pride. Catholic doctrine alone places you in your true position, without insult or adulation. It sees your greatness and proves it to you; it sees your wretchedness and shows it to you; it supports you against the pride that inflates and against the pride that dishonours you; in fine, it reveals to you at the same time the knowledge of your greatness and your wretchedness, in that single phrase which it alone has pronounced: Man is a creature, but he is the creature of God.

The creature of God! Why? What has moved that inaccessible being to look beneath Himself and call forth that

---

* Exodus iii. 14.

which was not? It concerns us to know, for it is evident that the beginning and end of our destinies lie in the motive of our creation. Lost as we were in the cold shadows of inexistence, unable of ourselves to rise from the depths of that tomb, we had no other hope, no other germ of life, than in the will of God, and the will of God could only turn towards us, pity, and call us, by virtue of a motive which determined it. No reasonable being, in fact, acts without reason under pain of acting at hazard, and of ignoring what he does by ignoring why he does it. Therefore St. Thomas of Aquinas, seeking before us the motive of creation, begins by laying down this maxim : " Every being acts for an end;" and he calls the end by the name of *final cause*, in order to show that, being the motive of the acts of the will, it is really the principle of that which the will produces. God, in creating the world, was then moved by an end, that is to say, by an object which He purposed to attain, and which was the term of His thought, His will, and His action. What was that end? If, in order to learn this, we study the springs of our own determinations, we shall easily find among them the motive of interest or of utility. We will and we act because we have wants; our movements are the efforts of a being which does not live of itself, and which seeks from without the support or the increase of its life. But God has no wants; He lives of Himself, and in Himself; nothing is wanting to the plenitude of His being and His felicity; how should He act from interest? How should He have created man and the world to fill the void of His nature, or to add to the infinite resources and delights not yet to be found therein? Evidently He possessed them all; He had nothing to gain, nothing to lose, in the creation of the universe. The outward manifestation of His omnipotence was a supremely disinterested act.

It is true—I have often heard, and you have heard it yourselves—that "God created the world for His glory." But that expression has two meanings, one which is exact, and which I will soon explain to you; the other, which is not admissible, because it supposes that the divine will may be moved by the reason of personal utility. Let us put aside, then, for an instant, terms ill-defined, and continue to seek what was the motive of God in calling the world into existence.

Man does not act from interest only: he is capable also of acting from duty, that is to say, of sacrificing his own to the common benefit, in the name of a supreme law regulating the relations between beings, and imposing acts upon them which turn to the benefit of others. This motive is infinitely more noble than the first: it draws the soul from egotism, and, as a moving principle, gives it an impulsion from above, which, being no other thing than the view and the sentiment of eternal justice, appears worthy to concentrate itself in God and to have commanded His resolution when He created the world. Nevertheless it is not so. God is justice itself. As soon as He acts, He acts under the empire of that law of equity which is comprised in His essence; but before acting externally for the first time, before founding the universe, He owed nothing to it. He was free towards it in all the liberty which being possesses before nothingness. He could communicate existence to it or refuse it, according to His pleasure, without affecting any right, without neglecting any duty. Man himself owes nothing to nothingness, and in drawing forth another man from his generous bosom, he performs an act of full and absolute sovereignty. He is a father because he has so willed it, as God is a creator because He has so willed it.

But did no motive then inspire the creative will? It cannot be so, and this we have already shown. The motive exists; let us not grow weary of seeking for it in the mystery of our own deliberations.

Above duty, if it be possible, or at least in a place not less elevated and sacred, lies another moving principle of our actions: it is love. We advance, because we love; we suffer, we live, we die, because we love. Love guides our most ardent designs, and if we sometimes feel ourselves able to do all things, if, urging life and death before us with a force almost sacrilegious, we sometimes think that already we possess the energy of immortality, it is love assuredly, it is love that persuades us and bears us along. No courser is more rapid, none will ever bound over more abysses with greater pleasure, none will carry us farther, higher, or give us a stronger sensation of a being about to create. Was it then love that moved the divine will, and unceasingly urged Him to create? Was it love who was our first father? But, alas! love itself has a cause in the beauty of its object, and what beauty could that dead and icy shadow which preceded the universe have possessed before God? That shadow to which we can give a name only by betraying truth! What could nothingness have said to the heart of God? How is it possible to love that which is not? Or even, how is it possible to love finite beauty when in possession of perfect and immeasurable beauty? Already love had produced in God its ineffable fruit; already the Father, Son, and Holy Ghost coeternally respired in the intimate colloquy of their triple, and single, and infinite beauty. They saw, they felt, they spake together their beatitude, and all three immutable in one and the same rapture, they could neither see, nor feel, nor hear anything which merited from them a single sensation of their love. The mystery was fully accomplished—great God! and what remained then to move Thy heart, and cause Thee to see us from afar in that complete inanity in which we did not even wait for Thee?

Something remained, do not doubt, something more generous than interest, more elevated than duty, more powerful than love. Sound the depths of your own hearts, and if you find it difficult to understand me, if your own gifts are unknown to you, hear Bossuet, who speaks of you: "When God," said he, "made the heart of man, He first placed in it goodness." This is divine language, and had Bossuet uttered but this single phrase, I should call him a great man. Goodness! That is to say, that virtue which consults no interest, which does not wait for the command of duty, which needs not to be solicited by the attraction of the beautiful, but which leans so much the more towards an object as that object is poorer, more wretched, more abandoned, more worthy of pity! It is true, it is indeed true, man possesses that adorable faculty. I appeal to yourselves as witnesses. It is not genius, or glory, or love, that measures the elevation of his soul; it is goodness. It is goodness that gives to the human physiognomy its highest and most invincible charm; it is goodness that draws us together; it is goodness that brings blessings to misfortune, and that is everywhere, from earth to heaven, the great mediator. See the poor cretin at the foot of the Alps: his eye has no lustre, he neither smiles nor weeps, he knows not even his own degradation, he seems as it were an effort of nature to insult herself in dishonouring her noblest production. Do not think that he has not found the way to some heart, and that his abjection has snatched from him the friendship of the universe. No, he is loved, he has a mother, he has brothers and sisters, he has a place by the cottage hearth, the best and most honoured place, because he is the most disinherited.

The bosom that nourished him holds him still, and the superstition of love speaks of him only as a blessing sent from God. Such is man!

But can I say: Such is man, without saying also: Such is God? If God were not the primordial ocean of goodness, and if in forming our heart He had not infused into it something of His own, from whence should we have obtained it? Yes, God is good. Yes, goodness is the attribute which in Him concentrates all the other attributes, and it is not without reason that antiquity graved upon the pediments of its temples that famous inscription in which goodness preceded greatness. But all perfection supposes an object to which it is applied. An object, then, as vast and profound as divine goodness itself was needful to it: God has found it. From the centre of His fulness He beheld that being without beauty, form, life, or name, that being without being which we call nothingness; He heard the cry of worlds that were not, the cry of immeasured misery calling to unbounded goodness. Eternity moved and said to time: Begin! Time and the universe obeyed the will of God, as the will of God had yielded, but freely, to the inspiration of goodness.

I say freely, because all the divine perfections operate within themselves in the mystery of the Holy Trinity, and because their outer action is thenceforth no longer necessary to their dilation, but a spontaneous effect of the free will of God. God was good before He created the world, and His absolute goodness was infinitely exercised in the eternal communication of the three uncreated persons. Therefore, when He made the universe, He made it from a free impulsion of His heart, and not from any necessity. He made it gratuitously, without the motive of interest, the constraint of duty, or the inducement of merited love, in the sole object of satisfying His goodness by communicating life. Therefore, St. Thomas of Aquinas, in treating this question, says that "God is the only perfectly liberal being, because He alone acts not for His own benefit, but because of His goodness."\*

This conclusion is of the highest importance for the whole course of Christian dogma, and it is needful to solve the difficulties which it presents, in the theological as well as in the rational points of view.

---

\* Summa, quest. 44, art. 4.

Theologically, a text of Scripture is opposed to us which is thus written: UNIVERSA PROPTER SEMETIPSUM OPERATUS EST DOMINUS—*The Lord hath made all things for himself.*\* These words possess a character of precision and clearness which would seem to overshadow all the ideas we have been placing before you. It is, however, easy to explain them. God could not, more than any other being, draw from outside of Himself the motives of His determinations. He finds them in His nature, and in yielding to them, if I may so speak, it is manifest that He acts for Himself, since He acts under the impulsion of something which is Himself. But goodness possesses that excellent and singular quality, that its object is the good of others, and that in acting from goodness we nevertheless act for others and in a disinterested manner. Therefore it is true to say that in creating the world from goodness, God has created it for Himself, since His goodness is Himself; and yet it is equally true to say that He created it freely, since He intended the good of His creatures, and since that good could not increase His own felicity. But even had it increased His felicity, the motive of goodness would still remain pure and irreproachable, for nothing is more perfect than to find happiness in communicating our own happiness. That egotism, if such it be, is that of great souls, and although the creature may be profitless to God, doubtless we must believe that our love is not indifferent to Him, and that, without increasing His happiness, it makes us dear and precious in His sight.

It would also be easy for me to explain that other expression to you: "God created the world for His glory." The inner glory of God is in His sovereign perfection; His outer glory consists in being known and loved by free intelligences; and it is beyond question that He has in fact given being to those intelligences in order to be known and loved by them. But why has He willed to call them to know and to love Him? Is it for their happiness or for His personal benefit? from the motive of goodness or that of interest? We have shown, with St. Thomas of Aquinas, that it was from the motive of goodness, and the expression under our notice decides nothing, since it does not even touch the question. It suffices to define the word glory in order to be convinced of this.

\* Proverbs xvi. 4.

Let us now approach the objections of rationalism.

So far from admitting that the world is a work of divine goodness, rationalism does not even see in it a work of justice. Is it just, say they, to dispose of another's condition without his sanction? When, in the exercise of His incomprehensible omnipotence, it pleased God to call intelligent beings into life, beings capable of judging whether existence was a blessing or a curse, had He the right to act without their consent? The Romans have written with as much eloquence as truth: NEMINI INVITO BENEFICIUM CONFERTUR—*There is no benefit without the will that accepts it.* By what right have we been drawn forth from nothingness to be thrown, without our consent, into that gulf of misery called life? What! we reposed peacefully in the eternity of our sleep, when suddenly an invisible hand seized upon us, a strange voice called us; it said with power: Come forth, see, feel, think, love! And, obeying that merciless order in spite of ourselves, after having spent hours or years amidst confused realities and vanished illusions, suddenly, again that hand which had dragged us from our first tomb, that hand rejects us! And the same voice which called us cries out to us: It is enough, lie down, close thy eyes, quit this world, begone! But if we were made for ourselves, should we not have been consulted in order to learn when, how, and under what conditions life was to be given to us? This has not been thought of: life came to us as death comes, with insult and scorn to us. Ah! let vain theology speak as it will, this is not the lamentation of the mind; it is the groaning of the soul, it is the sincerity of suffering and the accusation of the universe. Leave us, at least, to weep over ourselves, respect the desolation of ages, and do not add to the misery of our destiny that other misery of desiring to understand it.

I should be silent before the sound of those accents which have sometimes troubled you, and which perhaps still trouble many wounded hearts in this assembly. I should be silent, or rather I should lend my lips to the tremblings of complaint and ingratitude if I took in this question the same starting-point as yourselves. Yes, if this life were *the* life, if this light were *the* light, if this world were *the* world, yes, I should hide my forehead in my hands, and sink with you into an abyss of despair wherein I would hear no word of consolation. But do you believe this, and has Christianity so taught you? Do you believe that this life is *the* life, that this light is *the* light, that this world is *the* world? Do you believe it? and who has so taught you? Yourselves, none but yourselves. Learn then this from me: I do not believe you. I believe that this life is a road, that this light is a shadow, that this world is a prelude. I believe that life is God, that light is God, that the world is God. And I believe with all my soul, at the price of my blood, if needful, that God has created us to live by Him, to be enlightened by Him, to find in Him the substance of which all that we see is but an incapable and a painful image. This is my faith, it is this faith which I proclaim to you; and in order to dispute it you must deal with it such as it is, and not such as you take it in the injustice or discouragement of your own minds.

Yes, we all suffer: woe to him who denies it! But we suffer from the road and not from life. Life is abundance, peace, joy, fulness; when we love God we receive certain hallowed foretastes, certain yet imperfect delights, which suffice to make us forget the present world, or at least courageously to accept its passing trials. Is it meet, indeed, for a traveller awaited by unerring love, to complain of the road, to curse the dust he treads upon, and the sun that lights up his way? For my part, born to sorrow like the rest, charged with the two wounds of my forefathers—anguish of soul and infirmity of body—I bless God who has made me and who waits for me, I ask not to be consulted by Him about my condition; between the nothingness from whence He called me and the eternity He has promised me the choice is doubtful only to parricidal folly, and God should have counted upon my virtue as He counted upon His goodness. Eternal justice could not suppose the refusal of eternal beatitude: it was entitled to expect from us gratitude, love, and the acceptation of a trial without which love could not have been shown, and at least in ingratitude itself, silence and just remorse.

Nevertheless you continue, and you recall to me a thought which for a long time troubled the adolescence of my reason. If all of us, such as we are, intelligent and free creatures, attained the life of eternity, it is certain that the sufferings of the present life would vanish from our minds, not being "worthy," as St. Paul says, "to be compared with the glory to come, that shall be revealed to us."* But it is not so. Catholic

---

* Rom. viii. 18.

doctrine teaches that a portion of created intelligent beings do not attain to the reign of God, and thus that creation, instead of turning to their happiness, turns finally to their eternal woe. By their own fault, it is true, but what does that signify? God knew it, God had foreseen it. Was it an act of goodness to place beings in the world whom infallible foreknowledge beheld, whether or not from their own fault, excluded from the benefit of their primitive vocation, and hurled into a depth of ruin equal to the good prepared for them? If God, in creation, had intended to act only in virtue of His sovereignty, by an act of power and choice, it might perhaps be conceived that He had not looked to the result, and that the final misery of a part of His creatures, caused by their prevarication, might have appeared to Him as an accident incapable of disarming the right and efficacy of His will. But you tell us that the supreme FIAT was pronounced from goodness, from the desire to communicate life and glory to possible beings whom God perceived in the horizon of His thought. Are this end and motive compatible with the eternal fall of the lost intelligences? Doubtless we admit that Catholic doctrine does not teach as an article of faith that it is the smaller number of mankind who are saved. Much less does it teach that in the totality of intelligent hierarchies it is the lesser number who maintain their titles before the justice of God. But what of this? Were there but one man, but one single intelligence disinherited from the true life and for ever reprobated, it would be enough to accuse divine goodness, or at least not to attribute to it the creation of the universe. Seek then another motive for the omnipotence of God; say that He has done what He willed to do because He willed it; that He was Master, that crime and ingratitude could not deprive him of His sovereign rights. You may perhaps be listened to, but do not talk of the goodness of God in presence of that terrible image of eternal damnation: let us tremble before His justice, and be silent before His impenetrable majesty.

I shall not be silent, for what you have just said suffices to answer you. You admit that the creative power enters into the attributes which constitute the divine essence; it is impossible for God to be stripped of it by the disobedience of His creature. To say, in fact, that God has no right to create a being who might misuse His gifts, is to say that the wicked are able to destroy God by hindering the exercise of one of His essential attributes. What could be more vain or more unreasonable? Now, this admitted, the difficulty vanishes. In fact, even when God acts from goodness, He acts in the indivisible totality of His essence; He acts with His power, His wisdom, His justice, and all the inalienable totality of His perfections. Goodness moves Him, but goodness which abdicates nothing of the rest of His divinity. Goodness could not hinder Him from being wise, just, powerful, supreme, and if by His foreknowledge He perceive a creature so ungrateful as to turn His gifts against Himself, He will not withdraw the blessing from him, since He would then take from Himself the power to create under just conditions; this He should not do, this He could not do without ceasing to exist. You will say, perhaps: One thing is power in itself, another is the exercise of power; God could not lose power, but He is free not to exercise it. Assuredly; but you must understand that whosoever is free not to exercise a power, is free also to exercise it, under pain of not possessing it. If then you grant that God is free, all His attributes considered, to create a being who may abuse the blessing of life, why should you wonder that in fact He has exercised that liberty which belongs to Him and which you attribute to Him?

You still say, however this may be, metaphysically, the heart naturally rejects such a conclusion. Where is the father who would place a son in the world if he foresaw that life would even by his fault be a fatal gift to him? And is not God our father? Ought He not to feel more tenderness towards us than is felt by a mortal man?

Here the comparison wants force, because it is wanting in justice. God has not created isolated individuals, or even worlds; He has created one unique world in which all beings are linked together by relations of mutual dependence and service, and not one of these can be withdrawn without entailing the suffering of all the others. In the human race especially, each man contains a posterity in himself whose term is not assignable, and which makes of its generations one united assemblage in which no single member can lose his place without drawing after him the multitude of his descendants. To suppress a single man is to suppress a race; to suppress a wicked man is to suppress a people of just men who may spring from him. For good and evil are entwined together in the changeable course of mankind;

a virtuous son succeeds to a bad father, and the ancestor but too often contemplates in his distant progeny crimes which to him were unknown. Now, the glance of God perceiving at once all the successions of life, all the regenerations of good in evil and of evil in good, no destiny appeared solitary to Him; so that in cutting it off from the anticipated book of life, He would but cut off a course unworthy to be continued. In His sight Adam, a prevaricator, included the whole posterity of the saints. To refuse being to him because of his crime, even had that crime never obtained pardon, would have been to destroy in him all the merits of the human race. How could the goodness of God have required such a sacrifice? How could it have required that the wicked should have been preferred to the just, that life should be withdrawn from those who would make good use of it, because of those who would have turned it into a curse instead of a blessing?

I know God, I love Him, I hope in Him, I bless Him in life and death: why should the fault of one of my ancestors, eternally foreseen by divine goodness, have intercepted my birth, and not have permitted me for a single day to respire in the mystery of liberty from whence my beatitude might result? Why should I have been condemned to nothingness because one of my forefathers would have abused his existence? Where in this would have been justice, wisdom, or goodness?

God had not to choose between creating or not creating a wicked man, but between creating or not creating generations of good and evil together; and as all presented this mixture to His prophetic glance, He had to choose between creating the universe or not creating anything. The question is very different, and assuredly the most tender father would not choose to die without posterity, if God, revealing to him their future, were to show to him, in the transformations of his race, the inevitable alternatives of glory and shame, of happiness and misery. What would it be if, instead of a single generation, it were a question of all human generations? What would it be if to you were given the choice of destroying or creating the universe? For such is the question which was weighed in the counsels of God.

God has judged it, and heaven and earth proclaim how.

You may, however, judge it otherwise; you may complain of life and not consider it so great a gift. But learn that the life of which you complain is not that which God prepared for you, it is that which you have made for yourselves. You have cut off God from it, and you wonder that nothing remains. You have produced the void in your soul, and you wonder that the infinite is wanting to you. You have run after every vanity, and you wonder that nothing is left to you but doubts, darkness, bitterness, affliction. Ah! return, return to life, regain your rights in creation by the courage of faith, the holiness of hope, the divinity of love, and then, having returned to your place and your glory in the universal harmonies, you will repeat with all the worlds the testimony which God bore to Himself after He had finished His work: "God saw all the things that he had made, and they were very good."*

* Genesis i.

# THE GENERAL PLAN OF CREATION.

My Lord,—Gentlemen,

In our last conference we sought to discover by what process or from what motive the world came forth from the hands of God; we have seen that it was by means of creation and from the motive of goodness. Goodness is, in fact, the characteristic under which the human race has always preferred to conceive God, as it is also that of the men who have, in the highest degree, attracted the love and veneration of ages. Whosoever has not been distinguished by this august sign has not reached the fulness of glory, and neither the fame of brilliant conceptions, nor the success of arms, nor scorn of life, has sufficed without goodness to uphold the remembrance even of Alexander or Marcus Aurelius. That of God, more especially, rests upon the same basis, and nothing is more natural to us than to repeat with David: "The Lord is sweet to all, and his tender mercies are over all his works."*

God, then, having made the world from goodness, that is to say, in the design of communicating to it His properties, which are none other than perfection and beatitude, we must now learn the plan followed by Him in the realisation of that generous purpose. Now every plan is composed of two necessary elements; of the materials which served to found it and the ordinance to be given thereto. I have, then, to-day, to treat of the materials of creation and their general ordinance.

According to Catholic doctrine, God employed in His work; which is the universe, two perfectly dissimilar materials, namely, matter and spirit.

In the first place, what is matter? If I tell you that it is

* Psalm cxliv. 9.

something possessing weight, you will oppose to me the imponderable fluids. If I say that it is something possessing extent, you will reply: Many philosophers consider that it may be reduced to atoms, that is to say, to points indivisible and consequently unextended. If I say that it is something possessing colour, you will object that it may easily be conceived as colourless. So is it also in regard to taste and sound. But this work of spoliation, by which we successively deprive matter of its apparent attributes, has nevertheless a limit where the critical effort of our minds must halt. Whatever we may do, there will always remain to it the permanent susceptibility of receiving form and movement. I say of receiving them, for we see clearly that it possesses neither thought, nor will, nor liberty, no personal activity or command. It is at the same time active and inert: active, since it is a force; inert, because it does not act spontaneously, but under the empire of an irresistible necessity.

Spirit, on the contrary, has neither form nor movement of translation from one place to another; it does not fall under the investigation of our senses. It thinks, it wills, it is free; no necessity acts upon it. In vain is it commanded, if it does not command of itself, and all the assaults of power are as nothing against a single soul that respects itself.

Such are the materials of the world. Catholic doctrine knows none other; the senses and reason reveal to us only these. Shall we here also find rationalism in our way? Yes, we shall find it; and again I remind you that Catholic doctrine will never establish a single dogma without finding that rationalism sets up a negation against it. It is so now and always. It is the nature of error to create resources against all truth, otherwise the liberty of our intelligence would be but a chimera.

If anything is clearly proved it is certainly the coexistence in the world of matter and spirit. What is more manifest? Matter is the object of our senses; they see, they handle, they feel it, they make use of it as they please, according to invariable laws discovered by science and verified by experience. No effort of the will is capable of destroying the impression produced in the whole human race by the constant spectacle of the universe. Spirit is not less evident and eloquent to us, it is even more so. For, spirit is ourselves. We have no need to place ourselves in communication with it as with an object foreign to us; it is intimately present to us; each of its acts reveals it to us in its special faculties, in its empire over matter and ideas, in its spontaneity and its liberty. Yet, who would believe it? two contradictory doctrines have appeared in the history of human reason; one which denies the existence of matter, another which denies the existence of spirit. Idealism maintains that all, in nature, is immaterial; materialism affirms that all is body.

And truly, if ever error could be a noble and a sacred thing, we should be entitled to say so of idealism, which pretends to deny the existence only of the inferior part of creation, and fails to understand what relations a substance deprived of all intelligence and sentiment can hold with God. Why, in fact, did Mallebranche, that illustrious Christian philosopher, say that, without the authority of faith, he should not believe in the existence of matter, if it were not because he could not explain to himself the object of God in creating it? And have we not ourselves shown that the object of God in creation was to communicate His perfection and beatitude to beings the issue of His omnipotent goodness? Now, in what manner does matter, incapable of knowing and loving, respond to that view of the Creator? How is it able to reach even the frontier of the divine order, where all is knowledge, love, comprehension? We can conceive the motive and work of God in creating spirits, images of His own nature, endowed with the privilege of scrutinising the invisible world, presumptive inhabitants of eternal glory, vessels of voluntary praise, humble yet possible companions of the most holy Trinity. But who will ever conceive the office of matter in relation to God, and even in relation to created spirits? If not eternal, why should it have been created for a day? If it is to outlive time, what will be its part in eternity, that is to say, in the pure reign of God?

Some ancient sages, endeavouring to penetrate this mystery, had thought that the function of material substance was the limitation of spirits, which, from their nature, as they believed, had no barriers between them and the infinite. But sound theology rejects that interpretation. Created spirits have their measure in the divine will that produces them; since they are created they are limited, seeing that uncreated existence enters into the notion of the infinite. Let us suppose, however, that the immaterial and intelligent being meets with no limit in its personal essence, you cannot suppose that God would impose a limit upon it from jealousy—from fear lest it should become equal to Himself—and therefore imprison it in the sepulchre of a body! Can you suppose that men are but gods enslaved to a sensible organisation? Ah! had God been able to create infinite spirits, be sure He would have created them. He desired nothing more than to extend the orbit of creation; and you will soon learn that matter itself, so far from having become an instrument of restriction in His hands, has been one of the resources employed by His wisdom to enlarge the field of the universe.

Matter, like spirit, has been called to enjoy divine perfection and beatitude, and the more incapable it was of this the more God has willed to make naught of such difficulty, reserving to Himself the glory, if I may so speak, of stamping the seal of His power and mercy upon a substance in which nothingness appeared to dispute the empire with Him. However inert matter may be, however dumb, deaf, blind, insensible, it is indifferent thereto: listen to the Apostle St. Paul taking up its cause and speaking to you of its destiny: "All flesh," he says, "is not the same flesh. . . . there are bodies celestial and bodies terrestrial; but one is the glory of the celestial and another the terrestrial. . . . The body is sown in corruption, it shall rise in incorruption; it is sown in dishonour, it shall rise in glory; it is sown in weakness, it shall rise in power; it is sown a natural body, it shall rise a spiritual body."* You hear that St. Paul is not troubled about the meanness of our dust: he does not believe in its final wretchedness; he beholds it so transfigured as to become spiritual, and if you would hear him again foretelling its future, listen once more: "For the expectation of the creature waiteth for the revelation of the sons of God. For the creature was made subject to vanity, not willingly, but by reason of him that made it subject, in hope: because the creature also itself shall be delivered from the servitude of corruption into the liberty of the glory of the children of God."† What language! What splendour! What promises! Thus the most vile matter is in labour for its future greatness, as well as man himself; it awaits the final revelation, which will distinguish the children of God and mark out a place for them in the ages which have neither

---

* 1 Cor. xv. 39, 40, 42–44.  † Rom. viii. 19–22.

shadow nor turning; it will take part in the deliverance of spirits, and their beatitude will, in a certain degree, depend upon its own, since its own will serve to the liberty of their glory. What singular expressions, gentlemen, and how truly may the substance honoured by such prophecies hold in contempt the premature insults of ignorance and error!

The king of Macedonia once said: "If I were not Alexander, I would be Diogenes!" Let me say: "If I were not spirit, I would be matter!" For I should still be the work of God, the fruit of His thought and of His goodness. His eye would still be upon me, and, united in human nature to an immortal soul, after having served it here below in its need I should one day serve it in its felicity, which I should share.

In proceeding to expose to you the general ordinance of the world, I shall, however, hope to show you the part which matter fills there, and consequently enable you more clearly to see the reason of its existence and its creation.

The other rationalist camp denies the reality of spirit. It aspires to convince us that there is nothing in the world but the palpable, divisible, and miserable substance which falls under the investigation of our outer senses, and if it acknowledges the phenomena of thought and will, it attributes them to the very organism of the living body. You perceive that this doctrine is very different from the other. The first, although false, tended to the elevation of man; this tends to his abasement. The first induced us lowly to estimate the inferior part of our being; this tends to degrade, to immolate its superior part. What can have led sages—this is the name they bear—what can have led them to this parricidal act? The natural tendency of beings is to grow great; all, even those who obey only instinct, have a tendency towards pride. How is it that man, the visible masterpiece of creation, has employed his thought, which raises him above all the others, to destroy the very basis of his greatness, and to descend by his own choice from the rank of immortal intelligences? I know not whether there are any materialists in this assembly, and you know with what pious respect I am accustomed to treat, not error, but individuals. On this occasion, however, I cannot curb the liberty of my ministration, and I shall fearlessly say that materialism is a doctrine against nature, an abject doctrine, whose origin can only be explained by the corruption of the human heart. We are too manifestly spirits, there are not reasons enough against the dignity of our being to lead us to depreciate our own selves, if passions of a lower and dastardly order did not rise up within us against ourselves, in order to dethrone, with our spiritual essence, our ideas of truth, justice, order, responsibility—illustrious and incorruptible guests whose presence wearies vice and excites revolt. Vice knows no peace and wills to possess it. The soul opposes to it remorse, that last crown of corrupted man, that domestic and sacred voice which invites us to good, that good genius of the republic which inhabits ruins, and which appeared again to Brutus, in the fields of Pharsala, on the eve of the day when Rome was to fall. Oh!—pardon my doubts!—But if you were not pure, if remorse troubled you with its stern voice, in mercy and love for yourselves, do not drive it from you: as long as it is the companion of your soul you will not have lost the remains of your greatness and your hope; remorse precedes virtue as the dawn precedes the day, and vice should respect it out of respect for itself.

But when vice has no longer the instinct of its rehabilitation, remorse becomes its chief and last enemy, and spares nothing in order to extirpate its very roots, which is our mind itself. Materialism is the result of that exterminating war of evil against good; it is no other thing than the supreme effort to stifle remorse. And this is why I call it an abject and an unnatural doctrine. If this should seem rash, I offer no excuse for it. What! You attack my very essence, you reject me to the limits of mere animality, you treat me as the equal of a dog! What do I say?—you dare to write that "Man is a digestive tube pierced at both ends." . . . Ah! gentlemen, do not laugh; it would grieve me bitterly to have excited your laughter; hear, hear these things with the silence of scorn. What! men dare to write that "man is a digestive tube pierced at both ends," and, armed in all the greatness of truth against imposture, shall I not turn back in scorn and trample under foot that most vile doctrine?

I ought to say no more on this subject; I ought not to give so much honour to materialism as to ask it to explain itself. We will do so, however, with your permission. We will ask these proud gladiators of matter what they have seen in man to lead them to contest his intelligent and free nature. Do they deny the phenomena of thought? Are they blind to those of the will? No, they admit them; they admit that something extraordinary takes place within us which resembles nothing that falls under the investigation of the senses. But they consider that earth, having attained to a certain degree of perfection, is susceptible of producing sentiment, thought, and will, as it produces roots, flowers, and fruit. Nature, they say, is in a progressive labour which is nowhere interrupted, and which at each degree is manifested by a more perfect production. Man is the term of that fertile progression; he unites in himself all the anterior progressions, and his brain, the masterpiece of the wisest organisation, causes thought to emerge from it as naturally as the tree puts forth its buds.

How is it that this ingenious picture, for I will not call it analysis, has excited only coldness and incredulity in nearly the whole of mankind? How is it that the spiritualist philosophy has always obtained the glory of moving the heart of the people as well as that of the thinker; whilst materialism, a doctrine of decadency, seduces only a few souls in declining nations? Because spirit affirms itself with a presence so vigorous that reasoning and analysis perish before the splendour of that affirmation. How should it be otherwise? My spiritual being is myself: I feel the truth of it. I feel the distinction between my soul and my body with such force that my whole life appears to me to be but a confronting of the one with the other, and that each instant brings to me a conviction of their duality as strong as the certainty of their union. I see that I am two and one with a clearness which nothing diminishes, because nothing combats against the real presence of things. And what indeed is said against it? They oppose to it a progression of matter; but a progression is but the development of a germ which never changes its nature in that development. Elevate a force, according to the mathematical expression, to the second, the third, the tenth power; you will never gather in the force doubled, tripled, decupled, anything but the primitive element contained therein. In order that matter, transfigured in its form, may produce sentiment, thought, and will, the smallest material particle must be a being exercising feeling, thought, and volition, but in an inferior degree, susceptible of increase or of perfection as it is seen in the infancy of man compared with his maturity. Now, is it so? Does materialism even pretend that it is so? It does not believe that a grain of dust includes in miniature the intellectual functions of man, as a drop of water includes the properties of the ocean. Common sense too strongly rejects such folly, consequently matter elevated by organisation to whatever point you will, to the hundredth or the thousandth power, will never produce anything but the development of what it is, that is to say, more perfect forms, more complicated movements, sculpture and architecture more worthy of admiration.

Men wonder—and it is another objection against spiritualism—at the reciprocal influence which the soul and the body exercise over each other. Why not, if they are really united? This union may appear strange, inexplicable, but what of that? It is a fact. The fact once proved by the certainty which we have of our double nature, spiritual and material in one sole personality, it is very natural that there should be an action of one upon the other, without which there would be no communication between them; and if there were no communication between them, they would be separated instead of being united.

Thus even as exterior objects, acting upon the brain by the intermediary of the senses, convey to the soul impressions from without, the soul in its turn conveys to the brain, and by it to the rest of the sensible organisation, the rebound of its intimate and immaterial life. Thence arise those inveterate habits which take their source at the same time in the two parts of our being, both being in some manner bent thereto by the repetition of the acts, and become the slaves of our depraved wills after having been at first only their instruments. It is this which has given birth to that new science of phrenology, which abuses phenomena of the correspondence of the soul with the body and the body with the soul, in order to attack the free-will of man. I do not examine whether aptitudes and passions have really a representative sign in the exterior envelope of the brain; let us suppose it. What does it prove against human liberty? It is manifest that the soul and the body are in unceasing communication, and that every act—even an inward act—of vice or virtue, resounds somewhere in our mortal envelope and marks out traces of happiness or misery. These subtle traces, in their turn, react upon the profound seat of our internal activity, and solicit there the return of the same movements, that is to say, of the same thoughts and the same desires. Catholic doctrine consents to this; it does more than consent: it is the basis of its spiritual therapeutics, or, if you prefer it, of the medicinal treatment which it applies to the maladies of our soul. This is why the Gospel commands Christians to chastise their bodies in order to liberate and purify their hearts. This is why the Church imposes abstinences and fasts; this is why she commands labour, and why, after the example of Jesus Christ, her founder, she blesses those who weep and suffer; because, besides the benefit of an accepted expiation, there is in the afflictions of the body the infallible efficacy of reforming the senses. However ancient, however powerful, may be the traces of sin in the mysterious recesses of the body, the soul, aided by grace, fortified by penance, is able slowly to efface them, and to substitute the restoring vestiges of virtue. Thence, even in physiognomy, spring those singular illuminations which penetrate through the obscure traces of vice. The soul, after having ennobled the subterranean regions which crime had polluted, reaches the brow of man, and sheds upon it those serene and holy rays which soften the regard even of those who know not God. The gloomy shadows of sin fly away before the creative glory of virtue, and that which still remains of them in the premature sinking of the body is only a sign of mortality vanquished by the eternal beauty of Christ.

O visages of the saints! gentle yet firm lips accustomed to name the name of God and kiss the cross of His Son; regards full of kindness and love which perceived a brother in the most poor and lowly among creatures; hair silvered by meditation on eternity, sacred rays of the soul resplendent in old age and in death: happy are those who have beheld them! more happy those who have understood them and received from their transfigured glebe lessons of wisdom and immortality!

But what am I doing?—Am I pretending to demonstrate to you the existence of spirit, the reality of matter? God forbid! I do not stand before you as a philosopher, supported by his reason alone, and trusting only to the discoveries of his own sagacity. I stand here as the envoy of God, as one who bears His word to you, as one armed with the tradition and authority of the Church, and after having established the titles of my mission, I promised you only that rationalism should never oppose to a single Christian dogma negations more probable than the affirmations of faith. Once more I have kept my promise. For I ask, between the faith that affirms the presence in the world of two constitutive elements, matter and spirit, and the rationalism that denies the one or the other, where, even humanly speaking, lies the greater probability of truth? I do not say the certainty, because having found certainty in the order of the divine teachings, it is unnecessary for me again to seek it even there, where, in so many ways, I should be sure to find it. Against rationalism the semblance of truth will suffice for me, and I believe I possess it, and much more, in that question of the double nature of things. Let us hasten now to see the ordinance which God has given them; we shall gather here some rays of light upon the motives that induced the Creator not to content Himself, in the structure of the world, with only one order of materials.

We have said that God, in drawing beings forth from nothingness, proposed to communicate to them His perfection and beatitude. Now the divine perfection is of three kinds; it is metaphysical, intellectual, and moral, and consequently it should be reflected under this triple aspect in the production and disposition of the universe. Let us commence by the metaphysical aspect, which is naturally the first.

God is infinite, He is one, He is many; it is the reunion of these three terms that constitutes His metaphysical perfection. He is great in the depths of His essence, by infinity, unity, and plurality; and this also should be the fount of the grandeur of the universe. But even thereby, the creating thought appears at the very first to meet with an insurmountable obstacle; for, the infinite is incommunicable in its nature. As soon as a thing is created, however vast it may be, it does not exist of itself, and therefore the radical attribute of the infinite is wanting to it. Nevertheless, the world—the work of the infinite in person, the manifestation of his glory—could not be wanting in extent, representative of uncreated immensity. It needed a projection which manifested its origin, and by which every eye on beholding it revolving in the majesty of its orbit might recognise the hand that had launched it forth upon a course and in a space worthy of it. God provided for this. He devised—if I may be permitted to animate the divine action by these human expressions—He devised, between the infinite and the finite, something intermediary, which here below we call the indefinite. I will explain these terms if you will allow me. The infinite is that which has neither beginning nor end; the finite is that which has a beginning and an end;

the indefinite is that which expands between two terms infinitely distant, in such a manner as continually to draw nearer to them. God then resolved to construct the world upon the projection of the indefinite, and thus to impart to His work a figurative character of His unlimited essence.

Nothing opposed this design. Between God, who was about to create, and the nothingness whence being was about to emerge; between God, who is all, and nothingness, which is nothing, there existed of itself an infinite distance. It sufficed to fill it by a progressive creation, which, starting from a unique centre, should tend at the same time, and upon two different roads, towards the two extremities of things; towards nothingness by a graduated diminution, towards God by a constant ascension. But this plan supposed the existence of two quite dissimilar elements; one susceptible of constant diminution in descending towards the negative pole of creation, another capable of constantly perfecting itself in mounting towards the positive or divine pole. You anticipate me, you name matter and spirit: spirit, which is indivisible; matter, unceasingly divided: spirit, the element of the infinitely great; matter, the spirit of the infinitely little: both, in their diverse natures, sufficient to fill by their calculated elevation and degradation the infinite space which separates the supremely imperfect from the supremely perfect. It is St. Augustine who has revealed to us in a single phrase this beautiful law of the genesis of things: listen to this great man: DUO FECISTI, DOMINE, UNUM PROPÉ NIHIL, SCILICET MATERIAM PRIMAM; ALTERUM PROPÉ TE, SCILICET ANGELUM—*Thou hast made two things, O God; one near to nothingness, which is primary matter; the other near to thyself, which is pure spirit.* In virtue of that conception, which was as it were the exordium of the world, God created two lines or two series of beings; one series descending on the side of nothingness, the other ascending towards Himself. The one is known to you by your own senses and by the instruments with which science has endowed the eye of man; the other is revealed to us by faith, and also by the inductions of analogy. For how could we believe that creation stops at ourselves, and that having by our bodies an inferior kindred which extends even into the regions of the imperceptible, we should not have by our spiritual essence a superior kindred which penetrates even into the region of the substantial infinite? Faith teaches us this, reason confirms it to us, the order of the universe absolutely requires it.

Launched from earth to heaven upon that infinite projection, the world, as far as it was possible, had a relation of greatness with God; and by the innumerable multiplication of beings appertaining to each series, and to each degree of these series, it possessed also the divine character of plurality. But unity, the third term of the metaphysical perfection of God, was still wanting to it. There were two worlds, the world of matter and the world of spirit; the terrestrial and the celestial worlds: a supreme unfitness which deprived creation of all harmony and all possibility of being the mirror of its author. But how was this to be remedied? How were two orders so distinct, so radically separated as the material order and the spiritual order, to be really united?

God withdrew within Himself; He took counsel as it were, according to the beautiful indication of Scripture, and in presence of all that was accomplished, before the attentive heavens and trembling earth He pronounced the last creating word; He said: FACIAMUS HOMINEM—*Let us make man!* Man obeyed that voice which should never more cease to give him life and light. A being appeared participating in matter by which he became united to the inferior world, and in spirit by which he became united to the superior world; at the same time body and soul, the body acting with the soul and the soul with the body; not as being two, but as one only; not as brother and sister, but as one single personal being called by the same name, man. In man the mystery of universal unity was solved; placed in the lowest rank of the ascending line of beings, and on the first step of the descending line, concentrating in his personality all the gifts of the mind and all the forces of matter, communicating by his wants with the arctic and antarctic poles of things, the real centre of the creation—he, by his presence, stamps upon it the seal of its unity, and with unity the seal of perfection. Behold man; behold his place and his glory; behold why all the great religious scenes have been enacted upon the earth which he inhabits and in the very bosom of mankind. Rationalism is greatly troubled about the importance which man attributes to himself; it has not disdained to call astronomy to its aid in order to deprive us of the eminent position to which Providence has raised us, and, comparing the insignificance of our race and the inferiority of our planet with all the suns fixed in space, it is pleased to make of us pigmies, not to say the abortions of the universe. Let us leave to rationalism these pitiable gratifications of apostasy; and, as we are not afraid of being kings because we are not alarmed by the duties of the throne, let us learn to measure greatness by the essence and functions of beings, and not by their size or material rapidity of motion. The earth, it is true, is not the astronomical centre of the world; it suffices for it to bear mankind—the real centre of creation.

It is thus that God has communicated to His work the metaphysical perfection with which He is endowed. As to intellectual perfection, the second term of His total perfection, it was naturally to be found in man and in the spirits superior to man, since all of them, by their very essence, are capable of knowing. Matter alone, relegated to the frontiers of nothingness, seemed shut out for ever from the glorious privilege of thought. For God Himself cannot accomplish that which includes an express contradiction, and matter, an inert and divisible substance, rejects, with all the force of an absolute incompatibility, the idea of activity indivisible as thought, free as the will. But God, without performing an impossibility, performed a miracle. He willed then to spiritualise matter, according to the expression of St. Paul, by giving it a share in the most elevated functions of the human soul, and this is the secret which was faintly perceived by Aristotle, when he said: "There is nothing in the intelligence which was not before in the senses." Not that the soul does not receive, prior to all intercourse between itself and nature, a direct illumination from God, an illumination which is to its inner vision what light is to the outer eye; but, notwithstanding that divine communication, thought does not take its form, and, so to say, its outline, until the senses, by means of images and language, have brought to the soul, in its inmost sanctuary, the tribute of their exploration in the visible world. Man thinks only by means of the totality of his being, as he lives only by means of the totality of his being. All idealist or materialist systems are false, because they divide man by making him a simple intelligence or only a body. Man, in all his operations, is neither a body nor a spirit; he is man, that is to say, that marvellous unity resulting from two substances intimately interwoven, the material substance and the immaterial substance. Everything that separates these destroys man.

Thus matter is raised to an incomprehensible state of dignity. Contemplate that unnamed dust at your feet, which is the last degree of abasement that being reaches before your eyes. Contemplate it. You bore it along but just now without deigning to notice it; a puff of air will cast it into a field; darkness and light embody it in the frail tissue of a plant. It is already wheat. The same chance that cast it under your feet brings it upon your table in its new form. You recognise it no longer, and yet it will soon become a part of yourself. See, it flows in your veins; it penetrates the tissues of your body; it mounts even to the supreme seat of your exterior activity, to that calm and elevated throne, where, under the protection of a powerful shield, the purest elements of life are silently elaborated. There it encounters the reciprocal action of the soul and the body; it comes between them; it knocks at the august portal of your intelligence; it helps you to think, to will; it is yourself, and yet is the grain of dust under your feet.

I was then justified in calling St. Paul to bear witness to the grandeur of the world even in its lowest element. What if I were to advance yet further—if I pronounced to you that famous phrase: "The Word was made flesh"? If I showed you dust in its eternal wedlock with God? But let us not rob the future to serve the present; let us leave a shadow upon the Thabor of truth, and terminate this discourse by showing you how God has communicated His moral perfection to the world.

The moral perfection of God is resumed in two words: justice and goodness. In order for the world to receive its communication, it was not enough that man and the superior spirits were endowed with the double faculty of knowing and willing, of knowing good and realising it—another gift was needed, that of choosing between good and evil. For, without that free choice, what, in them, would justice or goodness have been? A necessary perfection stripped of all personal merit, which would have made of their life a succession of acts irresistibly ordered and accomplished. Now in God, whose total perfection was to be reproduced, that fatality does not exist. God is a free being. Naturally held in the immutable order of His essence, He acts without in full liberty; He creates or He does not create, He gives in the time and measure determined by His sovereign will; and even when He remains within His necessary operations, such as the relations of the three divine persons, He is subject to nothing exterior to Himself. He is neither commanded nor necessitated. If, on the contrary, man and pure spirits had no choice between God and themselves, between the infinite and the finite, their personality would exist only as an absolute dependence upon the divine personality; they would be others and not themselves. They would not give themselves from justice or goodness, but from subjection to an empire foreign to their own deliberation. They would be deprived of moral perfection, because they would possess a morality totally inamissible, and consequently impersonal.

In God, it is true, morality is inamissible, but it is so without being impersonal, because it is not the action of another that subjugates the divine will, whilst in the creature deprived of free will it would be the infinite who oppressed the finite. The human will would become absorbed in the divine will.

It is needless to add that matter itself, raised to the state of humanity, shares, by its association with the soul, the honours of free will, and that it thus enters into participation of the rights and perils of the moral order. You will have already drawn this conclusion if my words have but thrown a little light upon the ways of divine wisdom in communicating to the world its triple and adorable perfection.

The consequence of perfection is beatitude. God is infinitely happy, because He is infinitely perfect. Having then called the world to enjoy His perfection, He should also have called it to enjoy His beatitude; and as beatitude terminates all in God, it is also necessarily the final term of creation for every being who has not been unworthy of his destiny. Here I touch the Gordian knot of truth, and I venture to believe that you have severed it yourselves. You will not ask me why God has not given beatitude without conditions of merit; if I am not deceived, you know the reason. If, indeed, God had willed to communicate to the world all His properties, He should have communicated them in the order in which He Himself possesses them, and in the only order in which it was possible for Him to communicate them all. Now, the divine properties are simply perfection and beatitude; perfection, the cause of beatitude; and beatitude, the effect of perfection. If God had changed the order, in plunging us by the sole act of our birth into the possession of Himself, whence His felicity springs, He would have deprived us of the first of His properties, which is perfection. For, as we have seen, free will is a necessary element thereof, which the direct and beatific vision of God would not have permitted us to possess, even for a single instant. Lost at the moment of our birth in the abyss of an infinite attraction, we should have offered to divine goodness no representation of His own liberty, no virtue, no merit, no return worthy of His gratuitous and liberal dispensation towards us. God owed it then to us and to Himself to retard our beatitude in favour of our perfection. But to retard it was to hide Himself for a time from created beings, to clothe Himself before them in the veil of finite things, in order that, choice being possible to them, trial should be also possible with choice, and that from trial there should spring up within them justice worthy of praise, goodness worthy of love.

Thus the world was given possession of a sovereignty which placed it with glory in presence of God. Thus, having God for principle and end, it should gravitate towards Him by a voluntary and grateful perfection, even to the day when, the entire orbit of its trial being achieved, it will repose in the bosom of God Himself in a degree of beatitude equal to its fidelity.

I have traced for you the whole plan of Creation. I have shown you the materials employed therein, the ordinance they received, the reasons of that ordinance, and already knowing your beginning, you have learned to know your end. Your end and your beginning do not differ; God is your father, and God is also your end. He is the *Alpha* and the *Omega* of your destiny; you cannot look lower without losing yourselves, rise less high without perishing. In vain, being ungrateful, will you appeal to His goodness against His justice. I have just destroyed that hope by showing you in goodness itself the root of your duties. It is doubtless goodness that said: "Come, ye blessed of my Father, possess you the kingdom prepared for you from the foundation of the world."\* But it is also goodness that said: "Be you therefore perfect, as also your heavenly Father is perfect."† For the natural movement of goodness is to communicate its properties, and God having only His perfection and His beatitude, the effect of the divine

\* Matt. xxv. 34. † Matt. v. 48.

goodness is to communicate both to you in the same order in which they are in Himself. If you refuse perfection because it exacts sacrifice from you, at the same time you refuse beatitude, which is its consequence. That order does not depend upon God; it is His proper and rigorous nature; the very nature of goodness of which justice is but the sanction.

# MAN AS AN INTELLIGENT BEING.

My Lord,—Gentlemen,

We already know the two terms of the mystery of destinies; we know what is our principle and our end. But that knowledge, all-important though it be, is far from being sufficient for us. It is a great thing to be assured that God is the source from whence we spring, that our end is to attain to His perfection and beatitude; it remains, however, for us to be directed upon that perilous road of which God occupies the two extreme points; for if we are unacquainted with its secrets, we are in danger of going astray in our very way, and of descending towards death instead of advancing towards Him from whom proceeds all life, all perfection, all felicity. Where is then the road which we ought to follow? Is it traced out? Is it known with certainty?

You cannot doubt about it; God, who has revealed to us our principle and our end, must also have revealed to us the means of proceeding from one to the other, otherwise the object He had in view, which was to satisfy His goodness by communicating Himself to His creatures, would not have been realised. Here we quit the universe in order to concentrate our attention upon man in particular; for it is man who first interests us, and moreover, in seeking the paths which God has opened to us that we may mount towards Him, we unceasingly encounter the rest of creation either disputing the passage with us or opening it before us; and the theology of man, in virtue of the unity that co-ordains and combines every part of the divine work, will constantly blend with the theology of the universe. But man himself, within his proper nature, is an infinitely complex being. By his thought, he belongs to the intellectual order; by his will, to the moral order; by his union with his fellow-creatures, to the social order; by his body, to the physical order; by his entire soul, to the religious order: and, under all these relations, he has received means of attaining his end, which is perfection and beatitude. It is needful then, in order completely to unfold his destiny, to study man himself, and successively as an intelligent, moral, social, physical, religious being; and under these divers aspects to take account of the roads which eternal wisdom has prepared for him, and in which he must walk in order to avoid perishing. The course will be long; it will embrace not only the remaining conferences of this year, but all those which will follow even to the last day in which God may permit me to instruct you. In a word, the principle and the end of man being known to us, nothing remains in the development of doctrine but to expose to you, in all their historical and dogmatic course, the means given to man to attain his end.

I enter at once upon this subject, and man as an intelligent being will form my exordium. Intelligence is the faculty of knowing. To know, is to see that which is; and to see that which is, is to possess truth; for truth is no other thing than that which is, inasmuch as it is perceived by the mind. Whence it results that truth is the object of the intelligence, and that the function of the intelligence is to seek, to penetrate, to retain truth; to live by truth, and for truth; this is its perfection and its beatitude. In the first place, it is its perfection; for the mind out of truth is in the state of ignorance or error; it sees not or sees badly, and in either case it is deprived of its object and function. It is like an eye which looks without seeing, or which sees that which has no reality; an organ useless and dead in the first case, a false and dangerous instrument in the second.

But if truth be the perfection of the intelligence, it may be said without further proof that it is also its beatitude. For the one is the inevitable consequence of the other. As soon as a faculty is united to its object, as soon as it accomplishes its mission, it attains a state of repose because it attains its object; a glorious repose, because it is legitimate; full of joy, because it has been produced by God according to the pattern of His own operations, wherein all ends in transport. Therefore, in receiving the light of truth, the intelligence reposes, rejoices, exults; in fine, is happy according to the nature of the vision that enlightens and fills it. Daily we experience this beatification of the understanding. Even in the lowest regions of nature there is no being or phenomenon, how imperceptible soever it may be, how indifferent soever it may appear, the discovery of which does not cause us a kind of magic transport. You all know the history of that great geometrician who, after having long battled with a problem that arrested his genius, all at once penetrated its secret whilst he was in a bath. Forgetting himself, he rose, and, the folly of enthusiasm depriving him even of the consciousness of his nudity, he ran through the streets of Syracuse, exclaiming: "I have found it! I have found it!" This is the living image of those holy nuptials between the mind and intelligible light, when man has shown himself worthy of that immaterial alliance by a life which lessens the subjection of his double nature to the inferior order. Those blissful joys depend together upon the greatness of the mind and the greatness of the ideas that inundate it; they blend with the shores of the intelligence and the luminous course which flows between them.

Sometimes the mind is great without the light being also great; then come those times of mysterious sadness whose traces you may have observed on the generous brows of many of your contemporaries. Victims of doubt, they have drunk from the cup of knowledge without drinking from the cup of truth. They have studied past ages, interrogated the seas, followed the orbit of the heavenly bodies, nothing has escaped the perspicacity of their meditations, and yet a veil has remained before them which hinders them from thoroughly fathoming what they see, and from taking account of the illuminations of their own life. Light itself is darkness to them; each new discovery opens to them a new abyss; and like the labourer ploughing in the fields of Thebes or Babylon, who constantly strikes against unaccountable ruins, these mighty investigators of worlds, at each furrow which they trace in the immensity of things, raise up, even from the very bosom of science, great and painful obscurities. They have neither the peace of ignorance nor the peace of error; they see too much not to know, too little to understand, and however great may be the crime that hides truth from them, they have at least the honour of being unhappy because they do not possess it.

But after these long torments of doubt, if the veil be at last drawn aside, then the intelligence receives one of those vibrations whose voluptuous pain no tongue can describe. Then

Augustine rises, and, for the first time, finding even friendship irksome, he withdraws to give current to his feelings in a torrent of solitary tears. He, who was lost in the vain love of glory and creatures, sees all the charms that deceived his youth vanish in a moment. Truth enraptures him; the azure plains of Lombardy, the hopes of renown, the most tender professions of erring hearts, have no longer any power to move him; he departs, leading his aged mother by the hand, and already from the port of Ostia he sees the obscure solitude which he thinks will hide him for ever from the admiration of the world as from the dreams of his past life. Tears of great men, heroic sacrifices, virtues born in a single hour, and which ages cannot destroy, you teach us the price of truth! You prove that it is indeed the perfection and beatitude of the intelligence!

Therefore one of the most formidable crimes is that of betraying and labouring against truth; for it is to betray our highest good, to strike us at the very height from whence our glory and felicity descend. What is man without intelligence, and what is intelligence without truth? If you deprive man of intelligence, he is nothing more than the dethroned king of the animal world; if, leaving intelligence to him, you withhold from him the gift of truth, you dig out for him an abyss as deep as the infinite; you prepare for him a torment of hunger never to be appeased, an aspiration which can never attain to anything but grasping shadows in an immense and deceptive void. What can be more terrible than this condition? What more criminal than to be its willing instrument? Therefore, falsehood has ever been abhorred by the human race; and, even in things where its insignificance would seem excusable, it brings infallible scorn upon the lips which give it utterance. We do not forgive the man who, knowing truth, willingly substitutes for it the adulterous language of error. How much less will God and mankind pardon those who designedly stand up against the most holy doctrines that ages have bequeathed to us, and who, despairing of conquering them by calm discussion, arm themselves against them with all the resources of violence and cunning! This has too often been witnessed, and we must never lose an opportunity of protesting against those pusillanimous conspiracies of might; the powers instituted for the conservation of all rights and possessions have been seen to declare open war against the highest of all rights, the right to know; against the richest of all possessions, namely, truth.

Jealous of its power, which, indeed, is the greatest known in the world, they strive to dethrone it, in order to set up in its place and to their own profit the reign of interests and passions. Anything suits them better than truth; they accept, protect, give liberty to everything but truth. They pursue truth so exclusively, with so much art and perseverance, that they make it known by that same sign, and their very persecution becomes a mark of certainty which presents it to the legitimate adorations of the whole earth.

But do not wonder if truth some day or other takes vengeance upon its oppressors. As men are not able to ruin authority without striking at the root of the human understanding, sooner or later a kind of frenzy urges them beyond all fear and respect, and drives them with open arms against that which is. This is the time of reprisals, the time foretold by St. Paul when he wrote thus to the Romans: "The wrath of God is revealed from heaven against all ungodliness and injustice of those men who detain the truth of God in injustice."* Then kings grow pale and kingdoms are troubled; night gathers in Babylon; Baltazzar sees the hand that condemns him, and the sword of Cyrus waits not for to-morrow. I am not reciting history; no, it is not history. Look around you; we are in Babylon, we sit at the feast of Baltazzar! †

Must I ask your indulgence if I have allowed myself to yield to the emotions of a time so fertile in great lessons? Have I betrayed the interests of truth by showing you, in the catastrophes of our age, the avenging part which truth plays therein? If it be so, may you and truth forgive me, and let us remount together to the peaceful regions where nothing earthly disturbs the contemplation of causes and laws.

I have just proved that truth is the perfection and beatitude of the intelligence; and, since God in creating us has willed to communicate to us perfection and beatitude, I draw therefrom this consequence, that He has communicated truth to us. And it is, in fact, what Catholic doctrine teaches. If we listen to it, it teaches that God in sending us into the world did not abandon our mind to the hazard of its own discoveries, but enlightened it from the beginning with such knowledge that truth really existed therein. What was that primitive knowledge which, without being infinite, was nevertheless truth? That

* Rom. i. 18.   † A.D. 1848.

question leads us back to the definition which I gave you on commencing this conference. Truth, I said, is that which is, inasmuch as it is perceived by the mind. We halted there without advancing that other question, which we can no longer avoid. What, then, is that which is? Do we understand by this the heavens, the earth, and the seas? Is this that which is? What? the heavens, the earth, the seas, mankind even, all that we see, is stamped with such a character of limit and change that we find there nothing of the grandeur contained in that powerful word—being: human tongues have exhausted their energies to express the nothingness of visible things, and however pride may desire to magnify the theatre upon which it acts, all that it can add to the universe is to discover in it a ray of being, and consequently a ray of truth. Where then is being? Where is that which is? Ah, already I perceive, and even know it. Being is absolute, eternal and infinite unity, plurality without division, the ocean without shores, the centre without circumference, the plenitude that contains itself, the form without figure; the whole, in fine, without which all that is, is but an act and a gift. But in so speaking whom have I named? I have named Him who has said of Himself, EGO SUM QUI SUM—*I am who am.** I have named Him who said also, EGO SUM VERITAS—*I am the truth.*† I have named God. Behold being, and behold truth. God alone is truth, because He alone is being; He does not possess truth as something foreign to Himself, but He is substantial and personal truth, because He is being, possessing Himself; because He is at the same time, and by the same act, the eye that sees, the object seen, and vision. Whoever knows Him knows all; whoever knows Him not knows nothing. What know you indeed out of Him? The phenomena of the world, their laws, the composition and decomposition of bodies, the science of dust. You do not even reach so far; for, to attain to this, you must at least penetrate the last reason of an atom, and where will you find it if you ignore God, the principle and the end of all?

From thence come those lamentations of the greatest minds about the poverty of science, lamentations so eloquently expressed by Solomon, one among them, when he said: "I have seen all things that are done under the sun, and behold all is vanity and vexation of spirit."‡ It is, in fact, because

---

\* Exodus iii. 14.   † John xiv. 6.
‡ Ecclesiastes i. 14.

truth is not under the sun, it is above; it is in God, without whom man knows nothing, neither earth, nor heaven, nor present, nor future, nor man, nor even his own heart. And the more he learns without God and out of God, the more he enlarges, with the circle of his investigations, that of his doubts and torments. On the other hand, the man to whom God is revealed finds himself at the same moment in the centre and at the circumference of things; he sees their initial germ, their development, their term, their reason; if he knows nothing of the detail, he measures the whole, and his mind peacefully reposes in the double joy of knowledge and certainty. In a word, God, being truth, is the proper object of our intelligence, He is its perfection and beatitude; and when I said to you but now, that from the first He had given to us the gift of truth, I said that from the first He had revealed Himself to us.

I find a beautiful confirmation of this in the first page of the Gospel of St. John—". There was," says the Evangelist, " a man sent from God, whose name was John. . . . He was not the light, but was sent to give testimony of the light. That was the true light which enlighteneth every man that cometh into this world." If indeed there exist a supreme light, mother of all minds, its first act, when they come into the world, should be to enlighten them, and it can enlighten them only by making known to them their principle, which is God; their end, which is God; truth, which is God. If it failed to do this, what means would they have of accomplishing their destiny by tending towards their end? They would have none. And thus truth is not only due to them by right of the perfection and beatitude of the intelligence, it is due to them also as the first and necessary means, without which, being ignorant even of the object of their life, it would be impossible for them to advance towards that object, still more impossible to attain it. It is then with justice that Catholic doctrine makes truth—that is to say, the knowledge of God—one of the primitive gifts of man, the starting-point, and I shall add, the milestone of his destiny.

To this, what does rationalism oppose? You shall hear.

Eighteen hundred years ago a Roman proconsul called a prisoner before him, and after having attentively examined him as a man whose appearance was remarkable, he spoke to him these few words: "Thou art the King of the Jews?" The accused replied: " My kingdom is not of this world. If my kingdom were of this world my servants would certainly strive that I should not be delivered to the Jews; but now my kingdom is not from hence." The proconsul continued: "Art thou a king, then?" . The accused answered: "Thou sayest that I am a king. For this end was I born, and for this cause came I into the world, that I should give testimony to truth." The proconsul stood up and said: "What is truth?"\* This terrible question is the same that rationalism even now addresses to us whenever we speak of the basis of all faith and knowledge. Like the Roman, it asks: What is truth? And it must ask this question under pain of not protesting against the very foundation of the whole religious edifice, which is the idea of truth in itself. Now how could rationalism avoid protesting up to this point? How could it permit truth to affirm itself without being contradicted? How could it refrain from digging out under truth an abyss as deep as itself, and from making of the intelligence a faculty without certainty and without any other object than that of an incomprehensible enigma? It would be too weak on the part of rationalism, or too disinterested. It has not committed this fault, it has advanced straight to the question that precedes all others, and whilst the universe proclaims the works of truth, ages repeat its name, minds contemplate it, and its action is perpetuated by evidence and faith through the whole course of human generations, rationalism, opposing to that triumph the imperturbation of some of its sages, has boldly and fearlessly asked: What is truth? It has not denied; for to deny boldly is also to affirm. It has not said: There is nothing; but, Is there anything? It has not said: I know not; but, What do I know? In a word, it has raised up against absolute truth the icy arm of absolute scepticism.

Must we listen? Must we do so much honour to the reason which abdicates its throne, as to listen and reply? Yes, let us listen; let us learn how far intelligence afraid of God is able to annihilate itself from fear of adoring Him. Scepticism reasons thus: Man sees in his mind something which he calls ideas, some, secondary and deduced, others, primordial without a generating principle, and which constitute the inscrutable foundation of his reason. All the ulterior conclusions of the understanding flow from this primary source, wherein analysis readily discerns the notions of being, unity, the infinite, the

---

\* John xviii. 33, 36-38.

absolute, order, justice, which together take the august name of truth, or a still more august name, that of God. This is the fact. But because the mind possesses such ideas, does it follow that out of itself there are realities which correspond to them? It is not the mind itself which is being, unity, the infinite, the absolute, order, justice; nor does the mind directly perceive these. It sees but their shadow, if we may so speak, and the very word idea, in its origin, means only an image. But who can assure us that the image is exact, or even that it is produced by a real object? How can the intelligence, which is limited, be the mirror of the infinite? How, being contingent, relative, fallible, can it be the mirror of the necessary, the eternal, the just, the perfect? What proof have we that the ideal vision does not deceive us, and that it is any other thing than the permanent dream of a passing being? We believe that it is not so, but we believe this without demonstrating it, and we vainly endeavour to establish that demonstration; for every demonstration supposes principles upon which it is based, and these very principles of the understanding we have now to verify. Man encounters there an invincible obstacle; he may be able to ascend the Nile of his thoughts even to the elements which begin its course; beyond this, he becomes lost in a contemplation which renders to him but the sterile repetition of the ideas which he employs to enable him to advance farther. The mind becomes an echo which answers to itself, and its voice appearing to it to come from a greater distance adds only an illusion to its powerlessness.

I do not think that scepticism has said anything stronger than what you have just heard; it has perhaps said this in a more scientific manner, that is to say, in a more obscure manner, but not with more energy and sincerity. And I confess in the first place that it is impossible to demonstrate the primary ideas which form, as it were, the intimate substance of our reason. If they could be demonstrated, they would not be primitive; others would be so, and the same difficulties would arise in regard to them. We demonstrate only that which is a consequence, and not that which is a principle. Now our intelligence, being the faculty of a finite being, can be enlightened only by a transmitted light, a light which begins at a certain point and ends at another, a light which has a principle and an end. As principle, light is an axiom; as end, it is a mystery. Both of these, the axiom and the mystery, are indemonstrable, but the axiom is so on account of its clearness, the mystery on account of its obscurity. As the obscurity of the mystery is insurmountable, the clearness of the axiom is irresistible, and thus the understanding, at the two extremes of the horizon which it embraces, encounters a limit where its power is broken, or where its liberty ceases. It is powerless against the splendour of primary truths, and against the obscurity of final truths; it is exhausted before the former, and yields inevitably to the latter. This is why absolute scepticism is an effort against nature, which terminates only in self-deception, and in placing the actions of the man in perpetual contradiction with the reasonings of the sage. "If," said Pascal, "there is an impossibility of proving, which is invincible to all dogmatism, there is an impossibility of doubting, which is invincible to all pyrrhonism." We make no higher pretensions. For, what is certainty, but the impossibility of doubting? What is rational certainty, but the rapture caused by evidence which captivates the mind? Scepticism, it is true, stands up against the evidence of primordial ideas; it accuses this evidence of being purely subjective, that is to say, speaking so as to be understood, not attaining to a vision of the object which the ideas represent. But what matters it, if that evidence assures us naturally and invincibly of the reality of the things which the ideas represent? There is none but God, who—as being, unity, the infinite, the absolute, order, justice— confounds in His vision the subject and the object, the subject seeing and the object seen. For us who possess truth without being truth, we have no other natural means of beholding it and of being sure of its presence, than the light by which it appears to us, an intervening light which identifies itself with our minds, and which, seizing it as a part of itself, leaves it no other room for doubt than the resource of an act of suicide, so much the more powerless as it is never accomplished.

Indeed it may be said that there is nothing to reply to absolute scepticism; because there is nothing to reply to those who make objects of doubt of their ideas, their words, their very doubts. To reply, is to suppose a reality, were it only that of the objection. Now, as the sceptic destroys all reality, his objection becomes lost with him in the void which he hollows out for himself. It suffices to be silent before a shadow; to live before a dead body. So much the more as scepticism is but the malady of a small number of depraved minds, who, notwithstanding all the energy of their pride and all the glory of their aberrations, have never been able to escape from the chastisement of solitude. The generality of intelligent men have constantly disdained their sophisms, and believed with incorruptible faith in the reality of truth. What need you more? Error is something only by the adhesion of men; wherever mankind is not in a certain measure, nothing is left to error but a little noise in an empty tomb. It is a phantom which hopes to scare us, but the laugh of God and man render justice to it. This suffices for God and mankind; it is sufficient also for me.

If, however, absolute scepticism is but an unimportant chimera, it is not so of another kind of scepticism, which, attacking truth from a lower point, and not contesting its principal basis, produces a serious state of mind which it is necessary for us to notice. Absolute scepticism places in doubt the primitive notions that form the basis of human reason, and consequently the very idea of God; relative or imperfect scepticism gives its adhesion to these ideas, but refuses its faith to certain consequences which flow from them, and which embrace the nature of the divine acts. Absolute scepticism is atheism under a negative form; imperfect scepticism implies only an ignorance of the attributes and operations of God. It believes that God exists, but it does not take account of what He is, of what He does, or of what He wills to do. This is vulgar unbelief, and this very expression teaches us that it is no longer a question of a rare and chimerical condition, but a condition too real, in which man, so far from abdicating his intelligence, derives from it, on the contrary, forces for resisting truth, that is to say, God. Now God, we have said, manifests Himself to man from his cradle, not in an incomplete manner, but to the full extent required by the need in which we stand of knowing our principle, our end, and the means of attaining it. How, then, should a certain portion of mankind be ignorant of God, or are they in a state of doubt with regard to Him which hinders them from appreciating and accomplishing their true destinies? Is it the fault of man or the fault of God? It is needful for us to know this, in order that obscurities may not be left in your minds, which would be so much the more grievous, as it is now our object and yours that you may be instructed in the intellectual ways which God has opened to us that we may ascend towards Him.

I repeat, then: Is that imperfect scepticism—such as I have defined it, and in which so many reasonable beings pine—the work of God or the work of man? Has God been sparing of light, or is it man who has retreated from it? In order to solve this question, we must seek to learn by what means and in what measure God primitively communicated truth to the human race.

Doubtless God could have shown Himself to us face to face, in all the brightness of His essence, and, in this case, scepticism would never have appeared upon earth. Every veil being withdrawn, truth, which is but the divine nature, would have taken irrevocable possession of our intelligence. Intelligible light, instead of appearing to us between the axiom and the mystery, that is to say, with a principle and an end, would have risen for us in all the ineffable plenitude of its own immensity. Evidence would have been ecstasy, certainty would have taken the character of immutability, truth would have become the eternal life of our minds. But that state, so far from being our original state in the divine plan, was precisely the supreme term to which we were called. I have already told you for what reason. I have shown you, in exposing to you the general ordinance of the universe, that God, moved by His goodness, willed to communicate to us His perfection and beatitude, and that beatitude, given without the previous condition of free will, would have deprived us of the merit and glory of perfection. From whence it follows that a state of trial should precede the final state of beatification, and that state of trial, founded upon free will, necessarily included the possibility of believing or not believing, of admitting or rejecting truth, that is to say, the liberty of the understanding. Now, the liberty of the understanding was incompatible with a direct vision of the divine essence, and consequently it was needful that God should veil Himself from our sight, and be for us at the same time a hidden God and a God known, hidden without envy, known freely.

But how are we to see that which is unseen? How are we to know that which does not fall directly under the eye of the mind? If this difficulty could not be solved, the plan of God in creation would be impossible to realise. Can it therefore be solved? God possessed in His double nature the pattern of a double vision, the intuitive vision and the ideal vision. Present to Himself by the intuitive vision, He discovered by the ideal vision the things which He should one day create. These things evidently formed no part of His essence under their positive and realised form; He did not then behold them in Himself under that substantial form; nor did He behold them out of Himself before communicating to them the being which was wanting to them. Where then, and how, did He behold them, if not, as I have just said, by way of image, of representation, under that intelligible and mysterious form which we call an idea? St. Thomas of Aquinas proposes this question: "Are there ideas in God?" And he answers: "Yes; for as the world was not made by chance, but by the action of the divine intelligence, there must have pre-existed in the divine intelligence a form or likeness of the world, and that form or likeness is the idea itself."\* Now, if God beheld the sensible world by the ideal vision, why did not man see the divine world by the same kind of vision? Why, without discovering the very substance of being, unity, the infinite, the absolute, order, justice —all of which things are God under different aspects and under different names—did he not receive the idea of Him in his mind, and with the idea a distinct knowledge of Him, worthy of being called truth? Can we say that we do not understand what is being, unity, the infinite, the absolute, order, justice? And if we do understand this, if this is the very torch that enlightens all the rest, what is within our soul and what is without, can we accuse God of not having enlightened us, of not having cast before our life the pale and uncertain light of visible things? Yes, whilst hiding Himself from us, that is to say, whilst leaving a veil upon the substantial fount of His being, God has fully given Himself to us, by the exact impression of His likeness in the living flesh of our understanding. He has traced out in it luminous furrows, and with a generous hand has sown that incorruptible germ of truth which teaching, reflection, experience, and even the course of our years, unceasingly develop, so far as to cause us to attain, save by our own fault, to divine maturity; to that glorious moment when the image of God, fully formed within us, bursts the envelope which covers it, and rejoins in immortality the ineffable type which was its father, and which recognises its son.

---

\* Summa, first part, quest. 15, art. 1.

It is not then the want of light that precipitates a part of mankind into scepticism and keeps them away from truth, it is the abuse of their free will. The darkness wherein they lose God, is voluntary darkness; God shows Himself, and they fly from Him; God is the object present to their intelligence, and they choose to make of their intelligence a sepulchre or a chaos, rather than adore the star that shines upon it. They abandon that inner light, the only true light, to pursue the obscure and powerless attractions of the material universe from which they expect the joy of apostasy in the pride of false science. And yet the universe, all limited as it is, all pale and silent as it rises before our minds, is itself full of God. If it be not His likeness, it contains at least a vestige, a lineament of Him; from the hyssop to the cedar, from the dew of morning to the evening star, all nature is a reflection of the divine power, beauty, and goodness. God, who in the body of man has associated matter with the most subtle operations of the mind, has willed, in the body of the world, to associate it with the revelation which His mind perpetually makes to our own. To each ray of ideal light there corresponds a ray of sensible light; to each vision of the uncreated world, a vision of the created; to each voice of the one, the voice of the other. But man separates what God has united; enlightened by a double light, because of his double substance, he does not perceive that both meet in a single fount, as our double substance terminates in one single personality, and, dividing truth by a divorce which destroys it, he opposes the revelation from without to the revelation from within, nature to God, matter to spirit. Or at least he disdains the superior light, as a sort of vague apparition in a badly defined horizon, whilst he cleaves to the inferior light as to the only one which possesses a precise and positive character. From that moment, all that relates to God, His attributes, His acts, becomes obscured in that adulterous understanding; even if he does not descend to absolute scepticism, he clearly distinguishes only that which strikes the senses, and the true, in his eyes, is that alone which bears the stamp of a palpable and vulgar reality.

Are there then really more obscurities in the mind than in the body? Does the sensible world possess more clearness than the intelligible world? Is earth instead of heaven the great illuminator of man, and has God erred in the construction of our being so far as to have sacrificed the part which tends towards Him to that which tends towards nothingness?

You do not think so: Catholic doctrine affirms the contrary for us, and the most simple observation of the exercise of our faculties will show us that Catholic doctrine is in the right. Even natural science—that is to say, that which occupies itself only with the visible order—would be unable to subsist without employing notions which it draws from the invisible or metaphysical order. Despoil man of these fertile principles, take from him the ideas of being, unity, extent, force, relation, what would the universe be for him? Precisely what it would be for an animal—a spectacle. He would behold it without thinking about anything but beholding it; so far from penetrating its laws, he would not even have a confused presentiment of what a law is. A purely instinctive being, rendering to the world nothing superior to the world, he would stand mute before it, and his hand, which now leads the distant stars, would never beforehand have traced out for them the inevitable course which they unconsciously follow. It is the mind that sheds light upon the obscurity of nature; it is the mind that discovers the connection and the cause of phenomena; it is the mind that measures, calculates, analyses, defines, dictates orders to matter; in fine, that unravels in that labyrinth the thread left there by God, and by which He still holds it suspended to the will that created it. But the mind without the idea is but an unlighted torch, and the idea without a germ sown from above, greater and clearer than all the worlds, is itself but the powerless reflection of nature upon a faculty which, possessing nothing, has nothing to respond thereto. In vain materialism tells us that sensation becomes an idea on falling into the intelligence; it is as if it said that limit on entering into void becomes infinite. Sensation, because of the intimate union between the soul and the body, may awaken the intelligible grain that reposes in the depths of the mind; it may draw it forth from a kind of solitary abstraction, which is not in relation with the constitution of a being at the same time spiritual and material; but it is impossible for it to give to the mind what it does not possess, or to receive from the mind that which itself had not. Two lights become strengthened by uniting; a ray of light does not become the sun by passing through darkness.

It is then by an abuse even of the forces of the intelligible and divine order, that man withdraws from the exalted regions of the mind to bury himself in the science of terrestrial phenomena. He draws from his intelligence treasures of knowledge and harmony; he scatters them with profusion upon the world; next, beholding it reinvested with that sublime beauty which he has made for it, he believes that it is the world which has enlightened him, that in it alone is full certainty, that it alone merits the honour of assiduous cultivation, and, banishing God to an inaccessible throne, he is not slow to lose sight of Him, to forget Him, to misunderstand Him, to have no other notion left of Him than a notion vague and profitless. Thus is imperfect scepticism formed from the voluntary predominance of the material order over the ideal order.

But there is another cause of this, about which I must not be silent, and the exposition of which will fully make known to you the means which God has employed to initiate our intelligence to the perfection and beatitude of truth.

In depositing within us the ideal or intelligible seed, in placing us by our senses in relation with the phenomena and laws of the universe, God enlightened us by a double revelation, the one interior, the other exterior. This was a great gift; but it was not to communicate Himself to us personally, inasmuch as He is truth; had He remained there and given us nothing more, we should have known Him only by means of nature and ideas, that is to say, indirectly. He willed to advance further, and, without however revealing to us His essence, to establish personal relations between our minds and His own. He spoke to us then. It is a fundamental point of Catholic doctrine that a word of God was, from the very first, shed upon mankind, and that it has never ceased to exist and to spread in the world, either adulterated or in a pure state, as an immortal echo of truth; an echo often weakened, often corrupted, but rising again from its ruins through all generations, and recalling to us, with the eloquence of perpetuity, the existence of God, His nature, His acts; that He is the principle, the end, the means, the key of our destinies. Traditions, common to all nations and all ages, continually attest that oral revelation primitively made to the human race; human language itself, constantly transmitted by hereditary succession, and neither historically nor logically permitting the possibility of an origin by way of invention to be even perceived, bore testimony also to the reality of an anterior and a divine language, from whence our own issued. In the forests man has been found lowered to the rank of animals, from a precocious abandonment which had deprived him of all teaching. Language from his lips was nothing more than a vague, an inarticulate sound, a barbarous cry indicating the presence of sensations and incapable of transmitting ideas. All these facts confirm the page of Scripture which shows God speaking with man; and by the effusion of oral light achieving that which the gift of intelligible and sensible light had commenced within him. But it was reserved for our epoch to acquire from that truth a demonstration as marvellous as it was unlooked for.

Towards the end of the last century, a French priest, touched by the misfortunes of those poor creatures who are born deprived of speech because deprived of hearing—a circumstance which again bears witness to the close connection between the mystery of language and the mystery of a previous instruction—a priest, I say, touched by the condition of the deaf and dumb, devoted his life to leading them out of their sad solitude, by seeking an expression of thought which might reach their own and succeed in drawing from their bosoms, so long closed, the secret of their inner state. He attained this object. Charity, more ingenious than misfortune, had the happiness of opening the issues which nature held closed, and of pouring into these obscure and captive souls the ineffable, although imperfect, light of speech. The benefit was great, the recompense was still greater. As soon as these unknown intelligences were penetrated, investigation discovered in them nothing resembling an idea. I do not speak only of a moral and religious idea, but of a metaphysical idea. Nothing was found there but an image of what falls under the investigation of the senses, there was nothing of what falls from a higher region into the mind. Sensation was caught here in the very fact of powerlessness. What do I say, sensation?— the intelligence itself, although endowed with the ideal seeds of truth, although assisted by the revelation of the sensible world, the intelligence appeared in the deaf and dumb in a state of sterility. Men already ripe in years, born in our civilisation, who had never quitted it, who had been present at all the scenes of family and public life, who had seen our temples, our priests, our ceremonies, those men being interrogated on the intimate working of their convictions, knew nothing of God, nothing of the soul, nothing of the moral law, nothing of the metaphysical order, nothing of any one of the general principles of the human mind. They were in a purely instinctive state. The experiment has been repeated a hundred times, and a hundred times it has produced the same results; and hardly do we perceive, in the multitude of documents published up to this time, a doubt or a difference of opinion on so capital a fact, which is the greatest psychological discovery the history of philosophy can boast of. Has thought then received in language an auxiliary so indispensable that, without its help, man was condemned to incapability of emerging from the reign of sensations? Was language, for all the operations of the intelligence, the point or means of junction between the soul and the body? Did our double nature require that sort of incarnation of what is most immaterial in the world, or had God willed to make us comprehend the dependency of our mind by rendering it incapable of becoming fertile without the exterior action of oral instruction?

Whatever may be the explanation of this, it has always been found certain that man does not speak before he has heard language, and that he thinks only after the ideas contained in language have awakened the intelligible germ deposited in the depths of his understanding. If he did not possess this intelligible germ, language, in passing through the organs of his hearing, would vainly solicit his intelligence; he would hear it only as a sound, and not as a living expression of truth. But truth pre-exists in him in the same manner as the tree pre-exists in its seed and as the consequence pre-exists in its principle. Just as after-teaching causes to bud forth within each of us an innumerable multitude of deductions included in primary ideas, but of which our mind had no consciousness, so initial teaching causes the primary ideas themselves to appear to our inner vision. You find it natural that language should reveal to you mathematics, although you possess them entire in the primordial notions of unity, number, extent, weight: why does it appear strange to you that language should cause you also to perceive notions of unity, number, extent, weight, which are the base of mathematics? One of these phenomena is not more remarkable than the other; perhaps even it is more easy to understand the integral and profound sleep of a faculty which nothing analogous to it had yet disturbed, than to understand why that faculty, once called into exercise, halts in its way, and waits for language to manifest to it the simple consequences of what it clearly sees. The fact, however, remains incontestable, and that language is always the primitive and necessary motor of our ideas, as the sun, in agitating by his action the vast extent of air, produces there the brilliant scintillation which gives light to our eyes.

Thence it follows that Catholic doctrine is true when it exhibits to us God teaching the first man, whether in causing the truth of his intelligence to emerge by the percussion of the verb, or in announcing mysteries to him which surpassed the forces of the purely ideal order, as we shall by-and-by perceive. In fact, since man thinks and speaks only after having heard others speak, and since, on another hand, human generations take their beginning in God, their Creator, it follows that the first movement of language and thought remounts to the hour of creation, and was given to man, who possessed nothing, by Him who possessed all, and who willed to communicate all to him. This movement once impressed, intellectual life began for the human race, and has never since ceased. The divine word, immortalised upon the lips of man, has spread like an inexhaustible stream divided into a thousand branches through the vicissitudes of nations, and preserving its force as well as its unity in the infinite mixture of idioms and dialects, it perpetuates in the very seat of error the generating ideas which constitute the popular fund of reason and religion. If human liberty vitiates its teaching, it is but in a limited manner; its efforts do not attain so far as to reach the lowest depths of truth. Language, by that alone that it is pronounced, bears in its essence a light which seizes the soul and renders it an accomplice, if not in all, at least in the fundamental principles without which man altogether disappears. Therefore, God, by the effusion of His word continued in our own, does not cease to promulgate the gospel of reason, and every man, whatever he may do, is the organ and missionary of that gospel. God speaks in us in spite of us; the mouth that blasphemes still contains truth; the apostate who renounces Him still makes an act of faith, the sceptic who mocks at all employs words that affirm all.

However, if absolute scepticism is powerless against the revelation of language, it is not the same with imperfect or vulgar scepticism, which does not disavow human reason, but contests only certain applications of it relative to the superior order which does not fall under the investigation of our senses.

This kind of scepticism rejects in particular all personal relation between God and us by means of language; and maintains that our ideas spring of themselves from the living sources of the understanding, and in supposing that language may be necessary to their intimate emission, does not recognise in that marvellous functionary any traditional and divine character. God has not spoken to man; man has spoken of himself. He is the son of his own works, and all that he possesses of truth he owes to the success of his own investigations.

I have refuted this system, which is the corner-stone of rationalism, and which explains to you the blindness wherein so many creatures destined to know and love God live far from Him. God has given light to us under three forms, which are perfected by each other—the intelligible form; the sensible form; the oral or traditional form. Now rationalism admits only the two former, and rejects with tradition the invincible certainty found in the dogmas affirmed by God. It opens to its adepts the field of unlimited speculation, to which the best disposed bring but an imperfect intelligence, obscured by prejudices of birth and education, still more dangerously vitiated by the domination of the senses over the mind. But were all these obstacles surmountable, there would still remain the greatest of all, namely, the order established by God in the communication of truth which He has made to man. If man were a pure spirit, he would see truth in intelligible light, without the help of any sensible element. If, being unity composed of body and soul, he had not been destined to hold personal relations with God, he would probably have seen truth in the combination of intelligible and sensible light, independently of all oral tradition. But he is at the same time spirit and matter, and in addition he is called to live in society with God; and this is why truth has been communicated to him under a mode which is triple and single, corresponding to his nature and vocation. Would he think as an angel thinks? He cannot; some exterior image always intervenes in his most subtle operations. Would he think as an animal? He is equally unable; the height of his speculations elevates him even in the act by which he degrades himself, and even in concluding that he is only matter he proves that he is spirit. In fine, would he think like a being separated from God, independent of all personal relation with Him, supported by his reason alone? Doubtless he can do this, but only by losing at the same moment the equilibrium of his intelligence; he seeks, he hesitates, he deceives himself, and even when he touches truth, the clouds that cover it and the horizon that limits it take from him the hope of lifting by himself alone the immense weight of earth and heaven. The history of the human mind offers on every page superabundant proof of this. Two systems of philosophy dispute for empire—religious and traditional philosophy, and rationalist or critical philosophy. The first, even when it is mixed up with errors, settles minds and founds nations; the second, even when it affirms a portion of truth, destroys what the other builds up.

In a word, God, who is truth, has made Himself known to us by three revelations which are but one, by ideas, by the universe, and by language. Whoever breaks the bond that unites these, confuses and divides the light that lightens every man coming into the world; he condemns himself to a state of ignorance which knowledge does but increase; he will live at hazard like a being without principle or end, because he will voluntarily have abdicated, with truth, that is to say, with the knowledge of God, the highest means given to us to accomplish our destiny—which is to tend towards God, and, by imitating Him, to obtain the perfection of His nature and the beatitude of His eternal life.

# MAN AS A MORAL BEING.

My Lord,—Gentlemen,

Man is not simply an intelligence, he is not simply a contemplative being. If God had given him only the activity of contemplation, his life would have been limited to a simple and perpetual vision, to an impassible adoration of truth. But man is also an affective and an operative being; he is endowed with a second faculty, which is the consequence of the first, and has two acts, one expressed by the words: I love; the other by: I command. This faculty is the will. We have then to learn what God did for the will when He created man, and what means He has communicated to us, in and by the will, for attaining our end, which is perfection and beatitude.

But before entering upon this grave subject, gentlemen, I have two requests to address to you. I pray you first, never to applaud me, whatever may be the sentiment that moves your hearts. Not that I do not comprehend the involuntary movement which, even at the feet of the altars, causes an assembly to stand up, so to say, in unanimous witness of its sympathy and its faith. But although on certain occasions these acclamations might appear excusable, so much do they spring with piety from the souls of an auditory, nevertheless I conjure you to respect the constant tradition of Christendom, which is to respond to the word of God only by the silence of love and the immobility of respect. You owe this to God; you owe it also perhaps to him who speaks to you in His name. Although he may not have been tempted into pride by your applause, he may be suspected of not being insensible to it; it may be supposed, that, instead of giving freely to you that which he has freely received, he comes to seek its price in the glory of popularity, a recompense sometimes honourable, but always fragile, and still more fragile, more vain, between those who receive and him who gives the lessons of eternity.

The second request I would address to you is in favour of a nation to which on more than one occasion, and even from this place, I have already proved my respectful attachment. Yesterday, three noble sons of Poland visited me; they told me that four thousand of their companions, after fifteen years of exile, were about to approach their country, with the consent of France, which opens to them her gates, and of Germany, which permits them to pass through her territory. They asked me, after having obtained permission from the chief of this diocese, here present, to beg of you in their name, a last proof of your pious fraternity; for, if time has respected their glory and not lessened their courage, it has left them those precious remains, and nothing more. I bent before their desire as before their misfortune; I present them to you together. You will not give them alms; for although that word is dear to your Christian hearts, there are times when the heroism of misfortune constrains you to seek a higher title. You will not pay them tribute; although that word supposes a debt, and a debt of an important character, yet it does not sufficiently express the unction of Christian language. Therefore, borrowing a celebrated expression of the Middle Ages, I ask you to give them a viaticum, that is to say, the travelling pay given in those times to the members of religious orders and to the knights who went to combat in the Holy Land for the emancipation of Christendom. You will give a viaticum to those sons of another hallowed land, to those soldiers of another generous cause; you will give them the triple viaticum of honour, exile, and hope.

This said, this double satisfaction proposed to your heart and to my own, I enter at once upon the subject which claims your attention.

As truth is the object of the intelligence, good is the object of the will. But what is good? What distinction is there between the good and the true? Is it not the same thing under two different names? I grant that the good and the true have the same root, the same substantial support, since the true is being, and the good is also being. But as the unity of the divine essence does not exclude the triplicity of persons, the unity of being does not hinder it from possessing many aspects. In the first place, it is light; and under that form reveals itself to the intelligence, and is called truth. Next it is order, harmony, beauty; and under that form it seizes the will, and is called good. Our nature thus corresponds to its own. Inasmuch as it is light, we respond to it by a faculty destined to know the true; inasmuch as it is order, harmony, beauty, we respond to it by a faculty destined to reproduce good in loving and practising it. And as truth is the perfection and beatitude of the intelligence, good is the perfection and beatitude of the will.

In the first place, it is its perfection; for outside of good all is evil, that is to say, disorder, confusion, deformity: and evidently the will which loves and produces disorder, confusion, deformity, is in a false or an unjust state, as, on the other hand, the will which loves and produces good, that is to say, order, harmony, beauty, is in a state of justice or perfection.

I add that good is also the beatitude of the will: for thereby and therein it produces the most powerful sentiment of man, that sentiment which moves and fills from its very depths the vast solitude of his soul. No doubt the joy of truth known is great; there is in the regard that encounters the splendour of the true a motionless thrill, almost ecstatic; but if it reach to ecstasy, to tears, be sure that the intelligence has not alone been touched, the vision has penetrated still further, man has received the supreme shock from on high, the touch of love which terminates all in itself as in God. In the intuition of truth, man did not emerge from himself, he regarded the light present to his mind, and entered into enjoyment of it as an element or a part of his proper personality. By the impulsion of love, he emerges from his own personality or his life; he seeks a foreign object, he attaches himself to it, he embraces it, he longs to be transformed and absorbed into another than himself. This rapture from self to self, which may be called an attempt at suicide, gives him a bound of unspeakable happiness, and the abandonment of his being becomes its plenitude. This is love. But what has caused him to love? What has been powerful enough to take possession of that being, and so to subject him as even to make him feel that death in another is the best and highest life? A power, gentlemen, has wrought this miracle, the power of good. Behind the light where being appears to him, or in that very light, man has seen order, harmony, beauty, and this spectacle drawing him from the sterile contemplation of his own excellence, he feels that he is led to divest himself of himself in order to live in the object of his vision.

Nothing is more familiar to us than this movement; of all those of our nature it is the most universal, the most common, and that which we most willingly push to extravagance. Our life is passed in undergoing or regulating it. Every being possessing a certain amount of good, that is to say, endowed with order, harmony, and beauty in a certain measure, there is not one which is not capable of exciting within us some impression of love. But from man to man especially that impression appears and increases. Man is here below the masterpiece of good. He draws to his noble form the charm of the two worlds to which he belongs, the world of bodies and the world of spirits. Superior in the ordering of his features even to the imagination, which has never been able to conceive anything more perfect, he also calls to them from the depths of his soul the reflection of thought and the expression of virtue. If he open his eyes, a spirit looks at you; if his lips are left silent, the grace of the heart animates in closing them; if serenity brighten his forehead, the peace of an upright conscience sheds upon it light and repose; every bend of his body, every movement of his life contains under a single expression of beauty the double empire of visible and ideal good. Thence come those attachments which make of human life a long course of sacrifices rewarded by the happiness of loving and being loved. We do not seek elsewhere the secret of being happy; we know that it is there, and even when we abuse it by culpable passions, in the very crime we still bear witness to that law of our nature. Should man refuse us the love which we need, rather than renounce that precious treasure, we shall seek it from beings placed beneath us, but distantly preserving in their instinct some likeness capable of beguiling our heart. The poor man who has no other friend, makes one of some creature more neglected than himself; he warms in his bosom that obscure and faithful animal which a Christian writer has so well called the poor man's dog. He smiles upon him with that ineffable look of the forsaken; he confides to him those unknown tears which no tenderness wipes away; he shares his daily crust with him, and that sacrifice made by hunger to friendship causes him even in his poverty to enjoy the great happiness of riches, the happiness of giving.

Nor is this the last effort made by man to give and receive love. The prisoner goes beyond the poor. Separated from nature and mankind by inexorable barriers, he perceives in the chinks of his dungeon some lowly insect, the imperceptible companion of his captivity. He draws near to it with the trembling emotion of hope and the delicacy of respect; he watches the mystery of its existence, marks its tastes, spends long days in teaching it not to fear him, in leading it from timidity to confidence, in order at last to obtain from it some reciprocal sign which will lessen the solitude of his heart and widen his prison walls. The dog consoles the poor, the spider melts the prisoner; man, the child of good, carries everywhere with him a love of it which turns into a resource and a joy even the very horrors of isolation.

Need I say more? Have not your souls passed beyond my words, and do you not see that good, real or apparent, disposes of our will and is its beatitude?

But what, then, is good? It is true I have already told you; I have said that good is the order, harmony, beauty, which the intelligence discovers in the light where being appears to it. Nevertheless, this definition, all exact though it be, is not the term where your minds halt. You desire a more profound explanation, you ask me where order, harmony, beauty, are to be found?

Where? Doubtless everywhere in nature, everywhere before your eyes. There is not a leaf of the tree, not a blade of grass, not a cloud skimming the heavens, which is not order, harmony, beauty; but not all order, all harmony, all beauty, not all good. Every being, even the one perverted by his fault, contains a portion of good, which is perceptible and excites our sympathy; it does not contain the totality of good. That is order, which includes in its essence the rule from whence all the relations of beings proceed; that is harmony, which has weighed the worlds, and has traced out for them in space roads in which they never wander; that is beauty, which has made man, and stamped upon his visage so much grace and majesty; that is good, from whence all good comes, and which has shed it so profusely in the universe, without being able to give it all, because it could not give the infinite. Order, harmony, beauty, good, in one word, is God. As He is being and truth, He is also good. Inasmuch as He is being, He has communicated to us existence; inasmuch as He is truth, He enlightens our understanding; inasmuch as He is good, He inspires us with the love, which, according to the language of the Gospel, is all the law and all justice. For we can receive nothing greater, give nothing greater, than love; it is the supreme credit or debt, and whoever is quit towards it, is quit towards all. Now the first to whom we are accountable for it, the first who has a right to this highest treasure of our soul, is God, since God is the only good, and since good alone is the cause of love.

Whoever has not loved God is certain not to love good. He may, I grant, love particular things which are good, his family, his friends, his country, honour, and even duty, if we take duty in the narrow sense which governs the relations of men among themselves; he will not love the universal and absolute good from whence proceed all the other phases of good to which he has devoted his heart. And this is why he will not attain to the perfection and beatitude of the will, which, being in the love of good, can be found only in the love of God.

You see that in the mystery of love as well as in the mystery of truth, we arrive at the same conclusion, namely, that in God alone lies our perfection and our beatitude. And it is impossible that you should wonder at this, since we have established, as the foundation of doctrine, and as the knot of our destinies, that God is at the same time our principle and our end. Being our principle, He is the principle of each of our faculties; being our end, He is also the end of each of our faculties. And that end identifying itself with the divine perfection and beatitude, it is necessary for each of our faculties, by the way proper to it, to draw from God the life which renders it perfect and happy. Nevertheless, the developments through which I have led you are not sterile repetitions of the points of doctrine which we have before advanced and demonstrated; for, besides causing you to see their application to each of the springs of human activity, they verify those doctrines superabundantly by the analysis of our acts and of their objects. What joy do we not feel, in simply defining the intelligence and the will, on meeting God at the term of their operations! What ecstasy to be unable to name either truth or good, without naming God Himself! And, in addition, those investigations lead us straight to the means which we must have received for attaining our end. Already, in the last conference, we have proved that the first of these means is the knowledge of God; we are now prepared to conclude that the love of God is the second.

In fact, that love being the perfection and beatitude of our will, and God having designed to communicate the one and the other to us, as we have seen, it follows that, according to the order of His design, He should create us in a state of love with Him; of initial love, it is true, subject to the trial of our free will, but preparing us and leading us, save prevarication on our part, to the final and beatific union of consummated charity. This is what Catholic doctrine teaches us, when it represents to us the first man being born in original charity or justice. Remark, I pray you, that beautiful alliance of expression; in Christian language, charity is the synonym of justice, and justice is the synonym of charity. I have just told you for what reason. Without that divine justice of love, man is separated from God, even in knowing Him; and, being separated from Him, he can but descend towards misery and death, by the road directly opposed to that into which the order of his creation calls him. According to that order, he has received God for his end, truth for his guide, charity for his motor. If he wander, it is not in default of means, but of will.

Here we again encounter the intervention of free will in our destinies, and, if its presence disturb you, I might limit myself to repeating that without free will the gifts of God would remain in us as we received them, with a character of fatality which would make of our perfection a work unworthy of God or of us. But this explanation, all sufficient though it be, calls for developments which would have been premature when we exposed to you the general plan of creation, and which are no longer so when we touch, in the question of the will, the foundations of the moral order. The will is the seat of free choice as well as of love; we love by the same organ which gives us the empire of our acts, and which, with that empire, imposes our personal responsibility. And these three things blended together, free will, love, and responsibility, are those which indivisibly constitute the moral order. Free will presents the choice, love chooses, man responds. Why is it so? Is it arbitrary wisdom that has enchained these three elements of our activity? Or is there some profound reason for this which it is our duty to penetrate, in order to illuminate with a final trait the mystery of God in the creation of this world?

You think I shall adopt the last conclusion; I do adopt it, and I ask that question which includes all the rest in itself: Is there any essential relation between love and free will which makes the one the condition of the other? To know this, it is necessary for us thoroughly to scrutinise love. It plays also so important a part in our souls and in Christianity, that we shall not regret the thoughtful regard which we shall have thrown upon its essence.

Nothing is more simple, more single, than love; and yet it includes three acts in the unity of its movement. In the first place, it is an act of preference. Man, however great his heart may be, cannot cleave alike to all; surrounded by objects which, in divers degrees, bear the stamp of good, he feels degrees in the attraction which inclines him towards them, sympathetic degrees, whose order does not solely depend upon the comparative goodness of the beings, but also upon their secret resemblances to ourselves. Often even we do not take account of the motives of our preference; what is certain is that we have preferences, and that love begins in us by that first movement, which is choice. What is also certain is that choice, in him who is its author, as in him who is its term, gives the impulsion to the elevated joys of love. We are happy in choosing, happy also in being chosen. Two beings meet in the immensity of time and space, through the numberless chances of creation; they meet as if they had given rendezvous to each other from all eternity; they are united by a reciprocal preference which honours both, and flatters in their pride that which is pure and venerable. Nothing surpasses the original charm of that instant which remains the first in our memory, as it was the first in our heart. After years had weakened other impressions, that still subsists in its serene youth, and carries us back to those happy days when we felt the glory of choosing and of being chosen. But what would choice be without free will? What would it be without the faculty of preferring what pleases us? Doubtless the motives of preference exist in the perfection of the being who is its object; but they exist also and equally in the will which makes the choice. It may despise, it may reject an excellence towards which it feels no sympathy, for another with which it corresponds, and herein consists the value of its act, a sovereign act which confers honour and produces joy only because it is sovereign.

Love, however, does not stop at the act of choice, it exacts devotedness to the being chosen. To choose is to prefer one being to all others; to be devoted is to prefer that being to ourselves. Devotedness is the immolation of self to the object loved. Whoever does not reach this point does not love. In fact, preference alone implies only an inclination of the soul which seeks to dilate in that which has caused it, an inclination honourable and precious, doubtless, but which, thus limited, results only in seeking itself in another. If many affections stop at this point it is because many affections are but disguised egotism; we feel an attraction, we yield to it, we think that we love, we have perhaps the glimmerings of real love; but when the hour for devotedness comes, the dread of sacrifice shows us the vanity of the sentiment which preoccupied without possessing us. We see frequent and lamentable examples of this in the passions which have for their principle the fugitive beauty of the body. Nothing intelligible and immortal intervening between the souls which yield to these sad seductions, their charm soon disappears in the very ardour which produced them, and they leave in the heart nothing but the devastations of egotism increased by deceptive enjoyments. Virtue alone produces love, because virtue alone produces devotedness. We see proof of this in all the affections in which virtue mingles the divine balm of its presence. It is virtue that inspires the mother bent night and day over the cradle of a child; it is virtue that inspires the breast of the soldier, and leads him on to death for the cause of his country; it is virtue that fortifies the martyr against the threats of tyrants, and causes him to recline in the tortures prepared for him as in the nuptial and joyful couch of truth. These are the signs by which the world, all corrupt though it be, recognises and admires love, and if love cannot always manifest itself by heroic sacrifices, it constantly shows by lesser immolations that it bears with it the germ which renders it as "strong as death,"* to use an expression of Solomon.

But devotedness is not possible without free will. To devote ourselves, we have said, is to prefer another to ourselves, is to give ourselves to another to be his own. Now, how can we give ourselves if we are not free? How can we prefer another to ourselves, if we cannot dispose of ourselves? A being, deprived of free will, is under the fatal ascendency of

* Canticle of Canticles, viii. 6.

a foreign domination; he thinks, he moves only by the thought and will which hold him captive, by that inner captivity in which nothing remains to the proper action of his personality. Does such a being, thus despoiled of himself, preserve the right to give himself? He may die, but he dies as the stone falls, the slave of death and not of love. Even then, as free will is the condition of love, inasmuch as love is a sentiment of preference, it is also its condition, inasmuch as love is the impulsion of devotedness.

There remains a third act which crowns the marvellous drama of which our will is the theatre and the author. After we have chosen the object of our preference, after we have given ourselves to that object by sacrifice, all is not achieved. That object must prefer us, must give itself to us, and from that reciprocal choice and devotedness results a fusion of the two beings in the same thoughts, the same desires, the same wills—a fusion so ardent and so intimate that it would attain even to consummating them in one unique substance, if that power of joining substantial unity to personal plurality were not the exclusive privilege of the most holy and indivisible Trinity. At least we feel as it were the foreshadowing of this, and the limit where, with the power of union, the power of created love expires, is most painful to us. Union is the term of love, the term where it has nothing more to produce but the perseverance of its acts and the immortality of its happiness. But union, as well as preference and devotedness, needs free will; for to unite it is necessary to be two, and we are two only on condition of preserving on either part the plenitude of our personality, and this we cannot do without free will. The soul in which free will does not exist, or has never existed, which has never been capable of emitting a thought or an act of volition of its own, that soul is absorbed in another; it is annihilated, by its powerlessness to be the equal of a free soul, and to give to it, in reciprocal love, the preference, devotedness, and union which it receives.

I know not if it be an illusion, but it seems to me that nothing is more clear than this essential relation between free will and love; and consequently nothing is more clear also than the reasons whence divine wisdom has drawn the resolution of placing us in the world with the perilous gift of liberty. God had no need of us; He has freely chosen to communicate His blessings to us and unite us to Himself; He has also freely loved us. Now, in its nature, love exacts love; it is impossible to prefer without willing to be preferred, to devote ourselves without willing that our devotedness should be returned, and, as to union, it could hardly be conceived without the idea of reciprocity. Reciprocity is the law of love; it is the law of love between two equal beings; how much more so must it be between two beings of whom one is the Creator and the other the creature; of whom one has given all, and the other has received all! God had an infinite right to be loved by man, because He had loved him with an eternal and infinite love, and consequently He should place man in the only condition in which He could render him preference for preference, devotedness for devotedness, union for union, that is to say, in the glory and trial of free will. It was the right of God; but, strange to say, it was also the right of man, or at least his honour, since, without that gift of free will, man would neither have been able to choose nor to devote himself, nor, consequently, to love in the true and generous sense of the word.

Ask, then, no longer why man is free; why he is not born in a state of perfection and beatitude without peril of failure. He is free, because he should love; he is free, because he should choose the object of his love; he is free, because he should devote himself to the object of his choice; he is free, because in the union which terminates love he should bring the stainless dowry of an entire personality; he is free, in fine, because God has freely loved him, and has willed to receive from him the equitable recompense of full reciprocity.

I do not, however, disguise to myself the difficulty which rises in your minds; it is grave, and I will endeavour to be its exact interpreter.

According to Catholic doctrine, the trial of free will ceases with the present life of man; once disappeared from this world and called before the supreme judge, man passes into a state of happy or miserable consummation which leaves him neither the honour, nor the danger, nor the resource of choice. If, then, free will be essential to the reality of love, it follows that the saints, in the beatitude of eternity, love God only under the form of incomplete and impersonal affection, which it is absurd to suppose.

Doubtless it is absurd to suppose, and I shall neither suppose nor say this. When the saints enter into heaven, vanquishers of death and life, they do not enter there deprived of their anterior existence, as beings without past, without future, without acquired habits; on the contrary, they enter into full possession of a personality laboriously perfected, with all their soul and all their works, according to that beautiful prophecy of the apostle St. John, who, by the Spirit of God, beholding the last days of the world, heard from on high a voice which said: "Blessed are the dead which die in the Lord .... for their works follow them."* Their works follow them because they are living like them and in them, living in the love which was their fruit, and which mounts with the saints to heaven, not to lose there its primitive character of choice and devotedness, but to preserve it there for ever in the immutability of beatific vision. The saints have not another heart in heaven than that which they had on earth; the very object of their pilgrimage was to form in them, by means of trial, a love which should merit to please God and subsist eternally before Him. So far from that love changing its nature, it is its nature itself, it is its degree acquired in the free exercise of the will which determines the measure of beatitude in each elect of grace and judgment. According as man brings to God more ardent affection, he derives deeper ecstasy, more perfect felicity from the vision of the divine essence. It is the movement of his heart, as death has seized it, which regulates his place at the seat of life, and it is the unalterable perseverance of that movement, caused by the view of God, which alone distinguishes the love of time from the love of eternity. God recognises in His saints the apostles, the martyrs, the virgins, the doctors, the hermits, the hospitallers, who have before confessed and served Him in the tribulations of the world; the saints in their turn recognise in God the being to whom they gave their undivided love in the time of their suffering and their liberty. Nothing is foreign to them in the sentiments which they feel, nothing is new to them in their heart. They love Him whom they had chosen; they enjoy Him to whom they had given themselves; they ardently embrace Him whom they already possessed; their love expands in the certainty and joy of an inamissible union; but it is not separated from the stalk that bore it. God gathers, but does not detach it; He crowns, but does not change it.

It is thus that the trial of free will ceases, and that, not-

* Apocalypse xiv. 13.

withstanding, love subsists entire in the soul where God rewards it. But up to this point there is a struggle in the heart of man between good and evil, between his tendency towards God by charity, and towards himself by the egotism of the passions. The outer world arms itself to overcome him by all the beauties which it has received in another design; it opposes the visible charm to the eternal order which should obtain all our regards and regulate all our acts. Balanced as we are between these two attractions, we need strength to keep us attached to the polar star of real good, and that strength we call by a still more illustrious name than that of love—we call it virtue. Love without virtue is but weakness and disorder; by virtue, it becomes the accomplishment of all duties, the bond that unites us first to God, next to all the creatures of God; it becomes justice and charity, two things which form but one, and which were given to us on the day of our creation, to be, after truth, the second means of responding to our destiny and attaining our end.

I should have nothing more to say to you if, now as always, we had not to seek in rationalism for the counterproof of the doctrine I have just exposed to you. This doctrine attests that there exists an infinite difference between good and evil, since good is God, inasmuch as He is order, and evil is opposition to order, that is to say, to God; it attests that good is the object of the will, its perfection, its beatitude, and that the will corresponds thereto by love, the disinterested fruit of free will and virtue; it affirms, in fine, that man, being free to love or to hate, to do or not to do good, is responsible for his actions before the supreme justice of God. Is this also the doctrine of rationalism? In affirming the contrary, I have no need to tell you that I take the word rationalism in its general acceptation, and not as representing this or that class of philosophers. Rationalism has but one principle, which is the sufficiency of reason alone to explain the mystery of destinies, but it has a thousand heads which contradict each other, and which consequently never bear together the responsibility of the same errors. This diversity discharges such philosopher from such condemnable system; it does not discharge rationalism, whose starting-point is the cause of all the dogmas that deceive thought by corrupting truth.

I wished to give you this explanation at the moment when rationalism is about to appear to you in its most odious form.

Already you have seen it denying the existence of God, the creation of the world by God, the primitive intercourse between God and man, and placing in doubt even the very notion of truth. After such ruins, could it respect the distinction between good and evil? That distinction is but a consequence of the idea of God; this overthrown, the moral order disappears of itself. However, it is one thing to attack moral order in its source, another to attack it in front and directly. Were there nothing of God there, or were He a God indifferent to the acts of man, the soul might still endeavour to take refuge in itself, and by its own strength create for itself sacred duties. Notwithstanding the profundity of negations upon which it rests, it might choose not to deny itself, but by a generous contradiction, acknowledge laws and impose duties upon itself. However feeble that barrier may be, it is a vestige of conscience, an honour for man, a safeguard for society. What a crime, then, is it to dispute our possession of it, and pursue the idea of good even to the ruins amongst which we have formed this last and miserable refuge! Rationalism has not been ashamed to do this; after having attacked moral order in its principle, which is God, it has seized upon our soul as upon the remains of a prey, and defying us in this our supreme refuge, it contests the reality of love and the reality of free will.

Ingenuous that I was, I spoke to you but just now of sympathetic attractions, of disinterested preferences, of voluntary sacrifices. I represented to you the ascendency of good over the heart of man; I deceived you, if we must believe rationalism, I deceived you cruelly, and myself with you. Would you know the truth? Man acts only from one single motive, his own interest; he calls good that which is useful to him, evil that which lessens the value of the things and enjoyments of which he is in possession. Duty, if he observe it, is but a means of preserving his rights; love, if he feel it, is but a sentiment of pleasure. Egotism is at the fount of every human act, under whatever appearance or whatever name it may be hidden; and those grand expressions of devotedness, abnegation, immolation of self, serve but to disguise our true inclinations under a show which flatters our pride. The mother loves and seeks herself in her child; the soldier idolises himself in the glory of his captain or his country; death even is atoned for by the admiration which causes us to live again, as we believe, in posterity. Assuredly, if we may hope to find in man a pure sentiment of personal interest, we should seek for it in the soul of the Christian, since Christianity reposes upon the mystery of a God who gratuitously died for us. And yet to what does the Christian devote his life? To labour for his salvation, that is to say, to avoid hell and obtain paradise. His most heroic works are but a bargain which he makes with God. He knows that they are all registered, that not one falls to the ground, and that he will one day find again the smallest particle in an increase of felicity. Is this forgetfulness of self? Is this that charity come down from heaven, immolated on a cross, and raised again from the tomb to live in the heart of generations? Alas! it would be better to confess our indelible egotism, and to recognise with the sincerity of true philosophy that every being, whatever it may be, acts and lives but for itself.

We are asked for an avowal; let us begin by making it. Yes, it is impossible for any being endowed with intelligence and will to separate himself completely from his acts. I think, I will, I love; in whatever way I take it, it is I, myself, who thinks, who wills, who loves, and it is not in my power to take that I from myself. Whether I perform a good or a bad action, I am present in it, and have the enjoyment of it. Yet more, I should not perform it if I had no enjoyment in it. For every action supposes an end, and the last end of man being beatitude, for which God has expressly created him, it is absolutely chimerical to imagine that he acts without having before him the thought and motive of his happiness. And let me ask you, was there no difference between Nero and Titus; between Nero killing his mother, and Titus contributing to the happiness of the human race? Is there no difference between the soldier who turns his back in a battle, and the soldier who dies with his face towards the enemy and his country in his heart? Leonidas at Thermopylæ, Demosthenes at Chæronea, are they the same? You may say so, but I defy you to think so. You will not even say so before an assembly of men who honour you by listening to your words; even if your conscience lie to itself, it would not be bold enough to lie in the face of mankind. If there is one individual here who confounds in the same estimation and the same contempt crime and virtue, let him stand up! let him speak! And yet it is most true: Titus, like Nero, sought his happiness; there was no difference between them on this head; and if egotism consists in willing to be happy, Titus was an egotist by the same title as Nero.

But does egotism consist in willing to be happy? This is precisely the question. It would be very strange if happiness and immorality should be one and the same thing. Happiness is the vocation of man; it is the natural and predestinate patrimony of all intelligent beings. Whoever among them comes into the world comes into it to be happy. It is his right: what do I say? It is his duty. For his duty is to obey God, and God has pointed out to him two equal and parallel orders in calling him into life; the order of perfection and the order of beatitude. But, remark attentively what I have said; happiness is the patrimony of all, of all without exception; it is the natal land and the future country of all those who have not voluntarily repudiated it. And from this a great consequence follows, it is that no one should attribute to himself the happiness of others, and that all being children of the same father, inheritors of the same kingdom, we are commanded to live together in the divine fraternity of one and the same beatitude. He who usurps the part of another, who would be happy at the expense of his brethren, who, by cunning or violence, divides the spotless and seamless garment of felicity, is guilty of a crime which includes all other crimes; he is guilty of egotism, and since the beginning of the world he has borne a name and a mark—the name of Cain, and the mark of reprobation. He, on the contrary, who desires to be happy with all, who takes from another no part of his patrimonial right to happiness, who gives even of his own, he also, since the beginning of the world, has borne a name and a mark—the name of Abel, and the mark of charity. Charity does not consist in being unhappy any more than egotism consists in being happy; it consists in not troubling the good of others, and in communicating to them our own; a communication which, so far from impoverishing, enriches at the same time the receiver and the giver. Good has received from God that admirable elasticity, that the sharing it multiplies without lessening it, and that falling from the right hand, it returns to the left, like the ocean which receives all the waters of the earth, because it renders them all back again to the heavens.

This explanation, you will say, justifies the intimate sentiment of mankind, which has always placed an infinite difference between good and evil, which has execrated Nero and idolised Titus; but, in granting that personal happiness is the necessary end of all the acts of man, do you not destroy the very notion of love and devotedness? How can there be any sacrifice, any preference of others to ourselves, where we seek ourselves?

I have not said that personal happiness was the necessary end of all the acts of man; for that word personal excludes from the happiness of each the happiness of all, and I have declared, on the contrary, that happiness is a universal and indivisible patrimony, which no one could appropriate exclusively to himself without being guilty of the crime of egotism. Learn, then, that duty, love, devotedness, consist in making of our happiness the happiness of others, and of the happiness of others our own happiness, whilst egotism consists in deriving happiness from the misfortunes of others. Nero wished the Roman people had but one head, that he might take it off at a single blow: this is egotism. Titus considered that day to be lost in which he failed to render someone happy: this is love. "To love," Leibnitz has said, "is to place our happiness in the happiness of another." That sublime definition needs no commentary: it is understood or not understood. He who has loved understands it; he who has not loved will never understand it. He who has loved knows that a shadow in the heart of his choice would darken his own; he knows that nothing would be a sacrifice, prayers, tears, watchings, toil, privations, that would bring one smile upon the sorrowing lips; he knows that he was dead to redeem a compromised life; he knows that he was happy in another, happy in another's graces, happy in another's virtues, happy in another's glory, happy in that other's happiness, and that, had his blood been needed to increase that other's happiness, become his own, he would have given it, even to the last drop, with the sole regret of being able to die but once. He who has loved knows this. He who has not loved is ignorant of it; I pity him, and I do not reply to him.

I pity him, because he has known nothing either of human or of divine life; I do not reply to him, because the testimony of a dead man proves nothing against the living. What is it to us, Christians, if we must appeal to ourselves? what is it to be accused of indifference towards God by a man who has never loved God? Does he know what passes within us? Can he even conjecture it? He thinks that, with our eyes fixed upon heaven and hell, with our works in one hand, the scales in the other, we make a bargain with God for the price of our abnegation! He knows not that fear and hope are but the preliminaries of Christian initiation, and that in virtue of the first commandment, which includes all the others, according to the words even of Jesus Christ, the Christian ought to love God with all his heart, with all his mind, with all his strength, above all things, under the penalty, adds St. Paul, of "being nothing."* He knows not that beyond the threshold of faith the soul is touched by the invisible beauty of a love which the most heroic affections of this world will never equal, either in endurance, depth, or sacrifice; and that that love drawing us into the abyss of charity where God Himself respires, we draw therefrom the desire to associate all creatures in the perfection and felicity of which we have a foretaste, and of which we await the ulterior revelation. Who can deny this enlargement of the heart of man in Christianity? Who can deny it, save those who have never known what it is, and who, abased in the narrow passions of the senses, where all is egotism, measure by their own souls the soul of the Christian and the soul of man?

I am ashamed to prove to you the reality of love and devotedness, but rationalism compels me. It compels me also to say a few words to you on free will, which is, with disinterestedness, the principal condition of the moral order. As the moral order is destroyed if man acts only with a view to his interest, it is likewise destroyed if man be not master of his acts. Therefore, rationalism has not assailed our liberty with less ardour than our generosity; it needs our servitude as much as our egotism; our egotism to confound good with evil, our servitude to take from us the responsibility either of good or evil.

Are we free? Your conscience and mine answer: Yes. Rationalism says: No. And does rationalism give any proof of this? None. It asks us, on the contrary, to prove that we are free, and if we oppose to it the testimony of our intimate conviction, which knows apparently what it judges, that is condemned as blind and insufficient. It fears that our intimate conviction may be the victim of a superior power, which, unknown to it, makes it the instrument of its irresistible

---

* 1 Corinthians xiii. 2.

will. For us who believe in God, who, bending the knee before His adorable supremacy, have acknowledged Him as the Father, the Master, the principle, and the end of things, we do not entertain the strange doubts of rationalism in regard to what passes within us. Offspring of unequalled goodness and immeasurable wisdom, we do not imagine that God tortures His omnipotence to deceive the heart of His work, and give to it in servitude the illusion of liberty. We trust in the divine sincerity, and we do not seek whether it be in His power, even if He so willed, to lead us to so contradictory an impression on the subject of ourselves and our own acts. Truths, like errors, link together. God, once rejected or placed in doubt, I permit rationalism to mistrust the human conscience; the edifice being destroyed at its base, how can any detached part be sustained, and moreover, what interest would exist for so doing? What is man if God is not? What are good and evil? What the past and the future? It is needless for us to trouble ourselves about a dream in a night passed in sound sleep. But if God is, if the name that sustains all is written in the vault of our intelligence as in the vault of heaven, then I will no longer even listen to the rationalism which suggests mistrust to me on the subject of that liberty whose real presence I feel in myself. I take account of myself and of all things with me. My conscience is a sanctuary which gives me oracles; my life is a power which answers for itself; the divine solidity descends into all my being; and doubt, to my mind, is nothing but blasphemy and folly. I am free; I pass from good to evil, from evil to good. Suspended between these two terms which infinity separates, a voluntary captive or a culpable rebel, at each moment I choose and decide my condition. I choose to love myself, or to love God above all things; I withdraw, I return, I obey, or I resist remorse; and even in crime, I feel my greatness by my sovereignty. I need but a tear to remount to heaven, but a look to fall back into the gulf. This struggle is great, this responsibility is terrible; but woe and scorn to him who descends from the throne from fear of the duties that sit there with him!

Must I, in concluding, enlighten that other difficulty which rationalism opposes to the reality of free will, and which it draws no longer from the vanity of our conscience, but from the very attributes of God? I will do so rapidly, fearing to weary your attention, and hoping to abuse it but little. Truth is brief, because it is clear.

Catholic doctrine ranges amongst the divine attributes, that of foreknowledge, that is to say, the anticipated and infallible knowledge of the future, even of the future which depends upon our free will. Now, how can God foresee this last kind of future, if it be not because He is Master of our acts and directs them at pleasure? How does He know infallibly what I shall do to-morrow if not because He has decreed it, and because He possesses in His omnipotence the certainty of our determinations?

I shall have replied to this if I show, in the nature of God and in the nature of man, a means of foreseeing the effects of free causes which in no way destroys their liberty.

Now it is manifest that no reasonable being acts without motives, that is to say, without something that determines his actions. Hence these avowals constantly made by us: "Here is a reason, an interest, a circumstance, which decides me; in other terms, which persuades me to act." And when we examine the motives whose efficacious impression draws man from repose or uncertainty, we find that there are but two: the motives of duty and passion. Man decides either by a view of what is true, good, suitable; or by the inducement of a personal satisfaction independent of any idea of order. The question simply is to know who will decide him to the one or the other motive. If he were not free, the stronger attraction of his nature would decide him, as the greater weight brings down one of the scales of the balance. But man is free; between two attractions equal or unequal in themselves, it is he who pronounces sovereignly. Nevertheless he pronounces by virtue of a motive which persuades him, and not without cause, or arbitrarily. He knows what he does and why he acts; he knows even why he is persuaded to act. Persuasion reaches him not only from without, it comes to him especially from within, from the intimate state of his will, from his tastes, his virtues—the fruit of free will, free will itself in activity, such as it is formed, such as it wills to be, such as it presents itself to the outer attractions which come to solicit him for good and evil. It is the state of volition, the seat of free will, that decides the choice of man between the two motives of duty and passion. Suppose that state known, you would know what man would do in a given case, and in all the cases where the knowledge of the soul would for you have preceded its actions. Such is the basis of human, as well as of divine, knowledge. Have you never confided your fortune or your honour to the word of a man? You have done so; or, if you have never had occasion, you name within yourselves those to whom you would voluntarily give a high mark of your esteem. Whence comes that assurance? How are you certain that you will not expose your life to treason? You are sure of it, because you know the soul to whom you abandon your own; that knowledge is sufficient for you to see that in no case, under whatever peril or temptation, will your fortune or your honour be basely sacrificed.

They may be, however; the heart to which you give your faith is fallible, it is subject to unforeseen assaults; it matters not, you sleep peacefully, and no one accuses you of imprudence or credulity. If it happen that you are deceived, what will you say? You will say, "I was mistaken in that man, I thought him incapable of a bad action." Such is the chance which you would run, the chance of being mistaken; because, being a finite intelligence, you cannot read directly in the soul of another, nor even in the depths of your own. Whence it results that you possess only a moral certainty of your judgments, and of your foresight only an assurance of the same degree.

It is not the same with God. "God," to use the expression of St. Paul, "penetrates even to the division of the soul and the spirit, of the joints also and the marrow of our being, and is a discerner of the thoughts and intents of the heart."\* We are eternally naked before Him. He sees with infinite precision the state of our will, and, knowing in the same light all the outward circumstances to which we are exposed, He possesses an infallible certainty of the choice we shall make between good and evil, between the motives of duty and passion. From that moment, He knows our history, which is but a struggle more or less prolonged between the two opposite attractions, one which bears us towards our real end, another which turns us aside towards a base or false end. And that anticipated knowledge of ourselves being in no way the cause of our acts, no more obstructs our liberty than if it did not exist.

\* Hebrews iv. 12.

The error in this matter is in supposing free will to be a kind of abstract power, independent in its proper state, having no other movement than unlimited caprice. If it were so, man himself would not be capable of foreseeing his own actions an instant beforehand. His sovereignty would be but a state of permanent unreason. He would choose between good and evil without knowing why, and passing at hazard from crime to virtue, because of his liberty, we should find in him nothing more than an unregulated automaton. Such is neither man nor free will; I have shown you this, and I have but to leave your conscience to choose between the ethics of Christianity and the ethics of rationalism.

Christianity leads to charity and liberty; rationalism to egotism and fatality. If in the preceding questions, which appeal only to reason, some slight cloud still obscured your need of light, that cloud has vanished. The abyss of error has enlightened the abyss of truth. As the speculative dogmas of the existence of God, the Trinity, creation, the substantial diversity of matter and spirit, the vocation of man to perfection and beatitude, lead to the practical dogma of the distinction of good and evil; so the speculative dogmas of pantheism, dualism, materialism, scepticism, lead to the practical dogma of the confusion of good and evil, the supreme term which discerns all, and where darkness becomes light.

# MAN AS A SOCIAL BEING.

My Lord,—Gentlemen,

When God had made man, and when, after having animated him with the breath of life, He also shed in his soul light and justice—the light of truth and the justice of charity, He halted, if I may so speak, to contemplate His work, and seeing the eyes of man opening, his ears hearing, his lips trembling with the first vibration of speech, that clay, in fine, which He had touched with His mighty hand, become a sensible and a reasonable creature, He remained thoughtful, as if something were wanting to the masterpiece He had just produced. In fact, the mystery of our creation was not accomplished; God withdrew a second time within Himself to stamp our nature with the seal of a higher perfection, and beforehand He declared His design by saying: "NON EST BONUM ESSE HOMINUM SOLUM"—*It is not good for man to be alone.*\*

Why was it not good for man to be alone? In what manner was he to cease to be alone? This is the object which I now propose to your meditations, and in which you will see that society is the third primitive gift with which God has endowed us, the third means given to help us in the fulfilment of our destiny.

No being is alone. Whether we look above or below us, in God or in nature, we see plurality and association on every hand. God, who is one, is not solitary; He includes three persons in the unity of His substance, and the inferior world, divided into an innumerable multitude of different groups, presents none of which the condition and law of the creature is solitude. At each degree of existence we find number and

\* Genesis ii. 18.

union, that is to say, society. Number without union would still be only isolation; but when beings, distinct by individuality, alike by nature, approach and give each other their life, blend together reciprocally, act upon each other by mutual relations, then there is society, and such is the state of all creatures inferior to man; such is the state, under a more perfect mode, of the divine persons in heaven. Endeavour to imagine an absolutely solitary being, that is to say a being who has no resemblance or relations to anything, you will but create an abstract phantom in your imagination, a sort of God—nothing, because it would be at the same time infinite and void, infinite from want of bounds, void from want of activity. Isolation is the negation of life, since life is a spontaneous movement, and since movement supposes relations; still much more is it the negation of order, harmony, and beauty, all perfection and all beatitude, since none of those things can be conceived without the double idea of plurality and unity. Plurality without unity is positive disorder; unity without plurality is negative disorder. In the first case, the bond is wanting to the beings; in the second, the beings are wanting to the bond. Now, wherever there is disorder, it is evident that harmony, beauty, perfection, and beatitude vanish at the same time. It was then with justice that God, regarding man in the solitude of his creation, pronounced the words: "It is not good for man to be alone."

It is true that, by his intermediary position between the superior and inferior worlds, man—body and spirit—found himself in relation with nature and God; but that double relation did not the less leave him alone of his species, alone in the rank he occupied, a sort of stylite lost between earth and heaven. Even had nature sufficed for the wants of his body and God for the wants of his spirit, man, deprived of relations with beings of the same form and degree, would not have sufficed for the greatness of the position which he was charged to occupy. His history would have been too short, his perils too limited, his virtues too restrained; as he had a world above and below himself, it was needful that he should become a world, and that in this manner all the parts of creation, although unequal in themselves by their place and their essence, should answer to each other in a certain proportion of immensity. Man was to extend without being divided, to increase in number in order to increase in union, and to become, in the majesty of number and the harmony of union, a theatre of virtues such as the perfection of the universe and his own perfection required. Circumscribed in isolation, God alone would have been the object of his duties; member of a body composed of beings like himself, his offices embrace, with God, the whole of mankind. The law of love, the sum of all justice, no longer radiated only from the creature to the Creator; it animated with its life all the orbs of creation.

This great work is before your eyes; for sixty centuries human society has covered the field of history with its institutions. Stronger than time, it has resisted all disasters, and has constantly recovered its youth in the ruins under which degenerate nations have buried themselves. It is human society which has led our infancy through the hazards of the primitive emigrations, which divided the earth for us, and, after having dispersed us upon all the habitable shores, drew us together in spite of the jealousy of the deserts and the tempests of the ocean. It is human society which has built celebrated cities, encouraged arts, founded sciences, propagated letters, raised the mind of man to perfection, and given to his heart the glory of all virtues with the occasion of all sacrifices. In fine, human society is the permanent mode of our terrestrial life; and if, in the depths of forests or on the rocky shores of distant isles, the traveller discovers groups of people deprived of all civilisation, he still finds among them some rudiments of the social state, certain vestiges or outlines of relations which show how incapable man is to live alone.

And yet, who would believe it? the dogma of society has not been subject to fewer attacks than the rest. As sages have been found to deny God, creation, the distinction of matter and spirit, truth, the difference between good and evil, there have also been found men who maintain that society is a purely human institution, and, yet much more, that it is an institution against nature. They have endeavoured to persuade us that society is the source of all our evils, and that with our civilisation our decadency began. Who among us, in the time of his youth, has not imagined himself wandering freely in the solitudes of the New World, having no roof but the heavens, no drink but the water of unknown streams, no food but the spontaneous fruit of the earth and the game which fell by his hand, no law but his will, no pleasure but the continual feeling of his independence and the chances of a life without limits on a soil without possessors? These were our dreams. Our heart, recognising itself, thrilled when our eyes fell upon that passage in a celebrated book, where the man of civilisation says to the man of the desert: " Chactas, return into thy forests; take up again that holy independence of nature which Lopez will no longer deprive thee of; were I younger, I would follow thee." On reading these words it seemed that we heard them ourselves; our oppressed soul soared with them into ideal regions, and returned but with pain to the monotonous burden of reality.

Were we then in the true? Was that movement of our soul out of society an aspiration towards the primitive state which God had made for us, or a revolt against the order established by Providence in our favour? It was a revolt, a bound of egotism impatient of the limits which universal communion with our fellow-creatures imposes upon us, an attempt to subject the universe to our individuality alone. Whilst, in the plan of divine goodness, happiness is the right and patrimony of all, we sought to leave mankind in order to withdraw from sharing its blessings and evils, and rid ourselves of the duties which inevitably result from a great assemblage of relations. We hate dependence and labour in society. Dependence first: for society exists only by unity; unity is formed by ties; those ties, when intelligent beings are concerned, change into obligatory laws for the conscience, and are maintained by the double authority of public power and opinion. This is a yoke accepted by the virtue which does not separate its condition from the condition of others, but which weighs upon the egotism that lives only for itself; and therefore, as solitude is destructive of all laws because it destroys all relations, egotism seeks solitude in order to escape from dependence. In no less a degree it hates labour, another consequence of civilisation. A few men scattered over an immense territory live at little cost. Nature, abandoned to herself, supplies their wants, and isolation lessening in them the attraction which reproduces life, their number increases so slowly that it does not disturb their indolence. The man of society, on the contrary, has a paternity as prolific as his heart; he sees, under the blessing of God, the family changing into a tribe, the tribe into a community, the community into a nation; the tents are sheltered under walls; territories are defined by boundaries; nature fails before the increase of mankind. Art must supply its want of space and vigour. Assiduous labour must second the inventions of art. Numberless employments solicit the arms of men, and the arms of men in their turn solicit employment. Our veins are filled with the fruit of our toil. Each drop of our blood is purchased from the land at the price of a virtue.

This is more than enough to alarm egotism, and persuade it that social order is but an imposture in a state of martyrdom. I do not refute it, I simply explain to you how it is that the Christian dogma of society has contradictors and enemies. Dependence, labour, are hard words, I cannot deny it; and whoever does not accept them is necessarily in revolt against the reality of human things.

But a few days ago you engraved upon the monuments of your capital that memorable inscription: *Liberty, equality, fraternity.* It is, in fact, a part of the primitive charter which has united men together and founded the human race; but it is not the whole of it. It is the charter of rights, not that of duties. Now man, living in society, can no more deprive himself of duties than of rights. If liberty is necessary, that he may remain a moral creature, that he may not be overwhelmed in the pressure of an exaggerated and unjust domination, obedience is also necessary, to enable him to keep his place, by the help of a common and sacred law, in the living home which a nation makes for him. If equality is necessary, that he may not decline from the rank in which God has placed him by a common origin with all his fellow-creatures, hierarchy is also necessary that he may not, in default of a chief and a commanding authority, fall into the powerlessness of individual dissolution. If fraternity is necessary in order that confidence and love might widen the narrow ties of social order, that mankind might remain one great family sprung from one common father, veneration is also necessary, to acknowledge and strengthen the authority of age, the magistracy of virtue, the power of laws, in those who possess this character whether as legislators or as sovereigns. Write then, if you would found durable institutions, write above the word liberty, obedience; above equality, hierarchy; above fraternity, veneration; above the august symbol of rights, the divine symbol of duties. I have said this to you elsewhere; right is the selfish side of justice; duty is its generous and devoted side. Appeal from it to devotedness, that devotedness may respond to you, and that your work may triumph over the ardent passions, which, since the origin of society, have never ceased to conspire for its ruin.

Human society is not only hated for itself, on account of the duties that it imposes, it is also hated for another reason which it is important for you to learn. God, who was the founder of society, is its preserver. He maintains it by the power of His name, which is perpetuated under the guardianship of dogmatic traditions and religious observances. No nation has been able to exist without that venerated name, no community has been built up without that corner-stone of the temple. And vainly will the impious hope to abolish the memory of God until that society be abolished which is its depository, and which lives upon this hereditary treasure of mankind. Human society and religious society are two sisters born on the same day of the divine word, the one having regard to time, the other to eternity; distinct in their domain and end, but indissolubly united in the heart of man, sustaining one another, falling together, rising again together, braving together by their common immortality the hatred that pursues both of them. Do not lose this point of view, if you would take account of the leaven of anarchy which rouses the heart of man against society. Society is no other thing than order, and order has in God its invulnerable root. Whoever does not love God has by that alone a permanent cause of aversion towards the social state, which could not do without God.

Thence it comes that anti-religious epochs infallibly produce anti-social theories. You witnessed this in the last century. Whilst the doctors of a superficial generation held up to ridicule Jesus Christ, the Bible, and the Church, others, with a pen no less bold, wrote against human society. The savage state was exalted as the primitive state of man, and incomparably the best; the effeminate gentlemen of the Trianon were invited to return to that state with bows and arrows in their hands. It was demonstrated that society was at least formed by a voluntary contract, and, with a gravity but too formidable, they sought the clauses of that fabulous contract.

Is it necessary for me to prove to you that social order is neither an institution against nature, nor a facultative institution? We are far removed from the time when men discussed these questions, puerile in themselves, but which were rendered important by the decadency of the monarchy under which they were treated. Now that this monarchy has disappeared in a tempest, and the epoch of reconstruction has succeeded to that of ruins, intelligent minds are interested much more about the economical problems of social life than about the circumstances of its origin and the primary causes of its establishment. Therefore I shall confine myself to the few words which are necessary rationally to confirm the dogma of society such as Catholic doctrine professes it.

A thing is natural when it is in conformity with the real constitution of a being. Now the social state is evidently in conformity with the constitution of man, since everywhere and always he has lived in society. It is true that some oppose to us the savage tribes of America, and of many islands scattered in the ocean; but those very tribes, although deprived of civilisation, live nevertheless in the unformed rudiments of community. They are branches accidentally detached from the great human trunk, and which deprived of the sap of traditions, withdrawn from the law of oral instruction, vegetate on the extreme confines of sociability without having burst the last link that holds them thereto. If truth and charity should seek them at the ends of the world; if the words of the gospel, borne by the clouds of heaven, should fall upon the uncultivated glebe of their souls, you will see them extending their hands to the apostolate, covering their nakedness, plunging the plough into their forests, assembling round the wood and sign of a cross, and bowing their heads before the invisible presence of God, of whom they know nothing save a remembrance as uncertain as their life. You are not ignorant that Oceania now witnesses the accomplishment of these marvels, and those fortunate islands send back even to our old continents the virginal balm of a civilisation which finds again a cradle in the ruins of the desert.

I do not mean to say that the savage passes easily, or that he always advances, to the state of social perfection; no, gentlemen, this is a difficult work which requires time, a combination of favourable circumstances, and which, on this account, is rarely crowned with success. An entire population is not drawn in a single day out of the torpor of an inveterate state of indolence and free indulgence of the passions. It is enough that it has been done, or even that it has been begun, for the savage state to cease to be an objection against the social temperament of man. The Iroquois, or the Huron, is not civilised, but he is fit for civilisation, and if he does not become civilised alone, by the aid of his proper forces, it is for the same reason that the deaf are dumb. No one is an initiator to himself; every man or every tribe having left society, which is the great and universal initiator, can return to it only by means of a legislator bringing from the common centre, truth, justice, order, and devotedness. We need not travel to the Pacific Ocean to find the savage; whoever rejects the social tradition, by ungoverned passions, is a voluntary savage; so much the more degraded as he touches the source of truth and goodness. You have met with those beings fallen by their fault below civilisation, and assuredly you have drawn no conclusions from their moral misery against the dignity of our nature and against its sociability. The exception has never destroyed a rule, and here there is not even an exception. The savage is to the civilised man what an abortion is to a plant which has received a regular development; by its very deformity it bears witness in favour of the normal type to the plenitude of which it has not attained.

Man lives then socially by virtue of his native constitution; he is naturally sociable, and consequently naturally social. It is not a facultative contract which has placed him in society; he is born in society. And if it happen that he leaves it by a lamentable accident which separates him from the common stock, it is impossible for him to return to it of himself under the form of a contract or a deliberation. He vegetates in that state until the civilised man touches his hand, and raises him by the fraternal sovereignty of language to the rank of an intelligent being enlightened by God. For it is God who first initiated the human race to the social life, and who, after having with truth and love deposited in mankind the germ of mutual attraction, gave to it the first impulsion. Truth and love are the basis of social order; wherever souls meet, having received these gifts, the principle of society meets in, and tends to unite, them. But this principle may be deadened or degraded, and this is why it exacts, all pre-existing though it may be, an initiatory intervention, to rouse it if it be deadened, to purify it if it be degraded. So that these two things are equally true, namely, that society is natural to man, and that it is nevertheless of divine institution. It is natural to man; because man, an intelligent and a moral being, has received in his creation the intelligible germ of truth and love : it is of divine institution;

because it is God who first placed man in active possession of truth and love, and who, the first also, gave him the opportunity of applying truth in relations of like to like, of equal to equal.

It is time for us to arrive at that supreme moment of the drama of creation, and see human society unfolding under the blessed hand to whom we owe all.

When God had uttered that beautiful expression: "It is not good for man to be alone," the Scriptures tell us that He caused a deep and mysterious sleep to fall upon Adam, our first father. It would seem that God, so to say, feared to be troubled by the look of man during the sublime work He was about to perform; He willed that no other thought than His own should intervene in the act which was about to give plurality to man without destroying his unity. For such was the work which His sovereign power purposed to accomplish. Taking the eternal order of the divine society as the pattern of human society, He designed that there should not only be moral unity in the relations between man and man; but that those relations should take their source in one substantial unity, imitating as much as possible the tie that unites the three uncreated persons in an ineffable perfection. Mankind was to be one by nature, by origin, by blood; and, by means of that triple unity, to form but one single soul and one single body of all its members. This plan was in conformity with the general end of God, which was to create us in His image and after His likeness, in order to communicate to us all His blessings; it was worthy of His wisdom as well as of His goodness; and when I think that vulgar impiety has been able to laugh at the magnificent act which realised it, I am overwhelmed with pity for the abasement to which the intelligence falls that misunderstands the intelligence of God.

Man was, then, at the feet of his Creator and Father, overcome by the inertness of a superhuman sleep, knowing nothing of what was intended for him, and God looked thoughtfully upon him. Was it necessary to divide that beautiful creature in order to multiply him? Was it necessary to create by his side an image of himself, without other community than likeness, and cause the human race to spring from one primitive being associated with a second? It would have destroyed unity in the very root from whence it should blossom. There would have been two bloods, and only one was required. It was needful that all mankind should come from one single man, in order that living plurality should spring from living unity, and that man, multiplied without division, should recognise in his fellow-creature, emanated from himself, "the bone of his bones and the flesh of his flesh."* With this thought God bends towards man and is about to touch him: but where will He touch him? The brow of man, where, with his intelligence, reposes the eminent seat of his beauty, naturally presents itself to the creating hand, and seems to invite the new benediction about to descend upon us. God did not touch it. However beautiful the faculty of intelligence may be, it is not the term of our perfection. Calm as light, and cold also, it was not from the point which corresponds to him in the outer architecture of man that God was to draw forth the miracle of our consubstantial plurality. He knew a better part, He placed His hand upon it. He placed it upon the bosom of man; there, where the heart by its movement marks the course of life; there, where all the holy affections have their echo and rebound. God listened for a moment to that heart so pure which He had just created, and by a thought of His omnipotence removing a part of the natural shield that covered it, He formed woman of the flesh of man, and her soul of the same breath which had made the soul of Adam.

Man saw his fellow-creature. He saw himself in another with his majesty, his strength, his gentleness; and with an additional grace, a delicate tint that manifested a dissemblance only to produce a more perfect fusion between the two parts of himself. First regard of man upon his fellow-creature, what was it? First nuptial moment of mankind, who shall reveal it? We will not endeavour to paint it, we will not lessen by vain poesy the solemnity of that wedlock whose consecrator was God; but imitating the austere simplicity of Scripture, we will repeat what it says to us.

After, then, God had led to man his companion, according to the expression of the sacred pages, He pronounced over them in these terms the blessing of inexhaustible fecundity: "Increase and multiply, and fill the earth."† And with these words, efficacious like all the words of God, man received the gift of producing and perpetuating the miracle of the diffusion of his being, in offshoots personally distinct from himself, but one

* Genesis ii. 23. † Genesis i. 28.

with him in form and blood. Mankind was founded, and the man in whom it had just become being, the man king, husband, father, bearing in himself the innumerable posterity of his sons, sang the hymn of the first nuptials, the song of the first love, the law of the first family, the prophecy of all generations. Listen, gentlemen, listen to our forefather speaking to his race in the name of God; listen to those first words of man which have traversed ages and taught the human race. "This," said he, "is bone of my bones, and flesh of my flesh; she shall be called woman, because she was taken out of man; wherefore shall a man leave father and mother, and shall cleave to his wife; and they shall be two in one flesh."* Such is the law of family, society, civilisation; such is the oracle which will for ever regulate the condition of mankind. Every legislator who may despise its commandment will but found barbarism; no nation that withdraws from it will ever attain to the era of justice and holy morality. It is upon the constitution of family that the progress or decadency of society will in all ages depend; and the constitution of family, signed by man and God, is written in the charter which has just been proclaimed to you. Woman is not to be the slave of man; she must be his sister, bone of his bones, flesh of his flesh. Wherever she may be degraded from this rank, man himself will be degraded; he will never know the pure joys of true love. Subjected to the domination of the senses, woman would be nothing to him but an instrument of sensuality; she would not speak to him of God with the authority of tenderness; she would not soften his heart by the constant charm of her own; she would not adorn his life by the innate delicacy of her voice and gesture. The domestic threshold, as the symbol of servitude, instead of recalling to man the holy and happy hours of his terrestrial passage, would recall to him only the inconstancy of his pleasures, the tyranny of his passions.

But woman is not only to be the sister of man by virtue of community of origin, she is to be his wife; in the virginity of her body and her soul she is to bring to him an inestimable gift, a gift which man will not be able to receive from another until death shall have broken the oath which purchased it. "She shall be called woman," said Adam; "therefore a man

---

* Genesis ii. 23, 24.

shall leave his father and mother, and shall cleave unto his wife; and they shall be two in one flesh." They shall be two, and not more than two; they shall be two even to being but one flesh; and as death dissolves the unity of the flesh, death alone also shall destroy the unity of marriage, the source of life. Should the frailty of the human heart forget that order, should it profane marriage by daring to elevate adultery to the sanctity of marriage, woman would no longer exist either as wife or as mother. The infant born of her by an imperfect union would recognise in her only a dishonoured victim, and in his own days nothing but the fruit of selfish paternity.

Therefore, fraternal alliance between man and woman, exclusive and indissoluble alliance, in which, however, man exercises the chief authority, because he is the trunk whence his companion was taken, and because she was given to him by God, according to the language of Scripture, as "a help like unto himself."\* Such is the regular constitution of family, without which there is but oppression of the woman and child, weakening of the sense of moral obligation, sensuality instead of love, selfishness instead of devotedness, and in fine, barbarism or decadency, according to the age of the nations which have been led to despise the fundamental laws of society. Society is but the development of family; if man leave his family corrupted, he will enter corrupted into the community. If the community would destroy family in order to regenerate itself, it would substitute an order factitious and against nature for the order established by God, and fall into the double abyss of unmeasured tyranny and licentious dissolution. It would be the high road to death.

Society being but the development of family, the general laws that regulate family regulate society also. As at the domestic hearth woman is the sister of man, the citizen at the forum is the brother of his fellow-citizen; as man is only the husband of one wife, the citizen belongs only to one nation; as, in fine, the wife and child owe obedience and respect to the father, the citizen owes obedience and respect to the magistrate. If from the community we survey the human race, we shall recognise there, notwithstanding the difference of language, customs, and physiognomy, the dispersed council of a single race, the branching out of a single stem, and

---

\* Genesis ii. 18.

shall say to each man: Thou art my brother; to each nation: Thou art my sister; to all, whatever may be their colour, their history, or their name: This is bone of my bones, and flesh of my flesh. It is true we shall no longer find in the human race the unity of one single father, common obedience, unanimous respect; that order has been destroyed. The fields of Babylon saw the branches of man breaking off with great noise, and heard our forefathers utter in confused language the adieu of a separation which still exists. But the hour of the unity prepared and begun by Christ seems to draw near; the mountains bend, the seas diminish, the Christian family, with the vicar of God at its head, urges on, and, by its superiority henceforth assumed, enlightens the nations which have not yet adored the regenerating language of the gospel. The desire for peace keeps the sword in its sheath; fraternal language is exchanged from one end of the world to the other; the negro sits down with the white man in the great assemblies of nations; everything forebodes to attentive minds an era of reconciliation and the age in which, without destroying the variety or liberty of nations, the antique prophecy will be accomplished which announces to us, "one single shepherd for one single fold."*

I halt before this glorious hope which should console all who are concerned about the future of the human race. How is it that here also I find rationalism as the adversary of the truths which so greatly interest the dignity and happiness of man? Not content with having presented the social state as a state against nature, rationalism has attacked its constitution under three important relations: it has denied the unity of the human race, the unity of marriage, and its indissolubility. I shall not notice the last two errors, having had occasion to touch upon them in the conference in which we treated "of the influence of Catholic society upon natural society in regard to family;" and I shall limit myself to confirming, in a few words, the substantial unity which makes of the human race a family issued from a single love, and from one and the same blood.

It seems that in the age we live in, an age wherein ideas of equality and fraternity generally predominate, if there is a dogma which should escape from negation, it is the dogma

* St. John x. 16.

that gathers into unity all the nations that form mankind. But rationalism thought to seize Christian truth here in the very fact against the documents of science, and could not lose the opportunity of compromising it in those minds which attach more weight to the appearance of things than to the evidence of their laws. It endeavours then to establish the absolute diversity of the human races by the comparative study of the profound dissimilarities that mark their most important branches. These dissimilarities cannot be denied; the ignorant discover them as well as the learned. The Malay, the Mongol, the negro, have characteristic features which do not permit us to confound them either among themselves or with the European. This is true. The whole question is whether the difference is substantial, or only an accident, whether it constitutes a separate nature having an origin of its own; or whether it is but a shade caused in a primitive uniform type by the circumstances of time, place, customs, and even by fortuitous events whose effect and impress are afterwards perpetuated.

It is incontestable that sensible varieties appear in beings of the same kind and of the same progeny; it is the result of two forces which keep life in a just equilibrium, namely: spontaneity and immutability. Without spontaneity, that is to say, without a proper and original movement, beings would remain in the monotonous mould of barren uniformity; without immutability, they would lose the type of their true organisation under the force of their individual action. They are, then, at the same time free and restrained; they become modified without losing their nature. Such is the case of those changes of physiognomy which have no name when they are not perpetuated; and which are called varieties when they are powerful enough to be transmitted and maintained. For, as the primitive form of the living being resists all mutations, the secondary or acquired form may also share this privilege when the causes that produced it are inveterate, and have passed, so to say, to the very roots of life. The father or mother, and sometimes both together, communicate to their children the features and expression which they themselves received from their authors. If this hereditary vestige promptly disappears in families of little distinction, it acquires an obstinate persistence in the more strongly marked races, which guard their blood with more watchful care. It is above all remarkable in the particular physiognomy of each nation, whatever approximation of climate or customs may exist between them. The Frenchman, the Englishman, the German, the Italian, the Spaniard, who touch each other on a soil limited in extent, who drink the same waters, and are invigorated by the same sun, who adore the same God, who have been mingled by an uninterrupted communion of from twelve to fourteen centuries, have a type of face personal to each, and by which they are instantly recognised by the least attentive observer. If it be so among nations subject to the influence of common elements, what must it be of those separated by distance, light, heat, food, religion, customs, all those material and spiritual causes, in fine, which act upon life and produce profound modifications? And if the dissimilarity of two European nations does not manifest the diversity of their primitive origin, how should the dissimilarity between the negro and the white man manifest anything but the diversity of their religious, political, and natural history? That which makes man is an intelligent soul united to a body endowed with certain proportions. Now has not the negro the same soul as the white man, and has he not the same body? Who will say that the soul of the negro is not human, and that his body is not human? And if the soul of the negro be human, if his body be human, is he not a man? And if he be a man, why should he not have had the same father as yourselves?

A physiological law, promulgated by the illustrious Cuvier, has also decided the question. It is known to science that all living beings which unite together, and whose posterity remains indefinitely prolific, belong to the same nature and remount to a primordially unique stem. In order to maintain the great lines of creation, God has not willed that beings of diverse origin and kind should be able, by means of capricious alliances, to confound all bloods. Should this irregular event happen, it may obtain from deceived fecundity a first result; but it never advances beyond this; order immediately reassumes its empire, and sterility punishes the fruit of a connection reproved by the will of the Creator. Now this anathema does not reach the union of the negro and the white man; their oaths received at the feet of the same altars, under the invocation of the same God, obtain in an indefinite posterity the glory of an act legitimate and holy. Much more, the two bloods recognise each other; the purer elevates to its splendour the one that had contracted an adulteration; from degree to degree, from alliance to alliance, all disparity vanishes, and the sons of Adam find themselves again, as sixty centuries ago, in the fraternal features of their common father.

Away, then, with those shameful attempts of fratricidal science. Let us no longer listen to the voices which do not respect the inviolable unity of the human race! Rather, Christians, let us hail from afar, and on every hand, let us hail our brethren dispersed by the tempest on such diverse shores. Let us, who have better preserved the primitive tint of our creation, who have received with a softer influence of natural light a better share of uncreated light; let us, the elder sons of truth and civilisation, hail our brethren whom we have preceded only to lead, whom we have surpassed only that they may one day equal us. Let us hail in them our past and our future unity, the unity which they had in Adam and that which we wait for in God. Let us stretch out our hands to the Malay and the Mongol; to the negro, the poor, and the leper. All together, uniting our blessings and our misfortunes in one immense and sincere act of brotherhood, let us draw near to God, our first Father. Let us draw near to God who made us from the same clay, who vivified us with the same breath, who has penetrated us with the same spirit, who has given us the same word, who has said to all of us: "Increase and multiply, and fill the earth, and subdue it, and rule over it." He alone can bless us; He alone can open to us a veritable era of liberty, equality, and fraternity. Without Him you will write those sublime words in vain upon your public monuments. Thirty centuries ago, they were written on the tables of Sinai by a more powerful hand than yours, and yet the tables of Sinai fell from the hands that carried them, and were broken in pieces at the foot of the mountain. It was because their laws were written in stone, and not in the heart of man. Write not then yours upon stone, write them with the finger of God in your own hearts, that they may speak therefrom to the hearts of all, and so insure a durable immortality.

# THE DOUBLE WORK OF MAN.

My Lord,—Gentlemen,

It remained for me to treat of the condition in which God created man as a physical being, and afterwards as a religious being. Under the first head, God endowed him with immortality; under the second, He prepared him for sharing the divine life itself by a gift which Catholic doctrine calls grace, that is to say, the gift *par excellence*. This should then be the present object of your attention. But having at a future period to treat before you of the mystery of the resurrection of the body, I reserve for that period all that concerns the exterior immortality of man; and as to his vocation to sharing the divine life by the effusion of grace, it is too vast a subject to be dealt with on the day which will close our conferences for this year. I reserve it also, then, and I am consequently led to the expression which in the Scriptures closes the account of creation. That expression is singular; it is as follows: "On the seventh day God ended his work which he had made; and he rested on the seventh day from all his work which he had done: and he blessed the seventh day, and sanctified it: because in it he had rested from all his work which God created and made."\*

By this you see that the world was not the work of a moment, but that God produced it in a progressive order distributed in six epochs, which the Scriptures call days. I shall not stop to expose or to justify that order, which is already known to you. Science has taken this upon itself during half a century; each of its discoveries comes unawares to prove the profundity of Biblical cosmogony; and at length the bowels

\* Genesis ii. 2, 3.

of the earth, brought to light by tardy investigations, have revealed, in the state of their different strata, the reality of the successive formation which is the basis of the account in Genesis. It was necessary to acknowledge either that Moses was inspired by God, or that, fifteen centuries before the Christian era, he possessed a science which was not to be disclosed until three thousand years later. I would willingly treat of this magnificent triumph of our faith, if the nature of my labours permitted me to add thereto the weight of a personal authority, and if it were not more fitting that whatever concerns scientific developments should rather be treated in a book than from a Christian pulpit. I confine myself then to this incontestable fact, that the Christian cosmogony is henceforth assured of the respect of all who do not despise the testimony of the most authentic realities. But this testimony, which suffices to confound the reproaches of the mind, does not suffice to satisfy its desire to know. It still asks why God created the world gradually, why He in a manner diminished His power to restrain His action. It is easy to conceive that time may be necessary to a finite cause; it is not easy to conceive its utility to a cause which can do all things of itself. How is it that God abased Himself to the measure of a common workman? How is it that He began, quitted, and returned to His work? How is it that He rested from it? All these ideas are strange, and in seeing them united to the first act which has revealed God to us, to the act of creation, the intelligence vacillates and remains under the weight of unappeasable wonder.

I dare to say that your instinct deceives you, and that there is nothing greater in God than His abasement. Yes, God abased Himself in creation, as we shall see Him at a later period abasing Himself in the incarnation and in the redemption; He abased Himself because He laboured for us and not for Himself, because strength and greatness are communicated only by descending. Yes, God had no need of time as an auxiliary to His eternity: no motive drawn from Himself induced Him to divide the formation of the earth into six periods, and to await the help of ages for that which depended upon an act of His sovereign thought. But if it were the same for Him to act suddenly or slowly, it was not so for man. Destined, in our passage upon earth, to a work which ends only with itself and us, it is important for us to know the general law of labour; and God, in establishing outside of Himself the operation whence all ulterior operation was to flow, willed that His manner of proceeding should for ever contain and reveal the rule of our own activity. That rule indeed has never been effaced from the memory of the human race. It has outlived the wreck of the most sacred traditions, and its vestiges are found in the division of time observed by most of the ancient and modern nations. But in order to comprehend in what it consisted, what was its object and its importance, it is necessary to take account of the labour even of man.

This word labour seems to awaken an idea incompatible with the primitive state in which God placed us; a state of perfection and happiness which I have represented to you, and which bears the image of perfect repose. Does not labour imply fatigue? Is not a chastisement imposed upon man in consequence of a prevarication which caused him to fall from the prerogatives of his primitive state? And moreover, before that catastrophe had impaired the harmony of our faculties and drawn down the divine malediction upon earth, what would have been the object of labour to us, either of body or mind? These reflections so much the more prove to me the necessity of exactly defining the labour required of man in the design of his creation.

To labour is to act. We may act with pain; but pain is not a part of the essence of labour. Its essence is summed up in that energetic and glorious word: to act. Now, you do not suppose that God, who made all things, has destined man to eternal idleness. The most insignificant being, in coming into the world, brings into it a mission corresponding to the end for which it was created, a mission or a function which it accomplishes by labour. The very worm of the earth does something, it performs its task, it co-operates for an end; it belongs to the sacred band of useful creatures. How should man, raised so high by his faculties and by the place which he occupies in the universe, have received no other function than that of sterile idleness? It could not so be, and it was not the language of idle repose that God addressed to man when at the hour of his birth He said to him: "Increase and multiply, and fill the earth, and subdue it, and rule over the fishes of the sea, and the fowls of the air, and all living creatures that move upon the earth."* It was not a lesson of idleness that God

---

* Genesis i. 28.

gave him in bringing before him—according to the history of Genesis—" all the animals of creation, that he might give them a name which should explain their nature and remain to them for ever."* In fine, when He led him to a dwelling-place, called by Scripture the Paradise of Pleasure, it was not to slumber there in the sleep of inaction; for it is said God placed him there *to dress it and to keep it*—UT OPERARETUR ET CUSTODIRET ILLUM.† Do not then unite in your minds the idea of perfection and happiness, or even the idea of repose, with that of inactivity or idleness. God was infinite activity before He assumed, in the creation and government of the world, a work worthy of all His attributes; by an eternal action He produced in Himself the Word which ever speaks to Him, the Holy Ghost which responds to both; by a fecundity as ancient as Himself He diffused between three the unity of an essence whose inner movement is perfection, beatitude, and repose. So far from the idea of action—which is that of labour—being incompatible with the notion of a happy and perfect state, it is the necessary element which constitutes all that we know of that state; for, to think is to act, to will is to act, to love is to act, and apparently none of these acts will be rejected from the definition of happiness and perfection.

Placed in the centre of created things, belonging by his soul to the higher world of spirits, by his body to the lower world of nature, having the earth for passage and God for end, man was indebted by a double labour to a double function. His first function was to tend towards God, who had given him truth that he might know Him, charity that he might love Him, the participation of His own life as perspective and term; but with all these gifts the gift also of liberty, which raising him to the glory of a person master of himself, permitted him to repudiate his legitimate end, and opened before him the honourable but perilous career of virtue. This was the first work, the great work of man. However pure he might have been in his soul and body, he was free; he could withdraw from God and perish. Prayer, reflection, vigilance, perpetual care of his heart, were necessary for him to prevent his falling from the virginal splendour in which God created him.

Our present state includes other difficulties, which leave us no doubt as to the importance of the spiritual work imposed

* Genesis ii. 19. † Genesis ii. 15.

upon the human race. The abuse of liberty has covered every part of our being with ruins; our intelligence is darkened, our love has grown cold; the struggle between good and evil has assumed a character of alarming depth, with the development of generations. God, without disappearing from our midst, has found amongst us enemies conspiring against the remembrance of Him, and employing all the resources of the mind and the passions to destroy that remembrance. There is no tradition which has not been denied, no duty which has not been outraged, no divine institution which has not been subjected to the violent attacks of mad impiety; and if God has remained visible during the whole course of ages, if He still reigns over the posterity of His first creature, it is but at the price of a combat rife in tears and blood. You are engaged in this divine war, you form part of it, and, victors or vanquished, I have nothing to teach you on the painful price of truth.

Even had we but the work of the soul; if man could extend towards God a look free from all other care, a hand free from all other burden! But it is not so. From the first, a function and a labour of a different order have been confided to us. God, because He would not leave us without occupation for the forces of the body by which we hold to the inferior world, called us to share His temporal government. He gave us the earth to guard and fertilise, not at first at the price of our toil, but by an administration which partook of the nature of empire and added to our other prerogatives the glory of useful command. In exchange for a royal and blessed culture, the obedient earth rendered back to us a substance necessary to sustain our immortality during its earthly existence. "Behold," said God to us, "I have given you every herb bearing seed upon the earth, and all trees that have in themselves seed of their own kind, to be your meat."* This reciprocal intercourse between nature and man possessed nothing primitively which was an obstacle to the relation between our soul and God. The soul rather found therein a spiritual aliment, a source of joy which sprang forth without effort and reached even to its author. But that state did not last, and you know what temporal labour has become for the posterity of Adam. A curse has fallen upon it; the earth, which yielded to our

* Genesis i. 29.

desires, refuses to us all that we do not pay it for beforehand in toil and fatigue: it doles out its gifts to us with avarice that nothing can move, with uncertainty that nothing can disarm. Nearly the whole of the human race, with brow bent towards it, implores it with assiduous devotedness, and gathers for recompense only the bitter bread of hard poverty. Now, poverty of the body easily entails that of the soul: it has created modes of servitude which draw all the human faculties together in their many folds, and by pressing upon their action, plunges them into a state approaching to death. Man descends towards the instinct of the animal; absorbed in his material wants, he forgets his origin and his end; he throws to the winds the divine life whose germ is within him, and his only care is to force the earth to render to him the blessings of eternity.

We can only accuse ourselves; God is not responsible for our faults and our blindness. He foresaw them, doubtless; and I have told you why, notwithstanding that prevision, He did not refuse us the blessing of liberty. But, since He foresaw them, His wisdom and His goodness commanded Him to come to our help, and, by a primitive, fundamental, and imprescriptible law to regulate the relation between temporal and spiritual labour, both necessary to mankind, the one as the principle of its divine life, the other as the principle of its terrestrial life; both of which should be reciprocally limited in an equitable proportion. Now, who should have discovered this, and who should have established that proportion, if God had not done it? Who should have had wisdom to determine the time which man owed to his soul, and that which he owed to his body? Who should have possessed the authority necessary, in so difficult a matter, to obtain the sanction of universal respect? Who should have saved man from the tyranny of his own cupidity, and from the tyranny, not less to be feared, of one stronger than himself? In the question of labour lies the root of all servitude; it is the question of labour which has made masters and servants, conquering and conquered nations, oppressors of every kind and oppressed of every name. Labour being no other thing than human activity, everything necessarily has relation to it, and according as it is well or ill distributed, society is well or ill organised, happy or miserable, moral or immoral. We have now before us a proof of this which the most blind are obliged to comprehend. What has agitated the world during the last twenty years? What is the cry of the civil wars which we now witness? Is it not: "Organisation of labour"? Is it not also: "Live by labour, or die fighting"? And, if we examine the chain of historical revolutions, shall we ever find for them, whatever may be their name, another primary cause than the question of labour? The migrations of nations, the invasion of the barbarians, the servile wars, the troubles of the forum, all the great human agitations, hang directly or indirectly upon that terrible question, which rises again from its own ashes with obstinate immortality. It is the axis upon which the destinies of the world turn.

And, consequently, the first religious and civil law is the law of labour. Now who should, who could, lay it down? Who, save He who owes nothing to anyone, but who, having from love made Himself the Father of minds, willed to be the light whence they should derive their direction? Who, save He who has created the soul and the body of man, who knows their wants, who has measured their powers, and who alone possesses the secret of limits, because He has none? It was just that, in the act of creation, God should promulgate all the bases of the physical, moral, and religious orders, and that He should promulgate them by acts sufficiently powerful for the remembrance of them to bear their commandment even to the last generations. Language alone would not have sufficed; God was not content to proclaim His laws by language alone, at the origin of things any more than on Sinai and Calvary. He has constantly graven them in acts whose eloquence is more enduring than brass. The cross of Calvary, the tables of Sinai, the waves of the deluge, the days of creation, are the four great monuments of divine legislation; imperishable monuments, which, after so many ages, exist in all the vigour of the first day. The cross of Calvary covers the five divisions of the world; the tables of Sinai are read in all the places crowned by the cross; the waves of the deluge have left their traces from the Alps to the Caucasus, from the Caucasus to the Himalayas, from the Himalayas to the summit of the Andes; and the days of the creation, religiously preserved in the strata of the globe, in the furrows of our ploughs, revive that magnificent law of labour which has preceded all others, and which we must now more clearly define to you.

You have already heard the terms of this law: "God," it is said, "ended on the seventh day the work which he had made, and he rested on the seventh day from all his work which he had done, and he blessed the seventh day and sanctified it, because in it he rested from all his work which God created and made." Such is the proportion of temporal to spiritual labour, of the labour of the body to the labour of the soul, according as God determined it by the sovereign example of His own work. And, indeed, if the question had depended upon man, we may be sure that it would not have been solved in this manner. Knowing the law, are we even capable of explaining it to ourselves? Why should the number seven express the totality of the two kinds of labour? Why should spiritual labour amount only to a seventh part of temporal labour? Why should the one occupy six consecutive days, and not a longer or a shorter time? Is there nothing in the powers of the body and the soul that leads us to this proportion of six to one? Or is it nature that reveals it to us by the general harmony of its laws? No, gentlemen, neither do the phenomena of nature, nor the necessities of the body, nor the wants of the soul, give us the elements of such an induction. When the rationalist dictators of the French Revolution, from hatred of all traditional and sacred origins, resolved to efface the ancient period of seven days from the calendar of a great people, they knew not where to take the basis of a new calculation, save in the convenience of a system of numeration. They decreed that the week should be ten days, in order to introduce the uniformity of the decimal mode into labour, as into weights and measures. The French citizen was to labour for nine days and rest on the tenth, simply because a like division had been established in things of number, and because it is easier to compute figures by this mode than by any other. No one troubled himself to learn whether the body of man would bear such an increase of labour; and, had they done this, it is manifest that every precise limit would have been the result of an arbitrary choice, and not the fruit of experience or reasoning.

The number seven, chosen by God, has no relation to any mathematical fitness. Nor is it justified by the degree of the bodily forces; for it is not easy to see, for instance, that man would not have been able to labour for seven days and to rest on the eighth. It is a number taken from a higher region than physical order; and so it should be, since it was a matter of regulating the relations of two kinds of labour, one material and the other spiritual. Evidently, between two kinds of things so completely diverse, the mediator could come only from a point which governed both, that is to say, the soul and the body. Now, God alone governs all the beings which compose the hierarchy of the universe; He alone, in His universal and creating essence, possesses the pattern of their own, the reason of their existence, the law of their relations, the principle of their harmony. It is then in Himself, in the higher and mysterious mathematics of His own nature, that God has chosen the number suitable as the rule of our double activity. This number does not appear in the work of cosmogony only, it plays an important part in all the rest of the divine operations, as the Scriptures show us. We see it shining in the seven weeks of years of the Hebrew jubilee, in the seven branches of the candlestick of Jerusalem, in the seven gifts of the Holy Ghost, in the seven sacraments of the Church, in the seven seals of the Apocalypse, and in a multitude of occurrences which it would require too much time to enumerate. In almost every page of the sacred books its importance is manifested by the use which God has directly or indirectly made of it.

In short, to the eyes of pure reason the number seven is an arbitrary number; to the eyes of reason enlightened by faith it is a divine number; to the eyes of history it is a traditional number; to the eyes of experience it is a number which has reconciled the wants and duties of the body with the wants and duties of the soul. Six days of temporal labour have sufficed for man in all times and under all climates to gain his subsistence without weakening his strength, to fertilise the earth without compromising his health or his happiness; the seventh day, consecrated to repose in the worship of God, has also sufficed for him to refresh his soul, to preserve truth, to rekindle his love, and, in fine, to advance peacefully and joyously towards the august end of a creature blessed by God. Whatever metaphysical judgment you may pronounce upon this memorable division of temporal and spiritual labour, there are two things which you cannot deny, namely, its universality and its efficacy; so much the more remarkable, as we do not see any rational cause for it, whilst we are forced to conclude that that cause exists. Would you destroy the balance of human activity, engender the degradation of souls, the oppression of the weak, the cupidity of all, and the misery of the greater number? Would you do this? It is easy; touch the law of labour as it was promulgated by the work of creation; increase temporal labour; lessen, by violence or artifice, spiritual labour; abandon man to the inspirations of his covetousness and the will of his masters; do this, and you will be sure to gather its fruit in a generation which will satisfy you, if you like the moral and physical degradation of mankind.

I say the physical as well as the moral degradation; for the observance of the seventh day was not established simply with a view to religious sanctification, but also and directly with a view to terrestrial preservation. This is why Scripture employs two remarkable expressions at the same time; it says that God "rested" on the seventh day, and that He "sanctified" it. And as the object of God was to trace the rule of our activity by His example, it follows that He recommended two things to us at the same time, repose and the sanctification of the seventh day. And if you doubt this, if you do not think that God has so great a regard for the equitable well-being of the body of man, hear it again proclaimed by Moses, at the foot of Sinai, in the great law of the Sabbath: "Six days shalt thou labour, and shalt do all thy works; the seventh day is the day of the sabbath, that is, the rest of the Lord thy God; thou shalt not do any work therein, thou, nor thy son, nor thy daughter, nor thy man-servant, nor thy maid-servant, nor thy ox, nor thy ass, nor any of thy beasts, nor the stranger that is within thy gates."* This is the law. Now listen to the reason which God immediately gives for it: "that," He says, "thy man-servant and thy maid-servant may rest even as thyself."† And going still further, He said on another occasion to all the assembled people: "Six days thou shalt work; the seventh day thou shalt cease, that thy ox and thy ass may rest, and the son of thine handmaid and the stranger may be refreshed."‡ Here God stipulates in favour of the animals who share the labour of man; He associates them in the benefit of His merciful providence, and since they are fatigued with the reasonable creature, He wills that the repose of the reasonable creature should extend even to them. You recognise here the heart of God, and if your intelligence still doubted of the temporarily philanthropic sense attached by Scripture to the law of the seventh day, there remains no longer any excuse for you before texts which from their clearness defy interpretation. Listen

* Deuteronomy v. 13, 14. † Ibid.
‡ Exodus xxiii. 12.

again, however. After God had recommended to His people the observance of the seventh day in favour of the poorest and most laborious, He terminates by this solemn adjuration: "Remember that thou also didst serve in Egypt, and the Lord thy God brought thee out from thence with a strong hand and a stretched-out arm: therefore he hath commanded thee that thou shouldst observe the sabbath day."* Thus it is in remembrance of the bondage in Egypt, and in recalling it to them, that God imposes upon the posterity of Jacob the charter of rest from labour, that is to say, the first and fundamental charter of all liberty. For what is the liberty of a man attached to the glebe of unremitting labour? What is the liberty of a body never uplifted towards the vault of heaven, and the liberty of a soul never raised towards the light of God?

It is to you, gentleman, to all generations of masters, that these formidable words are addressed, which, three thousand years ago, resounded in the deserts of the Red Sea: "Remember that thou also didst serve in Egypt!" All of us, in our forefathers, have served; all of us, in our posterity, shall serve in Egypt. In vain do we wear the signs of emancipation, and ask from the future the fidelity which it refuses to kings; we are of a blood which servile labour has formed, which servile labour will form again. See in your hands the trace of earth; we come from the earth, and to it we shall return. There is no exception for any one of us, for the child of the palace any more than for the child of the cottage. Sooner or later the long hand of misfortune will again seize upon us and bring us back to the obscure labour which was our cradle. And if it was so in the ages of stability, how much more now when every corner-stone has been destroyed, and we build in the tempests of equality the shifting edifice of our destinies! Hearken then to the words which remind you of the bondage of Egypt, respect in your brethren living in service the service which was your own, and which will return to you again. Take not away from them the day of relaxation which was prepared for them from the beginning as the liberty of their souls and bodies, and with a degree of munificence of which you do not perhaps form an idea.

For remark that God has not made of the seventh day a private institution, a day to take at hazard by each of us in any

---

* Deuteronomy v. 15.

particular course of occupied days. No, He has made of it the great social institution; He has convoked the human race on the same day and at the same hour in the whole course of ages, inviting it to repose, to rejoice, and be exalted in Him. In a word, He has founded a periodical and perpetual festival for mankind. For man needs festivals. Withheld far from the permanent city which is the term of his pilgrimage, and bearing in his heart the sadness of this trial of absence, he needs, by certain emotions, to leave the monotonous shadow of his life. Like Saul, he needs to hear the sound of the harp, or like David, to dance to music, before the ark of God. But who will give these festivals to the poor of this world? Who will give them palaces, statues, paintings, voices, and lights? Who will give them emotions worthy of them, and that rare joy in which the conscience is enraptured as well as the heart? The people are poor and without art; they posess nothing great but themselves and God who protects them. The people and God come together and form the festival of mankind. For sixty centuries these two have been faithful to this meeting, and enjoy together without interruptions that festival which costs nothing to the people but their assembling, to God but looking down upon them.

The legislators of nations have recognised this popular want of common and public enjoyments; they have sought to satisfy it by religious pomps, by spectacles, triumphs, games, and combats. But instead of instructing and elevating man, nothing has helped more to degrade him; the most shameful passions came there to seek gratification and applause. Sensuality and blood met together there before the sacred images of country; and publicity, the mother of modesty, is there for the multitude only an additional debauch. This is because, in fact, the pleasures of the crowd turn easily towards all the vices. A celebrated politician has said: "Whoever assembles the people makes them factious." It may with no less truth be said: Whoever amuses the people corrupts them. In modern times rationalist legislators have been seen endeavouring to create festivals in order to replace that of the seventh day which they had abolished. They have only succeeded in inventing imitations of antiquity with the addition of ridicule and without the people. Public common sense was too just and too profound, under the inspiration of Christianity, to enjoy these puerile renovations. It then became necessary, in the great occasions of civil life, to limit them to vulgar amusements, and God alone remained to give to the human race grave solemnities which draw men together, move, ameliorate, and bring them repose.

Is there any one among you who has not been touched by the spectacle which a Christian population presents on the day consecrated to God? The public places covered with a multitude of beings dressed in their best apparel; all ages appearing there with their hopes and fears, each tempered by a sentiment higher than life. The eyes that meet each other are animated by fraternal joy; the servant is nearer to his master; the poor less removed from the rich; all by the community of the same duty accomplished and the same grace received, feel more fully that they are sons of the same Father who is in heaven. The silence of servile labour is compensated for by the joyous and musical sound of the bells, which make known to thousands of men that they are free, and prepare them to endure for God the days when they will not be free. No austerity clouds their features; the idea of observance is moderated by that of repose, and the idea of repose is embellished by the image of a festival. Incense burns in the temple; lights shine upon the altars; music fills the vaults and speaks to all hearts; the priest goes from the people to God and from God to the people; earth mounts upwards and heaven descends. Who does not leave the temple more calm? Who will not return to it better? Oh! for my part, gentlemen, this day has never passed without having moved me; and even here, in this capital, where so many souls do not respect it, I never witness its popular effect without lifting my heart towards God in an aspiration of gratitude and love.

Such is then the sense, such is the result of that great law of labour which God willed to promulgate and to hallow in the very act of creation. After having interpreted it to you, can I withhold a painful sensation which oppresses me? Can I refrain from complaining that there is a Christian people which despises this law, and that people is our own? Is it really France that, in this point, neglects the most sacred of duties between man and man? Is it France that tears in twain the fundamental pact of mankind, that delivers over to the rich the body and soul of the poor to use at their pleasure, that tramples under foot the day of liberty, equality, fraternity, the sublime day of the people and of God? I ask you, is it really France? Do not excuse her by saying that she grants to each the free exercise of his own worship, and that no one, against his consent, is constrained to work on the seventh day. For it is but to add to the reality of servitude the hypocrisy of freedom. Ask the workman whether he is free to abandon his labour on the dawn of the day that commands him to rest. Ask the young man who consumes his life in a daily lucre of which he does not profit, if he is free to breathe only once in the week the air of heaven and the still purer air of truth. Ask those withered creatures who people the manufacturing cities if they are free to save their souls in comforting their bodies. Ask the innumerable victims of personal cupidity and of the cupidity of a master, if they are free to become better, and if the gulf of toil without physical or moral reparation does not swallow them up alive. Ask those even who repose, but who repose in the degradation of unregulated passions, ask them what becomes of the people in that rest which is not given and protected by God. No, gentlemen, liberty of conscience here is only a veil that covers oppression; it covers with a golden mantle the cowardly shoulders of the most vile of all tyranny, the tyranny that abuses the toil of man by cupidity and impiety. If liberty of conscience were a reality here, doubtless Protestant England would have perceived it; doubtless the democracy of the United States of America would have learned it: and where in the world has the right of the seventh day been more respected? Learn then, those who know it not; learn, enemies of God and of the human race, whatever name they bear, that between the strong and the weak, between the rich and the poor, between the master and the servant, it is liberty that oppresses, and law that gives freedom. Right is the sword of the powerful, duty is the shield of the weak.

It is high time for us to remove from France this lamentable error, which has lasted but too long. The tempests also warn us that it is not good to violate commandments which were promulgated with the creation, renewed in the thunders of Sinai, and reinvigorated by the blood of Calvary. Whosoever is against God is against mankind, and if a few unhappy men, armed with what they call reason, fear not to make these two enemies, we may trust to the vengeance of the future alone—that future which is already the present, and which warns us all to think of our faults and generously to combat them by a salutary reparation. France will do this! Yes, Lord, France will do this! We see its foreshadowing in the respect she pays to Thee in the midst of the ruins she has so suddenly made. She will listen to the forewarnings of experience, she will rise again towards Thee by the difficulties which surround her, she will recognise the principle of her salvation in that beautiful saying which Thou hast pronounced to all nations of the earth by Jesus Christ Thine only Son: "Seek first the kingdom of God, and his justice, and all other things shall be added to you."* Hearken, O God, to that voice which speaks to Thee from France; and when another year fallen from Thy eternity upon our short life shall bring us again together in this temple, grant that we may find here more steadfast, stronger, and more glorious than ever, our country and truth!

* Matt. vi. 33.

# GOD AND MAN.

# GOD AND MAN.

## THE SUPERNATURAL INTERCOURSE BETWEEN GOD AND MAN.

My Lord,*—Gentlemen,

We will begin by establishing the point we have reached in expounding the mystery of destinies, as it is professed by Catholic doctrine. According to that doctrine, there exists an infinite, eternal Being, subsisting of Himself, who is one without being alone; for He finds in His own essence relations whence, with the necessary movement of His life, results the absolute plenitude of His perfection and His happiness. A Being unique and complete, God suffices to Himself. No necessity, no utility called Him out of Himself; He saw in His intelligence the inexhaustible image of a multitude of beings variously limited; He felt His power to cause them to pass from the possible to the real state; but being perfect and happy in the inner development of His triple personality, He was free not to exercise His power, and, in the depth of His mind, to leave in repose the eternal spectacle of the worlds which were not. Goodness alone incited Him gratuitously to communicate life; and therefore, on the day when it pleased Him, or rather in that indivisible day which has no distinct movements save for the passing beings who behold it, God created the universe. He created it so as to realise the indefinite perspective of the possible, as He beheld it in His intelligence,

* Monseigneur Sibour, Archbishop of Paris.

and man, who in his double nature drew together all its elements and all its features, was placed in the centre of that work, as its connecting link, and its most complete representation. God is thus the principle of things. But by the same reason which determined Him to be the principle of things, He is also their end—that is to say, their term or object. For, having created from goodness, He willed to communicate His own perfection and beatitude to His creatures, and this can be accomplished only by the intimate union of their life with His own. Whence it follows that the general law of all created beings is to aspire towards God—minds, by a free and direct effort; bodies, by their association with minds in the person of man. And in order for that ascension of the finite towards the infinite to be possible, on the very day of their creation, God, the author of intelligent beings, gave to them truth and love—truth, to know Him; love, to love Him—and the Father of beings became altogether and at the same moment their principle, their means, and their end.

Such is the first plan of Catholic doctrine, and the first plan of our destinies.

But is this all? Has God, in order to attract us towards Him, limited Himself to spreading out before us the spectacle of nature, and to lighting up in our intelligence the sun of reason? Is all other communication between Himself and us —communication more direct, nearer, more profound—impossible? Have we nothing more to hope for or pretend to, until the day when the mystery of our creation will be consummated in eternity? Rationalism affirms this; it declares —and this it is which separates it from us in the very fount of its essence—that there is no communication between God and ourselves, save by the intermediary of reason, that every other mode is chimerical, all other intercourse an imposture or an illusion. Catholic doctrine does not accept this decision—it believes, it teaches that nature and reason form but the peristyle of truth, the first torch of the temple, and that man, with this help alone, however great he may be, is an incomplete being, who would be incapable of attaining the term of his destinies—that is to say, God. Behold the formidable question now before us. All that I said to you last year of the Christian dogmas contains in itself only a spiritualist philosophy; there are sages who bend with respect before that portion of religious truth, and if we did not advance further, we should remain within the limits of human wisdom. Catholic doctrine does not permit us to do this; it constrains us to pass these narrow limits, and to show you that beyond and besides the creating act to which we owe the elements of life, knowledge, and love, which are within us, there exists in regard to us an action of God more penetrating and more profound. What is that action? Does it exist in reality? This is what we must now endeavour to learn.

My Lord,

You are the third Archbishop of Paris before whom I have here announced the word of God. Your two last predecessors were both struck by the thunderbolt; they both prematurely carried to God the account full and yet incomplete of their episcopacy. One of them saw his palace razed to the ground by the hands of the multitude, and, after having responded to that act of violence by ten years of good deeds, he died without having obtained from the justice of men the reparation due to his piety, his courage, and his goodness. The other offered himself as a holocaust; he fell in disarming civil war, and the people, moved by that victim who had become their peacemaker, brought him back into this temple, and made here for him a sepulchre greater than his throne, and a resurrection as glorious as his death. God has chosen you, my lord, to succeed these two men, and to continue the history of the See of St. Denis; He has considered you worthy to occupy a place which henceforth can only be filled by the charity that makes the martyr, and the greatness of soul that makes the citizen. I wish you happier days than theirs, a glory less agitated, and an end less precocious—not that I doubt of your heart, should God call you to equal them in the peril and honour of tribulations, but because it belongs only to God to desire for men, and send to them, tribulations as great as their virtues.

Gentlemen,

I shall not render an account to you of my public acts in the memorable year which has just closed upon us. Time perhaps has taken upon itself to explain and ratify them—I shall not say more to you than time. My mission is not to speak to you of myself, but to speak to you of God, and of yourselves in your relations with God. This is the mountain upon which I have placed my life, and upon which I would place yours. Let us ascend it together, and from this height, which surveys time and the passions of men, let us proclaim to earth the only truths which are able to save it.

Since God is the end of man, since He has created us to be perfect and happy in Him, it is manifest that if the designs of the creation have not here below been entirely frustrated, there should be found men who tend to their end in seeking and loving God. And nevertheless, because of human liberty, there should also be found other men who neglect God, their principle and their end, and yield to the seduction of created things. Such, indeed, is the spectacle which the history of the world unceasingly presents to us. At whatever epoch it is consulted or regarded it will be found struggling with the two great parties which contend for the government of minds—the party of God and that of man—the party of saints and that of sages. Now, if it be true that we have no other means for arriving at our divine end than nature and reason, it is manifest that the party of God should take its basis in the sole resources of the natural order. And yet it is not so. The party of God exists, it has always existed, it is endowed with a force which none other has been able to destroy—neither ages, nor kings, nor sages. Ages have come with the empire and stratagems of duration; the party of God has seen them pass away, and made use of them but to outlive them. Kings have held in their hands all the power of man; the party of God has blessed or cursed their passage, and in the one, as in the other case, has covered their head with earth and remained living. Sages have written books, and made names for themselves; the party of God has taken possession of their books, and now that their renown is but a fruitless remembrance, it still uses their ashes to insure its immortality. And whence, amidst general decay, does this persevering and victorious party derive its imperturbable life? I have said that it is not from nature and reason. Doubtless it acknowledges their rights, it employs them to its own profit, but as principles which have no elevation corresponding to the greatness of our destinies, and which form but the dawn of a more perfect day. Its force, it declares, is in a doctrine which does not come from nature, and which disconcerts reason. It is there, from that mysterious fount, that the party of God derives the light which guides it, the virtue which purifies it, the courage which raises it above the persecutions of time. This it does not hide, it is its glory and its boast.

If we now, on the contrary, consider the other party—the party of man—and seek to know the basis of its convictions and its acts, it is no more hidden from us than the other; it boldly declares to us that there is no other science than that of nature, no other truth than that of which reason is the principle, the seat, and the demonstration. That if beyond the universe there exists an invisible Being, freed from the limits in which all beings are retained, the party of man pretends to have no idea of Him save by the inner revelation of the mind, or by the conclusion to be drawn from the phenomena of the world. But whether it admit or reject the existence of that superior Being, the party of man holds no real intercourse with Him. Those among the sages who, like Plato, have left a religious memory, were all penetrated with serious respect for the vestiges of a tradition whose history they ignored. They avowed the infirmity of human thought left to its own resources, and endeavoured to raise themselves towards God by the irrational effort of prayer. They belonged to the party of saints by desire, to the party of sages by ignorance.

Behold the fact! Wherever God is adored, He is adored in virtue of a supernatural doctrine; wherever He is despised, He is despised in the name of nature and reason. However strange the result may be, it is not possible to deny it. Turn your eyes whither you will, enter into whatever temple you please, you will find there on the very threshold Prophecy and Sacrament; prophecy—a word of God containing truths inaccessible to reason; sacrament—an act endowed by God with an efficacy superior to all the forces of nature. And you will see that whoever despises these two things infallibly bends towards earth, knowing nothing of God but His name, and holding with Him no other relations than ingratitude and forgetfulness.

Again, behold the fact! But what must we conclude therefrom? We must conclude that the intercourse between man and God is not founded upon the purely natural order, but upon an order more intimate and more profound, which places human personality and the divine personality in direct contact. If you refuse to draw this conclusion, you are free to do so, but learn that you thereby destroy all intercourse between man and God, since in reality there exists none other upon earth. Perhaps you will say it is of little importance to you, and that your opinion is precisely that this intercourse is no other thing than an imposture or an illusion.

Here the question changes its face. It is no longer a question of knowing what is really in mankind the mode of its religious acts, but what is the logical value of those acts, as the human race performs them. I say the human race, and I ought first to establish this in order to give a basis to my argument. Is mankind religious? Is mankind religious under the supernatural form?

It seems impossible to pretend that mankind is religious, since I have myself confessed that it is divided into two parties —the party of God and the party of man—the party of faith and that of unbelief. But it is easy to see that this division, all real though it be, does not destroy the universality and perpetuity of religious worship among men, and therefore does not deprive us of the right of affirming that mankind is religious. In fact, whilst no people appears in history without the sign and palladium of a positive faith, without temple, altar, priesthood—that is to say, without a constituted religion—unbelief appears only under an individual form, sometimes proscribed, sometimes tolerated, seldom powerful, and never becoming established as the public and social expression of a nation. Far from obtaining a character of universality, unbelief does not even acquire the honour of nationality; it leagues man to man, like a venom which inoculates itself, and which, were it even to become a plague, would still remain, in regard to its expansion, in the state of accident and scourge. There are considerable portions of mankind which have never known it; such is the East. There, under a glowing sky, man more naturally raises his eyes towards the invisible sphere inhabited by God; he believes, he prays, he adores, he contemplates, so to say, without thinking of what he does; and doubt or unbelief, if they enter into his mind, leave there rather the trace of a dream than of a temptation.

It is the same with epochs as with nations. Epochs, taken in their suite, are religious. If certain periods form exceptions —that is to say, present a greater number of individual apostasies—they are periods of decadency which, in performing their painful and corrupt cycle, soon bring back from the depths of eternity, with younger days, more respected faiths. And as there are races to whom irreligion is unknown, there are also epochs in which this mystery of iniquity has not even a name. Such were the first centuries of the Roman Republic; such was that memorable epoch when Christianity, having accomplished the baptism of Europe, held its ardent nations under the sceptre of a still unanimous faith.

Whether, then, we consider mankind in the numerous nations which form its total body, or whether we regard it in its secular development, incredulity shows itself only in the state of protestation, with the weakness of isolation even in number; with the powerlessness of attaining perpetuity even in duration; and, in his heart and his history, man remains in the eyes of all, a religious being.

But under what form is he a religious being? Nothing assuredly is more varied than the spectacle of the religions which fill the earth. They differ in doctrine, in morals, in ceremonies, in priesthoods, in their aversions, and it seems impossible in whatever light we may regard them, to bring them together into one common architecture. And yet there is not one among them which, in regard to form, has not the same starting-point and the same constitution. All require their proselytes to bend with the respect and obedience of faith before a sacred dogma—that is to say, before a doctrine descended from God by an inspired or a prophetic revelation. Whilst science starts from the observation of nature, and philosophy from the investigation of reason, in all times and places religion invokes prophecy—that is to say, the word of God, communicated first to an envoy, next transmitted by tradition to the lips of the priest, who delivers it as he received it, as an inviolable heritage from on high. The man of science, the philosopher, and the priest, are the organs of a threefold teaching, whose lights might aid one another by mutual reflection, but which have all their own principle and their incommunicable character. None will ever be deceived in this. The man of science verifies, the philosopher reasons, the priest affirms in the name of God. And thus the very definition of these three kinds of men shows to us, that all worship is founded upon a prophecy, whether the author were really inspired by God, or whether he may have usurped, by a culpable imitation, the title and the power of prophecy. We shall soon see the means of discerning the true or the false in a matter where imposture has such grave consequences;

but here the imposture itself proves the truth which I wish to establish. For, I ask, why invent falsehood in the name of God, if the name of God, called in testimony of the dogma, were not necessary to the life of all religion?

Thus as each nation preserves the memory of the legislator or conqueror who was its founder, each worship, true or false, has consecrated the history of the prophet who brought to it from heaven the word of God. Christians name Jesus Christ; the Jews, Moses; the Persians, Zoroaster; the Hindoos, Buddha; the Mussulmans, Mahomet; and if there are forms of worship which do not personally know their divine founder, that ignorance arises because they are, like the polytheism of the Greeks and the Romans, only a confused corruption of anterior systems.

See, then, that all religions—that is to say, mankind itself inasmuch as it is religious—confess that the intercourse between man and God reposes upon truths of another order than that of reason, upon a light different and more elevated than that which naturally enlightens created intelligences. This is not all; by the side of prophecy, that universal and perpetual torch by which faith is enlightened, sacrament, another institution reputed divine, imposes and manifests itself—an institution whose object is the purification, the elevation, the sanctification of the soul; its union with God, by a virtue which surpasses and astonishes the powers of nature. You who listen to me are the children of sacrament. Almost as soon as you drew the breath of life, before your eyes were opened to the light, before you thought, desired, or demanded anything, those who loved you, being full of anxious solicitude for you, took you from the first watchings of a mother, to bear you to the vast and solemn shade of a mysterious place. A man appeared, he poured water upon your head, and pronounced a few words; he commanded the evil spirit to go out of you; he entered into your soul to eradicate evil therefrom and sow the seeds of good; he gave you his faith and that of your fathers, an infinite hope, a love which the united beauty of all creatures would not have been capable of imparting to you; he drew you from the limits of nature and the obscurities of reason; he made you living members of an invisible community; sons and co-heirs of God, worthy of hearing and repeating His name, of contemplating His works, of finding them too limited for you, and of aspiring, in fine, to His eternity as to your natural and true country. All this was done for you without your concurrence. Your friends were in haste, they feared lest a single day might deprive you of the benefit of that incomprehensible action, and had it been necessary to choose between your present death and your future life, those who loved you most, and who loved you the first—your mother even—would not have hesitated to lose you in your birth, provided you bore away with you the sign of the cross in the symbol of water. You may now despise these gifts; but whatever your will may be, you have received them; whatever you may do, they exist; and the faith of three hundred millions of souls, based upon the faith of a hundred generations, affirms to you, that the consecration of your baptism is of an immortality against which no revolt has any power or effect.

I pass over the other sacraments of Christianity; you all know them, and none of you doubt that they are an essential part of the religion of Christ—the means which it offers to raise us from earth to heaven. But is it the same in other religions? Is sacrament everywhere the inviolable mode of communication between man and God? Yes, amongst all: from the sacred forests of Scandinavia to the grotesque pagodas of China; from the stone of the Druids to the altar of Greece; from the most modern periods to the most remote ages—in all times and places, worship is sacramental as dogma is prophetic. Sacrifices, lustral waters, expiations, initiations, bloody or joyous rites—these have formed the life of all liturgies and the function of all priesthoods. One single worship, that of Mahomet, has appeared sparing in this regard, because it is scarcely anything but a form of deism clothed in revelation, and yet Mahomet preserved the vestige of sacrifice when he made prayer the practical foundation of his religious edifice. Now, prayer itself is a sacrament, when it is supposed to possess a power of impetration which evidently surpasses the character of a natural act.

Instead, then, of supposing that morals should be the sole and true means of uniting us to God, if we consult only the light of reason, we see that, in order to obtain that supreme object, all religions present to us strange operations whose virtue lies solely in the will which institutes them; and as reason is subordinate to faith in the mental order, morals are subordinate to sacrament in the order of the will. Not that faith should destroy reason, or sacrament morals, but on the contrary faith is given to increase reason, and sacrament to perfect morals. Now, the more extraordinary this result is, the more its universality and its perpetuity, so far from inspiring us with sterile astonishment, merit from us profitable and respectful consideration.

Therefore I beg you to remark that prophecy and sacrament are not secret works, hidden in the depths of sanctuaries and revealed only to the initiated, but they both stand forth with the boldness of faith, and are both public like religion.

Now, publicity is not a slight thing, and above all, publicity which is universal and perpetual. Better than in any other age, you are now able to judge how formidable is its trial, since we are surrounded by the ruins which it produces daily, and by which it replies to the audacity of those who affront it with so much the less reflection, as there has never been in the world less of self-distrust and more facility for speaking boldly and without restraint, than now. Formerly, when a man, endowed with the highest intellectual gifts—Pythagoras, for instance—believed that he had received from heaven an idea useful to the happiness of human beings, he was somewhat alarmed: for a long time he carefully considered it within himself, then, uncertain of his own genius, he sent from sanctuary to sanctuary to interrogate the sacerdotal orders, famous by their tradition, the sciences, "silvered by age," according to the expression of Plato, and, after years nourished with those divine intercourses, he hardly felt entitled to open his lips and teach in his turn. He did not dare to deliver to the world the fruit of his long meditations, but only to a few disciples, proving himself with them in abstinences, fastings, and all the austerities of a life of seclusion from men. Therefore glory, at least, rewarded this respect for truth; the name of Pythagoras lived, if his doctrine did not survive. It is far otherwise in our age—the youngest of our contemporaries is not afraid, as soon as he discovers an idea in his mind, to deliver it to the wind of publicity; he speaks, he writes, he prints, he is dissatisfied if in eight days his idea has not made the tour of Europe. Publicity obeys him; it bears from the West to the East the light sheet which an intrepid conscience has confided to it, but on the morrow it brings back, even more quickly, silence and forgetfulness. Mystery would have protected it, publicity destroys it. It is true that publicity is the high-road of great men; but it does not suffice to follow a high-road, it must be followed to the end, and nothing is more difficult or more rare, to judge by the spectacle which we witness. Our age is the age of high-roads, but they are short.

It is in fact, because publicity involves an immense confronting of the idea with all minds, rights, interests, institutions, acquired truths, settled customs—with all that passes in space and time. It is a contest of the new against the old—of progress against stability, and reciprocally of the old against the new, of stability against progress; a terrible and a daily struggle wherein it is impossible for that which is vain long to resist. This is why, even now, error seeks its empire in the shade of secrecy. You think, perhaps, that the peril of the nineteenth century is in unbridled publicity, and it is true that this publicity occasions many evils, but they are not comparable to those formed in the invisible conspiracies of thought. Day is but the reflex of night, publicity is but the echo of silence. Before the thunder escapes from the mouth of the volcano, it has furrowed underground the courses whence it derives its energy. If Europe trembles, it is not because it speaks, but because it has long been silent in the gloom of secret societies. Now is the hour of judgment, for it is the hour of publicity. Doctrines must appear before the tribunal of the human mind and of historical experience; they must cast away the charm of the unknown and the evils of hypocrisy; they must answer every question, satisfy every want, be in open struggle with the inconstancy of mankind. Therefore, young as you are, of how many of them have you not already seen the end? How many more will die before your own mortality will snatch you away from this scene of powerlessness and change? This is painful to witness, but at least we learn therefrom the vanity of error before the test of discussion and duration.

Admire, then, with me, in the sacramental and prophetic institution, a publicity of sixty centuries. The temples were open, the smoke of sacrifice rose freely towards heaven, the blood and the water flowed upon the brow of the faithful in face of the unbeliever, the world beheld and still beholds. Nothing was hidden, nothing is now hidden from it. See, there is the baptismal font; there, the spot where faith kneels, avowing and repairing its faults; there, the tabernacle in which, under the appearance of bread, the living flesh of a God reposes: and you hear the word which reveals and animates all these things, it does not flee from you, it stands before you, urges you, commands you in the name of God. You may laugh, it is permitted to you, or you may smite your breast, for you are able to do so. But whether you respond by insult or adoration, prophecy subsists, sacrament perseveres; to-morrow you may die, and to-morrow they will seal your tomb. Is it not needful for you to think of it? Is it not needful for you to know whence that strange institution derives a duration equal to its publicity—duration throughout all ages before publicity throughout all times?

And yet publicity is not the last character by which we may judge of the part which prophecy and sacrament play in mankind. If mankind has destinies which have God for their end, it has also those which have nature for their horizon; if, by its relation with God, it forms a divine society, it forms, during its sojourn here below, a purely human society. Between these two societies, so different in their object, mode, and end, it would seem that there should exist no point of contact, or at least that the supernatural means of the one should be foreign to the natural effects of the other. It is not so. Prophecy and sacrament, which form the basis of religion, form also the basis of civil society. Such has been the estimation of all nations, since all have aggregated religion under one form or another to their public acts, and have venerated in the priesthood one of the principal instruments of the stability of empires. The priest, the warrior, the magistrate, have always been the three pillars of human society—the magistrate by justice, the warrior by the sword, the priest by the prophecy and sacrament, of which he is the living incarnation. Not that many other offices do not contribute to the stability as to the movement of social order; all even, whatever they may be, hold an honourable part there; but honour has its hierarchy as well as all the rest, and it is assuredly remarkable, not to say marvellous, that among so many human administrations, whose utility and glory are not questioned, the supernatural ministration of the priest should have obtained from nations so exalted a place in the organization of their temporal life. Even now, when for the first time, the idea of separating divine and human things is introduced, it is not thereby intended that religion should be banished from national affairs and interests, but only that it should act upon them by an action more independent of their outward operations. In this position it has lost nothing of its social influence, it is not less the recognised soul of actual civilization, and perhaps there has rarely been an epoch in which its necessity as a principle of the human order was more powerfully felt. What ruins surround us? For sixty years what has not the hand of France touched in order to destroy? What has it left standing? What is there which it has not at least wounded? Veneration has flown away from kings; neither war nor hereditary inheritance, nor the choice of revolutions, has been able to create a monarchy for us; we overthrow thrones without having the faith of the republican ages; we are wanting even in respect for our own works, and we have no longer strength save to disturb our ruins. I am wrong: something has remained great and honoured in this shipwreck of all institutions—the magistrate under his toga, the soldier under his banner, the priest in his temple. These remain to us, and because they remain, all is still saved.

What more is required in order to conclude with certainty that prophecy and sacrament have penetrated even to the root of the life of mankind, and thence that mankind is religious under the supernatural form? I do not think you can contest the fact; you can but reject its consequences, and those very consequences I am about to establish.

Already more than once in the course of our conferences, I have called your attention to the logical importance of every establishment which bears in itself the characters of universality, perpetuity, publicity, and organization. We shall find these significative characters in the prophetic and sacramental establishment, but with a new force which they derive from the very essence of prophecy and sacrament. For whilst the other institutions in which they are generally found proceed from the wants and faculties of man—that is to say, from the natural constitution of his being—here we can no longer explain their presence by that motive, since prophecy and sacrament belong to an order which confounds rather than satisfies human nature. We willingly understand that mankind may be religious; reason announces to us the existence of a Supreme Cause, to which we owe all that we are, from which alone we can hope for all that we need, and religion, being no other thing than an intercourse of dependence, gratitude, and love, with that Supreme Cause, it is easy for an upright heart to conceive its justice and to follow the inner attraction to it. But outside of this circle, reason only meets with abysses, or at least it discovers nothing in its own light that opens to it another mode of knowing, loving, and adoring God. Consequently it is not reason that urges mankind towards that other mode; it is not reason that opens before us the obscure career wherein priesthoods have led all nations and all times. Nothing is produced save by a principle of impulsion, no impulsion is given save in conformity with the spirit whence it emanates. Reason might create a worship of reason; it could not create a worship of which it possessed no element whatever.

But it is still more remarkable that in no age or place has reason ever created a rational worship. In all times and places, prophetic and sacramental worship has stifled rational worship and hindered its production. If this worship has existed in certain hearts, such as those of Pythagoras and Plato, it remained there uncertain of itself, in the state of an aspiration which vainly seeks to define itself—an incomplete and painful state, which drew from the greatest of sages that confession so often cited: "It is needful that a master should descend from heaven to instruct us."

How then should reason, incapable of forming a worship for itself, have led all mankind to a form of religion of which it had neither consciousness nor intelligence? And if reason be not the author of that religious form, who then is its author? Who has been powerful enough to impose it upon the human race? You will, perhaps, say—Man is made for God; he feels it, he knows it; he is so straitened upon this earth, which affords him but a poor and transitory shelter; by the natural impulsion of all his faculties, he aspires towards the infinite region, which is the term of his destiny. But he does not clearly know that term where he is waited for, he has a presentiment rather than knowledge of it; and, by the combined effect of what he desires and what he ignores, in order to attain to God, he creates for himself means which reassure him in his faith and console him in his desire. He believes that God speaks to him; he supposes that certain acts performed in His name receive in that sublime invocation an efficacy which nature alone cannot impart to anything. Prophecy is the dream of a truth, sacrament is the error of a hope. In the intercourse between a limited being and an infinite being, the impossible becomes natural, and extravagance seems to be an effort of reason.

Lucretius invoked fear as the creator of the gods and of their worship; you appeal to better sentiments in order to explain this mystery; and, indeed, if it were a question only of individual or local practices, we might, perhaps, consider positive religions as an aberration, more or less excusable, of religious sentiments. But that aberration, whatever may be the influence which caused it, and the names by which it has been distinguished, could not become the law of mankind. It is mankind that believes in prophecy and sacrament—mankind, without exception, that has submitted to dogmas of which the mind has no evidence, and to rights of which reason does not accept the concurrence; it is mankind, in its eminent nations as in its degenerate races, in its ages of civilization as in its ages of barbarism, in its sages as well as in its simple-hearted. It is impossible that all mankind has, in regard to God, suffered so persisting an eclipse of its true and natural light; it is impossible that God should have permitted this. Truth is the highest good we have received from His equitable beneficence—it is in all things the principle of our perfection and beatitude—we cannot lose it, without losing the root of all the divine gifts. And you would say that it is God Himself, His acts, His memory, His rights over us which have become the corrupted source of a universal and inveterate superstition!—that mathematical truth shall have been preserved, and religious truth shall have disappeared from the earth! Doubtless, human liberty has produced errors of every kind; but, besides that they have never universally destroyed anything necessary to the life of the human race, they still preserve traces of truth. We recognise in them the source from which the passions of men were turned aside, and its own inability to create even an error. Error is but a deviation from the truth, an adulteration of the natural order of things, which cannot be totally destroyed or changed, except by God.

Now a universal error is here supposed which, however, would have had no root in the physical, intellectual, and moral constitution of man. According to that constitution, as rationalism supposes it, man includes no element superior to reason—reason is the most elevated point of his being, the principle and moderator of all his other powers; beyond it he attains only to dreams, chimeras, and follies. Thence it is manifest that whatever is not rational is repugnant to mankind; and, consequently, it is impossible to conceive where mankind could have obtained the idea of holding relations with God issuing from any other source than reason.

But, say you, although reason is truly the most elevated point of human nature, yet it does not know God with sufficient clearness to unite to Him by its own powers, and hence it aspires to that union by means which are not its own, such as prophecy and sacrament.

Pardon me for so speaking to you, but it is impossible to concentrate in one single phrase more contradiction and unreason. What! reason has not in itself the means of uniting to God, and yet it desires to be united to God! But why does reason desire this? What obliges, what urges reason so to desire, since it does not possess the faculties which justify that ambition? Either God has willed that man should hold intercourse with Himself by the intermediary of reason, or He has not willed it. In the first case, He has evidently given to our intellectual movement a vibration powerful enough to raise it even to Himself; in the other case, reason, not being at all called to that high prerogative, would feel no more the need of it than the duty of exercising it. You must choose, and whichever you may choose, you will not explain how man, a purely rational being, tends to God by a mode foreign to his nature.

The vulgar among reasoners solve the difficulty by supposing that the human race has been the victim of a certain number of impostors, who from age to age, have abused its good faith. Primarily, they think, man had for prophet only his reason, for sacrament only his heart; he spake to God, and God talked with him in the sanctuary of the soul; philosophy and religion, being confounded together by their object and method, were but one and the same institution. There was no altar, nor worship, nor priesthood—there were only man and God. But as there sprang up an ambitious man to found the first throne, so there came another to found the first temple. A second followed; then a third, and soon the prophetic and sacramental leprosy, consecrated under the name of revelation, covered with its irremediable impurity the conscience of the human race. Philosophy separated from religion, some scattered sages preserved in their hearts the pure light and holy liberty of the first ages of the world; the rest, a vile herd of error, became captive under the yoke of a superstition which nothing could uproot, doubtless because it is supported by the habit, the antiquity, the name of God, and also by the innate weakness of the greater number of minds.

I will not expose the injury which that doctrine does to mankind; you know that it is common in those who separate from the multitude. Let us leave to pride the argument of scorn, and accept the glory of a logic, calm and worthy of truth.

That there have been false prophets is not doubtful, that many have succeeded, history proves and Christianity admits. But why have they succeeded? Have they not succeeded precisely because there are true prophets? Have they not succeeded, because, even in corrupting religion, they have accepted its dogmatic and practical basis, grafting into this divine trunk foreign branches which thence derive their life? Have they not succeeded, because they found in the heart of man, as God had made it, a ready accomplice? Imposture, like every other thing, needs a soil analogous to its grain; it germinates only in virtue of a fecundity which it receives from the unique source of all fecundity—namely, nature. Suppose an impostor, who recognised no received idea, no real sentiment, no pre-existing force: do you think he would succeed in deceiving a single man, a single hour? And yet, to explain by imposture the mystery which occupies our attention, it is necessary that it should deceive all ages and all generations. We possess the history of some of those extraordinary men who have set up false religions in the world; we know, very near to us, Luther and Mahomet; what were they, but plagiarists and falsifiers? Issued from a pre-existing religious institution, they laid their rash hands upon it, and in order to curtail it, they made use of the passions of their times. They have degraded the temple, they have not built it. A portion of mankind has believed them, because it believed before—it believed them to be prophets, because it believed in prophecies—it has received their sacraments, because it had sacraments before. They have been causes of error only by an effect of truth.

This is why the last rendezvous of the question is always in nature itself; imposture having no hold elsewhere, it is necessarily forced to seek its support therein, and in order so to do, it is needful that it should not contradict all the elements of human nature. Now you have seen, and I must again repeat it, if God has given nothing to man beyond his body and his mind, if reason is the supreme term of our faculties, it is clear that all which does not take its origin there is for us unnatural, chimerical, and vain. Such is prophecy—our adversaries avow it—such is sacrament. And therefore they cannot be the fruit of imposture, above all, the universal fruit of a continued imposture, since there would, in that case, be an effect without a cause, an edifice without foundation. It is not, then, by hazard that Catholic doctrine, after having shown us all that God has done for man in the sensible and intelligible order, warns us that this is not the limit of the divine action in regard to us, but that above those precious and first gifts there is another which raises us higher and places us in immediate communication with the Author of our being, with the principle and end of our destinies. By the creating act God raised us up before Himself as a living and free personality; by the act of revelation He entered into communication with us, and we with Him: He delivered to us the secrets of His thought, the plans of His will, and in that effusion at the same time exterior and interior—exterior by the word, interior by light and unction—He created the supernatural and religious order. And as the nature which left His all-powerful hand perseveres in the conditions in which He enchained it, so religion, no less faithful, perseveres under the form which it received from Him. As it is folly to act against nature, so it is equally vain to act against religion. The one and the other remain as God has willed; what the sun and moon are in the visible firmament, prophecy and sacrament are in the firmament of truth. You will not make the luminaries fall, and you will not silence the word of God. And if, jealous of the divine work, you aspire to create something by yourselves, you will succeed only in producing imitations, which, even in their powerlessness, will attest the dogmas you fear, and add lustre to the glory you would destroy. What has Luther done, but confirm the Church? What has Mahomet done, but increase the grandeur of Jesus Christ? What have all the usurpers of the prophetic title done, but maintain in shadows the remembrance and need of revelation? And what do you, in denying revelation, but prove by your example that religion is extinguished in every mind that denies the reality of a supernatural order?

The world has reached a remarkable epoch of its destiny. For a century it has endeavoured to found all human things upon nature and reason; it believed itself capable of reigning alone without the intervention of any mysterious idea, any indefinite power. You have before you the result of this grand attempt. Social discipline has fallen to pieces in your hands; the ingenious springs to which you purposed to subject it have been found too feeble against resistance and aggressions. What was generous in your plans of reform has had no better success than what was chimerical, and justice wonders that it cannot give to your works either duration or majesty. Will you linger much longer before you doubt of yourselves? Will you not suspect that something is wanting to you, and, painfully warned by the innate providence of things, will you not lift your eyes towards the eternal pole where you have left the science of the past and the future? It is high time: let us call God to our help; let us acknowledge that we have relations with Him more profound than those of nature, and that to renounce them, from weakness or pride, is to take from the human race, with its highest duties, its highest virtues and its most necessary faculties.

# TWO OBJECTIONS
AGAINST
# THE SUPERNATURAL INTERCOURSE BETWEEN GOD AND MAN.

My Lord—Gentlemen,

After having established that the intercourse between man and God is not based upon nature and reason, but upon a higher order, which Catholic doctrine calls supernatural, the course of ideas would lead us to seek why it is so, and what are the motives which have determined God not to include in our sensible and intelligible faculties all the means that we need for entering into relations with Him. But rationalism does not permit us to advance so rapidly. The question of the supernatural order is too grave for rationalists to yield to the demonstration which we have given without endeavouring at least to weaken it. Let us then hear their objections.

It is true, they say, that if we look only to the surface of things, prophecy and sacrament possess a character of universality and perpetuity by which they seem to advance side by side with nature and reason; but this is only an appearance which vanishes at the first serious glance thrown upon that illogical institution. In fact, before it could possess a real universality, a real perpetuity, the subject or thought that aspires to these great characters must be the same in all times and places; without unity, universality and perpetuity are impossible, since universality is but the expansion of unity in space, and perpetuity is expansion in time. Thus nature is really universal and perpetual, because her laws, in whatever age or place they are consulted, give to all who interrogate them an answer that never varies. At the pole as at the equator, under the instruments of Newton as under the eyes of Aristotle, physical light falls upon and emerges again from an object in forming a constant angle. It is the same with reason. As the faculty of a free being, it does not follow the caprices of the will, it approves or condemns according to rules which do not bend. Speak to the Athenian of Pericles, to the Arab of the desert, to the savage of unexplored forests, to the child of barbarism, or the full-formed man of civilization, all understand you, and even when they dispute their own opinions among themselves, they invoke uniform principles to maintain them, which are as clear and certain to the intelligence of the ignorant as to that of the learned. Is it so in regard to the supernatural order? Or, rather, is there anything comparable to the chaos of superstitions of which it is composed? Open yonder Pantheon; what see you there? Gods insulting one another; dogmas contradicting one another; religions disavowing, priesthoods anathematising one another; altars in violent opposition; discord infinite as the sacred object which those frightful controversies of powerlessness and pride pretend to attain. Behold the supernatural! Behold it as it appears in history and before our eyes! And this is called a divine thing, an institution not only equal to nature and reason, but which, superior to all created things, should serve as a law to the conscience, a light to the mind, a crown to the universe! For us, whatever may be the cause of this terrible phenomenon, we accuse it of being human; it is human, because it is not one.

If you reply that among all religions one only is the true one, of which the others are but impious or pitiful imitations, the difficulty will, perhaps, lose its force on one side, but only to regain it on the other, and with usury. For one single religion being true, one alone is good for the soul, one alone establishes an efficacious communication between God and man. Thenceforth it is necessary to discern it among the crowd of others, it is necessary to choose it without error. And what a task is imposed upon the human race in a matter where it is a question of finding or losing God! Can it be that to us feeble creatures, already wasted in the toils which our transitory existence costs us, an enigma to solve should have been given as the condition of our eternal life? Is it possible? Is it possible that eternity costs us anything but virtue, and that, sparing in regard to the infinite, God takes cruel delight in becoming a sphinx to man? Ah! if truth be our nourishment, it should fall from heaven like rain, pass on like the wind, swell its waves like the sea, grow like the harvest in the days when man waits for that blessing upon his labour which created the earth, and commanded it to serve us. Every man is able to trace a furrow and cast seed into it : is every man able to unravel the confusion of the innumerable religions that contend for the honour of coming from God and of leading mankind to Him? None will dare to advance such a pretension ; and, consequently we oppose to the supernatural order, as a double accusation, first, its want of unity; next, the impossibility of discerning the true among all the positive religions, supposing even that one of them is true.

Such are the difficulties which arrest us, and which I must solve before advancing another step.

It is certain that unity is an essential character of the works of God, not a dead unity which would exclude variety—that is to say, harmony in number and extent—but a fertile unity, which, coming from God Himself, brings back to Him, as to their source, all irradiations of light and life. Unity is but order, and order is evidently an attribute of God and of His works.

It is certain also that, considering the mass of religions, although they all spring from the idea and fact of a supernatural revelation, although they have among them the very significative relationship of prayer, their dogmatic constitution nevertheless establishes a flagrant contradiction between the greater number of them. Unity is at their base, it is not in their architecture, and that diversity necessarily suggests in the secondary origin of the greater number the presence of another hand than the hand of God.

Whose is that hand ? Who has touched the divine work after God ? What power has suddenly appeared behind the Creator, to introduce even into religion, which was the crowning work of the universe, the seeds of discord and death ? That power is yourselves. God did not place you among His works to remain there in the inertness of captive contemplation, but to be there the free co-operators of His thought and His glory ; He did not create you to adore Him in a servile manner, but to love Him so much the more as you are able to hate Him, to serve Him so much the better as you are able to rebel against Him, to be so much the more efficacious instruments of His name as you are able to dishonour it. This is why wherever God is in this world there are you also; wherever He works you work also, whether in the sense of His designs, or in a contrary sense. And it is not upon a part of His work only that this power has been given to you; you possess it upon the whole, in the natural as well as in the supernatural order, against nature and reason as against prophecy and sacrament. You are able to deny all; you are able to deny God as well as Jesus Christ, society as well as the Church, mathematical truth as well as revealed truth, visible good as well as invisible good, time as well as eternity. Nothing escapes from your empire, because, on the one hand, your liberty has no limits, and, on another, since all is linked together in the world, the blow which you give to one point is necessarily felt in all the spheres of creation and of the infinite. Nature, reason, and religion are three progressive laws whose light is reciprocal, and whose force is in common—the intelligence divides them only by a schism which wounds all the three, and pride obtains great success only in ruins which form a tomb alike for both. The will of pride is not to obey, and it obeys as long as a law exists, whatever may be its origin, its form, or its name. Thence it comes that pride rests only in its absolute sovereignty, and that, measuring its force by the greatness of its desire, it has not despaired of attaining to the two sovereign acts which belong only to God—the acts of destroying and creating, of destroying the world as God had made it, in order to create a world as man wills it to be.

You think that I exaggerate, and that if man has really attacked religion, because it is but a supposed part of the divine work, he has at least always respected nature and reason, which are that work itself in all its certainty and its sincerity. You have said this in opposing the constant uniformity of the natural order to the contradictory variety of the religious order; but, I ask, does not the sound of the world reach you? Do you not hear from this very place the secular clamour of its divisions? It is only at the portals of the temple that the combat is engaged between man against man and man against God? Stand upon the forum of nations, enter their academies, open their laboratories of science—wherever you meet with the human mind, you find war, doctrines against doctrines, politics against politics, history against history, facts against facts, affirmations against negations. Can you question this? And thenceforth in what is the natural order more united than the supernatural order? In what does it escape more from the attacks of our liberty? Religious contradiction even holds a rational contradiction; for the dogma which I accept and which you reject, I accept with my reason, and with yours you reject it. We differ in regard to faith only because we differ rationally. Say you that if we differ about consequences, we recognise the same principles, and that in them the immutable unity of reason survives and consists? But by the same title religion may pretend to unity and immutability; it also claims principles upon which all forms agree, such as the existence of a Supreme Being, His action upon man, His positive intercourse with us by revelation, ceremonies, laws, rewards and punishments. Where begins the contest if it is not in the dogmatical development of these common principles?

There is then parity between the two orders, and if your accusation concludes to the prejudice of the one, it concludes no less to the prejudice of the other. Therefore learn that the same thing you say against religion, scepticism has said against reason—even as you deny supernatural unity, because of the divergence of religions, scepticism denies rational unity, because of the multitude of opinions and practices which divides sages no less than nations. Pascal scornfully remarked it: "Truth on this side of the Pyrenees, error beyond them!" Survey then the whole abyss; see what in the hands of man that reason becomes which you do not doubt of, and if you refuse to believe in the avowals of philosophy, believe at least in what is passing around you. What truth is not denied? What instinct of nature is not outraged? What human institution, how familiar soever it may be to us either by tradition or by the heart, is not treated as an enemy? You wonder that Christ found contradictors and judges eighteen hundred years ago. Lift up your eyes, behold reason itself before the tribunal of Caiaphas and the Romans!

Be not alarmed, however, and in learning what man may do against the work of God, learn also what he cannot do. Yes, there is a great power in man, for God is with him; there is a great power in man, for Satan is with him; there is a great power in man, for man is with himself: but with God on his right hand, Satan on his left, and himself between, man is neither capable of destroying nor of creating an atom. An atom suffices eternally to arrest all his power: how much more the universe! Sixty centuries in the service of our liberty have not given us the glory of making or destroying a grain of dust; how much more will nature, reason, and religion resist us! Be not alarmed then; neither you who doubt, nor you who believe, be not alarmed. God is in all that is, He maintains all that He has once willed; and our liberty, however important, is but the rock upon which the ocean breaks, remaining still the ocean. Therefore, being a child of truth in this most troubled age, I hear the tempest unmoved; I receive light from the flash that falls upon the temple, and with my head resting upon the threshold of the parvis, I repose in the divine slumber of infallible faith.

Powerlessness to destroy, powerlessness to create, such is in man the limit of pride, such is the law which protects all that is—nature, reason, religion—against the attempts of liberty. And yet it is very essential that liberty, even in its abuse, should be a fertile power; for were it otherwise, it would be but a mainspring poised in the void, a responsible name of an imaginary activity. God, in assuring His own empire, that the world might not become the toy of unbridled disorder, should have left such an effect to our action that even in its errors it should not be the vain effort of an abortive being. What is then the part of God, and what the part of man? God, as we have seen, has reserved to Himself the substance of things; He has willed that man should never attain to it; for if the substance of things had been given to us, God would have remained only as the tranquil spectator of the ruins of the universe. But if substance escapes from us, what remains to us? If we cannot destroy a grain of dust in nature, a principle in the intelligence, an element in the supernatural order, what can we do in reality? In order to understand this, we must remark that all substance has a mode of being, and that the substance remaining invariable, the mode is subject to change. It is then the mode which our liberty seizes. The mode is the figure of things; being powerless against things, we have the resource of disfiguring them. We disfigure nature, reason, religion.

You have received from the Creator a visage in which power and goodness shine. Your lips become animated with a smile whose grace outlives their motion; your eyes flash forth a light which springs from the fount of a living intelligence, but which, tempered by modesty, excites respect without fear; your brow, pure and calm, crowns with its serenity the living charm of your features, and wherever the regard of a soul lights upon you, that soul knows and loves your own. O youth, these are great gifts! But a single hour is sufficient to tarnish them, a single crime is sufficient to dishonour them. Nature, whose masterpiece you are, will not resist the blows you inflict upon it in the secret of your conscience, beauty departs from you in proportion as God leaves your heart, and soon that head, the object of admiration and love, remains but the ignoble crown of a reprobate or a debauchee. You will not have destroyed in yourself the natural image of God, you will have disfigured it.

So also you may lay waste the earth, burn the forests, disperse the sources of rivers, infect the air, doom admirable portions of our common heritage to solitude and sterility, and you have done this but too often! The hands of barbarians withered Latium; the tyranny of the sons of Mahomet, touching the soil of Greece and Syria, dried up sources which were deemed inexhaustible, and destroyed charms which were believed to be under the eternal protection of the purest light that has ever shone upon creation. But how cruel soever those injuries may be, the earth subsists and nourishes man. Better generations may succeed those hordes which have not respected the common mother of the human race; they may rouse the fields of Attica and the hills of Messina from their involuntary sleep; shade, invited by cultivation, may descend again from heaven upon the deserts of Rome; life, which had but turned aside, may shoot forth on every hand, and the very ruins become witnesses to our inability to deal the blow that causes death.

So it is with errors and crimes against reason. A century dawns, it is bold in the things of the intelligence, it agitates ideas as the traveller, at the close of a long day, shakes the dust and weariness from his feet; it takes pleasure in doubting, pride in contradicting; it strikes the pillars which aforetime supported the structure of science and wisdom; tradition loses its influence upon it, conscience becomes but a mute or a suspicious oracle. A moment arrives when astonished minds ask if truth is not a dream and good an imposture. But in the very midst of this orgie of scepticism, reason is attacked only by reason; it triumphs even in the very wound which it inflicts upon itself. Negation affirms that the intelligence lives and sees, as the eye, closing before the sun, attests the presence and the power of his rays. It is needful to live, and notwithstanding the universal delirium, the course of human things follows its ancient ways; mankind marches before Phyrrho who denies motion. Mankind believes, hopes, combines its thoughts and its actions. Then, time sounds an hour; a new age opens which raises up truth again, as the freshness of morning raises up in the fields the grass which had drooped at evening. The altars of doubt are overthrown; the negations but yesterday idolized are scattered to the winds; those who despised are despised; they are forgotten who forgot; a period is marked in history, and the future mounts to the horizon of eternity. There was a deformation of the human mind, but no destruction.

Do you any longer wonder that religion, struggling with the liberty of man, should be subject to the same injuries and the same vicissitudes? Why should religion be more fortunate than nature and reason? Why, in drawing nearer to heaven, should our ambition for sovereignty lose the energy which permits it to violate the inferior sanctuaries? Whatever shores we may touch, higher or lower, we bear with us, as an indefectible attribute, the power of good and evil. And that very power increases in proportion as we rise in the hierarchy of things; it is greater against reason than against nature, greater against religion than against reason. This is because we can raise ourselves only by drawing near to the infinite, and because the infinite, by its disproportion to our personal limits, necessarily offers a greater obstacle to revolt and error. Who does not conceive how easy it is to substitute chimerical imitations for religious dogmas? Man has done this; he has done this from impatience under too heavy a yoke; from weariness of antiquity, from forgetfulness of tradition; from aversion towards a negligent or corrupt priesthood; from obedience to the ascendency of famous sectaries. But whatever may have been the motive of his separation, under whatever point of heaven and in whatever time it may have begun, never has man, living in the state of a people—that is to say, in the natural state—been able to abrogate religion or change its essential characters. He has always believed in the positive communication between the human race and God, by means of the word direct from God. The perverted religions prove this no less eloquently than the Christian religion. What was a temple, but an oracle in the minds of the Pagan nations? What an idol, but marble and gold speaking in the name of God? What a priest, but a body and soul inspired by the breath of God? What are they now in every part of the earth—priest, temple, idol—but an incarnation, more or less living and near, of the Divinity? The unity of the idea outlives the multiplicity of form; moreover, when that form is studied, there is found, in the variety of the signs, the mutilated remains of an identical tradition.

To faith in prophecies all religions have joined faith in sacraments; all, we have said, and proved it, called sacrifices, ceremonies, and prayer, to the help of the soul striving to tend towards God. Homer immolates victims with the liturgy of Leviticus; Delphos commands expiations in the same language which Benares speaks; the Etruscan augury blesses the Roman hills as the Druid consecrated the forests of Gaul; and above all those living rites of invincible custom, the sacrament of prayer rises towards God to demand miracles of Him in the name of all grief that hopes, and of all weakness that believes. Doubtless prayer has not always known God under the same name; it has not everywhere known His true and eternal history: but the want was everywhere the same, the aspiration similar, and when the heart was sincere, prayer did not fail to be efficacious. The suppliant charged with grief, on bending the knee before a deceptive statue, forgot the fable that education had graven in his mind; he remembered the unknown God whom Athens revered at the foot of the Parthenon, and that God who seeks uprightness and knows misfortune, heard the cry of faith in the lamentations of a humbled heart. The darkness of idolatry became enlightened; truth descended with grace, and the soul of man met the Spirit of God through the illusions of error.

Acknowledge then that you have no more destroyed religion than you have destroyed reason and nature; you have no more changed its essence than you have changed the essence of logic and chemistry. You have disfigured all, and God has saved all. Nature has resisted your mutilations; reason, your systems; religion, your unbelief; and all these, being universal and perpetual, attest so much the more the power which founded them, as that power has respected yours in permitting you not to respect its own. Tell me, what has withheld you? Why is it that so much life remains amidst so many ruins? You desired, you still desire, to destroy religion, in which you see only a chaos of baseless ideas and practices; why is religion still standing? You would exercise the sovereign act of destroying, in order to arrive at the sovereign act of creating, and, indeed, there is a greatness in that ambition which would entitle it to praise, if nothing could be great against justice and truth; why have you neither destroyed nor created religion? Look at Luther . . . Luther is an old shadow, but since we are permitted to evoke shadow, let me evoke him and call him to account for the mystery which holds my mind and yours in suspense. Well, Luther; since thou despisest the Church, since thou hast resolved to extirpate from Europe the faith which was once thine own, why dost thou not strike the only blow that touches the root of the question? Why not overthrow the architect with the edifice? Why not deny Jesus Christ?

Ah! why? Luther did not himself know. He obeyed faith at the same time as revolt, and was illogical in the one as in the other—he was the formidable expression of great weakness in great power. His conscience responded to the conscience of his time, as the conscience of his time to that of all ages. It included with an element of protestation an imperious want of belief, and the success of Luther, like all the other heresiarchs, was, that he struck at the very heart of his epoch, by taking from its faith all that it could lose, and leaving to it all that it wished to keep. Had he denied Jesus Christ, he would have been a Voltaire without ancestors—that is to say, a madman; and Voltaire himself, preceded by two centuries of Protestantism, could only attain to the position of a sage—that is to say, a chief of a school and not a chief of the people.

This example includes all the others. It initiates us into the secret of religious revolutions, which are so much the more sure of success as they swerve less from the primordial sacramentary and prophetic basis; so much the more decisive in favour of the truth of religion as they preserve it in violating it. For, in fine, if for sixty centuries the human race obeyed the same dogma and the same liturgy, would you not recognise in that tranquil unanimity the sign of a divine institution? Now the sign of unanimity combated, of unanimity contradicted and persevering, notwithstanding such controversy, is manifestly still more worthy to move an attentive mind. For the first unanimity may be explained by the absence of examination and the force of habit, whilst the second can only be explained by a power superior to all the springs of human thought and all the attacks of its liberty. To affirm in denying, to maintain in destroying, to consent in protesting, this is doubtless to rise up against truth, but it is also to render to truth the highest of all homage, since it is the homage of an enemy.

It remains to be seen whether God has not done still more for the preservation of His religion upon earth, and whether among all those who have adulterated its original purity, there is not one which has preserved that purity unstained, and which may be easy to recognise by inimitable characters of grandeur and sincerity. I hope to show you this without trouble as well as without delay.

Let us first of all banish from our minds the vain idea that there are an infinite multitude of different religions here below. It is not so. Nothing has been more sterile than the imagination of man in the matter of religions. As, in considering the common features of beings, we collect them with a certain number of primitive families, so also in comparing together the religious branches which spread out in mankind, we find them terminating in three principal trunks, the only ones really distinct by their physiognomy and by an invisible and mutual repulsion —I mean idolatry, Christianity, and Mahometism; I do not name Judaism, because before Jesus Christ it was but Christianity awaiting its crown, and since Jesus Christ it is but Christianity without its crown. There remain then the Christian churches, which cleave to the trunk of the Gospel and Christ; the idolatrous sects, neither of which excommunicated the other, and whose symbols vied with one another in mutual respect in the council of the Roman Pantheon—in fine, the branches of Islamism, which all bend at the feet of Mahomet and the Koran. Name me a religion, I will trace it either to the idol, the cross, or the crescent; but there is no peace possible, there is no common ground, between the idol, the cross, and the crescent—those memorable banners which still divide the generations of men, and which bear in their folds three theologies separated by a radically different conception of the intercourse between man and God. In fact, in this intercourse, which constitutes religion and supposes an approaching of two beings so naturally removed from one another, either the mind conceives an alliance between the divine nature and human nature that attains even to confounding them—which is idolatry; or it conceives that alliance under a form that excludes compatibility between the two natures—which is Mahometism; or, in fine, it admits the union of the two natures remaining distinct even in their intimacy—which is Christianity. Idolatry confounds man and God; Mahometism keeps them at a distance from each other; Christianity associates them: these three systems resume all existing and all possible religions.

Antiquity in general was lost in idolatry, and even the superstitions which had not begun in idolatry ended by falling upon it as upon an inevitable shoal. The reason of this is, in fact, that it is difficult to halt just at the point of Theandry—a name by which Christian theology expresses the participation of God in man and of man in God. As soon as the intelligence is no longer enlightened by the full light of religious truth, it vacillates before that prodigious mystery, and according as it yields more to reason or to remembrance, to the inspiration of nature, or the impulsion of theological instinct, it remains behind or runs beyond the true. Instinct, remembrance, and a confused presentiment vanquished the intelligence in the intermediary period of mankind—I mean in that comprised between the deluge and the coming of Christ. When Jesus Christ appeared, that wonderful restitution of the eternal type of the alliance between God and man struck the world with such a flash of light, that the pagan theogony, notwithstanding its twenty centuries of empire, was no longer able to maintain the honour of deceiving the human race. Error was obliged to take refuge upon another basis, and to assume another form. Arius prepared its edifice, Mahomet completed it—Arius denied the divinity of Jesus Christ, Mahomet declared the union between the divine and human natures in one single personality to be impossible, impious, idolatrous; and, separating, as far as possible, the two terms of religious intercourse, he pronounced the fundamental sentence of Islamism, or the new faith: "God is God, and Mahomet is His Prophet." God is God—that is to say, God can be only God; Mahomet is His prophet—that is to say, the divine action with regard to man is limited to prophecy, and the action of man in regard to God is limited to the faith which accepts prophecy by adoring and praying. No other religion has appeared since Mahomet; none other will appear in the future. For, below Mahomet there is but pure rationalism; above him we necessarily find idolatry or Christianity.

Christianity fills the middle place between Mahometism and idolatry. It humanises God without causing Him to descend, it divinises man without changing his substance, equally removed from the extravagance of pantheism, which confounds all beings in a divine chaos, and the coldness of theism, which relegates the creature to a hopeless distance from the Creator.

Here, then, lies the choice; here, the contest. For whoever would come out of practical atheism, there are in all history but these three doors open; he must be an idolater, a Christian, or a Mussulman; he must bend the knee before an idol, bear the cross, or hoist the crescent—the one or the other; or remain indifferent among the spectators who hear unmoved the name of God, and who regard the future without preparing for it.

The choice being thus reduced to these, the only possible terms, nothing is easier than to recognise where is the true religion, the religion instituted by God and preserved in the integrity of its dogmas, its morals, and its liturgy—that is to say, in the integrity of prophecy and sacrament. It is said that Tacitus abridged all, because he saw all. God is a still greater abbreviator, because He labours in eternity for creatures who have only time. You are in haste. God is so more than you. You are eager to know truth—God is still more eager to impart it to you. Listen then: you will need but a ray of light and an instant of good-will.

Although idolatry and Mahometism start from absolutely contradictory points, I place them upon the same line in the discussion, because they bear upon their front the same characters of shame and inanition. I do not say to you—Mahomet has wrought no miracles, nor has idolatry; idolatry has not prophesied, nor has Mahomet. This is the detail of the question. It requires time to examine it, and we must advance quickly. Now to him who wishes to advance quickly, God has prepared a way which shortens all. He has placed in religion, as in all other things, a physiognomy. Behold a man whom you have never met; his origin and his acts are unknown to you—who is he? What does he desire? What is the secret of his soul? You know nothing of it, and you have neither opportunity nor leisure to learn. Brought together for a moment, which may never return, you need to judge him by the light of a glance. You will judge him, in fact, and if some experience has initiated you to the play of the inner life upon the features which form the accent of the visage, you will not be deceived—above all, you will not be deceived if great vices or great virtues have ploughed their furrows in the moving flesh in which you study truth.

So is it with religion. Every religion has a soul which is reflected in the body of its doctrines and its history; and, consequently, every religion has a physiognomy. What is the physiognomy of idolatry and of Mahometism? Do you feel in them the pulsation of anything divine? Is your conscience moved by them, and with your eye fixed upon Jupiter or Mahomet, would you ask yourself that formidable question— May not God be there? No, gentlemen, no; not one of you has ever given to either of those religions the honour of a doubt; not one of you has ever interrogated himself in their presence, and been tempted to exclaim—Perhaps! The perhaps comes to you from elsewhere; it descends into your soul from another region, and if there were here below only idolatry and Islamism to represent God, you would not even give yourselves the trouble to deny—you would pass them by without hatred, without scorn, without pride, as you pass before a heap of stones which has not even the architecture of a ruin.

In the celebrated assembly which inaugurated the unachieved era of our revolutions, two men met together endowed with unequal eloquence, who both sat for a long time on the same side, and defended together the coming of the age from which we have issued. But, at length, the hazards of public life fell between them, and separated them; the day came when they were to ascend the tribune to combat there before the eyes of a population awaiting this trial, and who had prepared applause for the younger and feebler of the two. He appeared first; the popular movement, which he was sure of, raised his language above itself, genuine enthusiasm responded to him; he felt that he had nothing to fear, and that, at least, he should share the honour of the rostrum with the powerful enemy arrayed against him. This man ascended calm and collected; received by unusual silence he measured with his soul all the popularity which he had lost, and drawing from that obstacle, new to him, a power of desperation, he turned like a lion in the terrible lair of his eloquence. Involuntary bursts of applause taught him what he already knew— his triumph; when, suddenly, he turned towards his adversary, no longer as orator against orator, but like an eagle hovering over his prey, and hurled to him that sublime and crushing apostrophe—" Barnave, there is no divinity in thee ! "

This expression of Mirabeau to Barnave is the expression which ends the controversy with regard to Mahometism and idolatry; or, rather, controversy is not even possible, and from the first observation thrown upon those miserable corruptions of religious truth, the mind disdainfully turns, and exclaims—There is no divinity in you ! Why? How? What is it then that gives or takes away the divine physiognomy? I know not, perhaps. What I do know is, that there is a feature of baseness which descends even to the face of the brute, as there is a feature of greatness which rises even to a superhuman transformation. What I do know . . . but listen a moment. On a day known in history, a Roman proconsul appeared upon a balcony; by his side stood a criminal covered with wounds, a reed was tied to His hands, His brow pierced with a crown of thorns, His body muffled in a purple robe, which added to His humiliations the injury of ironical majesty. The proconsul turned timidly towards the multitude, and said—Behold the Man ! The people replied by an acclamation which called for His blood, and the Roman obeyed and delivered Him up to them. But behind that infuriated mankind has stood up; it has regarded the Man in its turn, the Man condemned, scourged, crucified; and striking its breast, it has exclaimed—Behold God ! On another day Greece assembled her artists to obtain from their genius an image worthy of their adorations. Phidias was chosen. He took his chisel—he cut out one of those famous marbles which well-nigh breathed before the hand of the sculptor had touched them, he gave to it light, thought, glory, repose, and when Greece drew aside the veil which covered the Olympian Jupiter, she cried with a serious and unanimous voice— Behold God ! But mankind has risen behind that gifted people; it has regarded the object of a memory which has remained so great, and pitying Athens still more than its statue, it has exclaimed—Behold man !

Behold man ! All the arts of Attica, all the poetry of Homer, all the grandeurs of Latium—nothing in twenty centuries of duration has been able to hide the ineffable misery of idolatry; and Islamism has conquered a half of the world only to exhibit in it, under a form opposite but equally vain, the powerlessness of all religions, save that which has made sages believe, and which makes the impious doubt.

This striking absence of divinity, which is the prominent feature of idolatry and Islamism, suffices to judge them. In fact, it is easy to understand that man, whatever he may do, will never be able to give to his works a really divine character. The more he mounts beyond his sphere, in order to attain a glory which surpasses him, the further he falls away from truth, in which alone is the source of the beautiful. As conqueror, legislator, philosopher—simple mortal, in fine—he has days in his history worthy of admiration; would he touch the holy arch by uplifting himself in imposture, he loses the secret of the grandeurs of this world and the elevations of the other. He makes a parody of the name of God; and that name, to be avenged, needs but itself. Not only have the false religions no divine physiognomy, but to this negative character they infallibly join the sign of flagrant immorality. Lift your eyes to the antique altars! Dare I even ask you to lift your eyes to these? Notwithstanding the distance which veils them from us, dare I counsel you a glance, however obscure, upon their mysteries and their ceremonies? I dare not—I dare not paint to you what those Greeks adored—those Greeks so delicate, our masters in the art of feeling and expressing the beautiful. I dare not describe to you the pomps wherein they exposed, in the name of God, their wives, their children, their own heart. That which was their religion we cannot even make a matter of discourse; that which was sacred for them, on passing from my lips to your ears, would be a sacrilege for you and for me. They had raised up their gods in such sublime infamy, that we cannot perceive them in it, were it but to accuse them. All those gods, I admit, were not of equally degraded mire; some of them drew near to man by their virtues. I believe even that a better image of the Divinity rose up from the conscience before those idols, and inwardly braved the public worship which was rendered to them; but this was the effect of antique truth—it was the groaning of God in the presence of falsehood, and falsehood did not the less subsist with the chastisement of its corruption.

Mahomet, I also admit, in his dogmatic and liturgical exposition of God, has not incurred the immorality of idolatry. His design, which was the reverse of the fables of polytheism, did not permit it to him. But that even renders more striking and more formidable against him the shameful materialism which has resulted from his work, and whose germ, although perhaps dissimulated, is nevertheless visible in the Koran.

Mahometan morals have not put to the blush the morals of paganism; and these in certain things—such as the unity and indissolubility of marriage—have left far behind them the habits of the children of Mahomet. Neither Islamism nor idolatry has known and taught the spiritual life; they have not drawn the soul above the attractions of this earth, in order to impart to it the joy of an immaterial aliment. Even in revealing immortality to the soul they have left it a prey to the passions, the torments, the virtues which death ends.

What other sign would you desire against those miserable religions? And yet there is another not less palpable, not less striking; it is their logical incapacity. Men may be wrong and yet discuss—it seems even that nothing is more easy, so common are its examples—what then shall we say of a religion which reasoning fails to defend? And if you believe that such an excess of powerlessness is not possible, take the trouble to seek for the theological, historical, and polemical works of Mahometism and idolatry. Where are they? In India, as well as in Greece and Rome, idolatry has had poets for theologians; and when Christianity taught it what was a religion that wrote and spoke, it had for defenders, philosophers who overthrew its mythology in attempting to justify it. Mahometism has in no greater degree dreamed of establishing its divinity by discussion; it has reigned where its scimitar was master, it has perished where its scimitar has been broken. Now, under our own eyes, it maintains the rest of its empire only by a law which interdicts the conversion of its followers under the penalty of death. Paganism, menaced by the preaching of Christianity, did not act otherwise under the Cæsars of Rome; it does not now act otherwise under the despots of China and Japan. What is the cause of this, if it be not logical incapacity, or, if you like it better, the incapability of reasoning? Pascal said, "It is easier to find monks than reasons." The true version was, "It is easier to find executioners than reasons." The history of Islamism proves it to the envy of the history of paganism. We ought to find there, by the disposition of God and the force of things, an incurable imbecility; by the disposition of God, who willed not that religion should be corrupted without preserving the cruel marks of its adulteration; by the force of things, which does not permit that an error of such magnitude should anywhere find foundations. The foundations of the true religion are an antiquity which mounts by certain monuments to be the very origin of the world; an uninterrupted course of miraculous and prophetic acts leave here and there their ineffaceable sign in the history of nations; a dogma serious and profound; a moral teaching which explains itself by revolutions in the morals of the human race; a priesthood worthy to speak of God to vice and virtue; a providence which governs this extraordinary whole, and, in fine, maintains it by a constant prodigy; a tissue wherein all blends together—wherein each sustains the other in a duration of sixty centuries, notwithstanding the magnitude of the obstacles and the weakness of the means. How could a religion issued from man by an accidental degradation, attribute to itself or preserve such foundations? We may give the appearance of truth to a system of philosophy, because it is but a combination of ideas; but religion being an immense order of universal and perpetual acts, how should we create these facts if they do not exist, or how should we call them to the help of error if they exist to the profit of truth? It would be more easy for man to create the world than to create a religion with divine characters; for the world had but to vanquish nothingness, and that religion would have to vanquish the essence of things.

Such is the reason of the logical incapacity which you remark in Islamism and in idolatry, and which would deprive them of all power upon the mind, if the vileness of their physiognomy and the spectacle of their immorality left them any chance of seducing an intelligence free to judge them.

Of the three religions which divide the world, two are out of the lists: Christianity alone is now before us.

Regard it, gentlemen, not to ask yourselves if it be true, but if it resemble the two others. Does it resemble them? Is there here the same logical incapacity, the same immorality, the same absence of the divine physiognomy? You may well combat it, you must combat it. For it teaches, it discusses, it writes, it has filled the earth with its language,'and your libraries with its works. Whatever you touch, you meet with it. It opposes its sages to your sages, its scholars to your scholars, its writers to your writers, its politicians to your politicians, its men of genius to your men of genius; during eighteen centuries, preceded by traditions and works for four thousand years, it follows your steps, never leaving one of your reproaches unanswered, any more than one of your wants unsuccoured.

If you deny, it affirms: if you despise, it honours; if you trample it under your feet, it rises up again; if you believe it dead, it comes back again to life. Is it wrong? I cannot say. Is it right? I know not. What I see, what all the world sees, is that it reasons and keeps the human mind in suspense. Sometimes the political authority has served it, sometimes it has ignored it; but in good as well as in bad fortune, under persecution as under protection, it has done its work and held on its way. None of the vicissitudes which it has witnessed have astonished it—it has seen the science of the times which ended with that of the times which began, and it will be accused of all, save of having been wanting in greatness and power of mind.

As much as the other religions have been incapable, I do not say of sanctifying, but of ameliorating public morals, so much has this religion raised and divinised them. Who will compare the life of the Christian nations with the life of the nations governed by the law of idols, or by that of Mahomet? Ah! doubtless I know the failing of Christendom, since I know my own; but notwithstanding the traces which flesh and blood leave upon it, what purity in numbers of chosen souls! What respect for virtue in the conscience of all! What a struggle in those even who fall, and who with their eyes fixed upon the model of all holiness, retain even in vice the hope and desire to become better! If the secret of this salutary labour is not sufficiently known to you by your own experience, if the history of souls in Christianity has not been revealed to you, judge at least from what you see; compare the pleasures, the amusements, the spectacles of the heathens with ours; place before your eyes our weaknesses and the abominations of the East. Christianity has not destroyed evil, since evil forms a part of fallen human nature; but it has dishonoured it in opinion, driven it from the public places, pursued it even to its repairs, attenuated it in the life of the greater number, and effaced it from the hearts of many. It is the only religion which has wrought a moral revolution in the world; all the others have adored the evil inclinations of man, or ineffectually proscribed them. And that moral revolution is not of an age or a nation; from the debaucheries of Augustus to the adulteries of Louis XIV., it has reigned over a multitude of nations which daily feel the persevering benefit it confers upon them. There is not a Christian mother who is not its instrument, and who does not communicate a virtue of purification and honour to the souls whom she has received from God. Before the Christian becomes corrupted he has passed by the joys of purity, and he preserves in his bones a remembrance of it, which all the profanations of vice are unable entirely to eradicate. Vice is so incompatible with the Christian faith, that that faith grows weak and languishes in those who will no longer combat their passions, and under this head, unbelief is one of the most glorious crowns of Christianity. Neither the Mussulman nor the heathen need to apostatise in order to be tranquil in the opprobium of their senses: the Christian alone has a God who forces him to blush.

And yet this God became man, He bore a flesh like our own; He was similar in His body to the idols of nations, and differing from all who had preceded Him, and from all who should follow him, He has exercised upon earth a regenerating power. In Him as in their source, in His form as in their centre, are reflected all the characters which have made of Christianity an incomparable monument. Lift up your eyes now: behold Jesus Christ! Who among you will blaspheme against Him without a certain fear that he may err? On emerging from infancy, perhaps, at the age when the eyes measure nothing because they as yet have compared nothing, you may pass before Him without halting or bowing your head; but wait a little. The shadows of life will increase behind you; you will know man, and returning from man to Christ with regards more humble, because they will have seen more, you will begin to discover in that physiognomy signs which will trouble you. A day will come when you will say to yourselves: Is God really there? Whatever may be the answer, your conscience will have asked the question. And what a question! What a man must he be who constrains another man to propose to himself the question of his divinity! And even should you not feel the presentiment of that doubt, think that for eighteen centuries it moves and divides mankind. Now more than ever it is the great question of the world. Behind the political quarrels which resound so loudly, there is another which is the true and the last—it is whether the nations civilised by Christianity will abandon the principle which has made them what they are, whether they will reach the point of apostacy, and what will be their lot. To be or not to be Christian, such is the enigma of the modern world.

And however you may solve it in your minds, it exists, and I leave it there. It exists, Jesus Christ reigns by that doubt suspended over our destinies, as much as by the faith of those who have given Him their whole soul. His divinity is the knot of the future, as it was of the past, and were it but a ruin, it is a ruin that bears all. We know what has become of the nations which have been converted from paganism to the gospel; we are ignorant of what would become of the Christian nations on the departure of the Gospel which has nourished and formed them. For we see no doctrine ready to receive them, but an abyss where matter would sit down alone upon the vacant throne of God.

All these things, gentlemen, require but one look—they are seen and felt as quickly as light is seen and warmth is felt. As it is impossible to confound life with death, it is impossible to confound Christianity with the false systems which have corrupted its traditions. Far from being obscured by the disfigurations which human liberty has formed, Christianity draws from them proof that it is indestructible and inevitable, and consequently divine. It remains so much the more great as it is brought into comparison, so much the more alone as it has rivals, so much the more easy to recognise as it ought to be discerned. Were there a thousand luminaries in the firmament of religion as in that of nature, the eye discerns there only one sovereign luminary. He who denies the sun is materially blind, he who denies Christianity is spiritually blind.

# THE NEED OF
# SUPERNATURAL INTERCOURSE

BETWEEN

# GOD AND MAN.

My Lord—Gentlemen,
    We have made a great advance. We required to know whether, in the intercourse between man and God, there existed an order of relations superposed upon the order of nature and reason. We have proved that such an order existed, since mankind, in all times and places, acts as if it were real. Afterwards, in replying to an objection drawn from the want of unity which the supernatural order presents in the mass of positive religions that divide the world, we have shown that in fact it was adulterated by the free action of man—which, however, is unable anywhere to destroy it—so that we have here in favour of truth the testimony of error itself. For error, notwithstanding its corrupting power, not only has not destroyed the supernatural form of the religious establishment, but it has in no greater degree attained to the point of giving a specious character of divinity to false religions. Christianity alone possesses a superhuman physiognomy which imposes upon the mind examination and respect; alone it appears between man and God as the possible expression of their relations.
    That done, gentlemen, the question of the supernatural order is not exhausted; we have only considered its outer

z

side, and rationalism calls us within. Rationalism asks what is meant by an order superior to nature and reason—an order which supposes that the intelligence is deprived of what is needful in order to know, and the will of what is needful in order to act. When Omar was consulted as to what was to be done with the Alexandrian library, he replied: "Either the books of the Alexandrian library say the same thing as the Koran, in which case they should be burned as useless; or they say what the Koran does not say, and in that case they should be burned as dangerous." So also, either the supernatural order blends with the light and activity of the natural order, and then what ends does it serve?—or it does not, and then, being unintelligible to reason, irreconcilable with nature, what further end does it serve? What motive, moreover, could have moved God to refuse to our inner organization the unity which He has placed in all His works, and to form for us a mind which, in order to fulfil its function, needs to be perfected by something from without.

In a word, the very notion of the supernatural order is disputed; it is accused of introducing into the plan of creation a motive, at the very least arbitrary and superfluous. Now in the name of the Church I affirm that this motive is necessary —absolutely necessary—supposing that God has willed to give us full knowledge and full possession of Himself, as from the beginning of things He has in fact willed and prepared. I shall prove this for the one and the other elements of the supernatural order—that is to say, for Prophecy, which is the complement of our inner light; and for Sacrament, which is the complement of our free activity.

When we consider the intellectual labour accomplished by man here below, we cannot refrain from a feeling of stupor and wonder. Placed upon this earth, as upon an island whose ocean is heaven, man has willed to know the route by which he is to pass; but innumerable barriers raised up around him have opposed his design, and forbade him to take possession of his empire and his exile. The sea opposed to him the jealousy of its waves; he looked upon the sea and passed over it. The prow of his genius has touched the most inaccessible shores; he has explored and examined them, and after a few centuries of daring, more stubborn even than tempests, peacefully ruling the waves, he travels where and when he wills upon the subjected surface of their immensity. He sends his orders to all the shoals now become his ports; by commerce which will never cease, he draws from them the luxury and pride of his life, blending all climates, how distant soever they may be, to make of them but one single servant obeying his will at every point of the globe.

Another sea, greater and deeper still, a treasure of infinite mysteries, spread out over his head its waves peopled with stars. He, a simple shepherd then, wandering after his flocks in the fields of Chaldæa, observed the heavens through the pure nights of the East. Aided by silence, he named the stars, learned their course, penetrated the secret of their obscurity, foretold their disappearance and their return; and all that luminous army, as if it had received its orders from the eyes of man, has never failed to appear in an exact cycle at the rendezvous where the observer waited for them. Even the star which appears but once in many centuries has not been able to hide its course from us; called forth at an hour fixed, it emerges from those unspeakable depths where no vision follows it—it comes, it shines at the point marked for it in our horizon, and, saluting with its light the intelligence which had foretold its appearance, returns back to the solitudes where the Infinite alone never loses sight of it.

But between earth and heaven—between the abode of man and the abode of the stars—a space intervenes different from both, less subtile than the one, less dense than the other, inhabited by winds and storms, and penetrating by its active influence all the springs of our life. Man has recognised those invisible companions of his being; he has decomposed the air which he breathes, and seized the gradations of the fluid which gives him light; the quickness of the one has no more escaped him than the weight of the other. In vain the thunder—that striking image of divine omnipotence—appeared to defy the boldness of his investigations; like a giant who has vanquished all around him, and is indignant against every obstacle, he has struggled hand to hand with this terrible array of the powers of nature, and, more than ever master, he has treated the thunderbolt like a child in leading-strings, causing it to halt respectfully on the summits of palaces and temples, forcing it to descend by inoffensive routes to the silent abyss of the earth. Earth, sea, heaven and all its luminaries, air and all its wonders, nothing within or without has been able to hide from the mind of man; observation revealed facts to him, and facts led him to causes and laws. And those particular sciences, rays diffused from a common centre, drew together and became enlightened in a more general science, which, in developing the abstract mysteries of number, extent, and motion, unveiled before us the eternal elements of all created things.

But is this all? Has the king of the world stopped there? Beware of believing it. Had he not advanced further, he would already have been poet, scholar, artist—already man, but not divine man. Now he was divine, and all the visible worlds did not possess in themselves the means of satisfying his intelligence, and of giving repose to his heart. He mounted higher; he asked himself what there is beyond the stars, what that orb is which moves all those orbs measured by his compass, and he replied—the Infinite! For the finite, not containing itself, can be limited only by the infinite. But what is the infinite? Is it an empty space unceasingly enlarging before itself, a boundless abyss calling to itself, in order to give them place, all real and all possible life without being itself living? Man, who had surveyed the sea and the heavens, fearlessly surveyed that other heaven and that other sea; whatever the nature of the intellectual space wherein his thought dilated above all sensible things, he comprehended that the principle of being, life, and movement, was not there. He advanced beyond it; he left the imaginary infinite, to contemplate face to face the real Infinite, and seeing, without fully seeing it, defining, without fully defining it, he exclaimed with a voice which was the first, and will be the last:

> Beyond the heaven, the God of heaven dwells!

Behold me, gentlemen, behold me trembling before the greatness of man! Just now he shook but the dust from his feet, and see, he touches God!

And yet is there not some trace of sadness in your soul? Is there in your intelligence nothing obscure and unknown? In the palmy days of Greece there once lived a sage who served his country with his sword, whilst at the same time he served it by lessons which merited the honour of preparing human wisdom to bend before the Gospel of divine wisdom. Socrates—for it was he—one morning went out of his tent, sat down before it, and with his head resting upon his hands remained thoughtful. The sun rose, the army was in motion, the coursers passed by, all the noise of a camp surrounded his reverie; but he remained motionless, and, as it were, enraptured out of himself, and it was evening before he had power or thought to remember his head weighing upon his knees. What was the subject of that great man's thoughts? What painful mystery was able to hide time from him and fill up the space of so lengthened a meditation? Alas! gentlemen, the same mystery that troubles you, and that brings you here. Without wishing now to insult your reason after having so highly exalted it, may I not ask with Socrates, What do you know? May I not ask you, the children of sages, the question which he addressed to the sages of his time? Have the twenty centuries that have passed since Socrates changed the condition of the human mind, and brought down upon you the plenitude of light which was wanting to the master of Plato? A light, indeed, a great light has shone upon the world since the mouth of Socrates was closed by a draught of hemlock; but it came from Calvary, and not from reason. Those who have not received it in the obedience of faith, so far from being enlightened by it, have seen the gloom and uncertainty of their ideas increasing; for a formidable question for them has been added to all the questions that perplex our understanding. I say to you then, without fear of contradicting myself or of offending you, There is something which you know not, when in order to know it you interrogate only your own intelligence. Philosopher or peasant, transcribing with a golden pen pages which will fill posterity with immortal incense, or obscure labourer in a life without morrow, whoever you may be, there is a thing which you know not. What you know, I have declared; what you know not is yourselves, your soul, the reason of your soul, your destiny. You know all, except the secret of your life. I do not yet seek the reason of this, I expose the fact, Is your soul imperishable in its nature? Why is it united to a body? Why does it withdraw from that body at a certain moment? Whither does it go on leaving its prison of a day? What is death? What is that place to which your fathers have gone, where they wait for you, that place which calls you, which tells you by the voice of Bossuet, "that the ranks are crowded there?" Do you know with any certainty? Do you know better than Socrates, placed by injustice face to face with the future, and drawing from his condemnation a new assurance of our immortality?

If I consult the history of human wisdom, I see it arriving

at this mystery by all its roads, but by very different roads. Plato affirms, Cicero doubts, Epicurus denies, and the human mind constantly dilates in these three zones of thought. Would it, after the ages of faith, restore in modern times the independent philosophy? Descartes begins by affirmation, Bayle continues by doubt, Voltaire ends by negation. Less than two centuries are needed by philosophical activity to accomplish that fatal cycle, the result of which is what you see, that is to say, a society without certain belief, divided by a thousand opinions, each of which claims to be true, each of which has its herald, its hopes, its reverses, and which, disputing in order to build up, meet together but to destroy! The Greeks presented its spectacle to the world, the Romans renewed it, and we, two thousand years after the lesson of these ruins, choose to receive from ourselves their formidable teaching. It is before you, gentlemen; examine it; learn from it at least the limit of your intelligence, and the need which you have of another light than yours to know your own selves.

But whence comes to us this ignorance of our own destinies? Whence comes it that, having penetrated so far and mounted so high into the mysteries of nature, our sight grows dim when we exercise it upon what is intimate and personal to ourselves? It is not difficult to understand the reason. All the phenomena of nature are facts present before our eyes, and the mathematical laws which govern them, besides that they are manifested in perceptible and limited bodies, appertain to the invariable essence of things, which is present to our mind and constitutes the intelligible light with which it is enlightened. The Divine Being Himself reveals Himself to us by the universe, which, all great though it be, constrains us to seek for it a cause, a cause which can only be the Infinite in a state of personality, that is to say, God. We thus hold the two ends of the chain, the finite and the Infinite, the world and God. But when it is a question of penetrating the secret of our destiny, all our natural means of knowledge fail us. Our destiny is not a phenomenon present to our observation; it embraces a past invisible to us, a future alike invisible. Nor is it a law belonging to the essence of things, since we may be or not be—live for a day or a thousand years. Our destiny is a revelation between two free beings, one of whom is finite and the other infinite. It depends upon the concurrence of two wills differently sovereign, one of which has given what it did not owe, the other is able to refuse what it did not expect.

Now how are we reasonably to know the will of another? How is reason to attain to an inner and a necessary perception of an act which may be or not be? Doubtless God has in His nature immutable rules of justice and goodness, whose reflection enlightens our conscience and places us on the road of His operations. But neither justice nor goodness impose upon Him, in regard to His gifts, a measure absolutely determined. He was free to create or not to create, free to call us into life sooner or later, free to unite Himself to us more or less durably and intimately. Who would say, for example, that the alliance of the divine nature with human nature by the incarnation was metaphysically necessary? Now if it were not necessary, it was free; and being free, how would the intelligence have perceived it otherwise than under the form of a simple possibility? And it is the possibility even which makes the mystery. Behold me, a living being, behold me in presence of the eternity which my mind discovers all around me as the natural horizon of my being: am I there for an hour, for a century, for ever? Is eternity, which is my principle, also my right and my object? If I saw clearly that it is not, there would then be no mystery; if I saw clearly that it is, there would be no greater mystery; but I hesitate before the affirmation and the negation, because both are possible. That which is necessary is visible, that which is possible is but dimly perceptible. That which is necessary is like the day, that which is possible is but as the night. Who is to solve the doubt? Who will say to us of two contradictory things equally realisable, This is realised, that is the real? Reason cannot, for reason could do this only by changing that which is possible into that which is necessary, which is absurd. I declare that between what is necessary and what is possible, stands the probable; but the probable does not give certainty, it inclines the mind without subjugating it. Socrates died avenging himself towards his judges by the hope of immortality, and the Phædo is the imperishable memorial of that heroic vengeance: but what sufficed for the remorse of his judges and the greatness of his soul, did not suffice for the consolation of his friends. Another death than that of a sage, another language than that of a man, was to give to the human race the certainty of its immortality.

But immortality is not all; many things therein still remain obscure, and were it even assured, the mind would still ask, What is immortality? Shall we see God in it? Shall we see Him there face to face? Will it be for our transformed vision what the yesterday of nature is for our mortal vision? The abyss of the infinite is fathomless, and this is the second cause of the powerlessness of reason to render an exact account to itself of the last ends of man, as Christianity eloquently calls the dogma of his destinies.

In every other science the question rises from the finite to the finite. Even mathematics are but the general laws of bodies, and if they are considered in an abstract manner, inasmuch as they subject undetermined quantities to their calculation, they attain to nothing beyond the indefinite—that is to say, beyond a supposed progression constantly increasing or decreasing, to which unity serves as a starting point. But in the science of the last ends of man, the question rises from nothingness to the infinite. It is a question of knowing whether death brings us back again into existence, or leads us to eternity; whether we are a simple phenomenon measured by time, or a luminary emanated from God to return to Him again; and what is the law of that curve which we describe round the centre which is our principle and our end. Even, putting aside the intention of God towards us, an intention evidently not to be sounded by reason, as I have just shown, there still remains the difficulty as to the infinite considered in itself. St. Thomas of Aquinas has said, "Truth is the equation between the intelligence and its object." Now how can a finite intelligence be in equation with an object which is not finite? And if that equation be impossible, how should we of ourselves possess truth in regard to God and to our relations with Him? We are able to affirm that God is, because our mind, superior to the universe, discovers therein the need of a cause superior to it. We can also affirm that that cause is infinite, because if it were not, it would be but another universe, equally incapable as the first of subsisting of itself. But our mind, although superior to the universe, is not equal to God; it floats between two extremes, surpassing the one, surpassed by the other, and not even knowing entirely that which is beneath its sphere; because the total knowledge of the phenomenon would require the total knowledge of the cause, which is God. God, says the Scriptures, dwells in "inaccessible light;" He is, at the same time, that which is most clear, and that which is most impenetrable. Remove the idea which we have of Him, all light disappears from our understanding; truth becomes only a dream, and justice a name. But, also, would we penetrate the Divine Essence to its very depths, our eyes grow dim, and we perceive in immeasurable distance only a sparkling that dazzles us, and veils light from us by light itself. For example, would we study the metaphysical nature of God, we ask, Is God a solitary being, or does He possess relations in Himself? Whatever may be the answer, it is a mystery. Would we study His moral nature, we ask, What, in God, is the proportion of justice and goodness? Whatever may be the reply, we must reply again by another mystery. And, yet, if I ignore these things, can I possibly know the law of my relations with God? Can I know what I ought to fear, or what I ought to hope?

Perhaps you will say to me, But why has God not given us a more penetrating mind? Ah! gentlemen, whatever penetration He might have given us, would it ever have equalled the profundity of His essence, which is infinite. Would it have answered to the definition of St. Thomas of Aquinas, "Truth is an equation between the intelligence and its object?" You have but two courses open to you, either to deny that definition, or to maintain that God had power to create spirits his equals—that is to say, God. In the first case, it is to affirm that the effect might be greater than its cause; in the second, that that which exists by another, nevertheless exists of itself. Yield, therefore, to evidence, and no longer contest against Christianity that great and powerful truth, that no created intelligence is of itself capable of attaining to a perfect knowledge of God, and, consequently, to a certain knowledge of its destiny. History proves this to you, and reasoning has just confirmed history by explaining it to you.

What, then, is wanting, in order that man may know himself and God? A mediating light must interpose between God and himself—a light which should aid his nature without destroying it, which should draw him near to the Infinite without being itself the Infinite. And if that mediation seems impossible to you, give me your attention yet a moment longer.

You to whom I speak are a soul, and I who speak to you am a soul also. Now do you know my soul, and do I know yours? The infinite is not between us, and yet, although by

our bodies we touch each other, an abyss separates us. What
are you, and what am I? What is the hidden motor of our
actions? Whence do we tend by our weaknesses and by our
virtues? What is our degree of power in good and in evil?
I repeat, What are you and what am I? You see plainly in
my actions, and I see in yours, a certain reflection of what
we are inwardly; physiognomy adds its revelation to that of
our works, but can you say that you know me as I know myself, and can I persuade myself that I see you as you see
yourself? The soul ignores the soul, inasmuch as their essence
is not seen by a direct vision. There is but one remedy for
this evil, namely, confidence or confession—that is to say, the
opening of the soul to the soul by means of sincere language.
Language is the mediating light between equal things which
are unseen; by a stronger reason is it, also, between things
doubly separated by their invisibility and by their inequality.
Why should not God speak to man? Why, seeing us incapable
of attaining to Him by the feebleness of our nature, should He
not condescend to unveil Himself to us in a confidence which
would reveal to us, with the mysteries of His being, the order
of His thoughts and designs? I have proved to you that this
supernatural or prophetic revelation was necessary to the
intercourse between man and God, and I have just shown
you the instrument of this revelation in language. I will
terminate this conference by proving also to you the necessity
of Sacrament, not to enlighten the mind, but to strengthen the
will—not to teach us our destiny, but to help us to fulfil it.

The mind is the remote principle of our actions, the will is
their immediate principle; the mind sees, the will commands,
man acts. What is it then to act? To act is to produce
something. If you have produced nothing—if no result has
been the fruit of your will, you have done nothing; it is the
expression consecrated by language itself. Therefore man
never moves but to produce, and each of his movements, even
when it is abortive, still produces something, were it only noise.
But why does he produce? Why is not man in a state of
repose? What does he seek in that incessant production
which is the effect of his activity?. What he seeks is life. If
he breathes, it is to live; if he digs the earth, it is to live; if
he walks, it is to live; if he sleeps, it is to live; if he dies, it is
still to live. And he never rests, because life escapes from him
in proportion as he produces it. He drinks it from a parsi-

monious cup, which contains and affords but one drop at a time. To halt is to die. But to die!—did I not say just now that to die was still to live? Yes, in the truth of our destinies death is the high-road of life, provided we have known the secret of the course on which we act, which is to produce in ourselves the very life of God—a life full, stable, each instant of which includes eternity, and which has no more need to produce itself because it is. This is the true and final object of all our actions. I have demonstrated it to you in showing you that God is our principle and our end. Whatever you may do, if you do not this you will do nothing. If you do not this you are but like the herdsman who sits down on the bank of a flowing stream and beats the wave as it passes, pleased with the noise which he himself causes. The present life, when it is not the instrument of the eternal life, has no other form, and is nothing more worth. In vain will you clothe it with the consul's purple; in vain will you call it glory, power, immortality—illustrious names which elevate nothingness only to exhibit it from a higher place and to a greater distance. History is full of these extinguished beacons, famous mortals who, because they conquered for a day the admiration of this world, esteemed themselves great in life, and expected from their tomb a persevering reign. Do this if you will. Build up pyramids for yourselves in the devastated solitudes of memory; surround your death with moats and barriers against time; eternity will permit you, as it permits the child who totters in his first efforts to reach the arms of his nurse that he may feel proud of being greater there than on his feet.

But if these puerilities wound you, if you are ashamed of adding ridicule to nothingness, consider that it is a question of producing in yourselves the life of God, and seek in your nature if you can find there the instrument of such exalted ambition.

The life of God is infinite; it consists in the perpetuity of an indivisible moment in which God, one and many, beholds Himself fully in His essence and loves Himself fully in His persons. Now we are totally incapable of such life. Subject as we are by our nature to succession and change, we cannot aspire to the indefectible state of immutable duration; neither are we more able to behold the Divine Being face to face, nor to love Him with that perfect love which, in Himself, results from the direct vision of His ineffable beauty. If we behold Him, it is through the obscurity of ideas; if we love Him, it is as the invisible principle of the incomplete blessings by which we are surrounded. But to behold Him in His substance, to love Him with that regard which possesses the object loved, to become blended so completely in Him as to feel only the steady movement of His eternal life, is a prodigy so far beyond our power to perform that faith alone gives us the certainty of its future accomplishment. Reason laughs at that hope, so much does it feel incapable of realising it. For reason, the most glorious future of man is immortality; that is to say, the attainment by the soul of a duration which the senses could no longer measure—a life the ideas of which alone would fill indefinite space. Or, if reason pass beyond this, it casts to us the dreams of pantheism, boasting that it creates God for us on condition that we lose ourselves in the abstract immensity of being. Christianity has marked our place between these excesses; knowing that God is our end, it commands us to begin to live imperfectly in Him, in order one day to live there in the fulness of vision, which, without confounding us with the Divine Essence, will give it to us as the present object of direct knowledge and of love in possession.

Now, whether in its initial or its final form, that divine life —I have just shown it—surpasses the forces of all mortal nature. As there is no natural equation possible between a limited intelligence and a truth not limited, so also there can exist no possible natural equation between the life of a finite being and that of an infinite being. If, then, God calls us to His eternity, if our destiny is to live by Him, in Him, and with Him, he must necessarily communicate to our soul a mediatorial element, by means of which it may be raised above its own limits, and borne towards Him by a movement of a supernatural or divine order. Our present life is the painful crucible from whence our future life should flow; if only matter be found there, even were it the most precious, nothing but mire will come from it; if spirit only be found there, even were it the most penetrating, nothing would result but human ideas and sentiments. Let God then intervene, let Him pour in the gold of His eternity, or, to speak plainly, let Him attract us towards Himself by a direct action upon our souls; let Him draw us without violence from the affections of nature, and inspire us with such a love that the present life may appear to us only as a burden, and this earth but a place of exile.

This love exists, you cannot deny it. David exhaled it

in his Psalms, the martyrs embalmed their sufferings with it, the saints have lauded and glorified it from generation to generation: all, in different modes, have poured forth before God the melancholy of souls oppressed by the workings of superhuman love. "As the hart," said they, "panteth after the fountains of water, so my soul panteth after thee, O God! My soul had thirsted after the strong and living God, when shall I come and appear before the face of God. My tears have been my bread day and night, whilst it is said to me daily: Where is thy God? These things I remembered, and I poured out my soul within me, for I shall go over to the place of the wonderful tabernacle, even to the house of God, with the voice of joy and praise, with the noise as of one feasting. Why art thou sad, O my soul, and why dost thou trouble me? Hope in God, for I will still give praise to him because he is the help of my countenance and my God."\* These accents are not of earth—they rise from hearts delivered from time, and which began already really to inhabit the region which gives a distaste for all the rest. But how did they reach that region? Is it by the natural effect of intellectual contemplation, or of a movement of enthusiasm? Assuredly not; and never, either in Orpheus or Plato, or in any mind possessing only the spirit of man, have such vibrations moved the sanctuary of our sensibility. They proceed from an art unknown to genius, from a tradition which reveals its secrets only to saints. Interrogate the saints; they are not jealous of their gifts, freely they have received them, freely will they give them to you. They will tell you whence they derive that painful but hallowed life which draws them above the world. Look yonder: under the shelter of a chiselled stone, under the still more lowly symbol of bread kneaded by man, lives the hidden virtue that gives holiness, and, with holiness, produces and fertilises in the soul the germ of the divine life. What Prophecy is for the intelligence, Sacrament is for the will. Prophecy reveals to us the impenetrable mysteries of the essence and mind of God; Sacrament communicates to us the spirit, the desire, and the hunger for God, the right to possess Him by grace, since we cannot by nature, and even a real foretaste of that possession.

If the experience of the saints does not suffice for you,

---

\* Psalm xlii.

consult the opposite experience. You who have only the heart wherewith to love God, as you have only reason wherewith to know Him, do you love God? I do not ask you if you love Him with tender and profound love, better than you love your dearest friends, better than a mother loves her son, better than all things and yourselves—not from the spectacle of visible blessings of which He is the author, but from an anticipated contemplation of the personal beauty that is in Him. I do not ask you whether you love Him so as to be able to address to Him some of those accents which David has just lent us. But do you love Him with the faintest and most feeble love? Are your thoughts always turned towards Him? Have you any secret pleasure in Him? Does He form a part, how small soever it may be, of the treasure of your heart? I venture to say, No, and that the falling leaf which the wind bears along touches you more than the immensity of the divine perfections.

Seneca has said, AMICITIA PARES INVENIT VEL FACIT—*Friendship finds or makes equals.* Such is the reason of your coldness towards God; you know that He is infinite, and you do not conceive what there can be between Himself and you. He is in His place, and you are in yours; you ask from Him only forgetfulness, and you give to Him but the same thing which you ask from Him. And never, by the sole effort of nature, will you rise from that state of insensibility. Nature will inspire you with ardent passions, or even with heroic affections, but for the things that are felt and for beauties seen; nature will prostrate you before a little dust; it will make of that dust the soul of your existence, your life itself, so that you would be ready to die, if in a last embrace, you lost that precious gift of love to which you have a thousand times vowed immortality. You would do even more, you would die for a beloved object; you would die joyfully, offering to that object your last sigh as a holocaust of eternal adoration. All this you are able to do, when God is not in question; but if God be in question, that great faculty of loving dies within you, and your heart, so prompt for all the rest, refuses the Infinite. If you loved nothing we should have but to pity you; being loving by nature, and placing in it the felicity of your short life, we must wonder to see you insensible to God, and conclude therefrom that something is wanting to you in order to attain that supreme affection. A sage has just told you what is wanting to you. As St. Thomas of Aquinas has defined truth—"an equation between the intelligence and its object," Seneca, with a precision not less eloquent, has defined love—"a fusion which finds or makes equals." Now as no equality exists between God and us, it is for Him to lean towards His creature by a movement of grace, and divinely to attract that creature to a life common with Himself. If we consent, it is our merit and our salvation; if we do not consent, it is our fault as well as our ruin.

These truths which I endeavour to demonstrate to you, were one day announced by Saint Paul before a Roman proconsul and a king of the East, assembled more from curiosity to hear him than from desire to know the ways of God. After having related to them the madness of his youth against Jesus Christ, and how He whom he had persecuted had appeared to him at the gates of Damascus to confide to him the Gospel of nations, he thus continued his discourse: "But being aided by the help of God, I stand up unto this day witnessing both to small and great, saying no other thing than those which the prophets and Moses did say should come to pass, namely, that Christ should suffer, and that he should be the first that should rise from the dead, and should show light to the people and to the Gentiles." Here the proconsul interrupted him, and with a loud voice cried out to him, "Thou art mad, Paul!" And Paul, unmoved, replied, "I am not mad, most excellent Festus, but I speak words of truth and soberness, and the king before whom I speak knoweth of these things, none of which were hidden from him, or were done in a corner." Then turning towards the king he said—"King Agrippa, believest thou the prophets? I know that thou believest!" And the king answered, "Paul, almost thou persuadest me to be a Christian."\* Gentlemen, the same dialogue is now passing between your soul and mine; neither the truths nor the hearers have changed. There are here many, like Festus, puffed up in the pride of reason, to whom the history of their own weakness is unknown, and who, having never felt any need of the help of God, marvel that it is necessary to treat with Him otherwise than as equal to equal. These say to me, "Thou art mad, Paul!" But there are also those, who, like Agrippa, more infatuated by their passions than by their knowledge,

---

\*Acts xxvi. 22 and foll.

secretly warned of the misery of man, sometimes lift their eyes towards the Omnipotent Goodness which has made them. These say to me, "Almost thou persuadest me to be a Christian." And I, making no distinction between either, between those who are near and those who are further away—confiding in Him who has died for us all, I say to all, imitating the language of Saint Paul, "Would to God that you were as I am!"* Would to God that, recognising the powerlessness of your nature abandoned to itself, you would sing in the peace of the joy, the certainty of the children of God, that short and consoling hymn, CREDO—*I believe!*

* Acts xxvi. 29.

# PROPHECY.

My Lord—Gentlemen,

The reality and necessity of a supernatural order, as a means of communication between man and God, having been demonstrated to you, it remains for us to penetrate the intimate nature of that order. You have already seen that it divides into two acts, one corresponding to our faculty of knowing—namely, Prophecy; the other relative to our operative faculty—namely, Sacrament. In causing you more deeply to sound the mystery of these two acts I shall attain my object, which is to lead you to a knowledge of the supernatural order, as far as its profundity and the limits of our minds will permit. I begin by Prophecy.

Prophecy is a word of God manifesting truths to man which his reason alone would not have attained, and which, however, are necessary for the accomplishment of his destiny.

That which predominates in this definition is language—language is the first prophetic element. But what is language?

A man comes into the world. His eyes, his ears, his lips—all his senses are closed. He has no idea of the nothingness from whence he is emerging, or of the being to which he is attaining—he is ignorant of himself, and of all the rest with himself. Leave him as nature has just sketched him, leave him there naked, dumb, dead rather than living; he will live perhaps, but he will live without knowing it, an unformed guest of creation, a soul lost in powerlessness to find its own life. His eyes will open, but no thought will be visible in them, and his heart will beat, but no virtue will be felt therein. Happily something watches over him. The providence of language covers him with its fertile wings—language incessantly bends over him, watches him, touches, turns him, strives by its vibration to awaken that sleeping soul. And at last, after days which have been ages, on a sudden, from that dull and insensible abyss, from that infant hardly able to express by a smile that he understood the love which had placed him in the world, language escapes and replies. The man then lives; he thinks, he loves, he names those whom he loves, he renders back to them in language all the love he had received from them.

But this is only the beginning of man. He, the predestinated of the Infinite, as yet knows only the bosom of his mother, his cradle, his chamber, a few pictures hanging on the walls, the space which his eye discovers from a window—an hour is for him history, a house the universe, a caress the last end of things. He must leave this limited horizon and prepare to mark his place in that restless society where all, having the same rights in the same duties, will dispute with him the glory of existence. Soon he will descend the staircase of the paternal house, he will appear in public, his ears will hear the painful din of clashing ambition and contending ideas, and like a leaf fallen upon the waves of a stormy sea, he will, for the first time, wonder at the cost of life, and the mysteries which it contains. Who will explain them to him? Who, rightly or otherwise, will teach him the science of man, that science whose elements are the past, the present, the future, earth and heaven, which by one of its poles touches nothingness, and by the other the infinite? It will still be language, no longer the language of his father and his mother, but perilous language, which will, perhaps, stifle within him the germs of truth; which will, perhaps, develop them according to the spirit of the masters who may direct his own. For he will have masters; he cannot escape from that second reign which language will exercise over him. Language launched him into the world, language roused and gave the first course to his ideas: whatever he may will, whatever he may do, for his happiness or his misery, language will perform its work; it will make of him a vase of faith or of unbelief, a victim of pride or of charity, a slave of the senses or of duty, and if he always remains free against evil, he will, nevertheless, be free on condition of calling to his aid the language of better teaching than that which had deceived him.

Such is the history of man; listen now to that of the people. A tribe is found slumbering in barbarism; they know not even the first of arts, which is that of subjecting the earth to their wants. Like the beasts, they live on prey. When they find it they lie down and sleep before the fire that warms, or under the tree that covers them, until hunger commands them again to dispute with the forests, and with chance, their precarious subsistence. They have no country. The very soil on which they wander has received no consecration from their labour, no limit from their power; and although it may hold the bones of their forefathers, they live there without past or future. If attacked, they defend themselves, like wild beasts in their lairs, but are unable, even of the staff with which they defend themselves, to form either a sword or a standard. Idea is wanting to them, and with it, virtue, progress, history, stability.

But behold a change! This people settles; they build tents, they dig out trenches, they place guards, they have something durable and holy to watch over. A temple offers to them, under a sensible image, the God who made the world, the Father of justice and the Indweller of souls. They adore Him in spirit, they pray to Him with faith. The sun no longer passes over their heads as a fire which becomes extinguished in the evening and is lighted up afresh in the morning, but as the grave measure of ages, bringing to each day its duty, to each century its duration. They count his revolutions, and distribute their own history in the cycle wherein all nations have included their own. In fine, they live as a nation, they reveal their presence by men of name—by acts of power. But what has raised them from their former lethargy? What has made of that barbarous tribe a regular and civilized society? What, gentlemen? The same power that made the man—the power of language. Orpheus came down from the mountains of Thracia, he sang, and Greece rose up full of life at the sound of his lyre. A missionary appeared in the desert with a crucifix instead of a harp; he pronounced the name of God, and the savages, simple even to nakedness, covered their nascent bashfulness with the leaves of the forest. Children smiled at the man who spoke, and mothers believed in lips which brought to their sons the blessing of the Great Spirit.

Shall we contemplate other scenes taken from more advanced communities? A people, after having long held with honour the sceptre of their destiny, lost little by little the sentiment of great things; they no longer knew how to believe, to deliberate, or to devote themselves; they were seen bending over a counter, weighing coins in a balance, instead of weighing the destinies of the world, having no longer any desire beyond the monotonous and senseless clinking of money. With abasement of character came servitude; tyrants sported with that people and imposed upon them laws worthy of their morals. Those tyrants found accomplices even in the traditions of liberty, and the forum, the tribune, the senate, were names with which they covered the degradation of souls and the opprobrium of their tyranny. But whilst this corruption and fear reigned over that degenerate race; whilst all was silent save falsehood, calumny, delation, baseness of heart and mind, at a moment unlooked for, that people awoke and looked around them : Domitian has disappeared, Nerva has succeeded him. What was it that thus suspended the course of ruins? What power recalled, even were it but for a day, honourable names and remembrances? Do not ask, gentlemen : language glided between the interstices of tyranny; here and there, as in a field harvested, it met with souls who had remained true even in their generation, and scattering by them the leaven of the antique power, it reanimated the senate, the people, the forum, the extinct gods, the fallen majesty, and altogether resuscitating at the same time, they gave to the living and the dead a sacred and a last apparition of country.

Beyond a people there is only the human race, and perhaps we shall find that the human race also has felt the magic power of language. Perhaps also the human race, plunged in corruption and servitude, may, once in the course of its long history, have felt the divine shock of resurrection. If you have forgotten it, recall to your minds what the world was at the dawn of the times which we call our own. Endeavour in thought to be present at one of those festivals to which it bore at the same time its gods and its morals, its ideas and its joys. Choose the circus or the amphitheatre, the games or the mysteries—any scene whatever of antiquity. Such was the world! That world is no more. Chaste altars prepare generations laboriously to restore their senses to their proper functions, and the cross, the sign of mortification and humility, instead of presenting the slave as a source of amusement to cruel and dissolute masters, advances before princes to teach them gentleness, before the people to give them courage to sustain a grave and impoverished existence. Bloodshed no longer excites applause, if it be not given in a great and voluntary sacrifice; the flesh, dishonoured by the shamelessness of the soul, is no longer presented as an object of public adoration, and in the very midst of great cities, spotless purity has built retreats which are not even celebrated, so much is the heart of man raised in the knowledge and sentiment of virtue. The eye no longer sees traces of mutilations on the brow of the passers-by; the ear is no longer shocked with the abject sounds of private executions, and even public justice appears but rarely before the respected gaze of citizens. A street is an asylum where creatures meet who all bear in themselves the sign of their rights, and the visible inequality of conditions in no way takes from the poor their place and their dignity. What more shall I say? The heart of man is still feeble and devoured by passions, and yet mankind is transformed; in the very depths of its being it bears a germ of good against which no crime can prevail, and which condemns to the scorn of all the same things which in the ancient world usurped the homage of all. What has accomplished this? Yet once more, and I grow weary of repeating it, it is language. A man came who called himself God, and who said in the name of God: " Blessed are the poor! Blessed are they who weep! Blessed are they who hunger and thirst after justice! Blessed are the clean of heart! Blessed are they who suffer persecution for justice' sake!"* He said that; and language, which makes man, which founds civilization, which emancipates nations, that same language from the lips of Christ gave a new force, or rather a new birth to mankind.

Hereby it is manifest that language is the highest power of the world; that it is the cause of all the revolutions, whether good or evil, whose succession forms history, and consequently you must not wonder to find it an element of supernatural order, and that to prophecy is to speak.

I have said, moreover, that Prophecy is a word of God. And here rationalism, which has up to this point consented to my discourse, does not permit me to advance further. Rationalism considers that the idea of God and that of language are two incompatible ideas; that as God is a purely spiritual being and language a simple vibration of air caused

* St. Matt. v. 5 and foll.

by the physical organs of the voice, we cannot, without degrading the Divine Majesty, attribute to it so insignificant an operation.

Is it necessary for me to reply to this? Is it necessary for me to show you that they degrade the notion of language in order to refuse it to God? Do you imagine that air agitated, no matter how, possesses the power of obtaining the prodigious effects which I have described to you? Doubtless, because of our present state in which the soul is united to a body, language also has a body; it occasions an outer action which vibrates the air. But this is only the phantom of language. Close your eyes, collect yourself, shut up your soul within itself. Do you not hear that it speaks to you? Do you not hear that without disturbing any physical organ it inwardly articulates words, pronounces phrases, forms a discourse within you? Do you not hear that it grows animated, ardent, eloquent, that it persuades you, and that, nevertheless, all is still in the centre and at the extremities of your body? Outer language is but the pale and dying expression of inner language, and inner language is thought itself engendering in the depths of the soul by an immaterial fecundity. Were it otherwise—if to speak were but to vibrate the air—could you conceive that air is the vehicle of ideas and sentiments, that it seizes upon your intelligence in its impenetrable recesses, and withdraws it from its proper conceptions? Language is a spiritual power, united in man to a sensible organ, and giving it impulsion, as the soul, in the totality of its forces, gives impulsion to the whole body. God, who is spirit, may then be language, He may speak to us inwardly without the utterance of any voice heard by the senses, and speak to us outwardly if it please Him to give His communications a character of publicity and authenticity. It is true that in Himself God is not united to a body, that therefore His language has not an organ naturally and personally subject to Him; but all nature is more obedient towards Him than our bodies are to us. Over nature He has the right of the whole creative power, and it is as easy for Him to use it, as it is for us to use the portion of organised matter subject to us.

As a spiritual power, then, language belongs to God. But it belongs to Him still more manifestly under another point of view. In fact, if, considered in its first root, language is no other thing than thought making its appearance within and before the soul; if it is the intercourse of the soul with itself, it is also the faculty by which the soul enters into relations with another soul, initiates that soul to its views, its tastes, its desires, spreads out within it, if I may so speak, and receives in its turn, by a systematic exchange, the plenitude of the foreign soul. Language is the bond of spirits, not only of spirits united to a body, but of pure spirits, and who are reciprocally visible in the splendour of their essence; for that brightness in which they are does not deliver them over to thé mercy of one another. They have their closed sanctuary— the free place where they think before themselves—and it is by voluntary language, by language abstract and sublime, that they communicate with each other in order to give themselves to one another in more abundant and more perfect effusion. Language is, at the same time, the intercourse of spirits with themselves and with other spirits; it is an outer as well as an inner faculty; it is the highest means of initiation and communion. Now, I ask, shall we refuse to God the power of initiation and communion? Shall we refuse to Him who has established all the relations between beings—from the grain of sand to the seraphim—shall we refuse to Him the power of holding relations with intelligent beings, of communicating His thoughts and His will to them—in fact, of speaking to them? "There is nothing in the world without voice,"* said the Apostle Saint Paul; there is nothing without voice, because there is nothing without communication, and God alone is to be at the same time silence and isolation! God alone is to be silent, and to stand aloof in an exile as immense as His nature! No, gentlemen, my reason can no more conceive this thing than my heart; and with the joy of evidence I repeat those words of the Book of Wisdom: "The spirit of the Lord has filled the whole world, and that which containeth all things hath knowledge of the voice."†

You hear! "That which containeth all things." In fact, God being the primordial type of beings, they possess nothing which God does not possess more perfectly; and since language is within us, it is necessary that it should be in God in an ineffable and infinite manner. This is also what Catholic doctrine teaches, and what the Apostle Saint John says to us with such profound elevation at the commencement of his Gospel: "In the beginning was the Word, and the Word was

* 1 Cor. xiv. 10.    † *Ibid.* i. 7.

with God, and the Word was God."* As your language is the fruit of your soul—the expression and effusion of your soul—there is also something in God which is the fruit, the expression, and the effusion of His soul, which is "God of God, Light of Light," to use the expression of the Council of Nice. And as all the force of your language is in your soul, all the force of the divine language is also in the source from whence it springs. Have you remarked that there are dead as well as living words—words that fall upon the earth like a spent arrow, and others that fall into the mind like a devouring flame? And certainly you have not believed that the difference between them sprang from the air more or less agitated by the mechanical force of the lungs. Their difference springs from the soul, which is the principle of language. Dead words are those which come from a dead soul; living language is that which comes from a living soul. When an orator, in a matter capable of eloquence, speaks without moving you, when he leaves you master of your resolutions, insensible to error or to truth, be sure that a soul has not spoken to you. For it is impossible, if a soul had spoken to you, that your own could remain a stranger to it; it is impossible for a soul to receive without emotion the expression of another soul.

And you would take from God that expression of the soul! From God, who is the soul eternally and infinitely living, who is all life, all effusion; you would take from Him that which remains to us under the icy walls of the flesh! Oh! how God abhors that prison wherein the unbeliever seeks to confine Him; and how eloquently He says to us in His Gospel: "Man does not live by bread alone, but by every word which proceedeth from the mouth of God."†

In fact, whilst the language of man, even the most enlightened and the most eloquent, contains of itself only verities insufficient for the life of the human race, the Word of God abundantly diffuses treasures of wisdom such as our own can only acquire by accepting it. It is the mediating light by which the infinite intelligence raises created intelligences towards itself, and communicates to them ideas which, whilst surpassing their nature, draw them nevertheless nearer to their end. This operation includes nothing which is not very conceivable and very simple. All language is necessarily in equa-

---

\* St. John i. 1.  † Matt. iv. 4.

tion with the thought which it expresses; as is the value of the thought of a being, so is it also the value of his language. Now, the thought of God is as great as Himself—that is to say, without measure—and consequently His Word, whether He retains it within Himself, or whether He produces it outwardly, necessarily contains truths which are inaccessible to our minds by means of evidence and demonstration. But things inevident and undemonstrable are not unintelligible; and when enounced by God, and affirmed by Him, they become an incomparable seat of certainty and light for the intelligence which receives them. The intelligence does not see the infinite, but knows it.

This phenomenon, in due proportions, is presented to us in the purely human order. What, indeed, is the action of human language upon man in a state of infancy? Does it not act upon infancy as the Divine Word acts upon mankind —that is to say, by way of affirmation and initiation? The infant believes his father, who communicates to him in simple but affirmative language truths which that feeble intelligence is not yet capable of demonstrating, and which nevertheless gradually draw him from the native ignorance in which he lies, form his thought, elevate his heart, and make of him a being moved by knowledge and love.

I will go further; I will say that in all language which teaches, there is a mystery of authority and initiation. I will say that you, my contemporaries, whatever degree of maturity you may have attained, are but men initiated in the language of the nineteenth century. You think, perhaps, that you have formed yourselves. You err; the nineteenth century has formed you. And what is the nineteenth century? A spirit expressed by language, which language becomes transformed into public opinion, lives in the air which you inhabit, penetrates even to your bones, and governs you without your knowledge, unless a more powerful language has emancipated you from it by causing you to respire other and higher truth. Whatever mental power you may think you possess, whatever greatness of character or genius nature may have endowed you with, not one among you is of himself independent of his age—not one among you, of his own power, speaks higher language than the language of his time. Even when in advance of it, you are but its echoes and its servants. So much does man need to be instructed by a mind superior to his own. So much is it part of his destiny to hear, to receive, and to obey. Now to whom, rather than to God, does he owe that obedience? The language of an age is doubtless an authority worthy of respect: it is the result of a great movement of the human mind, caused by a long course of events which have turned the scale of things and ideas. But this is only a station in vicissitude. The tempest of the future will soon bear the mobility of the world on other anchors, and although there is a certain degree of logic in that inconsistency, there is nothing even in all ages taken together possessing a character worthy of our faith. Nevertheless we give our faith to them because even the natural order, although pressing upon us on all sides, is so profoundly complicated that we require a master to teach us the secret of a single day.

And God is not to teach us the secret of eternity? But we oppose him in vain. There is in the world another teaching than that of ages, another language that that of man. This language changes and passes. Although so many ingenious lips have been its eloquent organs, although writing has lent its durability to the immortality of eloquence, the human tongue has not been able to found the temple of truth. The columns lie upon the ground, moved from age to age by constructions upon which men have graven the prophecy of their duration, and which turns to ruins under the hands of the builders who come after. Man destroys man, and time reaps time. One single edifice stands erect amidst the rubbish where the contradictory works of the human mind are heaped together. The inscription upon this edifice is "THE WORD OF GOD." It is that word which, after having created the world and man has not abandoned them to the mercy of their own thoughts, too feeble before such a work, but has taught them the mystery of their principle and their end. It is that word which, having once pronounced its secret, known to itself alone, has never ceased to repeat it before heaven and earth, calling ages and races by their proper names, creating prophets against all forgetfulness, apostles against all falsehood, circulating in the human mind as its very blood, often adulterated, never destroyed, drawing forth light from error and life from death. This word is Christianity,—the Church,—unity in stability,— all that remains amidst all that passes away. Take it from the world if you can, what would remain? Time and man: time which passes, and man who doubts. It is too little for a soul.

I have analyzed prophecy, gentlemen, inasmuch as language is its first element. My intention is to seek if it does not contain another, and what is the nature of that second element. Before doing this I will immediately examine with you the mechanism of language, as being the prophetic root in which we may be able to discover what we do not yet know.

The effect of language is the enlightenment of the understanding and the direction of the will. How is this miraculous phenomenon produced? By what process does language enlighten the mind and move the will? We must first suppose that it is addressed to an intelligent being, that is to say, to a faculty capable of knowing, for if it were addressed to a being of what kind soever, which was incapable of knowing, it would at most produce only a sensation. Thus the animal hears language materially—some even faithfully reproduce it—but it causes in them only instinctive movements connected with the sensible order of which they form a part. This first condition necessary to the efficacy of language being established, what passes between the intelligence that speaks and the intelligence that listens? Evidently the first presents to the second an intelligible object—that is to say, a truth. For every truth however profound it may be, is intelligible, and may be enounced by means of language, which is the mould and representation of the true. I suppose, for instance, that you are ignorant of mathematics, and that it is my mission to teach them to you—here is a truth of that order which I should have some day to present to you: If a square be constructed upon the hypothenuse of a right-angled triangle, the surface of that square would be equal to the surface of the squares constructed upon the two other sides of the same triangle.

This is a portion of elementary geometry which is incontestable and proved, yet those of you who have not studied the elements of that science have not even understood me; they have felt the sensation of the words which I have pronounced, and no more. Why is this? Is it because this proposition is not a truth? It is a truth. Is it because that truth is not within the comprehension of the human intelligence? It is within the comprehension of the human intelligence, and even within the power of a simple student of mathematics. Why then do you not understand it? Manifestly because, in order for language to have its effect of illumination, it is not sufficient that it presents to the mind an intelligible object. It is also necessary that the terms whose logical enchainment constitutes language should possess their individual evidence in order that the mind might seize their sense—that is to say—discover under each sound the idea which it contains, and next, the general idea which the discourse includes. This takes place by definition. By means of definition, language enlightens language by decomposing it into such simple elements, that each word becomes a light, or, if you prefer, a ray of that total light which becomes the evidence of the mind.

Let me give you proof of this by defining the proposition which I have chosen as an example.

A triangle is a figure determined by three lines which meet so as to produce three angles. When one of these angles is right—that is to say, formed by two lines which fall perpendicularly upon one another—the triangle is called right-angled. In this case, the side of the triangle opposed to the right angle is the longest of the three, it being manifest that as the angles increase the side corresponding to them increases in proportion. This long side of a right-angled triangle is the hypothenuse. If it be taken as the base of a square, and two others are constructed on the short sides of the same triangle, the surface of the square of the hypothenuse will be equal to the surface of the two other squares.

You now understand the proposition; it is no longer for you an enchainment of words, but of ideas, which by their connection form a new idea. Language has become enlightened by being defined.

But is this all? Is the mystery of initiation accomplished? Has your understanding become enlightened? Certainly not; you see clearly what the words would convey to you, but you do not yet see that what they say to you is true. Nothing convinces you that the square of the hypothenuse is, in fact, equal in its surface to the squares of the other two sides of the right-angled triangle; you possess neither the evidence nor the certainty of it. It is for language to give you these, and it will do so by demonstration—that is to say, by showing you that that idea, which is new to you, is nevertheless contained in other ideas which, by their invincible and primordial clearness form the very foundation of your reason. Language will take the obscure idea, will lead it step by step even to the intelligible seat which is the centre and the torch of your soul, will present it there to the principle from whence it emanates, and give to you in the sentiment of their unity that ray of light which is evidence, that repose of the mind which is certainty. Or even, if demonstration be not possible, whether because the truth proposed belongs to an order whose principle is not in the human understanding, or because it belongs to the profundity of a science which you have not the time or the will to acquire, then language, initiating you by a shorter road, presents a character of authority to you which will invest the idea with a sufficient and legitimate sanction.

Such is the natural strategy of language. And yet, notwithstanding that triple power of proposition, definition, and demonstration, language is not certain of success. You are able to resist it; you are able to refuse your assent to it, to brave its light; and, intrenched in the fortress of your own convictions, not even to feel, to the distant remorse of your conscience, that truth has spoken to you. You are feeble and free; feebleness and liberty protect you against the ascendency of language. Feebleness veils from you the splendour of truth which it contains, liberty permits you to refuse to accept its yoke. It is needful then to do more than propose truth to you, more than define it, more than demonstrate it to you; it is needful to persuade you. Persuasion is the eternal glory of language human and divine; this is the victory, of which Montaigne should have said, rather than of Marathon or of Platæa, "that it is the most glorious which the sun has ever seen," since it is the victory of thought over the two greatest powers of the world, namely, feebleness and liberty.

But how and by what are we to persuade? I will give you an example.

In 1738, England was ruled by a ministry who desired peace, and at any cost. Now, at that very time, an English sailor was captured at sea, outraged and mutilated by the Spaniards, and this event produced a great movement of public indignation throughout England. Nevertheless the ministry had resolved to preserve peace, and the British Parliament had formed the same determination. The sailor appeared in the streets of London, he showed the wounds and injuries which he had received, and so excited popular indignation, that the parliament could not avoid seeing him, and listening to his complaint. He appeared then in the House of Commons, and after relating with calm and simple brevity the history of the assault of which he had been the victim, he ended with these words—"When the Spaniards mutilated me in this way they wanted to make me afraid of death, but I accepted death as I had accepted outrage, recommending my soul to God, and my revenge to my country." War was declared. That unlettered man needed but a quarter of an hour to change the councils of his country, to force the ministry to draw the sword, the parliament to vote the subsidies, the nation to applaud, and human blood to be shed in order to avenge his outrage. He had persuaded.

And daily you witness these triumphs of language; or at least, if they are more rare than I say, you witness them sometimes, were it only in remembrance, on recalling to mind the famous exhibitions of eloquence. You hear Demosthenes obtaining the condemnation of Æschines, Cicero drawing from the hands of Cæsar the condemnation of Ligarius, and you ask in what consists that sovereign art without which reason and justice are not sure of victory, by which error and passion obtain it but too often. Yes, eloquent language is a dominating power which commands obedience; but what is eloquence? What can it impart to language but light and truth? Is there anything in the world more persuasive than light, more powerful than truth? Yes, gentlemen, what is more powerful than truth is the principle from whence it emanates; what is more persuasive than light is the centre from whence it springs; what is greater than language is the soul from whence it proceeds. Eloquence is the soul itself; eloquence is the soul bursting all the bands of the flesh, quitting the bosom that bore it, and casting itself headlong into the soul of another. Can you then wonder that it commands, that it reigns? It is a soul which has taken the place of your own. Is it not plain that that soul which is within you, which is yourself, more than yourself, says to you, Go! and you go; Come! and you come; Bend the knee! and you kneel?

In short, the mystery of language at the state of eloquence, is the substitution of the soul that speaks for the soul that listens; or to speak with justice that leaves nothing incomplete, it is the fusion of the soul that speaks with the soul that listens. Eloquence has but one rival, and yet that rival is one only because it is eloquent; it is love. Love, like eloquence, melts hearts, and their power, so dissimilar in appearance, has the same cause and the same effect.

Now, it is not sufficient, either for God or man, to propose to define and to demonstrate truth. For God meets with the same obstacles to His word as man to his own, and even greater. Whilst human language is but the organ of thoughts accessible to finite intelligences which have their root and their proof in the natural orbit of reason, the Divine Word, essentially revealing in its nature, bears with it truths of which the universe forms hardly the shadow, of which reason is but a reflection, and to which no measure is applicable but the infinite. If then man is feeble before the things which he sees and touches, if his own history is a labyrinth before him, and his own mind an abyss, what will he become before the infinite unveiled by a simple affirmation? If he is free against man, how much more free will he be against God, a being placed at so great a distance from him, and so much the less violent in His operations as He is absolute master of all? Doubtless in order to give credence to His word, God supports it by striking signs; but those very signs are subject to discussion, and even if the mind, mute in their presence, knows not what to oppose to the splendour of their testimony, it will always find within itself, whether from the obscurity of the thing revealed, or from the sole effort of liberty, a principle of resistance and illusion. The Jews, for three years, saw Jesus Christ acting among them as a supreme master of nature; for three years they brought to Him all the infirmities of the body to be healed by a word from His mouth, or a touch of His raiment; they witnessed the miracles of His death after having been spectators of the miracles of His life; and yet, notwithstanding so many signs witnessed by them, notwithstanding the anterior prophecies whose depositaries they were, and whose accomplishment they looked for, a veil remained before their eyes. They were not able to believe in the humility of God; the thunderbolt would perhaps have converted them, goodness made them blind and ungrateful. God made Himself too little for them, and the terrible majesties of Sinai hid from them the mercy that visited them. It is the same with that multitude of souls who exhaust or torture themselves into incredulity. The miracles of sixty centuries pass before them as a chance without cause; they admit that it is grand and wonderful, but without humbling their hearts before the mystery that covers those marvels lost to them. According to the expression of Scripture, "they see and they do not see, they hear and they do not hear:"* the book of life is in their hands with the inimitable seal of the Divine Omnipotence; they see it, they touch it, they think of it for an instant, and pass on.

And if here under the walls of Notre Dame, I were to raise the dead in the name of Christ, do you suppose you would all leave this place convinced and converted? No; I am sure you would not, and the whole history of Christianity is an undeniable proof of this.

It is not enough then for the word of God, in order to become established in souls, to be authorised by certain miracles it must also vanquish the resistance of man to divine truth; it is necessary for it to move, to touch—in fine, to persuade. The Spirit of God, the only Spirit capable of containing the infinite, must descend by an immediate influence into the narrow vase of our heart, must incite it, inspire it, produce in it, in a more powerful manner than human eloquence, the assimilation of the inferior to the superior soul. It is there whence springs all the intercourse between God and man, and man and God. If the eternal soul does not really approach the created soul here below, religion is but a dream over which we ought to weep. We should inscribe over the portals of its temples, as over the portal of hell, "Whoever enters here must leave hope behind him." It is the Spirit of God that gives life to the Divine Word, as it is the spirit of man that gives life to human language. Language separated from its spirit is nothing more than a dead body in a tomb. Now God being always living His word also exists always. Once sent from Him, wherever it may go and in whatever form it may subsist, it is aided by its Father who lives in it and it in Him. Whilst human language perishes on the first furrow which time makes, and gives to the ear of generations only an echo disdained by those who think they still hear it, the Divine Word sows its immortality in the ruins of the world. It is as fertile after a thousand years as on the day when it was first enounced; it inspires the same faith, creates the same works, is recognised by the same signs, and effaces them all by that of its own life.

That life has a name celebrated in the history of the

* St. Luke viii. 8.

relations between man and God; it is called grace—that is to say, the unmerited gift, the highest of all gifts. And what gift indeed can be greater than the Spirit of God Himself placed in intimate contact with the spirit of man! This is the marvel which began with the world, and whose consummation by Christ the prophets announced from hour to hour. David said, "Cast me not away from thy presence, and take not thy Holy Spirit from me."* Solomon said, "And who shall know thy thought, except thou give wisdom and send thy Holy Spirit from above!"† Isaiah said, "And the Spirit of the Lord shall rest upon him; the spirit of wisdom and of understanding, the spirit of counsel and of fortitude, the spirit of knowledge and of godliness."‡ Joel said in the name of God, "I will pour out my spirit upon all flesh; and your sons and your daughters shall prophesy; your old men shall dream dreams, and your young men shall see visions."§ The precursor said, "I indeed baptize you with water; but there shall come one mightier than I, the latchet of whose shoes I am not worthy to loose, he shall baptize you with the Holy Spirit and with fire."|| And Jesus Christ said, "When they shall deliver you up for my sake, take no thought how or what to speak; for it shall be given to you in that hour what to speak; for it is not you that speak, but the Spirit of your Father that speaketh in you."¶ He said also, "I will ask the Father, and he shall give you another Paraclete, that he may abide with you for ever, the Spirit of Truth whom the world cannot receive, because it seeth him not, nor knoweth him; but you shall know him, because he shall abide with you, and shall be in you."** Not that Jesus Christ, the Son of God and Very God, did not communicate to His disciples the grace and truth whose fulness He was; but because, being the eternal Verb, He was especially charged with the sowing of the Word, which is the first prophetic element, whilst the effusion of grace, the second element of prophecy, was reserved in all its plenitude to the third person of the Holy Trinity, coeternally issued from the Father and the Son, the fruit and bond of their love, the last term of their divine fecundity, and therefore charged with placing the final seal of life to the work

* Ps. li. 11.
† Wisd. ix. 17.
‡ Wisd. xi. 2.
§ Joel ii. 28.
|| St. Luke iii. 16.
¶ St. Matt. x. 19, 20.
** St. John xiv. 16, 17.

of God in time. It was fitting also that the two prophetic elements, the word and grace, although inseparable from one another, should, nevertheless, have had a distinct emission, so that mankind, warned by the grandeur of that double accession, should feel that it was not capable of communicating with God, even by means of His Word, without the perpetual and intimate assistance of the Divine Spirit. Such was the object, and such is the sense of that great day in which the Paraclete announced by Jesus Christ descended visibly upon the apostles, and taking from them the remains of weakness and obscurity which they had still in them, made of them those men whose blood, after that of Christ, has founded upon earth the reign of truth.

There are but few among you who have not known by personal experience the reality of the prophetic mystery. You have all received the seeds of that language, which resembles none other; all of you at some time or other, as children or as young men, have felt in your souls an unction that filled them with light, and brought to you in chaste tears the taste for good, forgetfulness of the senses, the peace and presence of God. On that day all was said to you. No man will ever give you back its joy; no love will ever bring you back its perfume, but the love which was then given to you, and, which, being the divine goodness itself, waits but for a regret and a desire from you to love you again. May you draw from your heart that desire and that regret, and, by a second experience of grace, become again and for ever the children and the apostles of that Word which alone never deceives!

# MYSTERY AS THE OBJECT OF PROPHECY.

MY LORD—GENTLEMEN,

It results from our last conference, that the things revealed by God through prophecy surpass the natural power of our understanding, and are therefore for us beyond all demonstration and above all comprehension. Were they only undemonstrable, the mind might perhaps accept this condition, since, even in the natural order, there are truths which may be attested but not demonstrated, such as the ancient events which form history; and since man obtains credence to his testimony in regard to human things, it is not easy to understand why it should be refused in regard to divine things. But there is this difference, that the object of prophecy is incomprehensible as well as undemonstrable, and this is what rationalism will not forgive. What! (says rationalism) you show forth prophecy as the light of the world, and yet you yourselves confess that you do not comprehend it! You call your dogmas by the significant name of mysteries; you seem to make a boast of the obscurity that reigns in revelation. After reading your books you exclaim, "O the depth of the riches of the wisdom and of the knowledge of God! How incomprehensible are His judgments, and how unsearchable His ways!"* Now, how can that which is mysterious, obscure, unsearchable, incomprehensible, in fine, be the light of the world? For us— that is to say, for every man who does not renounce his reason —mystery is at the same time useless and absurd; useless,

* Rom. xi. 33.

since its sense is not to be seized; absurd, since wherever the sense escapes nothing rational remains.

Such is the double difficulty which rises before us, and which requires from me a double explanation. We are told that mystery is useless—I shall prove its utility. They add that it is absurd—I shall prove its reasonableness.

It is certain, and it would be a great illusion to wish to hide it from you, that the Word of God reveals to us things which surpass our reason; and were it otherwise, God would have no motive in speaking to us, since we should be able of ourselves to discover the truths about which it may please Him to communicate with us. But God is greater than we are; placed on the horizon of the infinite, which is His essence, He sees what we do not see, and tells us what no one but Himself can say to us. Why does He communicate this to us? Being unable or unwilling to give us evidence of the things which He reveals to us, why does He reveal them to us? Where lies the utility of such communication? In proving to you in a former conference the necessity of the supernatural intercourse between man and God, I have already answered this question. But I did so metaphysically; and if you will permit me we will to-day leave metaphysics aside. Utility is a matter of fact. You deny the utility of the incomprehensible, I maintain it. It matters little now about the exact definition of those words—understand or not understand. To define them would perhaps suffice to put an end to the question; but I shall not do so. I leave them in your minds as they are, and starting from the vulgar idea that to be useful is to do good, I ask, Does the incomprehensible do good to man? If it does, if history proves it perfectly, whatever reasoning you may oppose to that result will fall powerless. In a question of utility, the result decides all. It matters not whether we explain to ourselves or do not explain the benefit; it exists. Is there anyone here who has ever despised a benefit because he did not render account to himself of the process by which his benefactor had served him?

I renew, then, my question. I ask myself and you: Does the incomprehensible do good to man?

There are some among you who think they owe nothing to this strange Benefactor. Disciples of reason, they think they are formed by themselves, and that nothing but evidence has entered into the structure of their minds. But even were this true, a man is not a man, and I speak of man. I speak of you all, contemporaries of the nineteenth century, connected by your fathers with the ages which have gone by; belonging altogether to a great historical movement, which has changed the face of the world, and prepared for each of you another destiny than that which the course of ancient civilisation would have formed for him. This is the real man, the man whom I interrogate, and not the ideal man who believes he has separated himself from the paternity of his times. Now, what has formed that real man? What has formed modern mankind? Is it not Christianity? And is there even one among you who would deny the superiority of the Christian man over those who have sprung from another generation? If you doubt this, I would say to you, Compare yourselves with the most illustrious and perfect specimens of mankind that the world has produced before and since you have occupied your place therein. Certainly that was a great race whose country was Athens and Rome—a race fertile in legislators, in sages, in heroes; memorable in war by its conquests, in politics by its institutions, in peace by its arts, and which, although extinguished for many centuries, draws us even now around its ruins to give us lessons. But however marvellous its history, which of you would consent to live again in that antiquity? Which of you would sacrifice the rights and duties of the Christian man for all the glory of the Greek or the Roman? On reading the most glorious things which they have left to us, we feel, from their gods to their virtues, that they were but infant peoples, and that the very excellence of their literature, so far from being a veil to their inferiority, is its striking and immortal revelation. The masterpieces of those two languages will live to the latest posterity as a testimony that habits of barbarism may be joined to an exquisite cultivation of the mind, and great feebleness of thought to marvellous science of style. Therefore, when Christianity, born with the world but unknown by it, rose up before that ingenious and powerful society which had never known an equal upon earth, it had but to speak and to die in order to ruin its civilisation. The man of Greece and Rome cannot hold his place before the Christian man.

And what, then, was the Christian man? What did he bring with him that was more powerful than Athens and Rome?—Athens, mistress in the science of speaking; Rome, mistress in the art of fighting and governing. What did he bring, gentlemen? One single thing—which contained all the rest—the incomprehensible. He announced to the world that the human race, defiled from the beginning, received and transmitted with its blood the joint responsibility of an inexpiable fault; but that God, one in three persons, had sent His Son upon earth to take our nature in the womb of a virgin, and, by a voluntary sacrifice, to redeem us from sin and death. He announced that this mystery was accomplished, that the Son of God, come in the flesh, had appeared in Judæa, that He had taught there, and that, having been put to death upon a cross, buried in a sepulchre, He was raised again on the third day, assuring by His death His triumph over sin, and by His resurrection His triumph over death. Such was the Christian dogma, and such also was the principle of the civilisation which has made you what you are, by overthrowing all the antique society. Either you must deny your superiority over the ideas and the things of paganism, or recognise the utility of the incomprehensible.

You may suppose that Christianity includes two distinct elements—the one reasonable, which is the source of the good wrought by it in the world; the other mysterious, which is but an envelope by which exalted truths and holy virtues have by chance been covered. In fact, does not the Gospel naturally explain itself? If it speaks of miracles and dogmas which alarm reason, it speaks still more of a sage who teaches the people simple and sublime morality, gentleness, modesty, patience, disinterestedness, justice, and that which includes all in a single precept—the sincere love of God and man. Must we wonder that a code so perfect, emanated from a pure soul which maintained even to death the lessons He had given, should at length have produced in the human race a salutary and memorable effect? It is impossible to read the Gospel without wishing at least to be better; and this desire, become that of a great number, has at length been realised in some, who, from age to age, have adorned the world by their virtues. The incomprehensible is here but an unimportant help; it is the fable that precedes or that clothes truth. I grant that Christianity results entirely in the love of God and mankind; and here lies the secret of the prodigious change which it has introduced and maintains among us. But this love, so long despised upon earth, so difficult even now to know by proper experience, is that revolution itself in its last, its most profound effect. The Gospel, you say, has caused you to love God and man: it is so—I know it, I proclaim it—but how did it produce this love for those who had not been loved for four thousand years? How has it drawn the human heart from the egotism of its passions, and above all from the egotism of its virtues? Is it because it has said, Love God, love mankind? Alas! if it had said but that, it would have exercised just the power which so many dead philosophers exercise over us, who honour us with their counsels. Men would have set up a statue of Jesus Christ at the door of an academy; they would have preserved his portrait in the museums of civilized nations; and, since the invention of printing, they would have written in all the languages of Europe that the Gospel is a great book; but the poor would neither have known the book nor the sage, and the hearts of all would have continued to find enjoyment in selfish sensuality and pride.

Would you learn how Jesus Christ has raised us towards God, and inclined us towards man? Leave the Church of Notre Dame, and turn to your left. Upon a building there, without architectural merit, you will read this inscription, HOTEL DIEU. Perhaps the inscription may have disappeared from the stone. I know not; but it subsists in the memory and language of the people, and that is enough. Cross the threshold, mount the staircase, raise your eyes to the image above the door, you will read, L'HOMME DIEU. Advance still further, enter the cell of one of those voluntary servants who devote their days to the infirmities of the poor. You are young, attractive, rich; she is clothed in beauty which comes from virtue; offer her your hand. She will answer you, To me, L'ÉPOUSE DE DIEU! If these three incomprehensible worlds—the House of God, the Man God, the Spouse of God —do not yet enlighten you, ask that soul why she has quitted the hopes of the world to consume herself in this hospital, amongst misery which is not her own; she will tell you its secret. Of whom would you learn it if not of those who possess the love whose cause you seek? She will tell you that she loves God, because God loved her even to death; that she loves mankind, because God, in taking their nature upon Him, and dying for them, has caused them to share in His adorable goodness. If God is not man, if He did not die, be sure there is no Spouse of God, or House of God; the virtue of the

Christian comes from the incomprehensible, as the flower from the earth. The incomprehensible is the soul of the Christian; it is his light, his strength, his life, his breath. Say that this is madness, if you will. I have not undertaken to prove that it is not so, but that it serves you. For sixty years you have been endeavouring to do without this madness, and to preserve the benefits of Christianity whilst repudiating its dogmas: it is for you to judge whether you have succeeded.

Man is a divine animal, and the incomprehensible is his food. Were this gift of heaven ever fully withdrawn from him, you would behold a spectacle which I cannot describe, because it has never been beheld. Even paganism, all divested as it was, included the confused remains of the primordial incomprehensible, and these very remains formed its greatness in certain nations, and in certain times. When Rome had resolved to set up the centre and foundation of her future power upon a solitary hill, she built there, at the same time, a temple and a camp, leaving between the two an empty space, which was, as it were, the seat upon which she held her place, with one hand resting upon her arms, and the other upon heaven. From that place she watched and governed the world, deriving therefrom wisdom as invincible as her courage, and when her victors brought to her the kings and the spoils of nations, they mounted to that Capitol as the tutelary spot where their victories had taken their birth in the will of the gods that dwelt there. This religious character lasted as long as the virtue and liberty of Rome. The sacred mysteries presided over all; they were borne even before the enemy, and those famous generals, who had received from fortune and from their genius so many assurances of victory, dared not trust to a battle without having consulted, through auguries, the impenetrable counsel of the gods of the world and the country. But when Cicero was able to declare that he could not conceive how two augurs could look at one another without laughing, Rome fell from the Capitol to the Palatinate, from the temple of the gods to that of the Cæsars; and soon, Tiberius, followed by Nero, heaped the scorn of his tyranny upon the living and dead of the people-king. Laugh as you please at the sacred chickens; but learn at least that when they were no more, there were no more Scipios. And you will find the same spectacle, resulting from the same cause, everywhere in the history of the world. Everywhere the decline of nations follows the decline of the incomprehensible, and the earth has devoured all those who have no longer regarded heaven save as the eye discovers it on the horizon.

I admire, then, the Egyptians, for having placed the Sphinx at the entry of their temples. It is the old friend of man, and his natural herald to the infinite. Despise it as much as you will, appeal from it to pure reason, to the sacred rights of the human intelligence; for my part I shall hold to the Sphinx, as long as I see it at the door of virtues that found, and glories that have, a posterity.

Yet you will say, Why the Sphinx? Why the incomprehensible? Here, gentlemen, you change the question; you no longer ask me to prove the utility of the incomprehensible, but to give you the reason of its existence in the human race. Now, I believe I have given you this in the Conference where I recently treated of the need of supernatural intercourse between man and God, and I shall succeed perhaps in enlightening you in regard to it by what I am about to say on the subject of the reasonableness of the things whose certainty we possess without understanding them.

Nothing absurd can be useful, and above all useful to all mankind; it suffices that the incomprehensible does good to men for us to conclude from it that it is essentially rational. Therefore, whoever says of Christianity that it is the benefactor of the world, says at the same time that the incomprehensible, so far from contradicting reason, is its last and most magnificent effort. I feel, nevertheless, that this proof, all-sufficient though it may be, does not respond to the want which you feel of fathoming so grave a subject. I will then take a more direct path, and show you that in every rational thing there enters an incomprehensible element, as in every incomprehensible thing there is a rational element. It will then be no longer permitted to you to think that reason and mystery mutually reject each other, since the one is never without the other, and as the shadow accompanies light in nature, so it is also in the infinite depths where our intelligence combats truth.

I affirm in the first place that into every rational thing there enters an incomprehensible element. Nothing is more within the comprehension of reason than the bodies that people space, and especially the bodies that form the globe which we inhabit; reason sees, touches, weighs, measures, confronts, analyses them, makes of them whatever it wills. And yet what do men call that which in bodies is subject to the investigations of reason? They call it a phenomenon—that is to say, something that appears. A forcible and sincere avowal, which proves that reason does not see all the body, and that if a part of it unveils to its curiosity, something also still remains hidden. Do you doubt this? Consider that other expression by which science designates the body itself, an expression much more formidable and despairing, and which is to the phenomenon what night is to day. It calls a body a substance—that is to say, what is under; that something which is under what appears. And what, indeed, is a body in itself? When you have proved its colour, its weight, the mode of aggregation of its parts, the action which it exercises on other bodies, do you know what it is? Modern chemistry and, before it, alchemy, have doubtless endeavoured to pursue substance to its last depths, and draw from it the secret of its composition. They have even succeeded to a degree almost prodigious, and which has opened to us mysteries long hidden by nature from our investigations. Nevertheless the shadow has but retreated without disappearing, and the place which it has yielded to light has not lessened for us the abyss of the unknown. We know that bodies, forced by analysis, resolve into a certain number of substances which we call elements; but what the element is we know not. Matter takes refuge therein as in a fortress, where it braves the pride of our experiments and the dictation of our will.

It is the same with the vegetable and animal germ as with the universal element, but with a circumstance which it is well to notice. Science has power over the universal element, in the sense that it is able to make it again constitute a body properly so called; but when analysis has decomposed the germs of the animal and vegetable order, it is powerless to recall the principle of life which was contained therein. Under its instruments only inanimate refuse remains. It sees, it touches, the mysterious dust from whence the mighty oak of the forest, or the agile inhabitant of their hidden paths, should spring; but that dust is henceforth dead. Why dead? Whence is it that the sepulchre being broken, the living being has disappeared? What is life? Life is in a germ; it will remain there for ages, solitary and silent, without becoming lost and without acting; but let analysis touch it, and life disappears, as if jealous nature determined to become more incomprehensible in proportion as its work became more perfect.

In man you will find too undeniable a proof of this. Man is a body, and he includes in his body all the unknowns of the material world, all the things that are visible but unexplained. But conjointly with this first mystery, in the complex tissue of a sole personality, he holds a second abyss more terrible than the first—the abyss of his thought. Man thinks, he wills, he is free, he governs himself, all things of which no trace is seen in the body, and all things which escape from the most ingenious researches of scientific analysis. Never has science been able to attract thought into its crucible, never has it been able to subject it to any instrumented power. The spiritualist affirms that it is not the fruit of the body, but of another substance which he calls spirit, and which, deprived of form, extent, colour, weight—of whatever is known to us by the senses—constitutes a reality of which nothing visible could give us the faintest and most distant representation. Therefore but just now, the lowest of beings—the universal element—although remaining under our eyes, escaped in its essence from the efforts of our investigation; a little higher, in the animal and vegetable germ, life retreated before our researches, and did not even leave us the consolation of catching a glimpse of the source from whence its activity springs; now behold spirit, which never, under any form, by any image, has permitted us to approach it, although it is ourselves. The materialist, it is true, denies spirit, and maintains that thought is a simple effect of the body attained to a certain state of perfection: but is this clearer? Do we thereby learn any more clearly how matter, which does not think at all of itself, derives in a certain organisation the faculty of thinking?

However it may be, we think, and in the personal mystery of our thoughts there arises another still higher, which we call the Eternal, the Infinite, the Principle—God. As nature is the natural horizon of our physical vision, God is the necessary horizon of our intellectual vision. We cannot open our eyelids without seeing the indefinite space wherein bodies move, and we cannot awaken our thought without disclosing the first cause that contains in itself all the possible and all the real. The infidel may refuse it the name of God; he may endeavour to confound the cause with the effect by transporting to the visible world the idea which we have of being subsisting of itself: but that despairing effort in no way lessens the depths of the mystery which dwells in thought, and, whatever thought may do, eternity is before it. However, gentlemen, I never address atheism; that forlorn hope of the last follies of the heart has too few representatives to render it needful to speak to it in a great assembly of men; your number alone tells me that you believe in God, and therefore it is my right as well as my duty to oppose to your ambition to understand all, the incomprehensible light of His nature and of His name. What intelligence placed before this last abyss can say, I have fathomed it? What soul, how vast soever it may be, does not halt, sad and pensive, before that short word, God? An atom confounds us—and behold us in the presence of the Infinite! Can you represent the Infinite to yourselves? Can you conceive a substance without beginning in its duration—without limits in its being—filling all with its presence and its action, although concentrated in an indivisible unity which has no place but in itself? The day would run its course before I could even name all the mysteries contained in this supreme mystery; in which, however, all life takes its birth with all light. For, such is our condition, we meet with darkness in the very things from which we desire light. From earth to spirit, from spirit to God, in the three spheres of our speculation and our activity, a sparing as well as a prodigal hand has wisely mingled the shadow that blinds us with the splendour that enchants us. In vain will reason grow indignant at this adulterous wedlock; it must accept the incomprehensible as the shore that contains evidence; or, renouncing truth, address to it, in scepticism, an irrevocable adieu.

Scepticism, gentlemen, is but the despair of a mind great enough to know that it does not see the "whole of anything," according to the expression of Pascal, but too feeble to respect in mystery the inevitable limit imposed upon the created spirit. Whilst the vulgar rationalist, inebriated by his own ideas, thinks he comprehends all that he thinks, the sceptic, with as much pride and more penetration, discerns the weak side of human science, and conceives a gloomy distaste for truth. Surveying with his melancholy regard the progressive enchainment of things, and halting at God, he asks himself, Do I comprehend God? No; remove Him then! But do I comprehend myself, my mind? No; away then with the mind. But matter, at least! Doubtless, I see matter. I make experiments upon it; and, yet, do I know what it is? Can I say that I comprehend it? Away with matter! Thus from one degree to another, from one kind of despair to another, reason "vanishes" within itself, according to the energetic expression of St. Paul, and upon the uncertain ruins of all reality, it exclaims with lamentable despair, What do I know, and what am I? Doubt, it is true, does not often descend to that depth where nothing subsists in the mind; but wherever it may halt it is the destroyer of the soul, and whether higher or lower, it has but one and the same cause, which is the refusal to consent to the incomprehensible as a necessity and an element of reason. For my part, if I were in this state, if I recognised the sign of truth only in an absolute light, I declare to you, I should not believe in matter any more than in spirit; any more in spirit than in God; I should be to myself a painful enigma, a puff of air in the desert, a lamentation in a sepulchre, the plaything of an existence without principle or end; I should advance in my days at the hazard of each sun, between the sadness of yesterday and the joy of to-morrow, expecting nothing more from life, nothing more from death. But, thanks to God, I adore in evidence the shadow that limits it; I know that truth, the single and sacred object of my entire soul, is as great as the infinite, and that the infinite, being only comprehensible to its equal—that is to say, to itself, it is natural that I should not see anything entirely, but in a measure sufficient to know without sufficing to exhaust.

And as in every rational thing an incomprehensible element is found, in every incomprehensible thing a rational element is also found—that is to say, the idea. The idea is all that which the mind sees; and the mind, seeing nothing but by its primitive light, which is reason; it follows that every idea, how problematic soever it may be, is a rational element. Now Christianity, whose dogmas we confess to be incomprehensible, bears evidently in its very dogma the treasure of the idea; and, if you doubt this, I will give you but one proof of it, namely, that it speaks. Christianity speaks, it has spoken dogmatically for eighteen centuries; therefore, however incomprehensible its dogma may be, its dogma is an idea, and consequently something rational.

Does this reasoning astonish you, gentlemen? Have you never reflected upon what it is to speak? To speak is to enchain words together, and words being only ideas living under an expression, to speak is to enchain ideas. Whoever speaks gives proof that he sees something in his mind, and transmits to the mind that listens to him the whole, or part, of the light by which he is enlightened. Were it otherwise, language would be but a continuation of sounds falling into the ear, and not into the intelligence; it would be noise, and yet noise without signification. But, you ask me, does not the absurd also speak? And, since it speaks, is it not a light, an idea, a rational element? Doubtless it is all that, and if it were not, it would be impossible to speak and to be understood. The absurd is the evidence of the false, and the false being only a truth which is abused, it is truth hidden in the false which consents to be enounced. An absolute error, representing nothing to the mind, would call forth no expression in the thought; it would be pure nothingness. The glory of truth is to live even in error, and to enlighten the language which expresses it, so that the absurd becomes manifest to the eyes of the understanding. So far, then, from there being no idea or rational substance in the absurd, it is found there in so elevated a degree that all at once exclaim, That is not common sense. The absurd is the second revelation of the true, more powerful perhaps than the direct revelation, and that is the reason why mathematics employ so often that form of reasoning which is called demonstration *ad absurdum*.

I return, then, to my declaration: Christianity speaks, it has spoken dogmatically for eighteen centuries; and, therefore, however incomprehensible its dogma may be, its dogma is necessarily an idea—that is to say—something rational. This is true, perhaps you will say, but it is something rational *ad absurdum;* for since the absurd speaks as much as the incomprehensible, what hinders it from confounding the incomprehensible with itself? What hinders it, is that the one is not the other, that the absurd is the evidence of the false, whilst the incomprehensible fails, at the same time, in the evidence of the false and of the true. The incomprehensible is something which reason does not explain, nothing more. Would you deny its existence? Would you deny that particular state of the human mind? But I have shown you that the incomprehensible follows us even into the objects of science ; I have presented it to you as the necessary term of our highest light. If the incomprehensible became confounded in its nature with the absurd, there would be no shadows, since the

GOD AND MAN. 383

absurd is as clear as a demonstration. It being then proved that the incomprehensible is a distinct category of the human mind, a separate condition, if you like it better, where the understanding has neither the evidence of the false nor the evidence of the true, there remains this difficulty: that to understand not is to see nothing. What have I to do against this difficulty? Must I show you that the incomprehensible is not the exclusion of all idea; and, consequently, of all rational vision? On this account I have said: Christianity is incomprehensible in its dogma; and, yet, dogmatic Christianity is an idea; it is an idea, since it speaks. Your reply to that is, The absurd speaks also. Yes, but it speaks with the character of the absurd—that is to say—with the absence of decisive clearness, whether for the false or the true.

If, however, the example of Christianity should embarrass you, from the notion which you may entertain that its doctrine manifestly bears the sign of the absurd, I shall withdraw it from a discussion into which it does not necessarily enter, and ask you, Do you comprehend eternity, the infinite God? Do you comprehend a Being who exists of Himself, who is because He is, without beginning and without end? Do you comprehend the union in one single person of two substances as opposed to each other as body and spirit? Do you understand the action of body upon spirit, and of spirit upon body? Assuredly no. These mysteries then which are so profound, so impenetrable—do they, or do they not, present any idea to your understanding? If you answer me, yes—and you cannot reply in any other manner—I conclude therefrom, that the incomprehensible, notwithstanding its obscurity, does not bear with itself the exclusion of every rational element, and this is what I had to prove. Now remark attentively, it is now a question between us only of the general essence of the incomprehensible. You have said that the incomprehensible considered in itself, in its very nature, is an absurdity; and, I, following you step by step, have had to prove to you that it is not so, and that to propose to man the contemplation of a mystery, so far from dishonouring his intelligence, is to elevate him to regions whose natural and sublime guest he is. For, I have said, reason itself includes an incomprehensible element, and the incomprehensible in its turn contains a rational element; evidence, in mounting towards the higher pole of things, to which it is the great road, meets obscurity there; and mystery, in descending from heaven, bears to us a light worthy of its proper name, which is revelation.

Hereby you see that the difference between the natural and the supernatural order does not consist in the idea that all is comprehensible in the first, whilst all is comprehensible in the second, but in this, that the truths of the latter are not susceptible of a direct demonstration, whilst the truths of the former flow as a consequence from the luminous germ which is our reason. Thus God, although inscrutable in His essence, is a dogma of nature, because we draw conclusions in regard to Him by the very light which is within us; but the unity of God in three distinct persons is a dogma of revelation, because it is impossible for us to deduce it from any rational principle.

At the very last, you will perhaps think that there is more, obscurity in the supernatural incomprehensible than in the natural incomprehensible. Now, I can but repeat to you those words of Jesus Christ, "I am the light of the world: he that followeth me walketh not in darkness, but shall have the light of life."\* And those other words, "I am come a light into the world: that whoever believeth in me may not remain in darkness."† And those of the Apostle St. Paul to the Christians of Ephesus, "You were heretofore darkness, but now are ye light in the Lord; walk then as children of the light." ‡ Everywhere in Scripture the natural order compared to the supernatural order is called darkness; and the supernatural order, light, life, the way, the truth. It is because, however far and however high the most pure reason may reach, it knows God only by imperfect notions derived from the spectacle of finite things, or from the contemplation of itself. Now, God is all. Whoever knows Him not, knows nothing; whoever knows Him imperfectly, knows imperfectly; whoever knows but little of Him, knows but little. And since reason approaches Him but imperfectly, as is too manifest, it is just to say that it is but a faint dawn of a bright day, an enigmatical and painful mirror of truth. But if God, touched by our natural ignorance, brings to us a knowledge of Himself; if He reveals to us what He is, what He sees, what He feels, what He wills; if He opens to us the depths of His eternity, His action upon time, the motives and plans of His Providence; then doubtless our inner vision will discern, but with difficulty,

\* St. John viii. 12.
† St. John xii. 46. ‡ Ephes. v. 8.

the infinite lines of such revelation; it will remain under the celestial horizon as it is under created immensity. And yet who will say that he does not know more? Who will not call his former state darkness, and his new state light? I grant that the shadow increases with the light, but that is the law of all science and of all light. Is there a man of science who does not discover more abysses in proportion as he penetrates further into nature? Is there a sun whose light, falling upon a body, does not draw a shadow from it so much the deeper as its rays are the more ardent? If the finite, itself, on becoming revealed to our vision, becomes so much the more mysterious as it is more visible, what must it be with the infinite?

Accept, gentlemen, with a firm mind, that condition of things, that necessity of the incomprehensible which pursues us everywhere. March on, like Israel, under the guidance of that column, half cloud, half fire, the only one that still enlightens and guides the human race. Watch the cloud, in order to learn in it the limits of your nature; watch the light, in order to learn there the greatness of your destiny. Should the one afflict you, take comfort in the other; should the West trouble you, turn to the East; and, in fine, lifting your eyes yet higher, wait in patience and faith for the pure day which is promised to us, and which will dawn from eternity for every soul worthy to behold it; for although the incomprehensible cannot even then disappear, since it belongs to the nature of the infinite considered by the finite, nevertheless the vision of God in His very substance will impart to us a possession of Him which will transform the mystery into the joy of ever knowing and ever exhausting our knowledge.

# THE HUMAN ACT CORRESPONDING TO PROPHECY.

MY LORD—GENTLEMEN,

Having explained the nature of prophecy, and solved the difficulties relative to its object, we must now consider the act by which man, prophetically taught by God, corresponds to that revelation; for as prophecy has no other object than to establish a supernatural intercourse between God and man, it is not sufficient that God acts on his side—it is necessary that man should respond to Him by a positive act. What is that act? What is the act by which man responds to God, inasmuch as God enlightens him prophetically—that is to say, manifests to him, by means of language, truths that surpass the power of his rational understanding? This act, gentlemen, could not be an act of knowledge, for knowledge supposes demonstration, and God, in prophecy, does not demonstrate, he affirms with authority. He affirms, and man believes. Faith is the answer which prophecy solicits; not blind faith, but faith based upon the divine characters that surround and penetrate the revealing testimony.

In our two last conferences of the year 1836—a year already so distant from us—I treated the question of Faith. It comes before us again, brought back by the inflexible enchainment of things, and I shall reject it so much the less as I must now consider it under a new aspect. It was necessary then more especially to study its nature; to-day, supposing that nature known, I will reply to two difficulties, and thereby explain to you what faith is.

We are told, in the first place, that the act of faith, by which man corresponds with the Divine Word, is an act which has no parallel in the natural order, where all takes place by way of knowledge and demonstration; and that therefore, under this head, there is an anomaly which destroys the synthesis between the two orders—the natural and the supernatural. Although the necessity of a constant synthesis, or similitude, between the two orders is not clearly manifest, I shall nevertheless prove that it exists in the case in question.

We are told, in the second place, that the act of faith, being irrational in its nature, since it is not the consequence of a demonstration, man is not able to produce it at will, by a simple application of his intelligence and liberty; but that it is the fruit of chance, custom, certain inclinations of the soul, and that therefore it cannot be an absolute duty upon which our intercourse with God depends. I shall prove, against this objection, that the act of faith is a regular power of man, and that, revelation being known to him, unbelief is a free refusal on his part, consequently a culpable refusal, and one that severs his relations with divine light and love.

Let us begin with the first difficulty—that of the synthesis between the natural and supernatural orders in regard to faith.

You have already seen that it is not the prophetic revelation alone that brings into our intelligence the element of the incomprehensible; reason itself is subjected thereto, and its most sensible rays merge on all sides into profound mysteries. At the same time that nature displays its phenomena, that science demonstrates, and the mind is satisfied by evidence, the incomprehensible appears and exacts from us an act of faith. I say an act of faith; for, in what manner soever the incomprehensible may be presented to us, even when a direct demonstration is given to us of its existence, it brings to our need of knowledge a limit which supposes on our part that submissive acceptation whose proper name is faith. Doubtless it is not faith of the same order as that which adheres to revealed dogmas guaranteed by the word of God; but it is a real faith given to the testimony of nature upon realities which it does not explain to us, and which are enveloped in shadows inaccessible to all the efforts of our penetration. Therefore as the word of God makes unbelievers, so also do nature and science. Scepticism is no other thing than a revolt of reason against obscurities wherein it becomes lost as soon as it wills to penetrate the depths of truth; and this is why science as well as religion requires from its sectaries that humility which is a great part of common sense. The true sage, initiated to the secret of his weakness by the marvels which he has interrogated, bends before Him who created the universe, and who alone knows the secret of all its forces. He avows that he knows nothing, not in an absolute sense, like the sceptic, but in the sense which implies a voluntary abasement of the mind of man before the Spirit of God, and that voluntary abasement is faith itself.

In fact, knowledge, however imperfect it may be, is not the general state of mankind; it is the privilege of a very small number of men scattered here and there. The multitude, subjected to labour which leaves them no leisure to cultivate their minds, are ignorant of the demonstration of the things which they employ and of the rules which they apply to their lives. Whether error or truth govern them, they are governed by persuasion and by authority—that is to say, by faith. They go whither they are impelled by the privileged battalion of the princes of the intelligence, itself impelled by an unknown ascendency which has its source in anterior ages, and in the logical current of all accomplished events. The revolutions of the human mind have no other cause, no other law; they never operate by way of demonstration, any more than battles are gained by the knowledge of the soldier. The soldier is ignorant of what he does and why he does it; immovable under fire, or marching towards the enemy, he gives and receives death by orders whose principle he does not know, whose result is a mystery to the very last moment. He obeys in perils an invisible thought in which he has faith, and that faith is half of his strength. An army that doubts is a lost army; an army that believes commands defeat and draws therefrom its safety. So it is with the battles of the intelligence, with those great movements of opinion that lead nations to new destinies—the throng follow chiefs who persuade them; they obey, believing that they command. You have proof of this in the history of which you form a part. Sons of an epoch fertile in vicissitudes, you witness a social revolution which shakes Europe in its very foundations. How many minds, think you, are there in Europe capable of rendering an exact and scientific account of it? A party was formed, which for sixty years directed opinion and dispersed popularity as a sovereign; this party was supported by most of the seats of science and learning;

its organs were a multitude of journals which bore its ideas to the extremities of the world; its subjects were governments and laws; all bent before it, and at length it felt sure of having founded an eternal empire by free discussion. But yesterday it still reigned; to-day it is hardly defended. Publicity, learning, science, liberty, its own strength and its own work, have turned against it, and see, it gathers around its ruins for its protection the ruins which it had caused, and which it proudly called the relics of the past. How has this power been brought to an end? By the same power which established it—by faith. A new language has risen up from the general lassitude of minds; it has boldly anathematised the language which preceded it, and which, although so long master, was found feeble in persuasion and authority. Doubtless there is a cause for this, and a logical cause, but the multitude who are led by it do not discern it. The multitude changed faith in changing their chiefs. And never upon this earth is the language that persuades and commands silent for a single day. It perishes upon the lips of one but to be reproduced upon the lips of another, and should the people cease to understand it, having no longer either faith or knowledge, there would remain to them of the human intelligence only the faculty of deeper degradation.

But reassure yourselves, whatever is needful to mankind, happen what may, will not be wanting to it. Knowledge will be subject to eclipses among men because it is the light of a small number; authority will outlive all its catastrophes, and if, after having been the organ of the opinion which it enounced, you lose that authority, no matter from what cause, learn that another will take up the sceptre as it falls from your hands, and that an interregnum of faith is no more possible here below than an interregnum of life.

How should mankind know its own history if faith from man to man could be subject to any real interruption? History is not of itself visible on the horizon of posterity; as soon as the actors and spectators of an age have passed away to the tomb, they disappear also to the generations that take their place, and the course of ages, following its rapid flow, rejects them more and more to the obscure solitude where death hides them. What has caused them to live again in spite of time? What is it that keeps the buried form of the ancestor standing erect before his most distant descendants? It is faith alone—

the faith of the man living in the man dead, the testimony of the man who has seen passing from memory to memory to him who has not seen. Try whether any demonstration, beyond human authority, will bring before your eyes Sesostris or Cyrus, Babylon or Memphis, or any other vanished object of antiquity. The instrument that follows the heavenly bodies in the immeasurable heights of the firmament, can discover nothing in the narrow orbit of the tomb; and the arithmetic that subjects numbers can neither count, range, nor sum up the dead. Eternity alone sees them in their order and in their secrets and history, that pale copy of eternity, presents a representation of them to every man who believes in man. If you do not believe in this, mankind loses all traces of itself for you, and its generations are nothing but a fall of leaves between two summers ignoring one another. If you do believe it, no longer blame religion because it asks from you for God that faith which you have in man; confess that it is very simple to know God by faith, since mankind has no other knowledge of itself.

You have seen the past; let us look now at the present. We are to-day upon earth a thousand millions of men spread over four or five continents and in a hundred nations. How do we know one another? How many have we seen of those beings, our fellow-creatures, who breathe the same air, who tread the same earth, who live in the same times, who form together, and in the same labour, the life of one single body? We have seen one or two thousand of them at most, and even of that number, so limited, how few could we name? All the rest escape us, save by relations which books and travellers bring to us—that is to say, by our faith in the recitals which they bring to us.

Let us go further; let us leave our absent contemporaries, and speak only of those who live with us, whom we meet in our public streets, and even, if you will, only of those who are here in Notre Dame, within the walls of this great cathedral of Paris. Assembled together in one place we see each other— it should be easy for us to know one another by direct knowledge, in which faith would have no part. And yet, is it so? What are you, and what am I? What are your sentiments, and what are my own? I shall vainly strain the powers of my mind in order to penetrate at a glance, and by a clear view, the folds of your being; the gleams that come from them suffice only to attract or to repulse me instinctively, but not to give me the knowledge of your heart. Man is a soul, and the soul ignores the soul until a word spoken in the ear, in the outpourings of friendship or religion, has revealed its mystery and merited to hear the response, "I believe you." Faith is the knot of our personal relations; an untiring and a cherished mediator, it passes from friend to friend, from husband to wife, from the child to the mother, from the right that commands to the liberty that obeys; and in the most solemn acts of empires, as in the most tender effusions of love, man expresses himself fully by these same words, "I believe you; I trust in you." It is never sold, it is given, because it is so priceless that whoever sells it is incapable of holding it. And upon those simple words, "I trust you," man risks his fortune, his life, his family, his honour. He believes or he is believed, and it is enough. Better would it be for him to lose all than to betray that faith, so low, even among the vilest actions, does the heart fall which is convicted of it. Even falsehood, although it may not bear the character of a treasonable act properly so called, but by that alone that it does not merit the confidence which an honest man owes to the word of another —falsehood excites scorn, and in the days of chivalry our ancestors considered as the highest of all insult those words, "Thou hast lied!" In fact, when a man has been guilty of falsehood, his word exists no longer, because he merits no faith, and, having no word, what remains to him of a soul?

But who would believe it, gentlemen, the most material thing in the world, that which seems to be entirely subjected to the laws of arithmetic, money itself, is an object of faith among men. It passes from hand to hand, it multiplies in a fertile circulation only by the effect of credit, and every event that lessens confidence in the future lessens at the same time the value of money. But just now it solicited the hand to take it; under the form and upon the faith of a scrap of paper it passed from one nation to another, everywhere accepted under that ideal form which gave to it a value far beyond its real quantity; and suddenly that paper falls, money is hidden, manufactories stop their works, commerce fails, labour becomes scarce—a kind of universal failing holds society in suspense, and seems to paralyse it. What powerful blow has it then received? I have already told you: there has been a withdrawal of faith. That nation has ceased to believe in itself;

its moral resources are not equal to its perils; and whilst Rome sold the field upon which Hannibal encamped, because Rome had faith in his virtue, this people, measuring its fate by its corruption, has given itself over to the chastisement of fear. It has hidden its gold as the ancients, in the catastrophes of their country, hid their gods. Remove fear, and money, appearing again and circulating, will stimulate labour, enterprise, commerce—wealth, in fine, which, as you see, is a daughter of faith.

I have said enough to show that faith plays an important part in the human as well as in the divine order, and that, therefore, there is no antithesis, but synthesis, between the two orders under this head. However, it will not be unprofitable for us, before leaving this part of our subject, to ask the reason of this; for, if we have understood that faith is necessary in the relations between man and God, we do not see clearly why it is necessary in the relations between man and man.

Let us learn, then, that the life of the intelligence proceeds from two poles—the one immutable and absolute, which is the pole of truth; the other movable, which is the pole of liberty. Without the first, minds detached from any fixed point would wander at hazard in the night of doubt and ignorance; without the second, being deprived of their own movement, they would be nothing but the obedient satellites of a fatal mechanism. Their life is then at the same time a work of truth and of liberty. As a work of truth, it is an object of knowledge; as a work of liberty, it is an object of faith. For as the ancients said, FLUXI NON EST SCIENTIA—*There is no science of that which passes*. Now, nothing is more unstable, more rapid, more unforeseen than liberty, and this is why it is so difficult to know ourselves, all-present though we may be to our own hearts. What shall I do to-morrow? Where will the inconstancy of my will lead me? To what temptations shall I be subject? Shall I yield to them, or shall I not yield? I may perhaps suppose, but I cannot be absolutely sure. A book which may fall into my hands, a word which I may hear, an insult which I may receive, a leaf which the wind may carry beneath my feet —I know not what, in fine—all and nothing may be capable of changing my sentiments and of inspiring my will with unlooked-for resolutions. You ask me to give you the knowledge of myself, and I do not even possess it. I myself am ignorant of it. I am to myself an object of faith !

It is liberty, gentlemen, that brings into human things the element of faith, and makes it the only means by which we reciprocally know ourselves. If we were not free, science would dispose of us as it disposes of the rest of nature; it would weigh a man in the same manner as it weighs a little earth, and, all the laws of mankind being reduced to numbers, we should require for our rules only an academy of mathematicians. Such is also the final dream of materialism in regard to us. Persuaded that there is nothing in man but organised matter, it seeks the supreme combination which, keeping the passions in an equilibrium, would produce a purely scientific order wherein crime and virtue would hold neither place nor name. Make all men equals, for example, by mathematical equality; make so many figures of them; distribute to them in the same measure the objects which flatter the senses and satisfy pride; what would they need in order to be equally and supremely happy? Nothing, doubtless, if they were but bodies; but if by chance a soul lives in them, and in that soul the liberty of volition, be sure that the heavens, the earth, and the sea, given in pasture to each of them, would not satiate the reciprocal jealousy of their felicity. A moment suffices for passion to devour worlds; and if liberty is not the infinite by substance, it is the infinite by desire. This is why there are no mathematics of liberty, and those who seek its equation in matter are like that child whom St. Augustine saw upon the African shore endeavouring to empty the sea with a shell which its waves had thrown up. These great calculators are the worst of men for the government of man: they are amazed at the resistance made against their genius, never suspecting that liberty is greater than any empire, stronger than any Cæsar, deeper than any abyss, and that faith alone commands it, because faith is itself an act of liberty.

Therefore, by the same reason that we are free beings, we are beings of faith, and we must say in the natural order what Jesus Christ said in a higher order, " Blessed are they that have not seen, and yet have believed."\* That is to say, blessed are they that have no need of demonstration, because demon-

---

\* St. John xx. 29.

stration is attained only by a few minds in things of secondary degree; whilst faith, altogether popular and sublime, passes from the soul of all to the soul of all, in things which, taking their root in liberty, are the foundation of human life !

I repeat that faith is the correlative of liberty, as science is the correlative of necessity; and to ask why we ought to believe, is to ask why we are free. From thence follows a consequence upon which I cannot be silent, and which will fitly explain to you the important part which faith fills in the purely natural order.

Science relates to necessity—that is to say, to what is immutable in itself; it suffices to have intelligence to be learned, it is not the same in order to be a believer. Faith is an act of confidence, and consequently an affair of the heart. It supposes in him who grants it the same uprightness as in him who inspires it, and no ungrateful man, no impostor, no egotist, nor any of those whom the Scripture energetically calls " the children of unbelief,"* were ever capable of it. To confide is to give oneself; none give themselves but the magnanimous, or, at least, the generous—not that faith excludes prudence, and that it is needful to give ourselves up to the first word that falls from unknown lips, but because, after prudence is supposed to be satisfied, another effort is still necessary to draw from us that difficult word—I believe.

Alexander, the King of Macedonia, was on the banks of the Cydnus. He was there attacked by a malady which threatened to save Persia, and his physician, whom he tenderly loved, was to prepare for him a decisive draught. But, in the evening, a letter, written by a known hand, warned the invalid to beware of his friend as a traitor who had sold his life. Alexander kept silence. On the morrow, when the cup was brought to him, he drew from his bed the accusing letter, gave it to his physician, took the cup, and swallowed its contents at a draught. All antiquity has lauded this act of Alexander, and his most celebrated victories—Granicus, Issus, Arbela—have not encircled his head with more admiration. Upon this a celebrated writer, whom I shall not name, asks what is there so worthy of admiration in this act so highly vaunted; for, in fine, Alexander was the chief of a numerous army engaged in an enemy's country, the master of a rising kingdom, the man

---

* Eph. ii. 2.

of Greece who was charged with its vengeances and its designs; he should, on every account, have respected his life, upon which depended the fate of so many others; and what merit was there in exposing it without defence to the chances of poison? But the writer whom I have quoted, after having made these remarks, goes on to say: "What is there so worthy of admiration in that action of Alexander? Unhappy men, could you understand it if it be needful to tell you? What is so worthy of admiration is, that Alexander believed in virtue—that he believed in it fully, at the peril of his life!"

This is a magnificent explanation of the faith of a noble heart, and it is also the explanation of all faith, whether exercised towards man or towards God. Whoever makes an act of faith, whether he knows it or not, drinks the cup of Alexander; "he believes fully, at the peril of his life;" he enters into that lineage of Abraham, who is called "the father of all those that believe,"* because when he was old—wasted in age, but not in heart—he raised his obedient knife upon his only son, who was all his love and his race, hoping against hope in that declaration which had promised him a posterity. And if there be a creature who, in opposition to these great examples, has never drawn from his soul an act of faith, you may fearlessly accuse that creature of having dishonoured in himself the work of God. For faith is not only a virtue—that is to say, a generous and an efficacious effort towards good—it is the sacred portico through which all virtues pass—the sanguinary prodrome where the sacrifices commence and where the victims justly immolated return to the sanctuary of God. There is no act of devotedness, no act of love, no honourable or holy act which was not at first an act of faith, and this is the reason why the Scriptures so often declare that by faith man is justified and saved. The Jews imagined that the principle of salvation was the observance of the law in view of the recompenses of God; St. Paul unceasingly tells them that their works are powerless if they are not vivified by a higher element. "It is one God," he exclaims, "that justifieth circumcision by faith, and uncircumcision through faith."† What are works, in fact, if they are performed under the impulsion of a purely scientific view? A simple calculation of interest, or of good government of ourselves and others. Men are just, sober, careful, industrious,

* Rom. iv. 11.    † Rom. iii. 30.

faithful keepers of their word, because this is an order whose exact observance produces more than it costs; but place these well-regulated minds before the cup of Alexander—that is to say, before a sacrifice which may be avoided without loss, before a virtue which has no visible reward—you will then learn the void in the heart where faith is wanting. I do not even mean divine faith, but that vague, unnamed, indescribable faith, which is the basis of all that is great. Therefore, when St. Paul pronounced that sovereign sentence, " Without faith it is impossible to please God,"* we may add—and men.

Thence comes the weakness of society in the present time. Never has science thrown upon things a more living and a more complete illumination than now; nor has the social tie ever been so easy to burst in the hands of those who, turn by turn, endeavour to bind society together. It is because science is not the principle of the human order—it is only one of its glorious ornaments—and where it oppresses instead of sustaining faith, it is but the parricidal instrument of ruin wherein man will learn too late that it is necessary to believe in order to live a single day, even were it not necessary to believe in order to live eternally. Human faith is the life of the natural man as divine faith is the life of the man supernaturalised, and those two men forming but one, divine faith maintains human faith as human faith supports divine faith, were it but in proving the synthesis which exists between the two orders whose distinct, but harmonious, elements compose our destiny.

This first difficulty solved, I am urged to notice a considerable difference between the faith that serves as a means of intercourse between men among themselves, and the faith that serves as a means of intercourse with God. In the former, they say, it is easy to see when and in what degree confidence should be given to purely human testimony, relating to things and ideas not removed from the sphere in which we are; in the latter, on the contrary, every thing surpasses our faculties —divine revelation itself—in its exterior signs, as well as the mysteries contained therein. We believe in man voluntarily and naturally, because man is ourselves; we believe in God by chance and with difficulty, because God is not ourselves. How, then, should we make of that faith the chosen instrument of our relations with the invisible world? Is it our fault

* Heb. xi. 6.

it does not subjugate our heart? You tell us that it is a work of persuasion: persuade us, then! Behold us at the foot of your pulpit; we listen to you; what hinders you from persuading us? Just now, in an apostrophe which you thought eloquent, you told us that, when language lost its authority in the world, it infallibly found a successor which took possession of its vacant throne. This is what happens to the teaching whose organ you are; but why impute it to us? Is it needful to condemn or pity us if human teaching has been substituted for divine teaching, if we are born in an age wherein man is stronger than God, wherein men listen to sages rather than to theologians? It is possible that our generation may be decried; but it is not the author of its darkness, it is its victim. Our fathers prepared the cup from which we drink: they mixed with it so much art and power that our lips are naturally inebriated therewith, and that our birth and error form but a single act in one and the same day. Instead of condemning us, let God, then, come to our help; let Him speak, let Him give grace to His word; and if it be true that His Son, heretofore visible among us, did raise the dead, ah! let Him, then, raise up the whole human race; this is the real corpse. You have said that eloquence is the substitution of the soul that speaks for the soul that listens: let God, then, be eloquent! Is it too much to ask of Him for the salvation of the world? And if He will not—if He does not do this—if incredulity remains our natural state, whilst faith is but exceptional, why should He complain? Is it because we are such as He has created us?

Gentlemen, your objection supposes that divine or religious faith is an accident of the human mind, and already many times, in the course of these conferences, I have proved to you that it was the universal, perpetual, and public state of mankind. I proved it to you again this very year, at the beginning of our quadragesimal reunion, and without returning to that historical demonstration, I will limit myself to one remark—it is, that there have been in the world only two epochs where incredulity has had any hope of domination: the Augustan Age and our own: the Augustan Age, which saw the Roman Republic perish, and our own, which has as yet produced only tempests—two epochs in six thousand years, both marked by the signs and the effects of decline. Not that I would prophesy your ruin; even in the Augustan Age it was not ruin: the unbelief of the ancient world was the happy forerunner of a new world, the Christian world. So will it be with you. Your bark quivers and sinks, but the wave that draws it into the abyss will lift it towards heaven, and your posterity, guided to the haven, will admire in your history and in its own a new proof that unbelief, so far from being a station of mankind, is hardly a danger for it. Already certain foreshadowings of the future justify this presentiment, and even if my hope be not a proof for you, it will always remain that the only epoch of incredulity of which we know the integral development was followed by the exaltation of Christianity— that is to say, of the greatest and most memorable expansion of faith which has ever taken place in the human race. This suffices to give me the right to conclude that divine or religious faith is not an accident of our mind, but its general and true condition, and that man believes in God as spontaneously as he believes in man. I do not say that he so believes without an effort, and even without a struggle. Nothing is more natural to man than to live, and yet life is not a thing that does not cost any effort. Life is a labour and a struggle; how much more should faith be so, since faith, in its very definition, bears the idea of a virtue, and since all virtue is a laborious effort, because of the passions which are opposed to its reign over the soul.

Do not wonder, then, that it requires some care to believe, as well as to be just, true, chaste, an honest man, and wonder even that so little is needed, faith being not only a human but a divine virtue, and the gate of all the virtues that lead to God. You do not believe, and you conclude that faith is impossible; for my part, I conclude that you do not do what is necessary in order to believe, and I shall prove this to you in a few words.

The first cause of unbelief is voluntary ignorance. Faith cannot be acquired any more than knowledge without a certain application of the mind. As soon as the mind does not apply itself, it is inert, it ceases to be a power, it is in regard to the object from which it turns away as if it were not. What are mathematics for a mind which has never reflected on the laws of number, extent, and motion? What is philosophy for a man who has never asked himself what are being, idea, the absolute, the relative, cause and effect? And, by the same reason, what is faith for a soul which has never seriously thought on the necessary relations between the creature and God?

Gentlemen, be true to yourselves; at what age and after what studies have you decided that religion is an error? At the age of forty? No, you decided it in the flower of your age, at the moment when, rising from infancy, reasoning and passion made their joyous appearance together on the agitated surface of your being. Simple and subject up to that time, pious adorers of the thoughts of your mother, you had interrogated nothing, contested nothing—you lived upon a faith as pure as your heart. But hardly had that double puberty of man made known its living sting to your senses and your mind, than, without giving yourselves time to ripen your power, impatient of the mysteries of nature and the mysteries of God, you were seized with shame at believing at the same time as you lost that other shame which is the divine guardian of innocence. As yet incapable of a virile act, you nevertheless pronounced sovereignly upon man and upon God; you doubted, denied, apostatized, despised your fathers, accused your masters, traduced before your tribunal the virtues and the sufferings of ages—made, in fine, of your soul a desert of pride. Then, that ruin accomplished, you chose for your object one of the ambitions of man—the glory of arms, letters, or of something less elevated, as the case may be, and all the effort of your faculties is employed towards the idolatry of your future. You have learned nothing more than to be one day the actual hero of your dreams. You have sacrificed your days and nights to that egotistical image, reserving no hidden, no unknown part of them, save only for that other egotism of man, sensuality. And never, during that double and sad dream, has religion appeared to you other than as a futile recollection of your early years, a weakness or hypocrisy of humanity. You have not deigned to give to it an hour, a thought, a desire; and if, perchance, attracted by a celebrated name, you have passed the threshold of a book or a temple, you have done so in the haughtiness of a mind which had judged and which did not intend to change its sentence. O confidence of youth in error! O security of souls who have as yet seen nothing of life but its dawn! Oh! how good God has been not to call us at that hour of ignorance and enchantment! For, already the greater number among you are not in the state of simple certainty; time has brought back to you doubt and obscure presentiments of truth. You understand that your unbelief is the result of a puerile act of weakness, and that for your honour and your repose it needs a ratification.

It is this second work, this work of return and examination, that founds faith in man and maintains it in mankind. Faith, doubtless, is also a gift of infancy; it throws out its roots in the soul entering into existence, but it is the tardy action of life that brings it to its maturity. When man has seen man during a long series of years, when he has known his weakness and misery by experience which leaves him no more doubt, and already the mighty form of death brings nearer to him the last of the prophecies, then his look becomes naturally more profound. He discerns better the divine trace, because he knows better what man cannot do, and the lassitude of present things creates for him also a taste for things unseen. Therefore a writer, whose name I cannot now remember, has well said: "At twenty, men believe religion to be false; at forty, they begin to suspect that it may be true; at fifty, they desire that it may be true; at sixty, they no longer doubt its truth." Light advances step by step with life, and death, by disabusing us of all things, completes that continued revelation whose first words we heard from the lips of our mother. The infant and woman are the vanguard of God; the full man is His apostle and martyr; you, young men, are but deserters for a day from Him.

I know that voluntary ignorance does not of itself explain the painful phenomenon of unbelief, and that there are men versed in religious things who do not attain to the happiness of faith. Such examples are rare, but I have met with them. They are victims of a passion which is the most obstinate of all, the pride of knowledge. The pride of knowledge is that infatuation of a mind intoxicated with itself, which sees itself in what it knows, like Narcissus in the lake, and which, considering every limit as an insult to its capacity, presumes to treat with God as between equal and equal. Such a man no longer studies from a love of truth, but against it; he rejoices in gathering clouds around it, in finding a grain of sand which may be made a blasphemy, and which he may hurl against Heaven. Does he watch the firmament, it is but to draw forth from it the secret of the eternity of the world; does he descend into the bowels of the earth, it is but to seek for arms against a great biblical fact; does he interrogate the necropolis of Egypt or the ruins of Babylon, it is but to endeavour to find there a voice that denies something of the most ancient traditions. His knowledge is but a stubborn duel between himself and God.

Who could remain true under the influence of such a passion? Who would accept it as a judge? Faith, we have said, is an act of confidence; it supposes the sincerity of an upright and a loving heart. Now, the men of whom I speak would not even believe in mathematical demonstrations if their object and end were the truths of their religious order. Like Jean Jacques, they would rather declare themselves to be mad than say they were convinced. And indeed this is not an imaginary picture. Consult the recollections of your own conscience. Have you never felt a thrill of joy on discovering something in history or in nature that appeared to you to be stamped with an anti-Christian sign? Have you never clapped your hands on hearing it said, Here is an argument against Jesus Christ? "Ask, and it shall be given to you; seek, and you shall find; knock, and it shall be opened to you."* Such is the first condition for arriving at faith. The sun halts in vain in the height of the firmament, if his light is but a reason for us to refuse to acknowledge his presence.

In fine, a third cause of unbelief is the depravity of morals. I will not say that all the weaknesses of our frail flesh are obstacles to faith, since faith is itself the principle of chastity, and since Jesus Christ pronounced against the Pharisees that divine saying, "The women whom you call lost shall go into the kingdom of God before you."† There is a form of vice which is humble, which knows itself, which despises itself, which beats its breast. I will not say that it is agreeable to God, but God is able to heal it, as he healed Magdalene. On the other hand, there is a vice poisoned with pride, which raises its head, which laughs and mocks. This vice God hates; it is an almost invincible obstacle to faith, because it is the re-union of two kinds of perversity, which naturally exclude one another, and whose meeting takes from the soul the last resources of good. Pride alone of itself is so insupportable to God, that He prefers humble vice to haughty virtue. How, then, must He regard proud vice?

* St. Matt. vii. 7. † *Ibid.* xxi. 31.

Now, nothing is less rare than that lamentable disposition of the heart; slaves as they are to the most vile inclinations and the most shameful practices, they plume themselves in the pride of a pure conscience; they appeal from it to their honour, their probity, their genius, and cover with the name of amiable weaknesses the prostitution of all the senses to voluptuousness. They employ half a century in perverting the ignorance of youth and the beauty of virtue around them, and, after having driven to shame a number of souls, whose ruin they do not even deign to respect in their memory, instead of saying to God with St. Peter, "Depart from me; for I am a sinful man, O Lord," * they complain of the little light which God has thrown upon His works, and impute to him their misfortune of not knowing and serving Him. Do you believe, gentlemen, that miracles are due to such complainings, and that God is at fault for not answering them otherwise than by silence and coldness? Oh, yes, "the women whom you call lost will go into the kingdom of God before you," because nearly all of them have been victims before having been mercenaries, and because from the depth of their abasement they sometimes raise towards God that plaintive and humble look which is more than remorse, if it be not yet virtue. God will hear them; He hears the faintest sigh that is sincere, and He perfects every tear which has begun to form for time. But He despises the pride of ignorance, the pride of knowledge, and the pride of vice; He will await them on the day when, in presence of the assembled universe, angels will sing again the hymn of God made man, " Glory to God in the highest, and on earth peace to men of good will." †

Gentlemen, I shall not conclude without casting a thought upon the great week whose doleful events we are about to celebrate. It was the week of our salvation, and it is so now. From that cross which the Church has just covered with a veil, not to hide it from us, but to make its mourning more apparent and more bitter to us, for nearly twenty centuries justice and love have appealed to you. Listen to them now, and do not disdain such great patience in so much light. You, to whom age gives warning of serious things, listen to the counsel of time, which for you joins to the voice

---

\* St. Luke v. 8.  † *Ibid.* ii. 14.

of God. You, to whom youth promises long hours of grace, listen to what is most touching for you in the cruel appeal of the Passion. It is written that after the arrest of the Saviour, when all His disciples had left Him, a young man was seen following Him having a linen cloth cast about his naked body. The guards seized upon him in order to take him, but, casting off the linen cloth, he fled from them naked. That young man was yourselves; it was the youth which should one day spring from Christianity no longer dishonoured by hopeless vices, but subject to seductions and returns to good, preserving in evil the search after good, incapable of persecuting the Just and following Him at a distance in the shadow of the world with sympathetic presentiments. Such were you on the eve of the Passion; in that young man your precursor, such are you now. You are naked, you are wrapped in the linen sheet of death and sin, and whilst here you listen uncertain to the spotless word of truth, perhaps Providence will touch you with that blessed hand which has made and which seeks man. Ah! I conjure you not to fly from Him; leave Him your linen garment by giving Him your hearts.

# SACRAMENT.

My Lord—Gentlemen,

Prophecy does not suffice for the supernatural intercourse between man and God. Prophecy enlightens the intelligence by elevating it to ideas which the spectacle of finite things would not inspire; but the intelligence is only a part of man, and in order to be moved, it depends upon a faculty which rouses it and is the mainspring of all our actions, although it is subject in its turn to the influence of the doctrines deposited in the understanding—I mean the will. The will is the principle of free activity. If it were to halt in the orbit of nature whilst the intelligence mounts higher, there would be discord in the tendencies of our being, and the work of divine communion would not be accomplished. It is needful that the will should receive a supernatural impulsion at the same time as the intelligence receives an illumination of the same order, and that thus all our faculties should advance together to the conquest and full possession of the infinite. This is why the Spirit of God, which is called the "Spirit of truth,"* is also called the "Spirit of power,"† and Jesus Christ, in promising this Spirit to His apostles, announced it to them under that double form—the one of light, the other of power, or virtue. And unquestionably, in the prophetic action, this double effusion is produced. Illuminative grace includes also an attractive grace, but which, although sufficient to aid the will, is not sufficient to found in it the constant reign of divine justice, life, and love. As Jesus Christ, after having revealed to His apostles the mystery of the Gospel and after having begun in them the work of regeneration, fulfilled it by the gift

* St. John xiv. 17.   † Acts i. 8.

of the Holy Spirit which was to confirm them by His omnipotent power, so every soul already prepared by the hearing of the word of God, should resort to Sacrament in order to derive from it the vivifying virtue which exalts the will, and establishes it in the plenitude of the rights and functions of the supernatural order.

What, then, is Sacrament? If I limited myself to showing you what it is in the religious sense, perhaps you would not understand me; but I am sure that in considering it in a higher manner—that is to say, in its metaphysical and absolute nature—you will be constrained to respect it, if even you are not yet induced to practise it.

I propose, then, again this question, and I ask in an abstract and general sense, What is Sacrament?

Sacrament thus considered is no other thing than an instrument—that is to say, an organism which contains a force. The idea of force is the parent idea of sacrament, and it is consequently impossible for us to reason about it if we do not know beforehand what force is. When we were treating of Prophecy, the fundamental question was, What is truth? When Sacrament is under discussion, the fundamental question is, What is force?

It seems, gentlemen, easy to answer this question; for ever since we have been in the world, and at each moment of our lives, we have performed, and we still perform, only acts of force or weakness; and weakness itself is but a force inferior to what is required for the object to which we apply it. If you walk, it is a display of force; if you sit, it is the display of another force; if you stand up, it is still force. And so it is with all our outward actions, with all those that are performed by the organs of the body. The movements of the soul, whatever they may be, depend upon the same principle, and follow the same law. Are you bold in danger? It is force. Are you above the seductions of the world and the senses? It is force. Are you firm in your resolutions? It is force. Are you cast down by grief or fear? It is force that grows less in you, and if you did not retain it by an effort against your impressions, life would slowly and painfully escape from you. Life is but a tissue of actions which proceed from a force more or less energetic, more or less imperfect, whose seat is at the same time the soul and the body.

If from man you pass to nations, you will find there no

other spectacle. Nations begin by an act of energy, they live upon a principle which formed them, and they expire from physical and moral exhaustion. Their history lasts as long as their power, and their power as long as that force lasts which collects all the others in its essence and in its name—virtue.

The universe, in its turn, says the same thing to us as man and nations. All those immense orbs which compose its architecture obey two forces—one of projection, which impels them in a right line; the other of attraction, which calls them to repose in a fixed centre—and, dividing between these two contrary impulses, they describe that constant and glorious curve which unceasingly dispenses to us light, heat, time, space, and harmony.

All is then force in heaven and upon earth, because all is action, and science, of whatever nature it may be, to whatever object it may be applied, is employed solely in calculating forces, some physical, others moral, mathematical, metaphysical or abstract, and, in fine, beyond all things and all number, the most elevated speculation encounters, under the name of God, the supreme, eternal, infinite, immutable force, from whence flows, in each being, by measured participation, the germ of activity. Consequently nothing should be more familiar and more known to us than force. And yet, precisely because force is a primary element of our thoughts, I can only imperfectly define it to you, less by its essence than by its effects. I shall say, then, that it is the energy of a being, holding existence in itself by means of an effort of concentration, or diffusing it without by means of a movement of dilation. Every act of force reduces itself to this. Either we restrain ourselves within ourselves, in order to concentrate our life, and give to ourselves the highest possible sensation of it, or we diffuse our life, in order to communicate it to others, and according to the degree of that double tension, we produce, to a greater or less degree, the incomprehensible phenomenon which we call force. The hand contracted to refuse is the symbol of the force of concentration; the hand open to consent is the symbol of the force of expansion; and if you recall to mind the acts perpetually renewed which form the life of man and nature, you will find nothing in them which does not conclude in that alternative movement which our heart unceasingly manifests physically and morally.

The force of concentration at its height, is eternity. He

alone possesses it who, in an unique, indivisible, and absolute moment, feels in Himself and for ever the infinite sensation of being, and is able to say, *I am who am.*\* The force of expansion at its height, is creation. He alone possesses it who, sufficing to Himself in the plenitude of existence, is able to call into life, without losing anything of his own, who and what He will—bodies, spirits, worlds—and this always in untold ages and unbounded space. Such is God.

Now God, in giving us being, has given us force, without which no being could comprehend itself, and he has given it to us in its double element—one by which we have duration, another which enables us to multiply ourselves; one by which we tend to the act eternity, the other by which we tend to the act of creation. But between God and ourselves, under this relation, there is a great and capital difference. God possesses of Himself the force of concentration and expansion, whilst we have it only as a loan, by means of the instruments which Divine Providence has prepared for us. Therefore, living beings as you are, you would make vain efforts to live by the sole aliment of your substance, and the sole command of your wants. Were you llke Ugolino, shut up in a tower, with your children at your feet crying to you in all the tortures of inanition —you men, you fathers—it would be impossible for you to draw forth from the most energetic action of your soul anything but despair or resignation. You would be compelled to fall powerless upon the bodies of your children who had fallen from the same cause. Doubtless the force of your will would more or less retard that catastrophe of hunger. The soul sustains the body combating against affliction and death, and martyrs have been seen in whom the divine assistance seemed to delight in braving tyrants, and in surpassing the genius of cruel inflictions by the patient courage of faith. But that exaltation of virility, whilst being the triumph of virtue, does but lead it gloriously to the tomb; it must succumb in the material order, and bear witness that no creature possesses of itself the right or power of immortality. Life is in us on condition of our maintaining it by something other than ourselves—that is to say, by means of the instruments to which God has communicated force to retain and sustain our own. If nature did not bear us like a mother in her bosom,

---

\* Exodus iii. 14.

if nature did not, with inexhaustible fecundity, prepare for us the milk of the plant and the blood of the animal, our life would not even be a dream. We subsist by the invisible force contained in a visible organism, and Sacrament, or the instrument, being no other thing, we must conclude that we subsist by the natural and daily use of Sacraments.

So it is in regard to the force of expansion. If you would act outwardly upon the being the least capable of resisting, you cannot do so directly by a simple act of the will. In vain would you command a grain of sand to move out of your way. God moves the universe without even speaking to it; as for you, an atom braves your commands. You call to it, you command it to be gone. It is silent, and it despises your orders. If you would remove it, your hand must bend even to the earth, and cast from you the insolent dust which scorned the desire and power of man. But the body is a limited instrument, a slight increase of resistance, and the force which your body contains no longer suffices to maintain your empire; you must seek help for it, and add to its action the foreign action of the lever. The lever itself must increase in proportion to the weight which it is required to lift, and with that material aid resting on a fulcrum, you build your palaces, your temples, your tombs, and all those monuments conceived by your genius, but executed by your hands aided by a mean organism. You might even, said Archimedes, displace all the worlds with the lever, by giving it sufficient length and finding for it a fulcrum capable of bearing its weight and the effort of its movement.

Glory to you, gentlemen, but glory to you because you know how to employ instruments capable of raising even to heaven the ambition of your works! Without their help, you would know nothing of the firmament but its appearances, of the earth but its surface, of history but a vague and limited remembrance, of yourselves but the narrow limit of your faculties. The instrument is your whole force, without as well as within, in the order of expansion as in the order of concentration. But the instrument and Sacrament being the same thing, what shall we say, but that man is nothing save by Sacrament—that Sacrament is his life, his power, his sovereignty, his immortality? I say this after having proved it, and that you may not be left in wonder thereat, I desire to learn why it is so, and to show it to you.

Why, then, does our force come to us from without? Why does it come to us from a source inferior to us?—or, at least, why can we only sustain and develop that which is our own by the help of something foreign to us, and which is contained in the lowest regions of nature? Why, gentlemen? Is it so difficult to understand? If we possessed the force of concentration and expansion of ourselves, as that double force is the essence of life, we should have life in us and by us; we should be to ourselves our subsistence and our reason of being, we should be God; or, at least, not having consciousness of the silent and insensible action by which God would inwardly infuse life to us, we should easily believe that we possessed it of ourselves, and that, instead of rising in humble gratitude towards the Author of that magnificent gift, we should halt at ourselves as before our principle and our end. Our greatness would deceive us, and nature being under our feet only an observant and a passive slave, we should draw from it the idea that it is not distinct from man, and by a pantheism which would justify its obedience, we should adore in nature the reverberation of our sovereign majesty. God was too just; he was too much a father to deliver us to such easy risings of pride; he made us first among visible beings, but in warning us of our dependence towards Him by the state of dependence in which we are towards the whole of creation. We command only on condition of obeying; we live only by soliciting life; we act only by the help of the dust which soils our feet. God, in giving us a soul greater than heaven and earth, has not permitted it of itself alone to vivify the glebe of the body which it inhabits, and to communicate to it an action equal to its volitions. He has placed an intermediary between us and force; He has hidden it in the bosom of nature, under forms which we accept without understanding them, and the employment of which necessarily but partially humbles our pride, because we have the glory of discovering them, and because we believe that we make them our servitors by proving the law by which we depend upon them. But since you despise the supernatural Sacrament, learn at least the value of the natural Sacrament. You, the kings of the world—you can live only by eating; only by sitting at a table, and devouring blood, flesh, herbs, which you dispute with the beasts of the field; only by bearing within you an inexplicable transmutation of inanimate matter into the glorious and living substance of man. You, the kings of the world, for whom this earth is too limited—you cannot lay two stones one upon another save by the help of an instrumentation which subjects your genius to a piece of dead wood. For what is a lever? A lever is a pole. Yes, proud men, mathematicians, savants, artists, to found this temple in which I speak to you, you require a pole! Your thought conceived it, but it was a pole placed across another pole that built it.

And yet, where is the scholar in philosophy whom the idea of Sacrament has not revolted? What young mind, exercising in mathematics by calculating forces, has not laughed at the idea of Sacrament? He who daily employs it with imperturbable faith, who advances surrounded by instruments, who counts, weighs, measures, observes by instruments—he who stands wondering before a machine, and who never contemplates a collection of them in the museums of science without a feeling of pride—he, that same man, passing before a church, cannot suppress a smile at the thought that there are reasonable beings availing themselves of something which they call Sacraments. Ah! yes, gentlemen, the Christian lives by Sacraments as you live by them—religion has its Sacraments as science has its Sacraments, and, before complaining of this, it would have been but just to learn whether such is not the universal mode of life; for it is hard to live by the very thing which we despise the most.

Had God created man only for time and space, he would have given to him only the force corresponding to time and space, and the only instruments known to us would have been natural instruments. But such was not the vocation of man. God having placed him in the world from a motive of goodness, willed to communicate to him His perfection and His beatitude—at first indirectly, under a finite, representative, and enigmatical form, which constitutes the order of nature; next directly, by a higher effusion of light and love, we should prepare man, by means of his free co-operation, to see and possess fully the Author of all good. In a word mighty and wonderful, but a word taken from Scripture, and brought even to us by Christian tradition, the final end of man is his deification—that is to say, so intimate a union with God that, without destroying our personality, it should make us partakers of the divine life and the divine nature. This is what the Apostle St. Peter wrote in these terms to the faithful of his times:

"Simon Peter, servant and apostle of Jesus Christ, to them that have obtained equal faith with us in the justice of our God and Saviour Jesus Christ: Grace to you, and peace be accomplished in the knowledge of God, and of Christ Jesus our Lord, . . . by whom he hath given us the most great and precious promises: that by these you may be made partakers of the divine nature."† And St. Paul, writing to the Hebrews, said to them: "For we are made partakers of Christ: yet so if we hold the beginning of our substance firm unto the end."* And at every page of the Gospel eternal life —that is to say, the life of God—is promised to us as the reward of our works performed in the faith and fulfilment of the divine plan in regard to us. Now, the life of God, consisting in an infinite force of concentration, which is eternity, and in an infinite force of expansion, which is creative charity, it is this double infinite force which should be initially communicated to us in order that we may respond, even here below, to the marvellous vocation of omnipotent goodness. I have not now to discuss that vocation. I have already done so, and if I had not it is unimportant. Is there any soul here who accepts time and space as his destiny? Do we not all, believers and unbelievers, hold the faith that space is not our horizon, that time is not our measure, that we pass beyond and higher, and that the present life is but the painful portico of a greater future? Yes, save the atheist—and ought I even to except him?—save the atheist, there is no man who does not feel a germ of divinity. Therefore, we are all able to die for our ideas and our affections, for truth and justice, because, all feeble as we are, we feel on certain occasions so vivid an impression of the God obscure who is within us, that death appears to us as a fiction, and the duty of dying an immortality.

Ah! I thank God, that in this great mystery of our union with Him, there is dissent among us only as to the mode and the degree! I thank Him, I bless Him for this; I feel happy and full of joy to find one point in hope and in the infinite, where, whoever we may be—ancients or moderns, pagans, Mussulmans, heretics, unbelievers—we meet, and for once understand each other! Hail, promised land of man, duration which will no longer be a beginning and an end, incomprehensible substance which will bear us without increasing or

---

\* 2 St. Pet. i. 1, and foll.      † Heb. iii. 14.

lessening, air, light, heat, respiration of our soul—hail! We do not all understand thee in the same manner, we do not all possess the same certainty of thee, but we all possess, even in the despair of suicide, thy inexplicable augury: and if thou art, if thy dawn seen from so far deceives not the heart of man, what canst thou be but God? What other land, what other heaven, what other ocean but God, could bring to our weary minds a better vision than the vision of the present? Yes, even here below, for all of us, God is our perspective, He is our aliment; even when we have driven Him from us, He still dwells in us plaintive and consoling, like those unknown winds which pass in the evening over the desolate summit of the high mountains, and gently agitate some solitary plant which the pious hand of the traveller has never touched.

God is our future, or we have no future; we shall fall into His life, or we shall fall into death—the one or the other. Immortality without intimate union with God is the abstract dream of beatification, or the adulterous dream of infinite materialism. I do not believe that your hope has fallen so low, and consequently you must eternally enjoy God if you are not to perish eternally.

To enjoy God, to be in God and with God, plunged into his bosom as we are in nature, such is the vocation of man, and that vocation cannot have been given without a corresponding force to prepare us, in this world, for our final state. As beings destined to a transformation in the infinite, we should somewhere derive the efficacious germs of that divine change. As nature pours out its treasures for us to maintain our terrestrial life, God necessarily pours out also His own to elevate us to His life, and, according to the general law of the communication of forces, it is by an instrument that supernatural energy is presented to, and incorporates itself in, us.

Jesus Christ, having sat down by a well in the land of Samaria, saw a woman come there who began to draw up water, and He said to her: "Woman, give me to drink. . . . Then the Samaritan woman said to him: How dost thou, being a Jew, ask of me to drink, who am a Samaritan woman? . . . Jesus answered and said to her: If thou didst know the gift of God, and who he is that saith to thee: Give me to drink, thou perhaps wouldst have asked of him, and he would have given thee living water." That woman, full of the obscurities of man, and who represents so well to us the poverty of our reasonings, replied to her interlocutor: "Sir, thou hast nothing to draw with, and the well is deep; from whence then hast thou that living water?" Jesus, not wearying of showing mercy, which had been twice rejected, replied to her: " Whosoever drinketh of this water shall thirst again : but he that shall drink of the water that I will give him shall not thirst for ever; but the water that I will give him shall become in him a well of water springing up into life everlasting."* Such is the difference between the Sacrament of nature and the Sacrament of grace—in the one and in the other the force is contained in a sensible element; but the first communicates only a passing life, the second gives a life that springs up into eternity, because it nourishes the soul with God.

Nourishes the soul with God! What an expression, you will say, and what reality can it signify? We can conceive that a body may be nourished by another body, since both are of the same nature and are composed of parts which may be indefinitely divided; but how can a simple substance, such as the soul, be nourished by another substance still more simple, such as the essence of God? Doubtless a spirit is not nourished like a body; yet it is not in vain that human tongues possess the tradition of those bold figures, and transport to the spiritual life the operations of the animal life. Being, in whatever rank of honour or inferiority God may have established it, lives only by the forces received from without. and the eminent act by which it receives and assimilates these forces, is the very act of receiving nourishment. Now the spirit receives and assimilates forces as well as bodies, consequently it receives nourishment; and if the forces which vivify or sustain it are given to it of God by an immediate effusion, it is eloquently and truly said to nourish itself with God. However, the expression is of little importance, provided that the thing exists. God, in the supernatural Sacrament, communicated to the soul a force of expansion which bears it directly towards Himself, and a force of concentration which attaches it intimately to Himself, and if you are weary of expressions borrowed from the physical sciences, I will say to you in the language of St. Paul: CARITAS DEI DIFFUSA EST IN CORDIBUS NOSTRIS PER SPIRITUM SANCTUM QUI

* St. John iv. 7 and foll.

DATUS EST NOBIS—*The Charity of God is poured forth in our hearts by the Holy Ghost who is given to us.*\* Charity, that is to say love, which does not come from flesh and blood but from the beauty of God presented to the soul by faith—charity is that force of expansion and concentration which united us supernaturally to God. By charity, we raise ourselves above the senses and above all the enchantments which the visible world offers to us; by charity, having once seen the divine personality in the figure of Christ, we find therein more pleasure, more peace, more joy, more delight than in any created thing, and as the patriarchs under the nuptial tent forgot the death of their mother, we forget ourselves and lose ourselves in that superhuman love. We pass into God, and embracing Him with all our strength in an inexplicable certainty of possessing Him, we draw from Him a part of His life in abandoning to Him all our own.

Who among you, having been loved, and supposing that we are able to love God, does not understand what I mean? Who among you has not known that movement of the heart, which pours out itself and finds itself again in another? Even inanimate creatures possess its instinctive secret; they seek each other, and unite by secret affinities, and those famous laws which lead the celestial bodies are but the sensible revelation of the forces which move us in God in the mystery of initial and consummated beatification.

Perhaps you do not deny these forces, or that love in all its degrees is their principle; but you wonder that, in the supernatural or religious order, they should be communicated to us under a form humble, so little in relation with themselves, as Sacrament. In the natural Sacrament or instrument, say you, there is proportion between the cause and the effect. I take a lever, I move a body, the effect is natural like its cause: but what relation can be discovered between a few drops of water poured upon the head of a man, and his transformation in God by charity.

The objection supposes that in the natural Sacrament there is proportion between the cause and the effect: I deny it. I now maintain that between the lever and the body moved by it, there exists no more relation than between the water which baptizes and the soul which is purified by that water. What,

---

\* Rom. v. 5.

indeed, is a lever? I have already said it is a piece of dead wood placed upon another piece of dead wood, which serves it as a fulcrum. This definition is not scientific, but it cannot be contested. Now, is it there, in this inert organism, where lies the force that will lift the weight? Not in the least degree. The weight would remain eternally motionless if my arm did not give an impulsion to the lever, and my arm itself would remain still if my will did not command it to move and strengthen it so much the more as the obstacle of the weight is greater. Where, then, is the force? It is not in the lever, since it needs to be moved by the arm; it is not in the arm, since it needs to be moved by my will: it is in the will which moves the lever by the arm—that is to say, in a faculty of the soul, in the mind. Now, I ask you, what natural relation is there between the mind and the movement of a body?

The lever alone could do nothing, my arm alone could do nothing; they were both inactive, incapable, dead: an order of my will weighing upon my arm, has weighed upon the lever, which, in its turn, has given an irresistible impulsion to the body. And you find that simple! And you say that the effect is of the same nature as the cause! For my part, I say that the cause is spiritual, the effect material, and that therefore the proportion which you fondly assume, is as foreign to the physical instrument as to the religious instrument.

But there is something more. It is true, my will moved the arm, which moved the lever: yet it can do nothing without the co-operation of the lever and the arm. If my will, however active it may be, had not these instruments at its service, it would have endeavoured in vain to communicate a movement. The force is in my will, and, nevertheless, the force can come from it only by means of an instrument which has it not; the living and first cause depends in its action upon a cause inert in itself. Withdraw the lever, withdraw the piece of dead wood resting upon another piece of dead wood, let it refuse its help to the will, the will would waste itself in powerless desires. Spirit needs matter, as matter needs spirit: the miracle is reciprocal—the effect becomes cause, and the cause becomes effect.

You have not, however, yet exhausted that strange complication of mysteries. If, whilst the will acts upon the instrument, the instrument were to double its length, its force at the same moment becomes doubled, without the soul making any other effort, and so on indefinitely, even to the power of raising worlds, according to the boast of Archimedes. The instrument which is not the principle of force multiplies it without measure: it receives the initiative of the mind, and gives back to it in exchange an increase which exhausts all calculation. Do you understand that force, springing from the will, passes into a pole, and there increases simply ·because the pole increases in length? What relation is there between the immobility of the soul and the progress of force—between a principle which remains at the same point, and a consequence unceasingly developed by the aid of something inert and dead?

I leave you now free to declaim against the water of baptism; ask, as often as you please, how a little matter applied to the brow of a man raises him from earth to God. If I know not, nature has prepared too many reprisals against science for me to distrust myself on this head. But I am not ignorant about it; I comprehend that force is essentially spiritual, that it resides in the omnipotent will of God, as in its first principle, and that from thence it descends upon every creature in order to communicate to it movement and life, according to fixed laws, and in a measure whence universal order results. I comprehend that the Spirit breathes where it wills, and how it wills, and that it is not more difficult for it to cause a saint to rise from a drop of water than a world from a word. I comprehend that under that action of the divine will, dust seeks dust, the plant rises from its germ, the animal devours and assimilates its prey to itself, the soul acts upon the body, the body upon the soul, the planet upon the planet, and that the entire universe in its most lowly atom, responds by a force to every hand that touches it, and asks help from it. God is all in all things, even in the liberty which rejects Him, for that liberty is His work, and He maintains it at the peril of the evil which it engenders in spite of Him. Without liberty the world would be but a mechanism: liberty, a supreme power, gives to it in the being which possesses it self-possession, government, responsibility, a real intercourse with God—an intercourse of which Prophecy and Sacrament are but the proof and the means. Prophecy reveals to the free man direct truth in regard to God, and inspires him with faith; Sacrament pours into his soul the fermentation of charity, which no image drawn from creation would be capable of raising up and maintaining therein. The one and the other, however feeble they may be in appearance, form the foundation of the divine life in the bosom of mankind, and for sixty centuries they have there resisted the unanimous conjuration of created forces. All has been tried against them, but all in vain. To the demonstrations of science, the brilliant dreams of genius, the sword of potentates, the judgments of the magistracy, the revolts of opinion, the children of faith and charity have replied in these short phrases: God has spoken to us! God has blessed us! Death has found them firm upon these two anchors, and their blood has been but another Prophecy and Sacrament. The world mocked at the word and at water; they added their blood, and proved to the world that a fluid shed was not so insignificant a thing. Language is air put in motion; but when the soul enters into it, it becomes eloquence, justice, truth. What will it become when God enters into it? Water is hydrogen mixed with oxygen: but when the genius of man penetrates it, it becomes vapour, celerity, commerce, power, civilisation. What will it become when God touches it? Glory to God, who has remained so great in such feeble means!

Gentlemen, I have yet to show you how prophetic and sacramental grace, how supernatural truth and charity were given to the ancestor of all our race: but the order of our conferences now arrests me for a year. We will resume them next year by this question, and immediately after, having learned the whole plan of man in regard to God, having scrutinised the gifts which were granted to him by the intermediary of nature, and the highest and most direct gifts which he has received from grace, we will halt before that splendid masterpiece of divine goodness, no longer to study that divine goodness in its gifts but in its acts. We shall see man struggling with liberty—a depositary in liberty of his own destiny and of the destiny of all his descendants—master to lose all, master to bless all; in fine, conducting in his heart the pious and terrible drama of our common destiny. There, under the virgin shades of the primitive Eden, I give you rendezvous. There, in the ignorance of evil, and in the all-youthful glory of God, we shall find our first Father; and we, His sons, who too fully prejudge by our misfortunes the possible issue of so much innocence in so much felicity, let us each return to our works, may we, in another year, be able to bring back into this place less of remorse than remembrance, fewer faults than virtues, a soul capable of understanding the fall of man, and worthy to repair it!

THE END.

www.ingramcontent.com/pod-product-compliance
Lightning Source LLC
Chambersburg PA
CBHW020546300426
44111CB00008B/809